Palgrave Studies in International Relations Series

General Editors:
Knud Erik Jørgensen, Department of Political Science, University of Aarhus, Denmark
Audie Klotz, Department of Political Science, Maxwell School of Citizenship and Public Affairs, Syracuse University, USA

Palgrave Studies in International Relations, produced in association with the ECPR Standing Group for International Relations, will provide students and scholars with the best theoretically informed scholarship on the global issues of our time. Edited by Knud Erik Jørgensen and Audie Klotz, this new book series will comprise cutting-edge monographs and edited collections which bridge schools of thought and cross the boundaries of conventional fields of study.

Titles include:

Pami Aalto, Vilho Harle and Sami Moisio (*editors*)
INTERNATIONAL STUDIES
Interdisciplinary Approaches

Mathias Albert, Lars-Erik Cederman and Alexander Wendt (*editors*)
NEW SYSTEMS THEORIES OF WORLD POLITICS

Robert Ayson
HEDLEY BULL AND THE ACCOMODATION OF POWER

Gideon Baker (*editor*)
HOSPITALITY AND WORLD POLITICS

Barry Buzan and Ana Gonzalez-Pelaez (*editors*)
INTERNATIONAL SOCIETY AND THE MIDDLE EAST
English School Theory at the Regional Level

Toni Erskineand Richard Ned Lebow (*editors*)
TRAGEDY AND INTERNATIONAL RELATIONS

Rebekka Friedman, Kevork Oskanian and Ramon Pacheco Pardo (*editors*)
AFTER LIBERALISM?
The Future of Liberalism in International Relations

Geir Hønneland
BORDERLAND RUSSIANS
Identity, Narrative and International Relations

Oliver Kessler, Rodney Bruce Hall, Cecelia Lynch and Nicholas G. Onuf (*editors*)
ON RULES, POLITICS AND KNOWLEDGE
Friedrich Kratochwil, International Relations, and Domestic Affairs

Pierre P. Lizee
A WHOLE NEW WORLD
Reinventing International Studies for the Post-Western World

Hans Morgenthau, Hartmut Behr and Felix Rösch
THE CONCEPT OF THE POLITICAL

Cornelia Navari (*editor*)
THEORISING INTERNATIONAL SOCIETY
English School Methods

Dirk Peters
CONSTRAINED BALANCING: THE EU'S SECURITY POLICY

Linda Quayle
SOUTHEAST ASIA AND THE ENGLISH SCHOOL OF INTERNATIONAL RELATIONS
A Region-Theory Dialogue

Simon F. Reich
GLOBAL NORMS, AMERICAN SPONSORSHIP AND THE EMERGING PATTERNS
OF WORLD POLITICS

Robbie Shilliam
GERMAN THOUGHT AND INTERNATIONAL RELATIONS
The Rise and Fall of a Liberal Project

Daniela Tepe
THE MYTH ABOUT GLOBAL CIVIL SOCIETY
Domestic Politics to Ban Landmines

Daniel C. Thomas (*editor*)
MAKING EU FOREIGN POLICY
National Preferences, European Norms and Common Policies

Rens van Munster
SECURITIZING IMMIGRATION
The Politics of Risk in the EU

Palgrave Studies In International Relations Series
Series Standing Order ISBN 978–0230–20063–0 (hardback)
978–0230–24115–2 (paperback)
(*outside North America only*)

You can receive future titles in this series as they are published by placing a standing
order. Please contact your bookseller or, in case of difficulty, write to us at the address
below with your name and address, the title of the series and the ISBN quoted above.

Customer Services Department, Macmillan Distribution Ltd, Houndmills, Basingstoke,
Hampshire RG21 6XS, England

After Liberalism?

The Future of Liberalism in International Relations

Edited by

Rebekka Friedman
University of Oxford, UK

Kevork Oskanian
University of Westminster, UK

and

Ramon Pacheco Pardo
King's College London, UK

First published 2013 by
PALGRAVE MACMILLAN

Palgrave Macmillan in the UK is an imprint of Macmillan Publishers Limited, registered in England, company number 785998, of Houndmills, Basingstoke, Hampshire RG21 6XS.

Palgrave Macmillan in the US is a division of St Martin's Press LLC, 175 Fifth Avenue, New York, NY 10010.

Palgrave Macmillan is the global academic imprint of the above companies and has companies and representatives throughout the world.

Palgrave® and Macmillan® are registered trademarks in the United States, the United Kingdom, Europe and other countries.

ISBN 978–1–137–30375–2

This book is printed on paper suitable for recycling and made from fully managed and sustained forest sources. Logging, pulping and manufacturing processes are expected to conform to the environmental regulations of the country of origin.

A catalogue record for this book is available from the British Library.

A catalog record for this book is available from the Library of Congress.

Contents

Figures

Acknowledgements

The idea for this edited volume came out of the Millennium annual conference "After Liberalism?", held in London on 17–18 October 2009. We, Rebekka Friedman, Kevork Oskanian, and Ramon Pacheco Pardo, proposed the conference in 2008. This publication is the result of extensive conversations and discussions generated at the conference and in the subsequent special conference issue of *Millennium: Journal of International Studies*, 38: 3 (2010).

The conference would not have been possible without the generous economic and logistical backing of the Department of International Relations at the London School of Economics and Political Science, LSE IDEAS, and Sage. We would like to thank them for their help. We are grateful to Michael Cox for his support in this book project. We would also like to thank Palgrave for their enthusiasm and assistance and an anonymous book reviewer for comments and advice.

We would also like to thank Sage, publisher of *Millennium: Journal of International Studies*, for giving us permission to reprint G. John Ikenberry's article, "The Liberal International Order and Its Discontents", 38: 3 (2010), pp. 509–521, and for allowing us to use portions of Jonathan D. Caverley's article, "Power and Democratic Weakness: Neoconservatism and Neoclassical Realism", 38: 3 (2010), pp. 594–614.

We are also grateful to MIT Press Journals for allowing us to use ideas contained in two articles published in *International Security* – Charles A. Kupchan and Peter L. Trubowitz, "Dead Center: The Decline of Liberal Internationalism in the United States", *International Security*, 32: 2 (2007), pp. 7–44 and Charles A. Kupchan and Peter L. Trubowitz, "The Illusion of Liberal Internationalism's Revival", 35: 1 (2010), pp. 95–109.

Finally, we thank Palgrave Macmillan for granting permission to use one figure from Peter Trubowitz and Nicole Mellow, "Foreign Policy, Bipartisanship, and the Paradox of Post-September 11 America", *International Politics*, 48: 2–3 (2011), pp. 164–187.

Contributors

Jonathan Caverley is Assistant Professor of Political Science at Northwestern University, USA. He is currently completing a book on democratic militarism, and also writes on globalisation and the defense industry, civil–military relations, and American foreign policy. His publications have appeared in scholarly journals such as *International Security, Millennium: Journal of International Studies and Security Studies*, as well as *Foreign Affairs*.

Philip G. Cerny is Professor Emeritus of Politics and Global Affairs at the University of Manchester, UK, and Rutgers University, USA. He is the author of *The Politics of Grandeur: Ideological Aspects of de Gaulle's Foreign Policy* (1980; French translation, 1984), *The Changing Architecture of Politics: Structure, Agency and the Future of the State* (1990), and *Rethinking World Politics: A Theory of Transnational Neopluralism* (2010). He has also been editor or co-editor of several other books, most recently *Internalizing Globalization: The Rise of Neoliberalism and the Erosion of National Varieties of Capitalism* (2005). He has published articles in a range of journals, including *International Organization, European Journal of International Relations, Review of International Studies*, and *Millennium: Journal of International Studies*.

Michael Cox is Professor of International Relations at LSE, UK, and Co-Director of LSE IDEAS – a centre for the study of strategy and diplomacy. He previously taught at Queens University, Belfast, and Aberystwyth University, UK. Professor Cox is author, editor, and co-editor of several books, including *Beyond the Cold War: Superpowers at the Crossroads?* (1990), *US Foreign Policy after the Cold War: Superpower without a Mission?* (1995), *E. H. Carr: A Critical Appraisal* (2000), *Empires, System and States: Great Transformations in International Politics* (2002, co-edited with Tim Dunne and Ken Booth), and *The Global 1989: Continuity and Change in World Politics* (2010, co-edited with George Lawson and Chris Armbruster).

Louise Fawcett is Wilfrid Knapp Fellow and University Lecturer in Politics at St Catherine's College, University of Oxford, UK. Her research interests and publications cover topics including comparative regionalism and the history, politics, and international relations of developing countries. She is the author of *Iran and the Cold War* (2009) and editor of *International Relations of the Middle East* (3rd edition, 2013).

Rebekka Friedman is a tutor in the Foreign Service Programme at the University of Oxford, UK. She was an editor of *Millennium: Journal of International*

Studies. Her research focuses on transitional justice, conflict and peace studies, international institutions, and human rights.

G. John Ikenberry is Albert G. Milbank Professor of Politics and International Affairs at Princeton University in the Department of Politics and the Woodrow Wilson School of Public and International Affairs, USA, where he is Co-Director of Princeton's Center for International Security Studies. He is also a Global Eminence Scholar at Kyung Hee University in Seoul, Korea. In 2013–2014, Ikenberry will be the 72nd Eastman Visiting Professor at Balliol College, Oxford. He is the author of six books, including *Liberal Leviathan: The Origins, Crisis, and Transformation of the American System* (2011) and the award-winning *After Victory: Institutions, Strategic Restraint, and the Rebuilding of Order after Major Wars* (2001).

Beate Jahn is Professor of International Relations at the University of Sussex, UK, editor-in-chief of *European Journal of International Relations*, and director of the Centre for Advanced International Theory (CAIT). She is interested in the role of liberalism in international theory and practice and in the use of classical authors in and for the study of international relations. She has widely published in these areas. Her latest book, *Liberal Internationalism*, will be published in 2013.

Charles A. Kupchan is Professor of International Affairs at Georgetown University, USA, and Whitney Shepardson Senior Fellow at the Council on Foreign Relations. His most recent books are *No One's World: The West, the Rising Rest, and the Coming Global Turn* (2012) and *How Enemies Become Friends: The Sources of Stable Peace* (2010).

Margot Light is Emeritus Professor of International Relations at the London School of Economics and Political Science, UK. She has been teaching and writing about the former Soviet Union for the past 40 years. Among her publications are *Putin's Russia and the Enlarged Europe* (2006, with Roy Allison and Stephen White), "Russia and the EU: Strategic Partners or Strategic Rivals?", *Journal of Common Market Studies* (2008), and "Foreign Policy", in *Developments in Russian Politics* (edited by Stephen White, Richard Sakwa, and Henry E. Hale, 2010).

Cornelia Navari, formerly Senior Lecturer, is Honorary Senior Research Fellow at the University of Birmingham, UK, and Visiting Professor of International Relations at the University of Buckingham, UK. She is the author of *Internationalism and the State in the 20th Century* (2000) and *Public Intellectuals and International Affairs* (2012) and has edited *Theorising International Society: English School Methods* (2009). She is currently editing, with Dan Green, *The Guide to the English School of International Studies*.

Kevork Oskanian is a Visiting Lecturer at the University of Westminster, UK. He completed his PhD at the LSE Department of International Relations, UK. His research interests include the politics of the former Soviet Union, constructivism, the English School, and regionalism.

Ramon Pacheco Pardo is a Lecturer in the Department of European & International Studies at King's College London, UK. His research focuses on East Asia's international relations and political economy, EU foreign and economic policy, and EU–East Asia relations.

Nicholas Rengger is Professor of Political Theory and International Relations, and Head of the School of International Relations, at the University of St Andrews, UK, and a Global Ethics Fellow of the Carnegie Council for Ethics and International Affairs, in New York City. His scholarly interests range across political philosophy, intellectual history, International Relations Theory, ethics, and philosophical and political theology, and he has published widely in these areas. His most recent book is *Just War and International Order: The Uncivil Condition in World Politics*, and he is just completing a collection of his essays, to be titled *Dealing in Darkness: The Anti-Pelagian Imagination in Political Theory and International Relations*.

Christian Reus-Smit is Professor of International Relations at the University of Queensland, Australia. He is the author of *Individual Rights and the Making of the International System* (2013), *American Power and World Order* (2004), and *The Moral Purpose of the State* (1999); co-author of *Special Responsibilities: Global Problems and American Power* (2012); editor of *The Politics of International Law* (2004); and co-editor of *The Oxford Handbook of International Relations* (2008). He jointly edits the journal *International Theory* and the *Cambridge Studies in International Relations* book series.

Nabarun Roy is Assistant Professor in the Department of International Relations, Faculty of Social Sciences, South Asian University, New Delhi. He gained his PhD in Political Science from Carleton University, Ottawa, Canada. His research focuses on International Relations Theory, especially Realism and the English School, Indian foreign policy, and the geopolitics of Asia.

Frank Schimmelfennig is Professor of European Politics at ETH Zurich, Switzerland, and member of the Center for Comparative and International Studies. His main research interests are in the theory of international institutions and European integration and, more specifically, in the enlargement and democratisation of the EU and in international democracy promotion. He has published, inter alia, in *Comparative Political Studies, European Journal* *of International Relations, European Union Politics, International Organization, Journal of Common Market Studies,* and *Journal of European Public Policy.* He is the author of *The EU, NATO and the Integration of Europe: Rules and Rhetoric* (2003). His most recent book is *Differentiated Integration: Explaining Variation in the European Union* (2013, with Dirk Leuffen and Berthold Rittberger).

Brian C. Schmidt is Associate Professor in the Department of Political Science at Carleton University, Ottawa, Canada. He is the author of *The Political Discourse of Anarchy: A Disciplinary History of International Relations* (1998), which achieved the Choice outstanding book award. He is the co-editor, with David Long, of *Imperialism and Internationalism in the Discipline of International Relations* (2005) and *International Relations and the First Great Debate* (2012). He is also the co-editor, with David Long, of the History of International Thought Series.

Peter Trubowitz is Professor of Government at the University of Texas at Austin, USA. He is the author of *Politics and Strategy: Partisan Ambition and American Statecraft* (2011) and *Defining the National Interest: Conflict and Change in American Foreign Policy* (1998). His work his has appeared in scholarly journals such as *International Security, International Studies Quarterly,* and *Political Science Quarterly,* as well as *Foreign Affairs* and *the National Interest.*

Ren Xiao is currently Professor of International Politics at the Institute of International Studies (IIS), Fudan University, Shanghai, China, and Director of the Center for the Study of Chinese Foreign Policy at Fudan. His research concentrates on theory of international politics, international relations of the Asia-Pacific, East Asian security, and Chinese foreign policy. He is co-editor (with Allen Carlson) of *New Frontiers in China's Foreign Relations* (2011). He worked at the Chinese Embassy in Tokyo from February 2010 to February 2012.

Introduction

Rebekka Friedman, Kevork Oskanian, and Ramon Pacheco Pardo

Liberalism – defined, in its broadest sense, as the Western paradigm of thought that posits the individual as the normative standard of political and economic activity – has long had a strange courtship with the discipline of International Relations (IR). Indeed, it could be argued that liberalism has come in and out of intellectual fashion, largely as a response to world events. After two world wars and the Great Depression, the founding fathers of the discipline of IR sought to distance themselves from the unfulfilled promises of Wilsonian liberalism by taking a hard and "scientific" look at power politics. A few decades later, its perceived "triumph over communism" in 1989 seemed to have provided it with a degree of ideological legitimacy uncommon in the history of political thought: both its twentieth-century totalitarian challengers lay at its feet, defeated. A "New World Order", based on the now-unquestioned precepts of liberal democracy and neoliberal economics, would propel the world into an era of peace and prosperity where Marx's historical dialectic would reach a premature end point (Fukuyama, 1993). If anything, this brave new world would be a boring place, bereft of ideological conflict and discussion, with technocratic governments "kept in line" through a combination of market forces and a US-led international society.

Twenty years later, hindsight – the critic's perennial friend – allows us to marvel at the hubris displayed in the intensity of the moment. Liberalism's detractors charge that the enlightenment's foundational ideology failed to deliver its promise of individual freedom and knowledge through its reliance on and reification of the state; that it has provided the few with prosperity at the cost of environmental degradation and poverty for the many (Heynen et al., 2007); that it has left the world with an economic system that is forever teetering on the brink (Gill, 2012); that it has fundamentally remained a Euro-centric imposition on a culturally and ideologically still-diverse world (Hobson, 2012); and that it has threatened the fundamental right to life of the many – mostly in the global South – who have fallen victim to liberal forms of warfare (Barkawi and Laffey, 2001; Mbembé and Meintjes, 2003).

Gaps between theory and practice have widened as national and domestic norms and institutions are confronted with the War on Terror (Desch, 2007). Those who presented the International Economic Order as the road to global prosperity face one of the worst financial meltdowns in living memory. Cosmopolitan-inspired interventionism is juxtaposed with the failure to prevent and react to humanitarian crises, and top-down democratising projects around the world have either stagnated or reversed (Jahn, 2007a, 2007b). Critics charge that the world is more "in flux", with less agreed-upon rules than ever before, with the (re-)emergence of distinctly illiberal great powers pointing to new divides between autocracies and liberal democracies in the post-Cold War world (Gat, 2007). To its detractors, Liberalism seems to be an ideology with universal *pretensions*, but without universal *answers* – as the hapless fates of its totalitarian predecessors have shown, not a desirable position over the longer term.

This book was born at the start of the greatest crisis of Liberalism since the Interbellum. Marking the twentieth anniversary since the fall of the Berlin Wall, the October 2009 Millennium Conference – entitled *"After Liberalism?"* – presented a unique opportunity to put recent developments in IR into theoretical perspective. As turning points in IR offer novel opportunities to take stock of dominant discourse and thought, drawing inspiration from previous reflective works on historical change in the discipline, notably G. John Ikenberry's *After Victory: Institutions, Strategic Restraint, and the Rebuilding of Rules after Major Wars* (2001) and Robert Keohane's *After Hegemony: Cooperation and Discord in the World Political Economy* (1984), the objective of the 2009 Millennium Conference and Special Issue was to raise questions about the direction of liberalism in this new century of uncertainties. It evaluated the significance of recent events, in particular the financial crisis, the rise of regional powers, the humanitarian fallout, and the international response thereto, as well as the ability of IR theory to make sense of the liberal order today.

The 2009 Conference and Special Issue inspired our subsequent proposal for this edited volume. After reflecting on the discussions generated by the conference and the chapters presented in the Special Issue, we identified important subthemes and implications for future consideration. Prominent among these was the remarkable staying power of liberalism: its ability to reinvent itself to fit the current order, albeit in different guises. Whether, as G. John Ikenberry argues, liberal structures will retain a benign form even as US authority wanes, or whether, as posited by other contributors in this volume, liberalism will react to systemic change through greater hegemonic control, liberal ideology has found a way to adapt in both theory and practice. That liberalism's robustness lies precisely in its malleability, in its consistent ability to metamorphose in a world perennially in flux, struck us as an important implication for future reflection.

This edited volume will address precisely this theme. If liberalism's strength lies in its ability to reinvent itself, this raises important theoretical, empirical, and normative questions for the student of IR. Part I deals with liberalism as theory – What is the continued relevance of liberalism as an explanatory theory of IR? Are critiques of liberalism sufficiently effective in their current form? Part II looks at liberalism and American hegemony – To what extent is American hegemony expressed in the form of a liberal international order? Does domestic polarisation spell the end of support for this order? To what extent will it be able to survive in this new century? Part III examines the diffusion of liberalism – What is liberalism's role in the international political economy? How does it feed into the policies and world views of established and rising great powers – China, Russia, and the European Union – as well as recent political upheavals in the Middle East? The concluding chapter sums up and reflects on the larger themes of the volume.

In Chapter 1, Beate Jahn questions the narrative of a "rise and fall" of liberalism in IR theory. The rise and fall of liberalism reflects the experience of liberalism in IR theory, rather than its fate as a political project. The penchant of liberal theory for dichotomies and oppositions – between the domestic and the international, theory and practice, and between liberalism's political, economic, and normative dimensions – fails to grasp liberalism's core premises. Jahn develops a Lockean understanding of liberalism, which highlights continuities of the liberal political project from the Cold War period into the present. Liberalism is dynamic and varied. While democracy is today widely seen as a core characteristic of liberalism, liberals were historically cautious about democracy promotion. Jahn subsequently discusses the intimate link between liberalism and colonialism. Current IR theory fails to recognise power politics as a constitutive element of liberalism. Jahn concludes that we are likely to see more liberalism, yet in a different guise. She identifies the "successful democratisation of liberalism", which forces governments to pursue economic growth to "provide the population with the economic benefits that maintain their stake in the system", as the major historical change in liberalism. The intimate linking of liberalism and democracy, however, has not resolved a core tension – centred on the fact that the maintenance of liberal policies in some parts of the world has been built on the illiberal expropriation of others. Today, this expropriation takes place in the international sphere, where the "political fallout of these economic policies has to be borne by other states". Liberalism is best recognised as a political project, carried out through the differential treatment of liberal and non-liberal actors in the domestic and the international spheres.

In Chapter 2, Cornelia Navari argues that while liberalism may be declining, democracy is on the rise. While many have pinpointed Wilsonian liberalism as the origin of a democracy norm, Navari argues that democratic governance only emerged as an international norm with the collapse of the Soviet Union, in 1989. She states that this mischaracterisation has to do with the influence of constructivist theory on IR, which focuses scholarship on norm construction and norm entrepreneurs. Navari draws on the English School as a helpful tradition with which to identify settled and emerging norms. She argues that an emerging democracy norm has significant implications for international society, rendering for example the possibility that democratic states no longer recognise the outcomes of elections in non-democratic states, and justifying military intervention into such states. While the implications of a democracy norm remain up for question, Navari argues that democracy is gaining determinate meaning in international society by setting a standard of regular elections between at least two competing political parties, which are fairly monitored. While human rights advocates call for a deeper norm of full political rights, Navari identifies most of the activity surrounding the creation of a democracy norm as one of setting standards. With the exception of the European context, Navari claims that the international standard is not being enlarged to allow external interference into domestic political processes. While the existing democracy norm has gained a wide institutional backing among international and regional organisations, thus far, there has been more reference to democracy *promotion* rather than *protection*, and more emphasis on *humanitarian* rather than *democratic* intervention.

In Chapter 3, Nicholas Rengger examines what he calls "dystopic liberalism". He distinguishes dystopic liberals from liberals who believe in one superior way of life and focus on justice, rights, and obligations, such as John Rawls. Dystopic liberalism, in contrast, is pluralistic in its recognition and endorsement of multiple modes of life. Rengger draws on Judith Shklar's "liberalism of fear" to develop an understanding of dystopic liberalism as guided by scepticism and suspicion of utopianism. Dystopic liberals seek as their end the protection of personal freedom. They take a prudent approach to IR, which often overlaps with their realist counterparts. Rengger questions the ability of dystopic liberalism to "deliver what it promises". There is an ambiguity running through dystopic liberalism, where scepticism and liberalism push in contradictory directions. For Rengger, scholars must ultimately take a stance. While scepticism and liberalism run hand in hand and feed each other in the work of Shklar, Rengger argues that for other dystopic liberals, scepticism trumps liberalism. For Shklar, in particular, liberalism is rare and fragile – the conditions able to support liberalism are far and in between – linking realists and liberals in their view of the human condition as essentially "tragic". Rengger questions this core assumption: " ... human life is not 'tragic', it is just life; and equally, one should see political life not as a 'Dystopia' but just as political life in all of its variety and messiness". He concludes that political philosophy should be sceptical first and liberal second. Drawing on Santayana, scepticism is the "chastity of the intellect and should not be relinquished too readily".

In Chapter 4, Brian Schmidt and Nabarun Roy analyse liberalism as a theory of IR by dissecting its approach to the rise and fall of great powers, while providing an extensive comparison with the manner in which realism describes this reality of world politics. Schmidt and Roy show that liberalism and realism concur in important ways. Both theories emphasise engagement with rising powers and avoidance of unnecessary confrontation. However, Schmidt and Roy explain, liberalism and realism have significant differences in the analysis of the impact of rising powers in the international system. Liberals acknowledge that the rise of new powers such as China and India today challenges the existing liberal international order, but they are not especially worried about this because they do not believe any major disruption to the order to be likely. In contrast, realists, whether classical, structural, or neoclassical, are acutely concerned about possible disruptions to the international order caused by the rise of new great powers. This has led to a debate within realism that is missing among liberals, with realists agreeing on a prognosis of instability in the international system, but not on the policy prescriptions for today's hegemon, the United States. For realists, the existing liberal international order will not necessarily integrate a rising great power; thus, appeasement, balance of power, containment, negotiated settlement, peaceful change, preventive war, and retrenchment are all available policy choices for the hegemon in response to the rise of new powers.

In Chapter 5, G. John Ikenberry – following his keynote speech at the 2009 Millennium Conference – responds to a growing literature arguing that the liberal order is under challenge. This literature foresees a return to multipolarity and new forms of conflict, especially between autocratic and liberal-democratic states. It emphasises historical grievances, with powers such as China and Russia reclaiming their international role. Ikenberry posits that the current crisis is one of American dominance, rather than being one of the liberal order itself. Power and authority will shift, yet there is no ideological alternative to liberalism. Building on his earlier work, he argues that the current American-led international liberal order is defined by its transparent rules-based character. States today have more in common both in the threats they face and in their interests. A gradual normative reorientation in favour of a universal conception of human rights and the "responsibility to protect", greater "security interdependence" based on more diffuse and complex transnational threats, and common interests – especially in health and environment – will likely increase demands for cooperation and institutionalisation. Where, for more than half a century, the United States has governed the liberal international order, today, rising states seek a greater position within this order. "The challenge of the liberal international order today is to manage this transition in its ownership and governance". The crisis of liberalism is a result of its success, rather than its failure. Instead of an E.H. Carr crisis, where realist critiques of the liberal project bear fruit, for Ikenberry, the current crisis is a Karl Polanyi crisis, where "liberal governance is troubled because dilemmas and long-term shifts in the order can only be solved by rethinking, rebuilding, and extending that liberal order". Ikenberry argues that this crisis of liberalism is ultimately likely to produce more liberalism.

In Chapter 6, Michael Cox examines the future of the liberal international order in view of the multiple challenges it has faced in recent years: the post-9/11 conflicts, the financial crisis, and the rise of China. Rejecting the notion that the 1990s marked a high water mark of a Liberalism now in decline, Cox adopts the "unfashionable" position that it is, in fact, *not* in crisis, given the persistence of democracy, global capitalism, globalisation, and the fact that "the American people actually decided to reject many of the policies associated with the Bush administration by electing the most liberal (and the first black) President in the history of the republic". Cox considers not only material but also "soft" power, including Research and Development spending and the concentration of leading educational institutions in the United States. Despite rising China's economic prowess and increasingly active role in the Global South, for Cox, the Chinese lack a conscious international strategy; moreover, while China may command respect, it has shown itself less strong in the sphere of soft power, with few imitators. In sum, the system of power underpinning the liberal order may be battered and less confident than at the end of the Cold War, but it retains enormous staying power.

In Chapter 7, Charles Kupchan and Peter Trubowitz document the decline of support for liberal internationalism in the country that created it – the United States. Kupchan and Trubowitz argue that this decline has consequences not only for American foreign policy, but also for the international system as a whole. They trace this decline not to the policies implemented by the George W. Bush administration, as commonly believed, but to the end of a bipartisan consensus on foreign policy emanating from the threat posed by illiberal states, be it Nazi Germany, Imperial Japan, or the Soviet Union. Absent the geopolitical and domestic conditions that sustained liberal internationalism – above all engagement in multilateral institutions – this approach to foreign policy has been eroded. The absence of bipartisanship at the domestic level hampers those seeking the restoration of liberal internationalism as the default foreign policy of the United States, as proved by the difficulties of the Barack Obama administration in doing so. Kupchan and Trubowitz explain that, given the distinct possibility that liberal internationalism will not enjoy broad domestic support for the foreseeable future, the United States has to design and implement a new grand strategy. This grand strategy should be more modest in terms of its goals and means, more pragmatic from an American point of view, so as to avoid creating more divisions at the domestic level. In its liberal internationalist form, liberalism has been weakened as a foreign policy option in the United States and is unlikely to return any time soon. In Chapter 8, Jonathan D. Caverley also focuses on liberalism as a theory of IR by examining other theories with which it has some prima facie similarities and differences. To this end, Caverley looks at neoconservatism and neoclassical realism in the context of US politics. The former is yet to be universally accepted as a valid theoretical approach for the analysis of IR, but, as Caverley shows, there are a number of central tenets to neoconservatism that allow it to be considered as a distinct and codified theory as well. Above all, neoconservatives believe in the spread of democracy to enhance stability in the international system. This would put them in line with traditional liberal thinking, were it not for one crucial difference: their belief on the *use of force* in achieving this goal. As Caverley argues, this specific feature brings it closer to realism's latest incarnation – its neoclassical variant. For while neoclassical realism does not specifically advocate spreading democracy through military means, it does share with neoconservatism a starting assumption about the nature of the international system being defined by (potentially violent) competition among states in an anarchic world. Neoconservatism is thus best described as a theory advocating a liberal goal – the spread of democracy – within a realist world view. The debate between neoconservatism and neoclassical realism that emerged as a result of the policies of the George W. Bush administration – especially the launch of the Iraq War – thus camouflages a shared world view that does *not* coincide with liberalism's.

In Chapter 9, Christian Reus-Smit critiques Ikenberry's conception of international order as a common set of rules and practices as incomplete: for Reus-Smit, institutionalised power and authority and a framework for constitutional social norms are additional characteristics. While Ikenberry puts less emphasis on the "purposive" dimension of international order, Reus-Smit argues that great powers construct orders to preserve their own security and peace. There is a contradiction in Ikenberry's conception of order as *stability* versus order as *institutionalised governance* between states. Smit argues that Ikenberry takes a sovereign state system as given, neglecting the extent to which the rise of the liberal order occurred "hand in hand with a reordering of how the international system's political units stood in relation to one another". Where Ikenberry casts the United States as the "sole architect and builder", Reus-Smit emphasises the agency of post-colonial states in driving the post-1945 normative revolution of self-determination, noting the United States' opposition to self-determination alongside European colonial powers. Drawing on Ruggie's embedded liberalism, the development of the liberal international order reflects broadly shared legitimate goals. Instead, what is novel in today's liberal order is the notion of universal sovereignty as the sole legitimate type of political organisation. Like Jahn, Reus-Smit identifies tensions between the sovereign state system and cosmopolitanism. Reus-Smit highlights the "Millian" quality of the liberal order and the perpetuation of a distinction between "civilised" and "barbarous" nations. "One of the great accomplishments of post-1945 anti-colonialism was to delegitimise not only the institution of empire, but also this explicitly racist division of the world's peoples into civilised and barbarian". Constitutional norms of ethical cosmopolitan universalism and "hierarchy without empire" push in different directions. While empire now has a stigma, hierarchy has not disappeared, but must be informal and negotiated.

In Chapter 10, Philip G. Cerny examines liberalism by focusing on a phenomenon that many consider to be one of its clearest manifestations: globalisation. Cerny argues that globalisation both enhances and weakens liberalism. On the one hand, globalisation creates new pathways closely related to the traditions of Enlightenment liberalism and the pluralisation of social orders. On the other hand, globalisation strengthens cross-border manifestations of collective action, thus undermining the states that IR considers to be the birthplace of liberalism. Cerny explains that five trends are the most prominent result of globalisation: a reduction of war and violence, economic interdependence, social inclusion and multiculturalism, new ideologies, and institutional pluralisation. These trends can be described as simultaneously neoliberal and neomedieval. They are neoliberal insofar a new international political economy built upon cross-cutting institutional and market relations is developing. This renders obsolete important political and economic functions of the state, which therefore might cease to be the foundational point of contemporary international politics. These trends are concurrently neomedieval in that competing multi-nodal political processes creating an overlap of boundaries and jurisdictions are becoming entrenched. Therefore, the state is once again undermined, further weakening liberalism. But globalisation, Cerny argues, need not spell the end of the state and liberalism with it. States can become part of multi-level systems of governance, bringing together sub-state, state, and supra-state actors. Meanwhile, liberalism in its Enlightened and plural forms is being reinforced in the form of the just-mentioned neoliberalism.

In Chapter 11, Ren Xiao analyses the liberal and realist aspects of the rise of China through the prism of the "peaceful rise", and later the "peaceful development" conceptualisations. Ren argues that the origin and articulation of "peaceful rise" and its eventual transformation into "peaceful development" demonstrate that China is not an entirely realist power. Indeed, Ren maintains, China has increasingly displayed foreign policy actions that are distinctly liberal. In particular, China is involved in a growing number of multilateral diplomatic initiatives, unafraid to engage with other countries and even to take on a leading role. This reflects domestic steps towards democracy, the free market, and an open society. In this context, there was some internal debate about whether China's more prominent role in international politics should be labelled "peaceful rise" or "peaceful development". The latter was finally preferred, mainly because it served not only to soothe critics of China's rise, but also to show that China does not wish to seek hegemony or challenge the existing international order. Ren thus argues that the rise of China is, above all, the rise of a *liberal* China. Contrary to realist assertions, this rise is unlikely to lead to a confrontation between great powers, militarily or otherwise. Even China's military build-up, which many see as a means to prepare for war, has led to deeper engagement in multilateral security issues. China's self-interest is based on a liberal, not realist, understanding of international politics.

In Chapter 12, Margot Light examines why liberalism has failed to take root in Russia. While past historical epochs and events have indeed shaped Russian political culture, more effective elucidations for Liberalism's still-born status can be found in the country's recent past: firstly, in the nature of the reforms undertaken in the 1990s and the consequences of those reforms for the majority of the Russian people and, secondly, in the mistakes that were made in the democracy promotion programmes launched by the United States and the European Union in those years. The failure of liberalism to take root can be explained through an unbalanced preoccupation with *neoliberal* economic reforms, a determination to prevent – through undemocratic means if necessary – the return to power of the Communists and the more general failure to promote robust liberal-democratic institutions. There was, consequently, nothing inevitable about the failure of liberalism in Russia. The chapter begins with a brief account of the rise and decline of liberalism in the 1980s and 1990s; a second section describes the neoliberal economic reforms implemented in Russia in the early 1990s and examines their economic and social consequences. The argument then turns to the problems that arose in promoting democracy in Russia and the rise and demise of liberalism in Russian foreign policy, before studying the retreat from liberalism and neoliberalism under President Vladimir Putin, and concluding with a brief evaluation of the liberalising potential of the 2011 post-election demonstrations.

In Chapter 13, Frank Schimmelfennig criticises the truncated nature of Liberal Intergovernmentalism (LI) as an explanatory approach to European Integration. Emanating from neoliberal institutionalism and including domestic politics in its accounts of European integration – in typically liberal fashion – it nevertheless builds on only one single variant of liberal theory: *commercial* liberalism. As a consequence, LI neglects the many facets of European integration that derive from the nature of the European Union as an *ideational* liberal community, where fundamental developments cannot be adequately theorised and explained in isolation from liberal values, norms, and identities. The author proposes a move beyond the limitations of commercial LI, formulating building blocks and hypotheses for an alternative, ideational liberal variant of the theory. A liberal international community is then defined as a community of states governed by liberal norms, including peace, multilateralism, and democracy, and based on a post-national, civic identity: ideational liberalism argues that these norms, rather than economic interests or material bargaining power, shape the constitutional developments in such a community. The chapter provides three brief case studies on Eastern enlargement to substantiate its argument, representing three different dimensions of integration (enlargement, institutional deepening, and policy integration) that have remained unexplained by "orthodox" LI. Thus, the role of democratic values is seen as crucial in driving Eastern enlargement; similarly, the parliamentarisation of EU decision-making processes is tied to the varying democratic national identities of the member states; these same variations in national identity are posited as underlying the differentiated levels of integration between member states.

In Chapter 14, Louise Fawcett starts out by probing the historical record for a better understanding of the Middle East's experience of liberalism: challenging ahistorical and simplifying assumptions about the region's "illiberal" past, she seeks to construct an alternative narrative based around key liberal or liberalising episodes from the late Ottoman period to the present. Liberalism's history in the Middle East was by no means continuous, its progress marked by crisis, retrenchment, reform, and renewal. Against this background – one of stunted or interrupted liberalism – the chapter goes on to examine the relevance and appropriateness of some of the dominant "universal" pretensions of liberalism, those advocated and practised by Western liberal democracies, in light of the regional experience. Here, it suggests that while Arab, Iranian, and Turkish liberals – both Muslim and non-Muslim – have undoubtedly embraced the language of liberalism and pluralism, it is also likely that any modern Middle Eastern reading of liberalism will look different in some important aspects. These differences, it is argued, relate to timing – the region's first embrace of liberalism came relatively late; culture – there was and is a tension between certain universal logics of liberalism and local cultures and practices; and, finally, external factors, which have had contradictory push-pull effects. In this regard, the Middle East is seen as by no means unique – other states and regions have embraced liberalism at different times and in different ways – though it has perhaps been unusual in the longevity of authoritarianism and persistence of illiberal practices.

References

Barkawi, T. and Laffey, M. (eds) (2001), *Democracy, Liberalism and War: Rethinking the Democratic Peace Debate*, Boulder: Lynne Rienner.

Desch, M. C. (2007), "America's Liberal Illiberalism: The Ideological Origins of Overreaction in U.S. Foreign Policy", *International Security*, 32(3), 7–43.

Fukuyama, F. (1993), *The End of History and the Last Man*, London: Penguin Books.

Gat, A. (2007), "The Return of Authoritarian Great Powers", *Foreign Affairs*, 86(4), 59–69.

Gill, S. (ed.) (2012), *Global Crises and the Crisis of Global Leadership*, Cambridge: Cambridge University Press.

Heynen, N., McCarthy, J., Prudham, S. and Robbins, P. (eds) (2007), *Neoliberal Environments: False Promises and Unnatural Consequences*, New York: Routledge.

Hobson, J. M. (2012), *The Eurocentric Conception of World Politics: Western International Theory, 1760–2010*, Cambridge: Cambridge University Press.

Ikenberry, G. J. (2001), *After Victory: Institutions, Strategic Restraint, and the Rebuilding of Order after Major Wars*, Princeton: Princeton University Press.

Jahn, B. (2007a), "The Tragedy of Liberal Diplomacy: Democratization, Intervention, Statebuilding", *Journal of Intervention and Statebuilding*, 1(2), 211–229.

Jahn, B. (2007b), "The Tragedy of Liberal Diplomacy: Democratization, Intervention, Statebuilding (Part 1)", *Journal of Intervention and Statebuilding*, 1(1), 87–106.

Keohane, R. O. (1984). *After Hegemony: Cooperation and Discord in the World Political Economy*, Princeton: Princeton University Press.

Mbembé, J. -A. and Meintjes, L. (2003), Necropolitics, *Public Culture*, 15(1), 11–40.

Part I

Liberalism and International Relations Theory

1
Liberalism – In Theory and History

Beate Jahn

Introduction

Liberalism's standing in the discipline of International Relations (IR), as well as in world politics, is, by most accounts, characterised by constant ups and downs, exalted expectations, and embarrassing failures. Hence, liberalism's "triumph" (Fukuyama, 1989) at the end of the Cold War and its subsequent rapid demise is only the latest instance of this history which has given rise to the question of what, if anything, comes "after liberalism"? Yet, I will argue in the following pages that the narrative of a "rise" and "fall" of liberalism fits, at best, the fate of liberal theory within IR, but certainly not the fate of liberalism as a political project.

In the first section of this chapter, I will show that liberalism is widely misconceived in IR. Confronted with its rich, varied, and, at times, contradictory manifestations, scholars tend to focus on particular aspects of liberalism. This practice results in a variety of liberal approaches and theories that, however, provide only partial conceptions of liberalism. And it is in light of these partial conceptions that liberalism indeed appears to go through constant ups and down.

In the second section of this chapter, I will therefore try to recapture the core of liberalism by bridging the very divisions that lead to these partial conceptions. To this end, I will return to John Locke's pre-disciplinary formulation of protoliberal principles, which explicitly theorise the connections between their core aspects and their political dynamics. This Lockean account of liberalism and its political dynamics, moreover, is broadly substantiated by the historical development of liberalism.

Viewed through the lens of this alternative concept, recent history shows neither a "rise" nor a "fall" of liberalism. Instead, the shifts that undoubtedly characterise this period simply indicate liberalism's adjustment to the power political opportunities and constraints provided by the international system. In short, they are shifts in form rather than substance. What comes "after liberalism", I therefore conclude, is simply a different register of liberalism.

Liberalism – Divided

During the 1990s, a wide range of policies was prominently associated with liberalism. Among them were the liberalisation, deregulation, and privatisation of the international economy, the development of the World Trade Organization (WTO), and the transformation of former communist into capitalist states – in short, neo*liberal* economic policies. Proactive democracy promotion, as well as the widespread attempt to establish liberal market democracies as solution to failed, conflict-ridden, or even simply authoritarian states played an important role in the foreign policies of liberal states, of NGOs, and of international organisations and institutions, and gave rise to the notion of *"liberal* peacebuilding". Liberalism was also associated with the proactive protection of human rights, not least in the form of humanitarian intervention as well as with plans to reform international law and international organisations in accordance with "a world of liberal states" (Clark, 2009; Keohane, 2003; Slaughter, 1995).

In contrast to this spread of liberal norms, practices, and institutions, power politics generally associated with realism characterised the prior Cold War period. Capitalism, free trade, and free market principles were confined to the Western sphere of influence and tempered, domestically and internationally, by considerations of political stability. Democracy promotion was equally restricted and generally trumped by power political considerations; hence extensive alliances with authoritarian states and interventions in support of sympathetic rather than democratic regimes predominated. Human rights were generally subordinated to the principle of sovereignty. In short, the "rise" of liberalism was associated with the increase in policies explicitly designed to spread liberal norms, practices, and institutions. And it was the retreat from these policies towards the end of the 1990s and a more explicit turn towards traditional power politics after 9/11 that seemed to indicate a "fall" of liberalism.

On closer inspection, however, liberalism cannot unequivocally be identified with these policies. While democracy is today widely seen as a core characteristic of liberalism, liberals were historically passionately opposed to democracy. Meanwhile, calling the recent policies of economic liberalisation, deregulation, and privatisation, "neoliberal" indicates some continuity with the laissez-faire policies of classical liberalism. And yet, the Cold War settlement of large parts of the world economy was also characterised as (embedded) *liberalism*. And even though liberal states are today associated with the protection of individual freedom and respect for human rights, the very same norms coexisted historically with the practice and justification of slavery.

These examples show, firstly, that liberalism is historically linked to a much wider range of policies, institutions, and norms than is recognised in the contemporary conception. Secondly, there is no doubt that liberalism is a dynamic historical phenomenon, which changes over time and from place to place. Thirdly, different liberal norms, institutions, or policies may well stand in tension to each other. And this provides a challenge for the definition of liberalism. Indeed, the fact that liberalism is "quite diverse", has not "evolved in a singular linear fashion", and is "marked by levels of disagreement and variation" is widely interpreted to stand in the way of an encompassing definition which would "paper over significant differences" (Tansey, 2008: 90–91). Consequently, scholars tend to focus on the one or other aspect of liberalism.

Broadly four different – albeit not exclusive but often complimentary – lines of division provide the basis for solutions. These are temporal lines of division, political and spatial lines of division, the distinction between theory and practice as well as that between substantive issue areas. The temporal solution holds that early conceptions of liberalism were immature and often still mistaken in the interpretation and application of liberal principles. With regard to the tension between liberalism and democracy, for instance, it is argued that early liberals did not yet realise – but subsequently learned over time – that extending equal political rights to all citizens was not only logically required by liberal principles and that it "need not lead to the outright plunder of the rich and the destruction of a productive economy and a civilised society" (Plattner, 2008: 60, 68). Contradictory historical evidence is thus interpreted as a (potentially even necessary) step on the road to contemporary mature liberalism, which "contains within itself the seeds of its own democratisation" (Plattner, 2008: 60). Liberal opposition to democracy is thus recognised as part of the history of liberalism, yet clearly distinguished from the proper contemporary identification of liberalism with democracy. Instead of undermining the assumption that liberalism and democracy necessarily imply each other, historical counterevidence here simply demonstrates its progressive development and learning capacity.

The second strategy of accounting for the rich and contradictory norms and practices of liberalism distinguishes between a liberal and a non-liberal context. Here it is argued that policies on the part of liberal actors that appear to contradict liberal principles – such as protectionism or the use of force to extract economic benefits as in the case of slavery or colonialism – have their roots in an uncompetitive, monopolistic, undiversified, in short illiberal, environment that lacks economic interdependence and encourages rent-seeking behaviour (Moravcsik, 1997: 529–530). Similarly, the democratic peace thesis argues that the aggressive behaviour of liberal or democratic towards non-liberal states has its roots in the "illiberal" nature of the latter (Doyle, 1996). The distinction between liberal and non-liberal contexts thus recognises that liberal actors may engage in "illiberal" practices. And yet, the latter do not enter into the definition of liberalism because they are triggered by "illiberal" environments. Consequently, an end to such "illiberal" behaviour even of liberal states requires the transformation of "illiberal" into liberal environments.

In a similar vein, the distinction between the domestic and international context is frequently used to explain contradictory practices. Liberalism's performance in the international sphere is characterised, Stanley Hoffmann argues, by ambition, insolence, rapine, brutality, racism, intolerance; no liberal state has ever behaved as liberal abroad as at home (1987: 397). The reason for this systematic tension is sought in the fact that liberalism is essentially a domestic political project – concerned with the freedom of the individual and its participation in government – which is only subsequently extended into the international sphere where it encounters very different kinds of demands (1987: 395). While unsavoury policies are thus seen as part and parcel of liberalism, they are generated by an international environment that is "inhospitable to liberalism" (Hoffmann, 1987: 405). In this view, the solution to the weak international performance of liberalism lies either in a proper development of liberal principles for the international sphere – as prominently undertaken in John Rawls' "Law of Peoples" (2001) – and/or in a "domestication" of the international system itself; that is, in developments that bring it into closer resemblance to the domestic sphere. This usually includes either the demise of the sovereign state as asserted in globalisation theories and/or an international sphere dominated by (more or less disaggregated) liberal states, which removes the incompatibility between the domestic liberal principles and the demands of international politics (Beitz, 1979; Slaughter, 1995).

Thirdly, contradictory evidence is explained by a distinction between liberal principles and norms on the one hand and liberal practice on the other. Thus, liberalism can be divided into a "radical" and an "elitist" strand with "radical liberalism" embodying the core liberal norms and principles and "elitist liberalism" embodying the betrayal of those principles in practice (Richardson, 2001: 205). Again, the distinction between liberal norms and policies, or theory and practice, recognises contradictory evidence, but it defines liberalism on the basis of liberal norms and principles only which therefore provide a solution to deviant and corrupt practices.

Last, but not least, contradictory dynamics have given rise to a distinction between the substantive dimensions of liberalism, with different theories focusing either on its political, or its economic, or its normative dimension. Neoliberal economic policies, for example, are widely regarded as potentially undermining policies of democracy promotion because of their social costs (Bermeo, 2009: 259; Przeworski, 1992). Democracy, in turn, often appears to stand in contradiction to liberal norms – hence, the recent "rise of illiberal democracy" (Zakaria, 1997) or suggestions to sequence the introduction of liberal institutions and democracy (Paris, 2004). Hence, liberal theories tend to focus on either one of these – political, economic, normative – dimensions of liberalism. Andrew Moravcsik, for example, identifies ideational, commercial, and republican liberalism (1997: 515); Robert Keohane and Joseph Nye speak of commercial, democratic, regulatory, and sociological liberalism (Nye, 1988: 246); Jackson and Sorensen of sociological, interdependence, institutional, and republican liberalism (2003: 108); Tim Dunne speaks of internationalism, idealism, institutionalism as well as their respective "neo"-variations (1997: 150–154); Michael Doyle of liberal imperialism, pacifism, and internationalism (1997: 206); Mark Zacher and Richard Matthew distinguish between republican, commercial, cognitive, sociological, and institutional liberalism (1995: 122–137), to mention but a few of these theories. Republican liberalism focuses on political institutions and regimes; commercial, interdependence and pacifist liberalism focus on the economic sphere while ideational and cognitive liberalism focus on ideas, norms, and culture. Though avoiding direct tensions between the political, economic, and normative aspects, these theories end up providing competing and partial conceptions of liberalism. Thus, the "democratic peace" is variously explained through the representative nature of democracy (Doyle, 1996); through the extension of liberal norms of nonviolent conflict resolution into the international sphere (Russett, 1996); or through mutual interests and cooperation fostered by economic interdependence (Barbieri, 2002).

In sum, these approaches to the problem of liberalism's rich and varied nature manage to account for contradictory evidence, but they do so by externalising its less savoury aspects which are variously seen as generated by an immature past that has long been superseded, by external – illiberal and international – contexts, by an imperfect practice, or by an economic instead of political, political instead of normative, and normative instead of economic conception of liberalism. The results are partial and unsatisfactory accounts of liberalism. First of all, these accounts fail to chime with the general use of the term "liberal" and its application to particular actors. Though liberalism is undoubtedly intimately linked to the political institution of democracy today, democratic institutions are not sufficient for a state to be generally recognised as liberal – Russia being a case in point (Zakaria, 1997). Similarly, neither liberal norms and principles nor the existence of private property and free markets alone – as in China – constitute a liberal state.

Secondly, on closer inspection it turns out that contradictory evidence cannot neatly be divided along temporal and spatial lines or between theory and practice. Thus, while empirical liberal theory is right to claim that liberal practice has to play a crucial role in its definition, normative liberals correctly assert that without reference to liberal norms and principles, the emancipatory potential of liberalism is lost (Long, 1995; Moravcsik 1997: 514). Similarly, the distinction between historical and contemporary liberalism fails to account for the prominent role of supposedly "historical" features of liberalism – such as arguments for imperialism – in contemporary liberal thought and practice (Cooper, 2002; Ignatieff, 2003). The distinction between domestic and international liberalism obscures the fact that some of the less savoury practices of liberalism – such as human rights violations – occur in the domestic and not just in the international context (Roberts, 2004). The assumption that intraliberal relations are particularly conducive to the realisation of liberal principles overlooks the fact that these principles themselves may well constitute a specifically liberal barrier to liberal practice, such as the vertical integration of international law (Alvarez, 2001: 202). These distinctions thus capture neither liberal actors nor liberal practices and norms satisfactorily.

And yet, it is these partial conceptions of liberalism that underpin the story of the "rise" and "fall" of liberalism during the 1990s. Proactive policies of democracy promotion appear to indicate a "rise" of liberalism only if we exclude liberalism's un- or even anti-democratic record from the definition. If we take this record into account, Cold War alliances with dictators may well fit into liberal foreign policies, just as post-Cold War arguments that liberalism can exist perfectly well in the absence of universal franchise (Sartori, 1995; Vanberg, 2008). Neoliberal economic policies during the 1990s only indicate a "rise" of liberalism if the political regulation of the economic sphere – whether through Keynesian policies or the Bretton Woods institutions of the Cold War – are excluded from the definition of liberalism. Finally, the pitching of liberal norms and principles against the principle of sovereignty during the 1990s can only be interpreted as indicating a "rise" of liberalism if the crucial role of the principle of sovereignty in liberal policies – for instance its reassertion in the Responsibility to Protect (Bellamy, 2005: 33) – is disregarded.

Hence, a more consistent and encompassing conception of liberalism is required in order to assess the nature of recent changes. The development of such a concept of liberalism, however, faces the challenges that have led to the less than satisfactory approaches discussed above. For all their shortcomings, these approaches nevertheless show that liberalism is a complex cultural phenomenon in the Weberian sense: "a complex of different elements associated in historical reality which we unite into a conceptual whole from the standpoint of their cultural significance" (Weber, 1984: 47). In other words, we attach the conceptual term "liberalism" to the historical coming together of different elements that in combination play a significant role in shaping our cultural framework. Defining such phenomena is difficult, firstly, because they are multifaceted as the variety of approaches to liberalism shows; secondly, because their meaning arises from the relations of the different elements to each other which is generally obscured through the distinctions that underpin traditional conceptions of liberalism; thirdly, because they are changing over time and thus defy static forms of definition; fourthly, because they play a significant, often constitutive, role for the cultural framework and are thus difficult to isolate, delimit, and identify. Consequently, Weber argues that for complex cultural phenomena of this kind, the "definitive concept cannot stand at the beginning of the investigation, but must come at the end" (1984: 47). Ideally, a thorough historical investigation that traces the changing relations of the different constitutive elements to each other and to their effect on (our conceptions of international) society as a whole provides the necessary basis for the subsequent conceptualisation of liberalism as a complex cultural phenomenon. Alas, there is no scope for such an approach within the confines of this chapter (indeed, it would be a tall order even for a book). Instead, a theoretically well reflected and guided approach allows for a shortcut that can provide at least a first step in the right direction.

Given that complex cultural phenomena draw their meaning from the relations of their constitutive elements and in light of the fact that it is precisely these relations that have generally been severed in the familiar approaches, I start from the assumption that these relations have to be analysed in order to recover the dynamic core of liberalism. Since the distinctions to be overcome largely follow the fault lines of disciplinary fragmentation in the academy – history, political theory, political science, international relations, economy – I shall turn to the pre-disciplinary reflections of a great thinker in the liberal tradition, John Locke, in order to recover an explicit theorisation of the dynamic relations between core liberal principles. Armed with a preliminary understanding of liberalism based on Locke's work, I shall then show that the historical development of liberalism did indeed broadly follow Locke's conception – though not without significant changes in the nature of liberalism.

Liberalism – United

Although liberalism does not have one unequivocal founder, in Locke's work "the central elements of the liberal outlook crystallised for the first time into a coherent intellectual tradition expressed in a powerful, if often divided and conflictual, political movement" (Gray, 1986: 11; MacPherson, 1962; Rapaczynski, 1987). I will now briefly sketch precisely this merging of the central elements of liberal thought that is missing from contemporary accounts.

At the core of Locke's work we find the claim that by nature all men are in "a State of perfect Freedom" (Locke, 1994: 269). Yet, upholding this freedom requires self-preservation (Locke, 1994: 271). And it is this requirement, Locke argues, that can only be fulfilled if "every Man has a *Property* in his own *Person*" and "the *Labour* of his Body and the *Work* of his Hands" (Locke, 1994: 287–288). For only men who can preserve themselves through their labour, independently of others, are truly free. Upholding this freedom thus requires the right to private property, that is, the right to take "any part of what is common, and removing it out of the state Nature leaves it in, which *begins the Property"* (Locke, 1994: 289, 294). Individual freedom thus constituted by private property hence requires the consent of the individual to government (Locke, 1994: 336). And this government's "great and *chief end* therefore *is the Preservation of their Property"* (Locke, 1994: 351).

In these core assumptions, we can see the political, economic, and normative dimensions of liberalism come together in a mutually constitutive form. That is, the economic institution of private property constitutes individual freedom and this norm provides the basis for political government by consent whose main task, to come full circle, is the protection of the economic institution of private property, which ensures individual freedom.

Yet, these core assumptions of protoliberal thought immediately encountered a fundamental problem: they did not appear to be in line with the historical and political evidence. That is, most individuals did not own the fruits of their labour; they were hence not free in the sense of being able to independently preserve themselves. Consequently, most governments in Locke's time and throughout known history had not been governments by consent who concerned themselves with the protection of private property. Indeed, it was the very absence of these conditions in practice that motivated Locke to develop his theory and to propagate it against the prevailing conditions. Liberalism is thus a political project that *aspires* to the constitution of individual freedom through the protection of private property and government by consent. Yet, in order to achieve this goal, Locke was confronted with two problems: one was to provide a satisfactory explanation for the glaring disjuncture between his theory and the prevailing reality; and the other was to find a realistic way of bridging this gap. Concretely, Locke had to show how society could be based on the principles of private property and government by consent in the absence of a majority of individuals supporting such developments or, conversely, how the majority of the population could be made to establish and maintain such a polity. Locke, in short, saw himself confronted with the task of promoting "liberalism" in a non-liberal environment. It is this disjuncture between theory and practice that introduces the complexities, variations, but also contradictions so characteristic of liberalism.

Locke solved the first problem by developing a philosophy of history that provided historical evidence for his claim while at the same time accounting for counterevidence. As evidence of the natural freedom of the individual, the natural right to private property, and the natural right to government by consent, Locke cited the socio-political arrangements of indigenous American societies whom he depicted as representing human life in the state of nature (1994: 182–183). The freedom of the individuals in these societies, Locke argued, was based upon the right to private property: the labour bestowed on the common property (nature) "makes the Deer that Indian's who hath killed it" (1994: 287–288). And this freedom is subsequently reflected in the fact that these societies were governed by the consent of the people (1994: 336). "Thus in the beginning all the world was America" (1994: 301).

On the basis of these assumptions, Locke then develops a speculative historical narrative in order to account for the overwhelming counterevidence. The original state of nature was a peaceful state because "Man had a Right to all he could employ his Labour upon, so he had no temptation to labour for more than he could make use of. This left no room for Controversie about the Title, nor for Incroachment on the Right of others" (Locke, 1994: 302). And yet, since "nothing was made by God for Man to spoil or destroy" cultivation of the soil or intensive production could not be undertaken without violating that law (Locke, 1994: 290). The solution to this problem was the invention of money, which made it possible to exchange surplus production of goods that would spoil for metal, which would not spoil (1994: 301). "Find out something that hath the *Use and Value of Money* amongst his Neighbours, you shall see the same Man will begin presently to *enlarge* his *Possessions*" (Locke, 1994: 301). Economically, humanity as a whole benefited from this increased production through market exchange (Locke, 1994: 302) but politically "the Increase of People and Stock, with the *Use of Money* had made Land scarce" and generated a state of war. The answer to this problem lay in the establishment of states, which ensured internal appeasement and external defence (Locke, 1994: 299). It was this constitution of states that brought to power rulers who did not protect private property and justified their rule with reference to custom and tradition (1994: 329).

Having thus provided a speculative history that accounted for the disjuncture between his theory and the prevailing evidence, Locke was left with the task of establishing how such an "illiberal" society could be transformed into a "liberal" society. Faithful to his own theory, he argued that if private property was the basis of individual freedom, property owners would demand that government protect private property and hence their freedom. He thus advocated the extension of full political rights to property owners only, and the concomitant denial of these rights to those who did not own property (1994: 384). And yet, the resultant political oppression of the majority by a rich minority ran counter to the claim that all people were born free. Hence, Locke argued that an extension of the franchise could be achieved by turning more, and ideally all, sections of society into property owners who would then endorse liberal norms and help maintain a liberal polity.

This was a neat theoretical solution, but in practice it threw up the problem where all this additional property was to come from. Once private property had been naturalised and Locke had committed himself to its protection, redistribution was not an option. Locke therefore argued that since private property was more productive than common property (1994: 296–298), the latter could be privatised (Locke, 1994: 291). However, land – at the time the most important additional source of wealth – was too scarce in England to provide the vast and rising number of poor with property.

Locke therefore looked abroad where "there are still *great Tracts of Ground* to be found, which [...], *lie waste*, and are more than the People who dwell on it, do, or can make use of, and so still lie in common" (Locke, 1994: 299). This common land in America could be used, at least in principle, to furnish all individuals with property and thus make them eligible to full political rights. In short, "Locke [...] was offering the New World, specifically the colonial settlements of America, as validation of his socio-political philosophy" (Lebovics, 1986: 577). According to this theory, the establishment of liberalism and its subsequent democratisation required three steps: firstly, political rights were to be given to property owners only who would establish a liberal state; secondly, that state would support the privatisation of common property, which would lead to wider distribution of property in society; and thirdly, political rights could then be extended to the wider, now propertied, sections of society.

Locke thus provides explicit theorisations of the dynamic relations between core elements of liberalism. Firstly, and in substantive terms, he argues that private property is constitutive of individual freedom in the liberal sense; and this freedom in turn leads to a liberal political culture – that is, the pursuit of liberal norms and principles through political institutions. These political institutions in turn establish and protect private property. Hence, the political, economic, and normative dimensions of liberalism are mutually constitutive and only together amount to liberalism. Secondly, the disjuncture between theory and practice is addressed by a philosophy of history, which serves as a dynamic link between the two. The claim that liberal principles are derived from the state of nature (the distant past) and can be (re)established in the future prevents empirical weaknesses from undermining the validity of the theory and makes this temporal narrative an integral and constitutive part of liberalism. Thirdly, according to Locke, the practices that enable a bridging of the gap between theory and practice are based on the dynamic link between liberal and non-liberal, and domestic and international contexts. That is, establishing a liberal polity in a non-liberal environment requires differential treatment of "liberal" (i.e. propertied) and "non-liberal" (i.e. propertyless) citizens, namely the provision of political rights to the former and their denial to the latter. The unequal society resulting from this move, however, still contradicts the liberal theory of natural and therefore universal freedom and equality. This problem is solved by the spread of private property within society – that is, through the expropriation of common property within the domestic as well as, crucially, the international sphere. The international sphere thus plays a constitutive role for the emergence and development of domestic liberalism. In contrast to contemporary approaches to liberalism, Locke's work thus highlights that the relations between the different dimensions are actually necessary and constitutive of liberalism and ensure its continued historical development.

Historically, the establishment of liberalism broadly followed the trajectory outlined by Locke. Firstly, land owners and merchants who had become rich from the trade with the colonies – among them Locke's own long-time patron, the Earl of Shaftesbury – increasingly demanded political rights with direct reference to their property which led to a huge increase of members in the House of Commons (Acemoglu and Robinson, 2006: 350; Perelman, 2000: 175). These men subsequently used their political power to institutionalise the protection of private property on which their individual freedom rested. In other words, this development led to the establishment of a liberal state characterised by the transference of de jure political power into the hands of commercial and capitalistic interests and the stabilisation of property rights in seventeenth-century Britain (Acemoglu and Robinson, 2006: 349–350).

Once in power, these men used the state to protect and extend the private property on which their own freedom rested. That is, they systematically engaged in the transformation of common into private property – both in the domestic and in the international sphere. In the domestic context, Locke's work was frequently cited in Parliament in support of private enclosure acts which, between 1710 and 1815, transferred 6.5 million acres or 20 per cent of the total land from common into private property (McNally, 1988: 62, 8–9; Perelman, 2000: 175).[1] As a direct result of these policies, a large part of the population was impoverished and upheavals, rebellions, and the threat of revolution were widespread and integral features of early modern European societies (Kim, 1992: 24; Tilly, 2004). Hence, early "liberals" tended to be passionately opposed to the introduction of universal franchise or democracy on precisely the grounds that Locke had set out: namely that those who did not own property could not be expected to support and maintain laws protecting private property (Plattner, 2008: 64–65; Przeworski, 1992: 53). In short, the introduction of liberal principles within domestic society originally produced – or exacerbated – social and political tensions.

And yet, colonialism, just as Locke had argued,[2] provided relief for these tensions. Not only did colonialism offer an opportunity for privatisation, which did not add to the domestic tensions, but it also allowed liberal governments to export its poor, its orphans, its criminals into the colonies as well as to offer the middle and ruling classes opportunities for advancement in the administration of the colonies. Most importantly, however, colonialism provided common political ground for propertied and non-propertied citizens alike. Hence, it was Locke's theory of property that "preachers, legal theorists, and politicians" used to base first the land claims of the British colonists and then those of the American citizens on the enclosure and cultivation of land (Arneil, 1996: 169). The same argument was also influential in Australia, New Zealand, and Canada throughout the eighteenth and well into the nineteenth centuries (Ivison, 2003: 93).

These colonial policies thus allowed European colonists to acquire property and, perfectly in line with the dynamic outlined by Locke, in settler societies like New Zealand, the United States, and Australia, the promise based on such wider distribution of property – the introduction of universal franchise – was first realised.

Colonialism thus allowed the ruling elites in Europe to resist demands for extending the franchise for some time and thus ultimately guaranteed the liberal character of Western democracy (Ake, 1992: 33–34; Bova, 1997: 116). For the enclosure of commonly owned land domestically, colonial appropriation of land internationally (Marks, 2007; Washbrook, 1997), and the industrial revolution all contributed to economic growth that led to a spread of property in society – in line with the widely noted link between economic development and liberal democracy (Acemoglu and Robinson, 2006: 58; Przeworski et al., 2000). In other words, a sizable middle class slowly emerged and allowed liberals to lower the property threshold for voting rights gradually, thus extending the franchise – but only to those sections of society that had actually achieved a measure of individual freedom based on private property and who therefore had a stake in upholding the liberal character of government. Though private property was never spread to all members of society, the introduction of the welfare state ensured that ultimately even property-less citizens had a stake in maintaining liberal forms of government. It thus enabled the introduction of universal political rights into liberal states.

Yet, it is precisely the successful democratisation of liberalism that forces liberal governments today to pursue continuous economic growth in order to provide the population with the economic benefits that maintain their stake in this system. Perfectly in line with Locke's arguments, this growth is pursued through policies of privatisation (or expropriation), which in turn require unequal power relations. Hence, the last two decades have seen a remarkable revival of liberalism in the form of market economics, the privatisation of state-owned industries, and the trimming of welfare benefits by liberal democracies (Plattner, 2008: 68). This latest round of "privatisation" and "liberalisation" targeted communal ownership of water and electricity supplies, education, health care, and the establishment of "new enclosures" in the form of intellectual property rights over natural products and their uses (May, 2000). Policies of privatisation and marketisation also lie at the core of international organisations like the WTO regulating the world economy and of the development policies of international organisations like the International Monetary Fund (IMF) and World Bank as well as those of individual liberal states. And just as in the past, a successful realisation of these policies is not possible without recourse to power politics – which, for the most part if not always, today takes the form of weighted voting in international organisations, conditional aid, and the threat of exclusion from the major markets.

Liberalism is thus indeed intimately tied to democracy today which constitutes a major historical change. Yet, this change has not resolved the core contradiction of liberalism, which lies in the fact that the core policies that constitute and maintain liberalism for some groups – privatisation – simultaneously expropriate other groups and thus constitute non-liberal spheres. And since democratic liberalism has an even greater need than its non-democratic predecessor to avoid domestic political upheaval, much of this expropriation takes place in the international sphere where the political fallout of these economic policies has to be borne by other states, and can then be confronted as a matter of *foreign* policy that requires power political regulation.

Locke's theory, and the subsequent historical development shows, in sum, not only that the political, economic, and normative dimensions are necessary and mutually constitutive elements of liberalism, but also that this theory lacks empirical substantiation. This disjuncture necessarily turns liberalism into a political project that pursues its own realisation explicitly through the differential treatment of liberal and non-liberal actors, domestic and international spheres, consisting of economic appropriation and exploitation as well as of political liberation and oppression. The international/non-liberal sphere thus plays a constitutive role for the establishment of domestic liberalism and is in turn itself (re)constituted by it. And since communities generally do not knowingly consent to their own expropriation and oppression, power politics (whether pursued by economic, political, cultural, or military means) is an indispensable part of liberalism and has to be included in its definition just as much as its historical development, its relations with non-liberal actors, and its foreign policies.

Conclusion

In light of this Lockean conception of liberalism, the continuities between the Cold War and the post-Cold War period become apparent. Liberal actors systematically pursued the spread of liberal economic principles – privatisation, free trade, free markets – in both periods. The major international institutions regulating the world economy according to these liberal principles, such as the General Agreement on Tariffs and Trade (GATT), IMF, World Bank, were established during the Cold War and, like the WTO, further developed and strengthened thereafter.

Yet, a successful pursuit of these liberal economic policies requires a conducive political environment – that is, unequal power relations between liberal and non-liberal actors that allow the former to impose these principles on the latter. According to Lockean theory, therefore, liberal foreign policies, at a minimum, are concerned with the protection and defence of their sphere of influence (domestic and international) and, at a maximum, with its extension. Indeed, the foreign policies of liberal states during the

Cold War were largely concerned with the "containment" of the Soviet or communist threat to this liberal sphere of influence and pursued its extension where this appeared possible. Defence and consolidation of the liberal camp involved the whole gamut of foreign policy tools – from aid and economic incentives like the Marshall plan through political pressure to military support or even intervention in cases where domestic policies appeared to depart from the straight and narrow path of liberal economic, political or military policies. Attempts to extend the liberal sphere of influence generally took the form of competition with the Soviet Union over influence in newly independent states and involved economic, political, and military aid and incentives as well as pressure (Westad, 2005). With the demise of the Soviet Union, however, liberal foreign policies simply shifted "from containment to enlargement" (Lake, 1993), that is, to the extension of these policies into the former Soviet sphere of influence and heretofore relatively independent Third World states. In both periods, these policies involved the promotion of democracy – subject to its compatibility with liberal economic as well as foreign policies. Where democracy appeared incompatible with unequivocal liberal economic and foreign policies, Western foreign policies systematically supported "liberalism" against democracy (Jahn, 2007a, 2007b).

The Cold War period also saw the development and adoption of the Universal Declaration of Human Rights, which was to be realised through the institution of the sovereign state. Although the principles of sovereignty appeared to be under attack in debates on humanitarian intervention or globalisation (Jahn, 2012a), the foreign policies of liberal states during the 1990s systematically upheld the principle of sovereignty for liberal states even while rights of sovereignty were denied on an ad hoc basis to weak or "failing" states as well as to states explicitly resisting the projection of liberal power, that is "rogue states". It is this ambivalence, the possibility of a differential extension of rights and obligations, which the Responsibility to Protect has adopted (Bellamy, 2005).

Liberal states thus engaged in the pursuit of exactly the same substantive goals during the Cold War period and its aftermath. The differences that created the impression of a "rise" of liberalism thus pertain to the scope and form of these liberal foreign policies. The demise of the Soviet Union provided the opportunity to extend liberal economic and political principles into areas formerly closed to such advances. The absence of an economic and political alternative backed up by military power, moreover, allowed for a stronger "enforcement" of these principles – ranging from the institutionalisation of a dispute settlement mechanism in the WTO through conditional aid up to military intervention. Differences, in short, resulted from a shift in power relations, from the demise of the Soviet Union, which enabled a much broader and more forthright pursuit of liberal goals.

Yet, this shift in power relations was frequently interpreted as a historical validation of the core claims of liberalism (Fukuyama, 1989; Ikenberry,

2006: 161; Plattner, 2008: 24). The monopoly of liberalism after the end of the Cold War seemed to finally close the gap between liberalism's theory and practice; it "opened up a vast potential for movement toward realising the liberal vision worldwide" (Richardson, 2001: 2). The promise of individual freedom, government by consent, economic prosperity, and cooperation, as well as consequently domestic and international peace were going to become universally true (Jahn, 2012b). This optimism, however, arose from the partial conceptions of liberalism discussed in the first part of this chapter, which overlook the contradictory dynamics between its constitutive elements. Ironically, this optimism itself is what contributed to the developments that seemed to indicate the subsequent "fall" of liberalism.

Oblivious to the fact that the pursuit of liberal policies tends to produce prosperity, as well as poverty, involves political liberation as well as oppression, and is, in general, intimately bound up with power politics, this optimism at the beginning of the 1990s led to an intensive pursuit of liberal policies in all areas. Yet, the more neoliberal economic policies were pursued, the greater the gap between the rich and poor within and between societies became – resulting ultimately in a global economic and financial crisis. The missionary promotion of democracy involving political, economic, cultural and at times military intervention into nondemocratic states led to the establishment of democratic institutions – that frequently served decidedly "illiberal" policies. And the more liberal actors used their position of power to violate the rights of sovereignty of non-liberal states – whether in the name of human rights, democracy, or economic policies – the more they generated explicit and widespread resistance.

Moreover, these paradoxical outcomes were unanticipated due to the partial conceptions of liberalism. Neoliberal economic policies were pursued without regard to their political fall-out. Democracy promotion policies failed to pay attention to the necessary social preconditions. Humanitarian intervention, peacekeeping, and statebuilding largely ignored local political participation. Hence, neoliberal economic policies, democracy promotion, regime change, humanitarian intervention, peacekeeping, and statebuilding were, by the end of the 1990s, widely regarded as failures and generated calls for renewed attention to the necessary political regulation of liberal economics (Bhagwati, 2004: 239), the social preconditions of democracy (Rose, 2000/1), and the requirement of "local ownership" in the cases of peacekeeping and statebuilding (Paris, 2010). Consideration of these wider dynamics of liberalism in combination with resistance hence led to a shift away from "enlargement" and back to "consolidation" and "defence" (Deudney and Ikenberry, 1999). This shift is mistakenly interpreted as a "fall" of liberalism – mistakenly because, as this chapter has shown, the protection and defence of liberal achievements by means of power politics constitutes an integral and necessary part of the pursuit of core liberal principles and objectives. In short, after liberalism, comes liberalism, albeit in a different guise.

Yet, if the story of the "rise" and "fall" of liberalism does not reflect the fate of the liberal political project accurately, it nevertheless fits the fate of liberal theory, which excludes power politics from the definition of liberalism and thus fails to recognise or endorse these policies as liberal. The fate of liberal theory in IR is thus indeed subject to the winds of (power political) change.

Notes

1. McNally reports that in 1710 the first private enclosure act was presented in Parliament, followed by 100 between 1720 and 1750, 139 between 1750 and 1760, 900 between 1760 and 1779, and 2000 between 1793 and 1815 (1988: 11).
2. Locke's writings, political and theoretical, cover all aspects of colonialism and consistently defend it (Tully 1993: 140–141; Tuck 1999: 167; Arneil 1996; Armitage 2004; Boucher 2006).

References

Acemoglu, D. and Robinson, J. A. (2006), *Economic Origins of Dictatorship and Democracy*, Cambridge: Cambridge University Press.

Ake, C. (1992), "Devaluing Democracy", *Journal of Democracy*, 3(3), 32–36.

Alvarez, J. E. (2001), "Do Liberal States Behave Better? A Critique of Slaughter's Liberal Theory", *European Journal of International Law*, 12(2), 183–246.

Armitage, D. (2004), "John Locke, Carolina, and the 'Two Treatise of Government' ", *Political Theory*, 32(5), 602–627.

Arneil, B. (1996), *John Locke and America. The Defence of English Colonialism*, Oxford: Clarendon.

Barbieri, K. (2002), *The Liberal Illusion. Does Trade Promote Peace?* Ann Arbor: The University of Michigan Press.

Beitz, C. R. (1979), *Political Theory and International Relations*, Princeton: Princeton University Press.

Bellamy, A. J. (2005), "Responsibility to Protect or Trojan Horse? The Crisis in Darfur and Human Rights After Iraq", *Ethics and International Affairs*, 19(2), 31–54.

Bermeo, N. (2009), "Conclusion: Is Democracy Exportable?" in Z. Barany and G. R. Moser (eds) *Is Democracy Exportable?* Cambridge: Cambridge University Press, 242–264.

Bhagwati, J. (2004), *In Defense of Globalization*, New York: Oxford University Press.

Boucher, D. (2006), "Property and Propriety in International Relations: The Case of John Locke", in B. Jahn (ed.) *Classical Theory in International Relations*, Cambridge: Cambridge University Press, 156–177.

Bova, R. (1997), "Democracy and Liberty: The Cultural Connection", *Journal of Democracy*, 8(1), 112–126.

Clark, I. (2009), "Democracy in International Society: Promotion or Exclusion?" *Millennium – Journal of International Studies*, 37(3), 563–581.

Cooper, R. 2002, "The New Liberal Imperialism", http://www.guardian.co.uk/world/2002/apr/07/1/print.

Deudney, D. and Ikenberry, J. G. (1999), "The Nature and Sources of Liberal International Order", *Review of International Studies*, 25(2), 179–196.

Doyle, M. W. (1996), "Kant, Liberal Legacies, and Foreign Affairs", in E. M. Brown, M. S. Lynn-Jones and E. S. Miller (eds) *Debating the Democratic Peace*, Cambridge: MIT Press, 3–57.

Doyle, M. W. (1997), *Ways of War and Peace*, New York: W. W. Norton.

Dunne, T. (1997), "Liberalism", in J. Baylis and S. Smith (eds) *The Globalization of World Politics*, Oxford: Oxford University Press.

Fukuyama, F. (1989), "The End of History?" *National Interest*, Summer, 3–18.

Gray, J. (1986), *Liberalism*, Minneapolis: University of Minnesota Press.

Hoffmann, S. (1987), *Janus and Minerva. Essays in the Theory and Practice of International Politics*, Boulder: Westview.

Ignatieff, M. (2003), "State Failure and Nation-Building", in J. L. Holzgrefe and O. R. Keohane (eds) *Humanitarian Intervention. Ethical, Legal, and Political Dilemmas*, Cambridge: Cambridge University Press, 299–321.

Ikenberry, G. J. (2006), *Liberal Order and Imperial Ambition*, Cambridge: Polity.

Ivison, D. (2003), "Locke, Liberalism and Empire", in R. P. Anstey (ed.) *The Philosophy of John Locke: New Perspectives*, London: Routledge, 86–105.

Jackson, R. and Georg, S. (2003), *Introduction to International Relations. Theories and Approaches*, Oxford: Oxford University Press.

Jahn, B. (2007a), "The Tragedy of Liberal Diplomacy: Democratization, Intervention, Statebuilding I", *Journal of Intervention and Statebuilding*, 1(1), 88–106.

Jahn, B. (2007b), "The Tragedy of Liberal Diplomacy: Democratization, Intervention, Statebuilding II", *Journal of Intervention and Statebuilding*, 1(2), 211–229.

Jahn, B. (2012a), "Humanitarian Intervention: What's in a Name?" *International Politics*, 49(1), 36–58.

Jahn, B. (2012b), "Critique in a Time of Liberal World Order", *Journal of International Relations and Development*, 15(2), 145–157.

Keohane, R. O. (2003), "Political Authority after Intervention: Gradations in Sovereignty", in J. L. Holzgrefe and O. R. Keohane (eds) *Humanitarian Intervention. Ethical, Legal, and Political Dilemmas*, Cambridge: Cambridge University Press, 275–298.

Kim, K. (1992), "Marx, Schumpeter, and the East Asian Experience", *Journal of Democracy*, 3(3), 17–31.

Lake, A. (1993), "From Containment to Enlargement", http://www.mtholyoke.edu/acad/intrel/lakedoc.html, 23 February 2012.

Lebovics, H. (1986), "The Uses of America in Locke's Second Treatise of Government", *Journal of the History of Ideas*, 47(4), 567–581.

Locke, J. (1994), *Two Treatises of Government*, edited by Peter Laslett, Cambridge: Cambridge University Press.

Long, D. (1995), "The Harvard School of Liberal International Theory: A Case for Closure", *Millennium*, 24(3), 489–505.

Macpherson, C. B. (1962), *The Political Theory of Possessive Individualism*, Oxford: Oxford University Press.

Marks, R. B. (2007), *The Origins of the Modern World. Fate and Fortune in the Rise of the West*, Lanham: Rowman and Littlefield.

May, C. (2000), *A Global Political Economy of Intellectual Property Rights*, London: Routledge.

McNally, D. (1988), *Political Economy and the Rise of Capitalism. A Reinterpretation*, Berkeley: University of California Press.

Moravcsik, A. (1997), "Taking Preferences Seriously: A Liberal Theory of International Politics", *International Organization*, 51(4), 513–553.

Nye, J. Jr. (1988), "Neorealism and Neoliberalism", *World Politics*, 40(2), 235–251.

Paris, R. (2004), *At War's End: Building Peace after Civil Conflict,* Cambridge: Cambridge University Press.

Paris, R. (2010), "Saving Liberal Peacebuilding", *Review of International Studies*, 36(2), 337–365.

Perelman, M. (2000), *The Invention of Capitalism. Classical Political Economy and the Secret History of Primitive Accumulation*, Durham: Duke University Press.

Plattner, M. F. (2008), *Democracy Without Borders? Global Challenges to Liberal Democracy*, Lanham: Rowman and Littlefield.

Przeworski, A. (1992), "The Neoliberal Fallacy", *Journal of Democracy*, 3(3), 45–58.

Przeworski, A., Alvarez, M. E., Cheibub, J. A. and Limongi, F. (2000), *Democracy and Development. Political Institutions and Well-Being in the World, 1950–1990*, Cambridge: Cambridge University Press.

Rapaczynski, A. (1987), *Nature and Politics: Liberalism in the Philosophies of Hobbes*, edited by Locke and Rousseau, Ithaca: Cornell University Press.

Rawls, J. (2001), *The Law of Peoples*, Cambridge: Harvard University Press.

Richardson, J. L. (2001), *Contending Liberalisms in World Politics. Ideology and Power*, Boulder: Lynne Rienner.

Roberts, A. (2004), "Righting Wrongs or Wronging Rights? The United States and Human Rights Post-September 11", *European Journal of International Law*, 15(4), 721–749.

Rose, G. (2000/1), "Democracy Promotion and American Foreign Policy: A Review Essay", *International Security*, 25(3), 186–203.

Russett, B. (1996), "Why Democratic Peace?" in E. M. Brown, M. S. Lynn-Jones and E. S. Miller (eds) *Debating the Democratic Peace*, Cambridge: MIT Press, 58–81.

Sartori, G. (1995), "How Far Can Free Government Travel?" *Journal of Democracy*, 6(3), 101–111.

Slaughter, A. (1995), "International Law in a World of Liberal States", *European Journal of International Law*, 6, 1–39.

Tansey, O. (2008), "The Complexity of Western Diplomacy: A Reply to Beate Jahn", *Journal of Intervention and Statebuilding*, 2(1), 87–94.

Tilly, C. (2004), *Contention and Democracy in Europe, 1650–2000*, New York: Cambridge University Press.

Tuck, R. (1999), *The Rights of War and Peace. Political Thought and the International Order from Grotius to Kant*, Oxford: Oxford University Press.

Tully, J. (1993), *An Approach to Political Philosophy: Locke in Contexts*, Cambridge: Cambridge University Press.

Vanberg, V. J. (2008), "On the Complementarity of Liberalism and Democracy – A Reading of F.A. Hayek and J.M. Buchanan", *Journal of Institutional Economics*, 4(2), 139–161.

Washbrook, D. (1997), "From Comparative Sociology to Global History: Britain and India in the Pre-History of Modernity", *Journal of the Economic and Social History of the Orient*, 40(4), 410–443.

Weber, M. (1984), *The Protestant Ethic and the Spirit of Capitalism*, London: Unwin.

Westad, O. A. (2005), *The Global Cold War*, Cambridge: Cambridge University Press.

Zacher, M. W. and Richard, A. M. (1995), "Liberal International Theory: Common Threads, Divergent Strands", in W. C. Kegley Jr (ed.) *Controversies in International Relations Theory. Realism and the Neoliberal Challenge*, New York: St. Martin's Press, 107–150.

Zakaria, F. (1997), "The Rise of Illiberal Democracy", *Foreign Affairs*, 76(6), 22–43.

2
Liberalism, Democracy, and International Law – An English School Approach

Cornelia Navari

Liberalism may be in decline, but democracy is in the ascendancy. According to Freedom House, the US-based non-governmental organisation that conducts research and advocacy on democracy, the number of democracies has increased from 41 (out of 150) states in 1974 to 117 of 195 states in 2011 (www.freedomhouse.org). "Democracy" became the general call for reform in the former Soviet satellite states and dependencies, and guided the reform process in both. It has become the chief justification for secessions, as in East Timor; and the present Arab Spring is being dominated by calls for democracy. Most importantly, the United States has declared that it will give support to democracy movements in countries struggling to escape from autocratic rule, a declaration made in the face of a strong non-intervention norm.

The critical question is the nature of the political form, or forms, implied by the emerging transnational calls for democracy. Not only is democracy one of W.B. Gallie's essentially contested concepts (indeed one of the fundamental concepts that Gallie outlined in his 1956 article for the Aristotelian society), moreover, and notwithstanding philosophical disputation, what stands for democracy will be a highly political question. Another is democracy's relation to liberalism. Democratic states are not necessarily liberal states, as the emerging political form in Russia evidences, a quasi-autocracy legitimated by election. What, in short, is the emerging democracy norm and how liberal is it?

The chapter will begin by identifying the first uses of democracy as a diplomatic device, and the first appearances of democracy as a norm in international politics. It will then proceed to outline the major sources for identifying emerging international norms. From these, it will derive the definitional criteria to be used in identifying such democracy norms as may be considered settled, including the characteristics of liberal democracy. The major portion of the chapter will subsequently apply the aforementioned criteria.

Democracy in international politics

If by "democracy" we mean "asking the people", it should be noted that the first modern plebiscites in international relations were used primarily to determine state borders, the earliest being the annexation of Rome to Italy in 1871, which was legitimated as a result of a popular vote. The Rome franchise was so limited, however, that it would probably not be considered a true democratic vote in contemporary terms. Plebiscites were also mandated by the Versailles Treaty after the First World War to determine some of the borders of the post-imperial states of central Europe. The Upper Silesia plebiscite was carried out in March 1921 to determine a section of the border between Weimar Germany and Poland, in which about half the population voted.[1] The Carinthian plebiscite of 10 October 1920, with an equally impressive turnout, determined the final southern border between the new Republic of Austria and the newly formed Kingdom of Serbs, Croats, and Slovenes. The Schleswig plebiscites were two plebiscites in 28 June 1919, to determine the future border between Denmark and Germany.

The first appearance of a democracy norm, *strictu sensu*, is frequently placed with Woodrow Wilson's Fourteen Points, in the form of the much vaunted concept of self-determination. But Wilson's idea was limited to self-determination within an already de-limited territory. Moreover, democratic referenda applied only to determining the placement of a territory within this or that state, not the form of government; and the referendum was only used in cases where populations were mixed or indeterminate as to nationality. Democracy in the sense of an appeal to "the people" was a special treatment intended to delimit borders in difficult cases, and not to serve as a model of good governance, a sanction on bad governments, or to provide for regime transition. Finally, the "nationalities" norm as then understood did not outlive the experience of the interwar period, during which national minorities had been allowed to petition the League of Nations with their complaints. The new Declaration of Human Rights in 1949 deliberately excluded group rights and spoke only of individual rights. The Declaration, moreover, makes scant mention of political rights, and neither does the 1966 Convention on Civil and Political Rights, which primarily secures the individual against arbitrary imprisonment and torture.[2]

In its contemporary sense of a favoured form of government, an international norm of democratic governance began to emerge only with the collapse of the Soviet Union in 1989. The United States Agency for International Development became the first major aid donor to include democracy as part of its portfolio when it launched its Democracy Initiative in 1990 (USAID, *Democracy and Governance*, November 1991). The then European

Community, in the Charter of Paris, 1990, established democratic government as an essential condition for European Community membership, demanding that all the newly liberated states of central and eastern Europe aspiring for membership meet the democracy criteria as outlined in, and gain membership of, the Council of Europe. Generally summarised as "human rights, democracy and the rule of law", the conditions were "domesticated" when the European Union (EU) adopted the Charter of Fundamental Rights in 2000, and strengthened still further when the Charter became legally binding with the entry into force of the Lisbon Treaty in 2009.

Two models of norm evaluation

In terms of a "scientific" and objective approach to the understanding of international norms and norm evolution, the first inclination of the analyst will be to look to constructivism, and particularly American constructivism, with its interest in international norms, their statistical manifestations, and causal processes. The dominant constructivist approaches to norm evolution use a number of dramatic process models to describe the emergence of norms. In the constructivist literature, norms cascade (Finnemore and Sikkink, 1998), boomerang (Keck and Sikkink, 1998), spiral (Risse et al., 1999), and diffuse (Checkel, 2001). The relevant question from the perspective of this chapter has been posed by Cristina Badescu with reference to the Responsibility to Protect: "How long can a norm be described as 'emerging' before it truly 'has emerged'?" (Badescu and Weiss, 2010: 356).

In general, the dominant models call for evidence of "successful application to concrete cases" (Badescu and Weiss, 2010: 358). But the constructivist literature does not identify the criteria of "successful application" with any precision. Keck and Sikkink are content to quote Hedley Bull that an international society of agreed norms and rules exists. Finnemore and Sikkink (1998) identify a norm's emergence as the point at which it is "no longer disputed". Risse points to the enshrinement of the norm in an international "agreement", but neglects the varied obligatory (and political/legal) statuses of the varied texts. In general, evidence of the successful application of Responsibility to Protect, for example, has been most frequently referenced by General Assembly resolutions, but these are not only often loosely worded as to the locus of obligation and precise duties, they do not have a determinate legal status. The best set of indicators of a norm's relative *political* status remains Jack Donelly's "Human Rights: A Regime Analysis", and his method and categories are drawn from traditional institutionalism and not from constructivism (Donelly, 1986). This neglect is perhaps understandable. The main concern in the constructivist literature has been with identifying the processes of norm "construction", and with outlining the various strategies of "norm entrepreneurs". The precise nature of the end product has tended to get lost among these concerns.

The other major approach to the study of international norms is the English School. Norms are equally at the centre of the English School's intellectual preoccupation. International society is the central concept in the English School armoury, and international society is constituted by norms (see Jackson, 2000). Here, by contrast, the question of the nature of the end product is the major concern (and much less the processes of its establishment). The question of what constitutes a norm, how to characterise the norm, when a norm is established, and the strength of a norm are the central criteria for identifying the compass and nature of "international society". Accordingly, the "moment" of a norm's emergence and what precisely the norm entails, are, from that aspect, more important, and indeed critical, than the processes of its production.

Fortunately, the tradition from which the English School draws does have a vocabulary, and a fairly sophisticated set of criteria with which to identify settled norms, and even emerging ones. This vocabulary allows not only for the identification of a norm, but also for its characterisation. The result of their application presents a more nuanced picture of the advance of the democratic norm (as well as the construction of the norm) than is generally produced by constructivists' cascades, boomerangs, and spirals.

The English School, the norm, and international law

The English School has two answers to the question of how to identify a "settled norm" in international affairs. One is practice, constantly repeated, and the other is international law. Bracketing practice for the present, the English School's relation with international law goes back to C. A. W. Manning, one of the English School's founding fathers, the product of a legal training at Brasenose College, who lectured on jurisprudence at New College before becoming Cassell Professor of International Relations at the London School of Economics. A follower of Austin in the association of law with the commands of a sovereign, his own understanding of international law, which strongly influenced his younger colleagues, may be discerned from his selection of the German Legal Professor Julius Hatschek's *Outline of International Law* for translation into English.

Hatschek (1872–1926) was a product of the German historical school, which considered law to be the natural outgrowth of historical experience, emerging first as custom, and then as codified by the "rational" state into law proper. In the German historical approach, law is an immediate expression of the society in which it grows, and expresses the normative understandings of that society. Custom is the pre-legal version of law, but may have the same normative force; indeed, custom in the historical school is rated rather more highly than formally established law. For Hatchet:

> It is not the legal, but the social aspect of the state, which is the more important. The state is a species of social community which, bound up

as it is with the very essence of the process of historical evolution is conceived, fashioned, and brought forth – yea, even suffers extinction – without it being within the power of legal formulation either to embarrass its inception or to save it from its fall (1930: 18).

The historical school was intrigued by international law, which grew so thoroughly without a single sovereign, as well as by English constitutional law, also considered a "natural" growth. According to the historical approach, law and the norm are the same; and international law is no different from "domestic law" in that each expresses the normative understandings of a specific society.

Peter Wilson has recently expounded the main elements of this approach, beginning with its leitmotiv: "International law is a real body of law, no less binding than domestic law, and therefore no less deserving of the name of law" (Wilson, 2000: 167). He also, however, and importantly, distinguishes the two bodies of law. International law is *"sui generis"* in that it cannot be understood as command or control. On the contrary, its efficacy can only be understood in relation to the particular character of "international society"; that is, in the light of the anarchical nature of the international order, particularly with regard to the sovereignty of its members and to the requirement for "self-help" that the absence of regularised sanctions entails. In the domestic legal order, the law may be used to produce a new social norm, such as in anti-racist legislation or anti-smoking legislation. This legalisation process is intended to promote new social understandings. In the international legal order this is very difficult. There are aspirations to use international law as a form of social control – to enforce new norms (as e.g., "Responsibility to Protect") – but these remain primarily aspirations. Moreover, such aspirations are unlikely to be shared throughout the society of states. Its main purpose is to "facilitate, regular, continuous, and generally orderly international relationships" (Wilson, 2000: 172). It is a form of social communication, which allows for the signalling of intention, as well as a procedural framework for diplomatic activity and political initiatives. Quoting Hedley Bull, in his *Anarchical Society*, Wilson identifies the typical question asked by a state as not, "What does the law require me to do?", but rather as, "Does the law permit me to do this?" Or, put in another way: "how can I lawfully achieve this goal?" He identifies Terry Nardin's procedural account (Nardin, 1983) as the best expositor of this approach.

The import of Wilson's account in the present context subsists not so much with the nature of international law as with his identification of the *methodological implications* of the approach. These are, on the one hand, "the core propositions of nineteenth- and early twentieth-century legal positivism". Wilson does not list these in detail, recalling instead their major representatives: Austin and Oppenheim in the nineteenth century, and Brierly, Schwarzenberger, Fitzmaurice, Jennings, and Stone in the early twentieth century. On the other hand, there is another equally important factor in the present "aspirational" age. This is the identification, in addition, of an "aspirational law", whose identification he credits to the Japanese international lawyer, Yasuaki Onuma. Professor Onuma categorises some treaties as aspirational in that they, in Wilson's characterisation, "embody global aspirations shared by the overwhelming majority of members of international society" (Wilson, 2000: 170). Onuma considers these to be worth including in the corpus of international law because, in Wilson's characterisation, they "induce convergence, if not strict observance, of the behaviour of diverse members of international society over a period of time" (Onuma, 2003: 134). They are akin to the "declaratory tradition" identified by Dorothy Jones (1992), but whereas Jones considers the various declarations that have emerged from the General Assembly in the post war period to be more akin to moral philosophy than to law, Onuma considers them to be a genuine form of *emerging positive law* (under certain conditions).

Positive law and aspirational law

The identification of an emerging or developed norm in the English School begins by drawing from these two approaches their definitional criteria; that is, the qualities that declarations entailing norms should display, if they are to qualify as norm-producing. These may be summarised as:

Positive Law criteria – to determine an already existent norm:

1. Does the law oblige?
2. Is the phenomenon (in this case, democracy) sufficiently defined to allow a judge to determine derogation?
3. Does derogation give rise to a sanction of some sort?

Aspirational law criteria – to determine whether a substantive norm is taking shape:

1. One swallow doesn't make a summer: Are wordings in resolutions repeated, and do resolutions lead to further elaborations in later resolutions?
2. Is endorsement hearty/sincere, on the part of government, section of government, or section of the population of a state?
3. Does the injunction apply generally, or only regionally or specifically?

The site of these injunctions may be international treaties, resolutions, or statements.[3] They may also be located in domestic law, an accepted source of international law in the positive tradition, particularly of aspirational international law, and particularly when parallel legal orders, and the legal orders of large states, endorse similar normative goals.

The emerging democracy norm

The question of an emerging democracy norm is clearly critical for the complexion of and pattern of licenses and constraints accepted in international society. If it became compelling for its members, a democracy norm would, in the post-Cold War era, endorse liberalism as the dominant state ideology of the international order. It would determine autocracies to be at best transitional staging posts on the way to more satisfactory forms of political order; and it would qualify and render conditional the rights of non-democratic states. For example, it might well give democratic states the right not to recognise the outcomes of elections in non-democratic states, and it might allow them to intervene directly, even militarily, in internal political processes, and to justify such interventions.

If we apply these criteria to the issue of democracy among states, we will notice at once that a *variety of questions* arise in consideration of a democracy norm, and indeed that there is not a single norm but a *clutch of normative criteria*, or qualities, which give the idea of democracy (and by extension, "international democracy") a determinate shape. These qualities have been the subject of various normative endeavours, and the chapter will now consider these in turn. The aim in each instance will be to identify, firstly, the obligatory nature of the norm, and secondly, the area where the norm is "weak" or open to question. In all considerations of international norms, the question of who speaks out against the aspiring norm, and the grounds for their objections, is critical, since international law is overwhelmingly consensual. It obliges only those who sign up to such a law (or which gain the various agreed majorities necessary for its coming into force). Democracy is emphatically not, in the language of positive law, a peremptory norm or an *ergo omnes* obligation, but only, and only possibly, an emerging custom.

To take these questions in turn:

Is there a right to democracy?

The term "promotion of a right to democracy" first appeared in a Commission of Human Rights Resolution (CHR) 1999/57, in the title.[4] In the text, however, there is no mention of any right to democracy. A Cuban proposal to delete the term in the title was defeated on a vote of 28 to 12, but also with 13 abstentions, not a rousing defence of the resolution's language. In the subsequent resolution, CHR 2000/47, the term "right to democracy" was dropped in favour of "promotion and consolidation"; and in the General Assembly resolution adopting the CHR Resolution, the preamble takes a step backwards, then certainly sideways. The General Assembly resolution affirms, "there is no one model of democracy". Boutros Boutros-Ghali in his 1996 *Agenda for Democratisation* observed that any "right to democracy" was tainted by suspicion that it may be motivated by superpower competition. Such a statement by the Secretary General of the United Nations obviates any possibility that a right to democracy could be considered a universal right, much less any sort of peremptory norm. There is, as yet, no right to democracy in international law.

The features of democracy

In 1949, the emerging Council of Europe listed "devotion to individual freedom", rule of law, and political liberty as the basis of all "genuine democracies" in the preamble to its Statute. These are, however, loose categories, which give rise to multiple interpretations. The innovation came with the Commission of Human Rights Resolution 2000/47. The operative paragraph is 1(d)(ii), which deals with the right to vote in "a free and fair process... open to multiple parties".[5] This innovation is extremely important, given that the states of the Warsaw Pact, during the Cold War, were formally described as "peoples" democracies'. In effect, it "allows no further grounds for single-party states to claim that they have in place the mechanisms for functioning democracy" (Rich, 2001). The demand for multi-party contestation in regular election processes also disallows the use of single-issue referenda as sufficient evidence of democratic intent. The Commission passed the resolution by 45 votes to zero. There were eight abstentions – Bhutan, China, Cuba, Pakistan, Qatar, Congo (Brazzaville), Rwanda, and Sudan. Note, however, that these states *abstained* rather than out-rightly opposed; accordingly, their abstentions may be taken to imply that they did not object to such a *definition* of democracy, merely that they did not wish to be associated with it.

Is the notion of a democracy sufficiently defined to allow for a determination of what is not a democracy?

Though being a democracy is not a requirement to enjoy the protection of international law, a certain standard of being a democracy has been generally endorsed. Countries claiming to be democratic now must show evidence of elections, and these must be "fair". The by-now standard terminology is "free and fair". In the adoption of the Charter of Paris for a New Europe, in 1990, the European leaders stated: "We undertake to build, consolidate and strengthen democracy as the only system of government of our Nations.... Democratic government is based on the will of the people, expressed regularly through free and fair elections". The Charter of Paris went on to establish some basic liberal criteria, generally accepted as prerequisites for any state to present itself as a liberal democracy:

> Democracy has as its foundation respect for the human person and the rule of law. Democracy is the best safeguard of freedom of expression, tolerance of all groups of society, and equality of opportunity for each person.
>
> Charter of Paris (1990)

Election processes, it has been increasingly granted, should be subject to international verification. Writing in 1992, Thomas Franck advocated building the foundations for the "emerging right of democratic governance" by having national elections observed and informally ratified by the international community, a process whereby the resulting government gains international legitimacy through the procedural device of international election monitoring. In many ways, Franck was quite prescient, since international observation of national elections and referendums in countries claiming to be democratic has become the norm.

But it should be observed that the European conception of democracy goes well beyond the holding of periodic open elections. It insists that "proper" democratic states (formally designated as liberal-democratic states) will incorporate guarantees for the respect of human rights and fundamental freedoms. Membership in the Council of Europe is dependent upon meeting these criteria, and the Council recently threatened to suspend Russia under Article 8 of the Statute of the Council of Europe because of its actions in Chechnya. This followed a 1997 decision of the Parliamentary Assembly of the Council of Europe to suspend the participation of the parliament of Belarus because of the illegitimate way in which it had been constituted.

In 2000, an international Community of Democracies was established that, at its meeting in Seoul in 2002, issued the Seoul Plan of Action, which listed the "essential elements of representative democracy" as

> respect for human rights – civil, political, economic, social and cultural – including freedom of expression, freedom of the press, and freedom of religion and conscience; access to and free exercise of power in accordance with the rule of law; the holding of periodic free and fair elections based on secret balloting and universal suffrage monitored by independent election authorities; freedom of association including the right to form independent political parties; separation of powers, especially an independent judiciary; and constitutional subordination of all state institutions, including the military, to the legally-constituted civilian authority.
>
> Seoul Plan of Action (2002)

This list, though undoubtedly aspirational, extended the democracy criteria considerably, and associated democracy clearly with liberal democracy. It also established the Western conception of democracy as the international conception.

Democracy "promotion" or democracy "protection"?

Democracy promotion as a potential goal of the United Nations became generally touted with UN Secretary General Boutros-Ghali's 1996, *Agenda for Democratisation* report (see, e.g., Rushton, 2008). Defenders of this essentially aspirational document have paid insufficient attention to the care with which Boutros-Ghali defined democratisation, and to the conclusions of his report. Firstly, the report solidified the triad of peace, development and democratisation, affirming that they were indissolubly linked. Secondly, the "triad" had emerged during a series of heated General Assembly debates, which expressed clear concern that development was being downgraded as a priority for the organisation. Thirdly, in the conclusion on concrete action, the Secretary General proposed that development might be a necessary *pre-condition* for democratisation, and that both depended, in many places, on the success of internal peace processes. Boutros-Ghali, in short, ordered the triad as, firstly, peace, then development, and only thereafter, democratisation. He also observed, as noted above, that democracy promotion was tainted by suspicion that it was "motivated by superpower competition". In effect, democracy *promotion* remains a contested policy, part of the politics of UN agencies as they battle for legitimacy and resources, and expressive of the ongoing structural divide between developed and developing countries.

Protection, as opposed to promotion, came with the International Conference of Newly Restored Democracies, held in Manila in June 1988. An international conference of 13 new and restored democracies, it owed its inspiration and intellectual rigor to the late Philippine Foreign Secretary Raul Manglapus; its legitimacy came from its clear independence of great-power politics and the evident sincerity of its participants. At Manila, the 13 participating countries committed themselves to the "ideal of democracy"; that is, to democracy as an aspirational goal. At a second conference in Managua in 1994, the participant states, growing in number but still outside of the ambit of the great powers, called for the UN to become involved; with the result that the meeting in Bucharest, with now 80 states, was served by UNDP under the rubric of "democracy development". The substantive obligation was formulated in the Warsaw Declaration of 27 June 2000, at a gathering called "Towards a Community of Democracies", and which initiated the Community of Democracies. It stated: "We resolve jointly to co-operate to discourage and resist the threat to democracy posed by the *overthrow of constitutionally elected governments*" *[my ital.]*.

Something akin has been attempted in Latin America, again with a focus on election processes. In the Organisation of American States' (OAS) 1948 Charter, the preamble had named "representative democracy" as the "indispensable condition for stability, peace and development" (but without elaboration of any institutional details or definitions). The 1985 Cartagena Protocol amending the OAS Charter went further, proclaiming the promotion of democracy as one of its "essential purposes" and declared that "representative democracy" should be the basis for the political organisation of the states of the hemisphere. The Santiago mechanism of 1991 followed, allowing the OAS to react to situations where democracy was interrupted. The "mechanism" permitted foreign ministers to meet to decide on collective action in the case of possible threats to democratically elected governments; and the Declaration of 1993 committed the organisation to uphold democracy in its region (see Acevedo, 1993). In terms of positive reinforcement, the Unit for the Promotion of Democracy, established in 1990, has coordinated election observation missions and other activities aimed at establishing a "culture of democracy" in the Americas. The OAS immediately condemned a military coup in Haiti in 1994 against the legitimately elected government, attempted to negotiate a resolution to the crisis, and, when this failed, agreed to impose voluntary sanctions upon Haiti.

But the arguably significant sets of policies were those initiated by the Economic Community of West African States (ECOWAS). The 1999 ECOWAS Protocol Relating to the Mechanism for Conflict Prevention, Management, Resolution, Peace-keeping and Security, read together with related ECOWAS instruments, established a Mediation and Security Council that, by a two-thirds vote, may authorise "all forms of intervention" (article 10) including military intervention, in a member state. The potential conditions listed that could trigger action included cases of aggression or conflict in any Member State or threat thereof; conflict between two or several Member States; and internal conflicts that (a) threaten to trigger a humanitarian disaster, or (b) pose a serious threat to peace and security in the sub-region. Finally, action was allowed in the event of serious and massive violation of human rights and the rule of law, and also in the event of an *overthrow or attempted overthrow of a democratically elected government*.

It continues to be understood that no state can use force with regard to another state except in self-defence unless under a Chapter VII action endorsed by the Security Council. In the event, Security Council statements of 27 May (document S/PRST/29), 11 July (document S/PRST/36), and 6 August 1997 (document S/1997/42) called for immediate and unconditional restoration of the democratically elected Government of President Ahmad Tejan Kabbah of Sierra Leone, confirmed in Security Council Resolution 1132.

The efforts of ECOWAS have not been without their critics. It is noteworthy that these mechanisms have provided international support for West African states, and notably Nigeria, to intervene with force, now legitimately, in the internal affairs of their neighbours. Nor it is clear in the case of Nigeria that these efforts represent a sincere conversion to the values of democracy or to respect for electoral processes. The question of the legitimacy of individual efforts is, however, a different question from whether "democracy protection" in this form is on the way to becoming a norm.

Sanctions in aid of democracy protection

SCR 940, adopted on 31 July 1994, affirmed the goal of the international community to restore democracy in Haiti and authorised a US-led multinational force (MNF) under unified command and control to restore the legitimately elected President Jean-Bertrand Aristide and authorities of the Government of Haiti. The vote was the first time the United Nations sanctioned the use of an invading force to "restore democracy".[6] (It was also the first time the United States sought and gained UN approval for a military intervention in the Americas.) The mandate of the force was narrowly defined by the international community as the return of the legitimately elected government and the holding of elections.

Between 1990 and 2004, the UN was involved in a broad range of democracy promotion and statebuilding activities in Haiti, many of which involved the use of enforcement measures against various Haitian actors. The UN's engagement came in two waves: from 1990 to 2001 and from 2004 onwards. Its activities included electoral monitoring (1990), several peacekeeping and rule of law operations (1994–2001, and 2004-present), the imposition of sanctions supported by a naval blockade (1993–1994), and the delegation of Chapter VII powers to two US-led MNFs – one in 1994 and another in 2004 (Malone, 1999, 2004).

However, many Latin American countries saw the resolutions allowing the use of force as licensing external interference in the region, and objected to it on those grounds. (The OAS's own efforts at mediation in Haiti were conducted under its own mechanism, allowable since it did not then envision the use of force.) At a Security Council meeting called to discuss the resolutions, Mexico's UN ambassador, Víctor Flores Olea, charged that "it [SCR 940] sets an extremely dangerous precedent in the field of international relations" because the crisis "does not constitute a threat to peace and international security". Cuban Foreign Minister Roberto Robaina said that the resolution furthers "the repeated attempts by the Security Council to amplify its powers beyond those which were granted it by the Charter". Pointing out that the situation in Haiti posed no threat to world peace and security, Uruguay's UN representative Ramiro Piriz Ballon said his country "will not support any military intervention, unilateral or multilateral" (Security Council Meeting 3413, 31 July 1994). (Sanctions against Haiti were also reckoned to have imposed severe, and unjustified, impoverishment on the population.)

In 1998, ECOWAS, the regional body of West African states, intervened in Sierra Leone to restore President Kabbah to office. ECOWAS was created on 25 May 1975 purely as an economic organisation. By 1998, it had transformed itself into a regional collective security system with extraordinary authority to intervene militarily in the internal affairs of member states (see above). Both ECOWAS interventions in 1989 and 1997 in Liberia and Sierra Leone respectively were without the UN's authorisation. However, the UNSC Resolutions 788 (1992) and 1132 (1997) eventually retroactively sanctioned both interventions, and ECOWAS was commended for its efforts at mediation and sanctions enforcement, bringing to mind Albert's phrase in relation to Panama – "a continuum of lawfulness" (Albert, 1991). A letter, dated 7 October 1997, from secretary-general Kofi Annan addressed to the President of the Security Council (document S/1997/776) in which he assessed the current situation in Sierra Leone, established the principle: "At stake", the secretary-general concludes, "is a great issue of principle, namely, that the efforts of the international community for democratic governance, grounded in the rule of law and respect for human rights, shall not be thwarted through illegal coups." It was even then being predicted that, should similar circumstances arise again in the future, the UN would be likely, or at the very least would consider itself able to react as it did in Sierra Leone, provided the *regional organisation supported action against an illegal seizure of power.*

This prediction proved accurate. In 2004, the UNSC had sanctioned French intervention in the Ivory Coast, then under the rubric of "threats to international peace and security" (SC 1528), subsequently extended. In December 2010, after days of negotiations held up by Russia's refusal to interfere in domestic elections, the 15-member Council finally came to an agreement. US envoy Brooke Anderson read the Council's statement to the press: "In view of ECOWAS's' recognition of Mr Alassane Dramane Ouattara as President-elect of Côte d'Ivoire and representative of the freely expressed voice of the Ivorian people as proclaimed by the Independent Election Commission, the members of the Security Council call on all stakeholders to respect the outcome of the election."

She went on to say that the council condemns "in the strongest possible terms" any effort to subvert the popular will of the people or undermine either the integrity of the electoral process or the free and fair elections in Ivory Coast; and that the Security Council stood ready to impose sanctions on persons "who attempt to threaten the peace process, obstruct the work of the UN mission there, or commit serious violations of human rights and international humanitarian law" (Press statement, SC/10105). Anderson did not link sanctions directly to the overthrow of a duly elected person. But on 30 March 2011, the Security Council passed Resolution 1975 imposing sanctions on President Laurent Gbagbo and his close associates, and calling on "all the Ivorian parties and other stakeholders – including the security forces – to respect the will of the people and the election of Alassane Ouattara as President of Côte d'Ivoire, as recognised by the Economic Community of West African States (ECOWAS), the African Union and the rest of the international community following the November polls" (SCRes 1975).

Humanitarian intervention versus democratic intervention

Security Council Resolution 1244 (1999) authorising the intervention into Kosovo (after the event) made it clear that the primary goal of the intervention was to deal with the grave humanitarian situation and the acts of violence against the Kosovo population, and not with the limitations of democracy. The intervention in Libya this year was also under humanitarian law, quoting "the Responsibility to Protect", and not under any emerging democratic law; and proposals for interventions into the civil war emerging in Syria, now fading, are also based on the legal premises of Responsibility to Protect, which enjoins governments to protect their populations – in the concrete case not to use heavy weapons and artillery to put down civil unrest.

The United States and democracy promotion

Since in the English School, the advancement of norms has as much to do with the attitudes of the great powers as with juridical formulation, the United States' stance on democracy in its foreign affairs is relevant and should be noted. This is expressed in the legislation by the US House and Senate enacted on 30 July 2007, and signed by President George W. Bush on 3 August 2007. Entitled "Advancing Democratic Values", the Carnegie Endowment for Peace describes it as the most important piece of legislation in this field in two decades.

The act, among other things, requires the State Department, *working with local civic activists*, to *develop written strategies* for the promotion of democracy in all countries that are non-democratic or "transitioning to democracy" as defined in the legislation. It makes no mention of the use of force to promote democracy and demands evidence that locals desire democracy, and that local organisations are prepared to take action to procure it. The legislation's co-sponsors, senators Joseph Lieberman (I-CT) and John McCain (R-AZ) both stated that the Advance Democracy Act strengthens America's ability to promote freedom, the rule of law and social modernisation through the international order.

In its details, *Title 22*, Foreign Relations and Intercourse, Chapter 89, Advancing Democratic Values, defines the term "non-democratic country" or "democratic transition country" to include "any country which is not governed by a fully functioning democratic form of government, as determined by the Secretary, taking into account the general consensus regarding the status of civil and political rights in a country by major non-governmental organisations that conduct assessments of such conditions in countries"

The characteristics required of a democracy, listed in Chapter 89, are as follows:

(A) All citizens of such country have the right to, and are not restricted in practice from, fully and freely participating in the political life of such country.

(B) The national legislative body of such country and, if directly elected, the head of government of such country are chosen by free, fair, open, and periodic elections, by universal and equal suffrage, and by secret ballot.

(C) More than one political party in such country has candidates who seek elected office at the national level and such parties are not restricted in their political activities or their process for selecting such candidates, except for reasonable administrative requirements commonly applied in countries categorised as fully democratic.

(D) All citizens in such country have a right to, and are not restricted in practice from, fully exercising such fundamental freedoms as the freedom of expression, conscience, and peaceful assembly and association, and such country has a free, independent, and pluralistic media.

(E) The current government of such country did not come to power in a manner contrary to the rule of law.

(F) Such country possesses an independent judiciary and the government of such country generally respects the rule of law.

(G) Such country does not violate other core principles enshrined in the United Nations Charter, the Universal Declaration of Human Rights, the International Covenant on Civil and Political Rights, United Nations Commission on Human Rights Resolution 1499/57 [sic; should be 1999/57] (entitled "Promotion of the Right to Democracy"), and the United Nations General Assembly Resolution 55/96 (entitled "Promoting and consolidating democracy").

(H) As applicable, whether the country has scored favourably on the political, civil liberties, corruption, and rule of law indicators used to determine eligibility for financial assistance disbursed from the Millennium Challenge Account.

(H.R. 982 (110th): Advance Democracy Act of 2007)

The characteristics noted by the United States would clearly qualify as liberal democracy and, read by themselves, would not support the contention that the international order has entered a post-liberal phase. They also demonstrate, however, that declarations of democracy alone and even guarantees of "free and fair elections" are not sufficient to secure liberalism's future.

International law or international standard?

From the foregoing, it is probably fair to characterise much of the activity surrounding the creation of a democracy norm as one of setting standards. What has emerged is an understanding that claims to democracy cannot mean merely what any state claims they should mean. Democracy is gaining a determinate meaning, and setting a certain standard for what it means to be a democracy. That standard is regular elections where at least two competing political parties are allowed freely to petition votes and where electoral processes are not interfered with to the point of distorting, much less overthrowing voter preferences. Human rights petitioners would like that standard to go much further, of course, and to guarantee the full panoply of political rights; such as for example equal rights to media access and the disqualification of elections where *any* voters are being coerced in their choices, but so far the standard is not being enlarged, at least not so far as allowing external interference in internal political processes.

The existing norm is also gaining an impressive institutional carapace for ascertaining that the standard is being met. The United Nations, the European Community, individual governments, and a plethora of non-governmental organisations have all established monitoring systems, and rota of personnel, that may be called upon to check electoral processes. Hyde and Kelley in a recent account observe that the most active monitoring comes from the EU and the Organisation for Security and Cooperation in Europe, but that "more than a dozen organisations including the Carter Center, the International Republican Institute, the National Democracy Institute and the O.A.S. send observers to five or more elections each year" (Hyde and Kelley, 2011). Monitoring has become such an accepted feature of international political processes that refusing to invite observers has become a sign that an aspiring democracy has something to hide.

The latter must be stressed. The standard applies only to those who make the claim. States that do not claim to be democracies, and who indeed reject the values of democracy (much less liberal democracy), do not, on those grounds, lose their rights in international law, including their rights of non-interference. At the meeting of the Council for the Community of Democracies in Lisbon in 2009, 66 states signed the Declaration of Lisbon, reaffirming their pledge to "advance democratisation and to involve citizens in a transparent political process", among a host of other democratic aims. Seventy-seven signed a less ambitious pledge at the Council meeting at Vilnius in 2011. At present, the states claiming to be democracies, and who have undertaken international pledges to uphold democratic values, number at somewhat less than half the states in the international community.

But it is not an unimportant half. These are not only Western states or small states. They include major "non-Western" powers like India, Nigeria, South Africa, and Brazil. With the Philippines and Lebanon (and the aspiring state of Palestine) they include states from all regions. Moreover, the aspiration to democracy has come to be considered a legitimate aspiration of the community of states; that is, of the international community itself, and deserving of international protection on those grounds. Not all states have to be democracies, and beyond the minimum of "free and fair elections" the criteria of being a democracy are only beginning to be refined. But, in practice, non-democracies are being pushed, and not merely on the grounds of neglecting human rights or "inhuman" practices, but on the grounds of not being democratic (e.g., Morocco, a constitutional monarchy, had to be perceived as a democracy before receiving major loans and investments from Western states). Finally, and most significantly from the point of view of an international norm, the protection of democracy has become an international obligation on the part of other democratic states and a justification for intervention on the part of the international community, including non-democratic states (since such can sit on the Security Council). Internal coups against democratically elected governments are no longer a matter of internal jurisdiction or a reserved domain of state sovereignty. Legitimately elected democratic governments may now call on the protection of the international community.

Notes

1. As the results were somewhat confusing, the border was finally determined only partly by reference to the plebiscite.
2. The Covenant is noteworthy for its care to secure "peoples" their economic rights; that is, collective rights to equality of treatment in international economic relations.
3. The sources of international law are defined in Article 38 of the Statute of the International Court of Justice.
4. All official documents may be retrieved directly from the web using the resolution number/date, or the title as quoted.
5. 1 (*d*) To develop, nurture and maintain an electoral system that provides for the free and fair expression of the people's will through genuine and periodic elections, in particular by:

     (i) Ensuring the right of everyone to take part in the government of his/her country, directly or through freely chosen representatives;
     (ii) Guaranteeing the right freely to vote and to be elected in a free and fair process at regular intervals, by universal and equal suffrage, open to multiple parties, conducted by secret ballot;
     (iii) Taking measures as appropriate to address the representation of under-represented segments of society;
     (iv) Ensuring, through legislation, institutions and mechanisms, the freedom to form democratic political parties as well as transparency and fairness of the electoral process, including through appropriate access to funds and free, independent and pluralistic media.

6. The legal drafters felt sufficiently uncertain of the legitimacy of the action in international law to call up a plethora of precedents, including resolutions 841 (1993), 861 (1993), 862 (1993), 867 (1993), 873 (1993), 875 (1993), 905 (1994), 917 (1994), and 933 (1994).

References

(Official documents may be retrieved directly from the web using the official title, as used in the text, or document number and date.)

Acevedo, D. E. (1993), "The Haitian Crisis and the OAS Response", in L. F. Damrosch (ed.) *Enforcing Restraint*, New York: Council on Foreign Relations, 119–143.

Albert, D. (1991), "The United States Invasion of Panama: Unilateral Military Intervention to Effectuate a Change of Government", *Transnational Law and Contemporary Problems*, 1, 259 (recovered 29 May 2011).

Badescu, C. and Weiss, T. (2010), "Misrepresenting R2P and Advancing Norms", *International Studies Perspectives*, 22, 354–374.

Checkel, J. T. (2001), "Why Comply? Social Learning and European Identity Change", *International Organization*, 55, 553–588.

Donelly, J. (1986), "International Human Rights: A Regime Analysis", *International Organization*, 40, 599–642.

Finnemore, M. and Sikkink, K. (1998), "International Norm Dynamics and Political Change", *International Organization*, 52, 887–917.

Hyde, S. and Kelley, J. (2011), "The Limits of Election Monitoring", *Foreign Affairs*, 28 June (recovered 5 December 2012).

Jackson, R. (2000), *The Global Covenant*, Oxford: Oxford University Press.

Jones, D. (1992), "The Declaratory Tradition in Modern International Law", in T. Nardin and D. Mapel (eds) *Traditions of International Ethics*, Cambridge: Cambridge University Press, 42–61.

Keck, M. and Sikkink, K. (1998), *Activists Beyond Borders: Advocacy Networks in International Politics*, Ithaca, New York: Cornell University Press.

Malone, D. M. (1999), *Decision-Making in the UN Security Council: The Case of Haiti*, Oxford: Oxford University Press; (2004), "Look beyond the 'Republic of Port-au-Prince' Intervention in Haiti", *International Herald Tribune*, 3 March (recovered 29 May 2011).

Nardin, T. (1983), *Law, Morality and the Relations of States*, Princeton: Princeton University Press.

Onuma, Y. (2003), "International Law in and with International Politics: The Functions of International Law in International Society", *European Journal of International Law*, 14, 105–139.

Rich, R. (2001), "Bringing Democracy into International Law", *Journal of Democracy*, 12, 20–34 (recovered 29 March 2011).

Risse, T., Ropp, S. and Sikkink, K. (eds) (1999), *The Power of Human Rights: International Norms and Domestic Change*, Cambridge: Cambridge University Press.

Rushton, S. (2008), "Boutros Boutros-Ghali and Democracy Promotion", *Global Governance*, 14, 95–110.

Wilson, P. (2000), "The English School's Approach to International Law", in C. Navari (ed.) *Theorising International Society: English School Methods*, New York: Palgrave Macmillan, 167–188.

3
Realism Tamed or Liberalism Betrayed? Dystopic Liberalism and the International Order

Nicholas Rengger

That liberal political theory has enjoyed a remarkable resurgence in the latter part of the twentieth century will not, I suppose, be challenged by anyone who has even a nodding acquaintance with the intellectual history of the last 50 years.[1] In Anglo-American circles, at least, liberal thought is now the dominant voice and even in parts of the "European" world where, 50 years ago, liberalism was the political theory that dared not speak its name, it has risen to prominence (Lilla, 1996). Even those critical of liberal thought – as much post-structurally inclined theory of course is – often take their starting points from liberal claims or use liberal ideas as a peg on which to hang their own thoughts, however critical they may be; a sign, as Gramsci would have been quick to remark, of "hegemony", if ever there was one (Honig, 1993).

One area where this is often not supposed to be true, however, is International Relations. Here, or so the story has it, the dominant voice has been, and still is, something called "realism", and "liberalism" was, at best, a challenger to this hegemonic tradition; an important presence to be sure, but certainly not a dominant voice. I think, in fact, that this always underestimated the power of at least some versions of liberalism in international thought but in any event, today, liberal thought is increasingly influential and in certain areas could I think be said to be dominant. Certain liberal claims – the liberal or democratic peace thesis for example – have almost become the orthodoxy, even (at least in some circles) an unchallenged assumption. And in "international (or global) political theory" – to use this term to mark out a terrain of normative and ethical reflection on the substance of international relations – it is the liberal voice that is now the dominant one.

Of course, this rather begs the question of how we are to understand the term "liberal" in all of the above. For it is a truth as general as that of the revival of liberal theory itself, that the form of liberal politics is much disputed. Indeed, it seems sometimes that so many claims can be reasonably described as liberal as to render the term useless as a general term of art in political theory. When thinkers as disparate as Hobbes, Locke, Montesquieu, Kant, Bentham, Toqueville, Mill, Green, Aron, and Rawls can all, fairly enough, be seen as "liberal" thinkers, one must at least begin to ask about the continued utility of the term itself.

Important as this thought might be, I shall not pursue it further on this occasion. Rather, I want to explore one particular version of liberal political thought and offer a reading of it in the context, especially, of international politics. I do so both because I think that it is an especially interesting version of politics; but also because, in the ways in which it has been best rendered at least, it contains a powerful flaw that threatens to tip it into incoherence at precisely the point where it most needs to be most clear – and this flaw is perhaps most visible in the context of international politics. Indeed, to tip my hand in advance, I will suggest that, for all of its power, and despite what I would see as its clear superiority to more generally dominant forms of liberal thought, it ultimately shares one illusion with those dominant forms and it is this illusion that threatens its central insight.

The argument I shall make has three broad stages. In the first, I shall offer a general interpretation of what I shall call "dystopic liberalism".[2] It will, of course, be a composite, but will try and outline what I take to be the essential claims of this version of liberal thought. Not all of these claims would be endorsed by all the scholars I associate with it, but the most important ones certainly would be. The second stage will focus on how this form of liberal thought understands international relations. The third will then pose a problem that is potentially ruinous for dystopic liberal thought and see whether dystopic liberalism has a response to it. I will suggest that, at least in its present form, it does not. Finally, I will close the paper by offering an alternative thought about liberalism and suggest a rather different trajectory that might prove more fruitful – but that would also have costs that liberals, even of the dystopic kind, might not be prepared to countenance.

The faces of dystopic liberalism

The kind of liberal thought I want to discuss is best made clear if, to begin with, we contrast two distinct forms of liberal thought. The first I shall take to be expressive of the dominant forms of liberal thought in contemporary analytical political theory. Although, of course, it is a composite, one might suggest that paradigmatic versions of it can be found in Rawls, Dworkin, and other so-called "egalitarian" liberals, as well as – in a rather different form – in thinkers like Hayek. Its central assumption has been well spelt out by John Gray – who is himself a dystopic liberal of a certain sort – as essentially the idea that "there can be a rational consensus on the best way of life" (Gray, 2000), however that is understood. Bernard Williams also refers to it as "political moralism", a view of politics that sees morality as "prior" to politics in important ways (Williams, 2008).[3] This form of liberal thought is the form in which, in Anglo-American theory at least, it has become dominant, in part simply because it is the guiding set of assumptions that underpin Rawls' *A Theory of Justice* (Rawls, 1971) and its offspring – far and away the most influential liberal political theory of recent times. It is also, interestingly enough, the form that has now become dominant in international political theory as well, if we understand that term to indicate an area of ethical reflection on the circumstances and character of international politics. It is the liberalism of Rights and Obligations; of ever more complex accounts of distributive justice, domestic, international, and global; of the possibility of "realistic utopia"s and of "ideal" and "non-ideal" theory; in other words, of all the impedimenta of the still burgeoning Rawls industry.

It is the second form, however, with which I shall chiefly be concerned on this occasion, and again Gray has given a good rough description of it. He suggests that on an alternative view (which he favours), liberal toleration should simply be seen as a *modus vivendi*, predicated on the realisation that human beings can flourish in the context of many different forms of life and that thus liberal thought is best seen as a liberalism of "peaceful co-existence"; a way of allowing such multiple forms to exist without too much conflict (Gray, 2000: 2). Gray suggests that this form of liberalism owes a good deal to Isaiah Berlin, and I agree with Gray that Berlin is a powerful contributor, though he is hardly the only one. This version of liberal thought has been called a number of different things, and I am not sure that Gray's "*modus Vivendi*" is quite the best term for it, nor that he is right to suppose that it is simply a philosophy of peaceful co-existence. There could, after all, be a number of those and they need not be distinctively liberal; and some might say, for example, that Gray's current version is not (Rengger, 2007).

Perhaps the most arresting presentation of such a view that is distinctively liberal, however, offers the best general title for it: "the Liberalism of Fear", a phrase, of course, taken from the title of a famous essay by Judith Shklar (in Yack, 1996). Her version of it has, for many, become paradigmatic and for very good reasons, as we shall see.[4] However, as with the first version of liberal thought, there are subtly different readings of it. Shklar might have pride of place, but standing behind Shklar is, as Gray suggests, her friend Isaiah Berlin, and alongside her are her and Berlin's friend, Bernard Williams, and *her* friend and Harvard colleague Stanley Hoffmann. And standing behind *him* is his friend and teacher, Raymond Aron – and, of course, there are others, some more directly, and some more tangentially, related.[5]

While of course it is the case, that each of the aforementioned thinkers gives a subtly different reading of the essence of liberal thought and practice, it is, I think, fair to suggest that they share certain common assumptions, and in particular that they base their liberal thinking on one shared assumption above all others. This assumption is that liberal thought, properly understood, is resolutely anti-utopian; that, indeed, it is *rooted* in its anti-utopianism. George Kateb suggests that Shklar, for example, had what amounted to "contempt" for the utopian imagination,[6] a contempt that found expression in her borrowing of Emerson's terms, the party of memory and the party of hope, and defining herself (in her celebrated essay) as a member of the party of memory, specifically the memory of the atrocities of twentieth-century history. Aron, likewise, many times suggested that the essence of his liberalism was suspicion of utopian ambitions. As he says:

> among the freedoms proclaimed by the Atlantic Charter there are two that would have been ignored by traditional liberals – freedom from want and freedom from fear – because want and fear, hunger and war, were inherent to human existence throughout the centuries. "That poverty and violence have been as of now eliminated no one believes'. that one day they might be why not hope"? That the ambition to eliminate them is new and shows an arrogance that...Tocqueville would not have shared or approved is beyond doubt. For this ambition emerges from equating the tyranny of things with the tyranny of men...only men can deprive other men of the right to select a government and worship a god. But what men are responsible for – and what men can conquer want and fear?. No social condition must be accepted as independent of the rational will of men. This...expresses the common faith or universal illusion of modern societies.
>
> (Aron, 1983b: 231)

Similar sentiments can be found in Berlin, in Williams and in Hoffmann. So we can say, to begin with then, that dystopic liberalism is first and foremost anti-utopian (i.e., indeed, why I chose to call it dystopic).

But if it is indeed dystopic, is it also anything else? For after all, there are many anti-utopians who are not liberals. So what distinguishes dystopic *liberals* from those who are merely dystopic? Here again, Shklar perhaps provides the core assumption. "Liberalism", she announces, "has only one overriding aim: to secure the political conditions necessary for the exercise of personal freedom...apart from prohibiting interference with the freedom of others, liberalism does not have any particular positive doctrines about how people are to conduct their lives or what personal choices they are to make" (1998: 3). Shklar then makes clear how rare such a view has been in the history of both political thought and practice. It most certainly does mean that one cannot see – as some claim to do – "liberalism" as somehow expressive of the dominant ethos of "modernity" – a term Shklar thinks is riven with imprecision and dubious historical claims in any event. It also means that there is no direct relation of liberalism to either scepticism or the pursuit of the natural sciences (two other common claims that Shklar discusses). Of course, the sceptic *inclines* to liberalism, Shklar thinks, since "whether the sceptic seeks personal tranquillity in retreat or tries to calm the warring factions around her, she must prefer a government that does nothing to increase the prevailing levels of fanaticism and dogmatism" (1998: 7), but inclination is not the same as identity. As with scepticism, so with science. "The alliance between liberalism and science", she remarks, "was one of convenience... [they] were not born together; [science] is far older" (1998: 7).

There is, however, one interesting difference between the dystopic liberals, which might be worth commenting on at this point, since I shall want to return to it later on. One claim that a number of dystopic liberals – perhaps especially Berlin and Gray – would make is that while liberalism might rest at bottom on anti-utopianism, another scarcely less significant aspect to it is the recognition of value pluralism, of the fact that there are multiple, incommensurable moralities that exist both within and between political communities. This is, after all one of the most powerful reasons for seeing liberalism as *modus vivendi,* according to Gray. Shklar's response to this is characteristically brusque and leads to the core of her own conception of the "liberalism of fear":

> Whatever the truth of this metapolitical assumption may be she says, liberalism can do without it. The liberalism of fear does not rest on a theory of moral pluralism. It does not, to be sure, offer a *summum bonum* toward which all political agents should strive, but it certainly does begin with a *summum malum*, which all of us know and would avoid if only we could. That evil is cruelty and the fear that it inspires, and the very fear of fear itself. To that extent the liberalism of fear makes a universal and especially a cosmopolitan claim, as it has historically always done.
>
> (1998: 11)

Here Shklar is drawing on her earlier work, most especially *Ordinary Vices* (1984), where she states that "cruelty is the worst thing we can do to one another" and in which the phrase the liberalism of fear first appears. But this claim also maps out a series of assumptions about what a distinctively dystopic liberalism should do: in brief, reduce the scope of cruelty and fear, within society and, indeed, between societies, in international society. It is this insight that, for many, opens Shklar and other dystopic liberals to particular and concrete issues and questions within politics and political theory and which allows dystopic liberalism to be a species of liberalism relevant to modern concerns, which allows them to "link" as it were to other versions of liberalism including the two that Shklar most persuasively differentiates the liberalism of fear from, the liberalism of Rights (traceable to Locke), and the liberalism of personal development (traceable to Mill). Whilst dystopic liberalism would certainly be critical of notions of Natural Rights and of personal development (or rather, as Shklar does, suggest that whatever virtues they might have are, strictly speaking, irrelevant to liberalism), that does not mean that dystopic liberalism could not deploy such notions.

Bernard Williams, for example, argues that rights can follow as a central plank in "reducing the scope of cruelty and fear" since they can be seen as "one necessary protection against the threats of power",[7] and has further argued that if one sees rights so, they can be divorced from any specific liberal moral and/or metaphysical assumptions that might make them more problematic in terms of general acceptance (Williams, 2008). And, as Michael Walzer points out, in a characteristically perceptive essay on Shklar,[8] even Shklar's emphasis on the negative can be open to more positive readings. Walzer argues that the liberalism of fear invites us to build a "bulwark" against the onslaught of cruelty and fear. But a bulwark is a defence; it has no function or meaning apart from what it defends. So we have to fill in a picture of what it is such a liberalism would defend.

This would, I think, be more or less accepted by most of the advocates of dystopic Liberalism in one way or another. Even Shklar herself seems to edge towards such a claim in her later writings on obligation, loyalty and exile and on American citizenship. And yet in some respects it does not quite *feel* right. As Miller has said, Shklar's essays, even her later ones, are deeply unsettling and are meant to be; "I mean to be unsettling", Shklar once declared (1989). Her turn of phrase, and I would argue also her cast of mind, was very different from the liberals she otherwise found herself alongside, even friends like Walzer. To Walzer's claim that "inside the bulwark" are "men and women, complexly related, with their personal status and sense of themselves; families and their varied holdings; customary rights and privileges; established communities of different sorts; different institutional arrangements; different moralities and religions" (Walzer, 1996: 18), one can contrast, as Miller does, Shklar's acidic portrayal of human relations in her most important late work *Faces of Injustice* where, we are told, "we are intuitively evasive" and are "strangers to one another and ... too ignorant to judge each other" (Shklar, 1990: 27).

This ambiguity, a pulling on the one hand, of dystopic liberalism back towards more conventional liberalisms and, on the other, an ingrained scepticism that pulls it in another direction entirely marks many of the dystopic liberals. Bernard Williams, for example – for all his distrust and criticism of "political moralism" – does not want to break with other forms of liberalism completely. At the end of his essay, honouring Berlin (in which he borrows the title of Shklar's famous essay), he remarks that:

> [the liberalism of fear] is disposed not to be too sanguine about [how secure what has been secured is] ... particularly since it remembers to look

beyond national boundaries. It is conscious that nothing is safe, that the task is never ending. This part of its being, as Judith Shklar said, is resolutely non-utopian. But that does not mean it is simply the politics of pessimism that has not collapsed into the politics of cynicism. In the words that Shklar quoted from Emerson, it is very importantly the party of memory. But it can be in good times, the politics of hope as well.

(Williams, 2008: 61)

But that is the key question, of course. I doubt that Shklar would think that, in the relevant sense, dystopic liberalism either could or *should* be the "party of hope". Williams is correct, however, in one thing. One of the central planks of the dystopic liberal imagination is a recognition that you cannot rest secure "within national boundaries". It is that recognition that drives dystopic liberalism into thinking about international relations. How then do they understand it, when they do?

Dystopic liberalism and the international order: Between "realism" and "universalism"?

The dystopic liberals I have chiefly discussed so far have in the main offered only scattered remarks about international relations (though that is not true of Gray whose recent work is deeply engaged in thinking about aspects of contemporary international relations). But the two thinkers mentioned above who certainly have reflected with great acuity and at considerable length on the problems of international relations are, of course, Raymond Aron and Stanley Hoffmann. I want, therefore, to say something about how these writers have seen the problem of international relations in the light of dystopic liberal concerns and will begin with Aron. To do this, however, I need firstly to say something about how Aron understands the problems of international relations in general before turning once more to the way Aron as a dystopic liberal might see them.[9]

For Aron, any "theory" of international relations must include both an explanation of the topic and moral reflection on both the topic and the explanation offered: neither, indeed, is really possible without the other. Normative implications are inherent in every theory, he argues, before going on to say that, in his view, the essence of interstate relations raises two "praxeological" problems. He calls them the *Machiavellian* and *Kantian* problems and identifies their essence as, respectively, the problem of *legitimate means* and the problem of *universal peace*.

For Aron, legitimacy was always a tension-filled, contradictory concept in the international realm. Just as international society is a unique kind of society – the only kind, Aron thinks, which accepts resort to force as potentially legitimate – so the norms that govern such a society are unique, consisting of a compromise between – and not, please note, a synthesis of – what he calls the morality of struggle and the morality of law each of which is the rationale of, respectively again, the Machiavellian and the Kantian problems.

It is largely because of this that Aron's reflections on international relations came to have their particular form. Because these two problems together constitute the problem of international relations, one cannot offer an answer to that general problem that is in fact only an answer to one of the problems and not to both. It is for this reason that Aron cannot give a standard "realist" answer (that international relations is about power or material interests). Such a view ignores the necessarily central elements of moral choice in all political life, including the international. "The realist who asserts that man is a beast of prey and urges him to behave as such", Aron tells us in *Peace and War*, "ignores a whole side of human nature. Even in the relations between states, respect for ideas, aspirations to higher values and concern for obligations have been manifested" (Aron, 1966: 634). Nor, however, could Aron opt for any particular version of a reformist/radical answer that ignores the provenance of the Machiavellian problem (we can ignore/denigrate states and their problems, devise a new international order, create international justice, etc). None of these, he thinks, are in fact answers to the combined questions.

If we recall the earlier discussion of Aron's notion of freedom we will remember that Aron's concern was that the "traditional" liberal concern with freedom from despotism – rights, constitutional procedures and so on – was increasingly being conflated with what we might today call the liberal universalist or Cosmopolitan claim to master nature in order to make a much larger freedom, freedom from want and fear, possible; and that in fact this ambition was ruinous to liberal politics properly so called.

Aron's concern, I think, was that, in international relations, it is only the older liberal politics that can offer a way of responding to both of his questions without collapsing one into the other and since the Kantian problem can never, as it were, be completely solved that would run the risk of collapsing everything to some sort of a vulgar "realism". That I think is the significance of the epigram from Montesquieu that Aron chose for the frontispiece of *Peace and War*, "that, in time of peace states should do the most good, and in time of war, the least harm, as possible".[10] This had the corollary, of course, that interpreters of international relations must pay attention to the character of a political regime and the way in which it behaves, but recognise that its behaviour will in part be shaped by its context, its circumstances. "In our epoch", he writes, "instead of repeating that all states no matter what their institutions have 'the same kind of foreign policy' we should insist upon the truth that is more complementary than contradictory; no one understands the diplomatic strategy of a state if he does not understand it's regime" (Aron, 1966: 279).

Aron's own way of responding to the double problematic that he had sketched was to emphasise, as he had done in many other contexts, the importance of prudence, though it is a prudence which, as Anderson (1997: 143–158) and others have pointed out is, Aron shaped in a very particular way. As he writes:

> The only morality which transcends the morality of struggle and the morality of Law is what I would call the morality of prudence, which attempts not only to consider each case in its concrete particularities, but also not to ignore any of the arguments of principle and opportunity, to forget neither the relation of forces nor the wills of peoples. Because it is complex, the judgment of prudence is never incontestable, and it satisfies completely neither the moralists nor the vulgar disciples of Machiavelli.
>
> (Aron, 1966: 609)

It is this conception of prudence that guided Aron in all his concrete judgments on events or processes, people or personalities. He explained its origin in a central passage in his memoirs. Asked to talk to an undersecretary at the foreign ministry on his return from Germany in 1932, Aron gave a lecture, brilliant, I suppose, in the pure style of a student from ENS:

> [The undersecretary] listened attentively [...] he then answered [...] meditation is essential. Whenever I find a few moments of free time, I meditate. So I am grateful to you for having given me so many subjects for meditation [...] you, who have spoken so well about Germany and the dangers appearing on the horizon. What would you do if you were in the minister's place?.
>
> (Aron, 1983b: 42)

That question was never far from Aron's mind when he analysed political events, near or far, domestic or international, as a political commentator or an academic. It allowed him to steer a course between the competing poles of realism and universalist liberalism without in any sense ever giving a sense of drift or of simply going with the common view. Often, Aron's answer to that question would, indeed, be very critical of the "minister" – or indeed other political actors of various kinds – but there was always an attempt to see the situation whole, in all of its contexts and to recognise, therefore, the contexts of judgment for *this* or *that* actor.

This conception of prudence is central to Aron's thought as a whole, not just to his thinking on international relations, but it is perhaps most visible and most important there. It informs his analysis in his book on nuclear strategy, is strongly present in his works of contemporary history – perhaps most obviously *The Century of Total War* – and is central to his interpretation of Clausewitz, perhaps the most impressive work of his old age, and one of the most impressive readings of Clausewitz in any language of which I am aware (Aron, 1983a). And, of course, as we have already seen, it dominates the interpretation of international relations laid out in *Peace and War*. It is a profound refusal to collapse the antinomies of which human life and conduct are made up and it shares with other iterations of "dystopic liberalism" a resistance both to the utopian forms that increasingly (even in Aron's day) were dominating liberalism and to a "non-liberal" dystopia that Aron saw in unadorned "realism". Aron's prudence is the best way – perhaps the only way – in which the fear inherent in the international political condition might be confronted and reduced.

Hoffman's work adds powerfully to this sort of reflection on international politics.[11] He has offered perhaps the most sustained and illuminating set of reflections derived from the dystopic liberal imagination in International Relations. At least from *Duties Beyond Borders* in 1981 – indeed, in some respects, since *The State of War* in 1965 – Hoffmann has sought to grapple with the ambiguity he perceives as central to thinking about international politics. The "liberalism of fear" sustains both his commitment to liberalism and his unflinching realism when it comes to the analysis of international relations. As he puts it:

> Realists who are pessimistic about human nature and about the nature of states, but concerned about the survival, the welfare, and the freedom's and capabilities of human beings; idealists who are appalled by the huge gaps that separate ideal theory from reality, could meet around the non-metaphysical liberalism that Judith Shklar has called the liberalism of fear; a philosophy and ethics centred on the fight against and prevention of, cruelty, oppression, fear misery and injustice – evils experienced by most human beings.
>
> (Hoffmann, 2006)

In another essay, he spells out what that would mean in the context of international relations. Hoffman discusses two fears characteristic of – indeed inherent in – international relations. "One is the fear of anarchy – of a world without norms in which states are too weak to protect or are all too willing to terrorise their subjects...the other is the fear of unfettered superior power, that is of imperial domination presenting itself as the only alternative to chaos...Both Chaos and Imperialism breed violence and war...and war today in all its forms...is the greatest source of fear in international society" (Hoffmann, 2006: 38). Of course, there is no simple remedy against, or cure for, "the state of war", Hoffmann argues. But there are ways of reducing the fears they provoke. As with Aron, Hoffmann insists that such ways are always context dependent; they will require "guides and leaders" (i.e. a strong sense of agency in world politics), and, most of all, they will require the kind of prudence that, as we have already seen, Aron insisted was the indispensable handmaiden of a properly constituted liberal international theory. Hoffmann suggests that just as in domestic society, Shklar's liberalism of fear requires constant vigilance (one of the reasons, remember, why liberal politics is so difficult and so rare), so, in international relations, "the freedom from fear requires a network of inspections...in the never ending battle against fear, ignorance means doom; sharp light, transparency and publicity means hope for the victims, worries for the victimisers and encouragement for oppositions that fight against state or private violence". Quoting Camus' *The Pest*, Hoffman (2006) ends this essay with perhaps a prototypically dystopian liberal refrain, "we need, of course, to remember (he tells us) that after a plague, a new one would come some day to 'awaken its rats and send them to their death in a happy city". But our duty remains to fight the bacillus "that never dies or disappears with as much lucidity and ardour as we can muster" (Hoffmann, 2006: 41).

This attempt – to tie a certain sort of realism and a certain sort of liberalism together – is common to the other dystopic liberals as well. Berlin, for example, though he did not write much about international affairs in any organised way, was every bit as critical of "unvarnished realism" as Aron or Hoffmann, and for very similar reasons. "Whenever you here a man speak of realism", he famously said in one lecture, "you may always be sure that this is the prelude to some bloody deed" (see the discussion in Ignatieff, 1998: 225). Williams, in several essays, has tried to emphasise a pathway between a "naked" political realism and a dystopic liberalism that is aware of the intractable character of political power (Williams, 2008). Gray, in his most recent book, has explicitly urged a return to "realism" as the only way to cope with our situation, but it is a realism wedded to the dystopic liberal assumptions he has developed in other works (see Gray, 2007, Rengger, 2007). So here, we might say that we have reached the core of the dystopic liberal project in international relations; an attempt to navigate between the Scylla of universalism (whether liberal or of other kinds) and the Charybdis of a realism that is William's "pessimism become cynicism" come to life and all the while to retain the central element of the liberalism of fear in place. The question is whether such a middle way is possible, and whether it is possible to tame realism without betraying liberalism?

After dystopia: The illusions of a "liberalism without illusions"

It goes without saying that I think what I have been calling dystopic liberalism is enormously interesting and extremely powerful as a counterweight to other, how shall we put it, less robust forms of liberal political thought. Each of the writers I have discussed is justly celebrated as an acute and hugely rich scholar of political thought, international relations, philosophy and/or (in some cases) of all three. Their work contains insights that any student of political theory and international relations could not fail to learn from, and, for the most part, they are also prose stylists and writers of uncommon elegance and range, often in several languages.

I stress this because what I shall have to say in this final section will be seen, quite rightly, as sceptical of the ability of "dystopic liberalism" to deliver what it promises. But I should like to add that scepticism is not always the same as hostility. I share a good deal with dystopic liberals; I just think that there is a better way of understanding, and perhaps sustaining, what we jointly share than the way they have laid out.

In the end, I think, we come back to that ambiguity I noted at the end of the first section above; the resistance, even of those most committed to a form of dystopic liberalism, to give up on "the politics of hope" and the fate of dystopic liberalism if they do. Indeed, my own view is that this ambiguity runs all the way through dystopic liberalism. As noted by Shklar and as I drew attention to above, the one clear reason for this ambiguity is not in the form in which I now want to deploy it. One might I suppose put it this way: *The manner in which dystopic visions and liberal ones are related needs always to be spelt out.* A case in point Shklar's claim that scepticism and liberalism are not directly related even though sceptics may *incline* to liberal thought. The point, however, is what happens when those who are both sceptics *and* liberals (like Shklar) face a situation where scepticism and liberalism point in opposite directions; they must ultimately, I think, decide whether they are liberals first and sceptics second, or the other way around.

If the former, then the temptation of what Miller rather archly refers to in his review essay on Shklar as the "power that positive thinking confers" will always be present, however much dystopic liberals may also recognise the traps that lie ahead (as Berlin, Williams, and Hoffmann, for example, all certainly do). The result, I think, will be a permanently unstable mix of commitment to "classically liberal" ideas and practices, perhaps adapted to new contexts, and a constant backsliding as such ideas and practices seem to require ever closer approximations to the utopian thought dystopic liberalism must eschew. This ambiguity is especially clearly displayed, I think, in Williams' thought, perhaps all the more so because his explicitly political thought was late and only partially developed, though expressed with all his usual intellectual fecundity and persuasiveness of expression, but there is a good deal of it Hoffmann as well. His own defence – that he prefers ambiguous eclecticism to fundamentalism – is very human and attractive, but it does not solve the problem.

It is also possible, however, for dystopic liberals to see themselves as sceptics first and liberals second. This is how I, at least, read Shklar, despite her occasional protestations – as well as many of those of her friends and colleagues like Walzer and Benhabib. Miller suggests that we see Shklar, and cherish her as a classical kind of Pyrrhonist, "outwardly engaged, inwardly detached" (Miller, 2000: 819). Note that I do not suggest that this necessarily means that she is wrong about her own commitment to liberalism, only that, in fact for her, her scepticism and her liberalism did run together and never ran afoul of one another. The reason, I think, was rooted in her own history. Mark Lilla, a former student, suggested that her "vision of political life was deeply, perhaps too deeply, marked by the catastrophes of modern history" (Lilla, 1998). I think her sense of history certainly supported both her liberalism and her scepticism, and that for her, a choice never had to be made. However, that was, so to say, a contingent, rather than a necessary relation. Not everyone would be so lucky.

For some other dystopic liberals, however, it seems that sometimes the liberalism shrinks almost to vanishing point as the scepticism increasingly takes hold. This I think would be one way of reading John Gray's progressive evolution, from Hayekian liberal to liberal critic of the New right, to *Modus Vivendi* liberal, to dystopic liberal "proper" as it were and now perhaps to an almost Santayana-esque Naturalist and sceptic, who is certainly dystopic but appears increasingly less and less concerned with anything that could reasonably be called liberal.[12]

If it is to avoid such constantly jarring existential choices, the crucial assumption that dystopic liberalism must make is that it is possible *always* to steer between various different forms of universalism, on the one hand, and simple capitulation to power, force and interest – with all their ensuing cruelty and fear – on the other. This is the one illusion, or so it seems to me, that "liberalism without illusions" *must* retain, for if it is not true then there will be times when the choice between universalism and realism will *have* to be made. If this is so, then dystopic liberalism, while it does not exactly betray liberalism, cannot ultimately safeguard it (perhaps, after all, nothing can), since in as much as one cleaves to universalism we would have to let in utopian once more (and thus the central plank of dystopic liberalism falls); and it most certainly cannot "tame" realism as sometimes "realism" (in any of its various forms) will simply become the default position of those who have dystopic views about human relations and whose scepticism trumps their liberalism.

Yet it seems to me that on their own premises, one cannot assume that there is always a middle way; everything will depend on the context, on the history and on just plain brute luck. This, perhaps, is why liberalism, as Shklar understands it, is so rare and so fragile. The conditions for its emergence, and certainly the conditions of its being able to sustain itself over time, are going to be very difficult to find and almost impossible to deliberately create. That does not mean it can never happen. I – with Shklar – think it *has* happened, and that at least aspects of it still exist. With Shklar too, I think that there are good reasons for being pleased when such occasions, and such conditions, do occur.

But perhaps I also agree with the Shklar of *Ordinary Vices*, and of *The Faces of Injustice*, that much, perhaps most, of human life is lived outside of those sorts of conditions, and that we cannot stop living because the conditions for liberalism as she understands them are not present. This is also the point Gray makes towards the end of *Black Mass*, and it is perfectly well taken, even if I am not inclined to accept the diagnosis that leads Gray to make his prognosis. Such a view certainly does then suggest to an extent, at least, a politics with a good deal of negativity in it – one must deal with an intractable world as best one can, and with what resources one has at one's disposal, both "domestically" and "internationally". But I suppose where I would differ from Shklar and from Gray – and from dystopic liberalism in general – is that it does not seem to me that there is anything to bemoan in this, nothing to be "dystopic" about. It is simply what human life has always consisted in, for good and for ill.

In this respect, there is another illusion, or perhaps the shadow of one, hanging over dystopic liberalism. It is simply that "dystopic" visions always run the risk, after all, of becoming the mirror images of the utopian visions they reject. As Michael Oakeshott memorably said, apropos Hayek, "A Plan to resist all planning may be preferable to its opposite; but it is still part of the same style of politics" (Oakeshott, 1962). Perhaps the greatest danger for dystopic liberalism is that it will often become simply a "dystopic" counterpoint to the harmonies played by either realism or universalist, utopian, forms of liberalism, in which case it has nothing particular to bring to the table itself.

The point, I suppose, is simply to say that one can agree with much of what dystopic liberals claim – about the rarity and fragility of liberal thought and practice, about the importance of not being utopian, and about the centrality of freedom for liberal politics – without being in the least "dystopic". Indeed, I would go further and suggest that if one cherishes at least some of the things that dystopic liberals also cherish, it is much better *not* to be dystopic. In addition to mirroring utopia, dystopias have a rather pronounced tendency to exaggeration, shrillness, and an entirely non-Dionysian pessimism. Realists who constantly emphasise the "tragic" character of the human condition are cut from the same cloth in that respect, and as I have argued elsewhere (Rengger, 2012), it does not seem to me that one can see human life as tragic in any respect unless there is a kind of world where human life could be utterly different from the way it is here. If we cannot assume that, then human life is not "tragic", it is just life; and equally, one should see political life not as a "dystopia" but just as political life in all of its variety and messiness.

Of course, this does not mean that there are not political forms and actions we do (and should) prefer and political forms and actions we do (and should) excoriate. Such preferences are, however, as dystopic liberals would all accept, rooted in our histories – complex, multifaceted and hybrid as they are – and are not features of some universal condition of "humanity", whether actual or potential. We should accept too, I think, as perhaps not all dystopic liberals would, that even those political forms we (rightly) value will often be partial, compromised, or divided.

Let me close these remarks with one further reflection. If we abandon the "dystopic" character of dystopic liberalism, we are left, I think, with a form of sceptical liberalism that has no guarantees. It is also, I would say, necessarily more rooted in its scepticism than its liberalism. And this brings me back to my opening comments. For it seems to me that a sceptical, anti-perfectionist political philosophy – which both I and the dystopic liberals I have discussed would agree is the best way of understanding and grounding our political contexts – must be sceptical firstly, and only secondarily liberal, in part simply because of the ubiquity and multifaceted character of liberalism. I said at the outset that the term was now so wide it seemed almost useless as a meaningful descriptor in political theory. Of course, we are not about to abandon it; it has too great a hold on our imagination and our history. However, notwithstanding this recognition, we must be prepared to be sceptical about *all* forms of liberalism in particular contexts and on particular occasions, even a resolute and profound anti-utopian liberalism. Shklar was correct, I think, to say that the central political aim for a scholar like herself was to secure the political conditions necessary for the exercise of personal freedom. She was, however, wrong to ascribe this objective to "liberalism" as such; for, as she herself emphasised, there are versions of liberalism that effectively frustrate that aim. Rather, this is the political task of a certain sort of scepticism, for reasons that will overlap with those of the dystopic liberals but will by no means by synonymous with them. And scepticism, as Santayana once wrote, is the chastity of the intellect and should not be relinquished too readily.

Notes

1. I am grateful for conversations – always stimulating and, of course, ongoing – with Liz Ashford, Michael Bentley, Samuel Brittan, Chris Brown, John Gray, John Haldane, Tony Lang, Onora O'Neill, Noel O'Sullivan, David Owen, John Skorupski, and Jens Timmerman on the subject of the character, shape, and fate of various forms of liberalism. I do not suppose they would agree with my reading of it, or indeed that they would agree with each other, but I would like to thank them for helping me to arrive at it nonetheless. I would also like to thank, *in memoriam*, Alan Milne, for all he taught me on this topic. He is greatly missed.
2. Shklar's particular version has been termed this before – by Seyla Benhabib in her essay in *Liberalism without Illusions* – and while I share some aspects of Benhabib's view, I would not want to implicate her in the rather more general way I choose to deploy the term here.
3. Many who are not liberals share this view of the dominant face of liberalism, of course. See, for example, the discussion of Raymond Geuss in Geuss (1999) and Geuss (2002).
4. Another term for it has been coined by Bernard Yack, in a book of essays dedicated to Shklar's thought: he calls it a "liberalism without illusions"; see Yack (1996).
5. Some names who could fit here might include, George Kateb, John Skorupski, Stephen Holmes, and Pierre Hassner.
6. See Kateb's forward to Shklar (1998: viii).
7. See Williams (2008: 56).
8. See Walzer (1996). See also the very acute analysis of Shklar by James Miller in Miller (2000).

9. In the next few paragraphs I draw on the account of Aron given in Rengger (2000).
10. In the next few paragraphs I draw on the account of Aron given in Rengger (2000).
11. As indeed does that of his friend and fellow student of Aron, Pierre Hassner.
12. For a more extensive treatment of Gray, see Rengger (2007). I should add, by the way, that Gray has been a long-standing admirer of Santayana (as I am myself) and has published some characteristically elegant essays on him. Santayana, of course, was an extremely elegant and acerbic critic of liberalism all his life.

References

Anderson, B. (1997), *Raymond Aron: The Recovery of the Political*, New York: Rowman and Littlefield.

Aron, R. (1966), *Peace and War: A Theory of International Relations*, New York: Praeger.

Aron, R. (1983a), *Clausewitz: Philosopher of War*, London: Routledge & Kegan Paul.

Aron, R. (1983b), *Memoirs: 50 Years of Political Reflection*, New York: Homes and Meier.

Geuss, R. (1999), *Morality, Culture and History*, Cambridge: Cambridge University Press.

Geuss, R. (2002), *Outside Ethics*, Princeton: Princeton University Press.

Gray, J. (2000), *Two Faces of Liberalism*, Cambridge: Polity Press.

Gray, J. (2007), *Black Mass: Apocalyptic Religion and the Death of Utopia*, London: Allen Lane.

Hoffmann, S. (1965), *The State of War*, New York: Preager.

Hoffmann, S. (1981), *Duties Beyond Borders*, Syracuse: Syracuse University Press.

Hoffmann, S. (2006), *Chaos and Violence*, New York: Rowman and Littlefield.

Honig, B. (1993), *Political Theory and the Displacement of Politics*, Ithaca: Cornell University Press.

Ignatieff, M. (1998), *Isaiah Berlin: A Life*, New York: Metropolitan.

Lilla, M. (ed.) (1996), *New French Thought*, Princeton: Princeton University Press.

Lilla, M. (1998), "Very Much a Fox", *The Times Literary Supplement*, 9.

Miller, J. (2000), "Review Essay on Shklar", *Political Theory*, 28, 6.

Oakeshott, M. (1962), *Rationalism in Politics*, London: Methuen.

Rawls, J. (1971), *A Theory of Justice*, Cambridge: Harvard University Press.

Rengger, N. (2000), *International Relations, Political Theory and the Problem of Order: Beyond International Relations Theory*, London: Routledge.

Rengger, N. (2007), "The Exorcist", *International Affairs*, 83, 4.

Rengger, N. (2012), "Tragedy, Scepticism and the Anti-Pelagian Mind in World Politics", in Erskine and Lebow (eds) *Tragedy and International Relations*, Basingstoke: Palgrave MacMillan.

Shklar, J. (1984), *Ordinary Vices*, Cambridge: Mass: Harvard University Press.

Shklar, J. (1989), "A Life of Learning: Charles Homer Haskins Lecture for 1989", *American Council of Learned Societies Occasional Paper*, 9.

Shklar, J. (1990), *The Faces of Injustice*, New Haven: Yale University Press.

Shklar, J. (1998), *Political Thought and Political Thinkers*, Chicago: University of Chicago Press.

Walzer, M. (1996), "On Negative Politics" in Yack.

Williams, B. (2008), *In the Beginning Was the Deed*, Princeton: Princeton University Press.

Yack, B. (ed.) (1996), *Liberalism Without Illusions: Essays on Liberal Theory and the Political Vision of Judith Shklar*, Chicago: University of Chicago Press.

4
Rising Powers: A Realist Analysis

Brian C. Schmidt and Nabarun Roy

The rise and fall of great powers is an enduring pattern of behaviour in international politics. While historians such as Paul Kennedy (1987) have painstakingly chronicled its history, political scientists have sought a general theoretical explanation to account for this cyclical phenomenon. Political scientists are not only interested in explaining the rise and fall dynamic, but also numerous issues that are closely related to uneven rates of growth among the great powers. This is particularly true of theorists who belong to the realist school of international relations. Realists attribute important international outcomes and foreign policy behaviour to the relative distribution of power in the international system. Compared to liberal theorists, who generally seem to be unconcerned about shifting patterns of power, realists are very interested in relative changes in state power. Realists argue that changes in the distribution of power that are triggered by a rising power have significant implications for the overall stability of the international system. For most realists, rapidly growing states are inherently threatening. Their deep concern about rising powers should not be surprising because, unlike liberals, they consider power to be the main currency of international politics. Moreover, many of the topics in which realists are interested, such as the causes of war, the balance of power, and grand strategy, are directly related to changes in the relative distribution of power.

This chapter examines the phenomenon of *rising powers* from the perspective of realist theory. The chapter begins by noting the curious point that liberals are seemingly unfazed by shifts in the distribution of power caused by rising powers. Thus, while many liberal theorists concede that the rise of countries like India and China poses a challenge to the contemporary liberal international order, these scholars are not alarmed by these developments (Ikenberry, 2008; Moravcsik, 2008; Nye, 2001, 2011). Since these rising powers are already integrated into the global political economic order, liberals do not foresee any major disruption – and certainly no great power war – as resulting from their rise. Most realists, in contrast, are extremely anxious about the erosion of American power and the ascent of new powers. Historically, realists observe that rising powers have had a destabilising impact on the existing international order. Our survey of this realist perspective rests on the recognition that there is no singular realist theory, but rather a variety of different realist theories. While acknowledging this point, we also recognise that all realists concur that power is the most important factor shaping international politics.

Our survey of the realists' assessment of rising powers begins with a brief overview of the realist conception of power. Next, we scrutinise how specific schools of realism – such as classical, structural, and neoclassical – as well as specific realist scholars view the phenomenon of rising powers. While the historical record offers a number of reasons to be concerned about a sharply rising power, there are significant differences in how realists view the consequences of this phenomenon. As we demonstrate, realists do not speak with one voice when offering policy advice about how to deal with an emerging challenger. Thus, we examine the different recommendations, including appeasement, balance of power, containment, negotiated settlement, peaceful change, preventive war, and retrenchment, that realists have provided for responding to a rising power. Since our focus is on the consequences of, and policy prescriptions for, rising powers, we do not dwell on the factors that give rise to differential rates of growth. Instead, we concentrate on the timely question of what should be done when a state is stridently growing in power relative to the other states. While this chapter is largely theoretical, we do provide some insight about how realists view the rise of Asian powers like India and China and how their ascent is shaping the contemporary policy debate. In so doing, we show that while both realists and liberals acknowledge that international relations is entering a post-unipolar era marked by the "rise of the rest", realists have shown greater concern for the implications of such a transition. While liberals have located the "'rise of the rest" within the framework of the liberal order – with the United States as the liberal hegemon – realists have not confined their analyses to the constraints and incentives that the liberal order presents to rising powers such as India and China. Moreover, compared to liberals, realists have been much less sanguine about the ability of the United States to maintain its preeminent hegemonic position.

Liberalism and the rise of powers

Despite that international politics has witnessed the periodic rise and fall of powers, and numerous wars among them, contemporary liberal international relations theorists do not appear to be greatly concerned with rising powers. While liberals, like realists, are interested in providing policy prescriptions aimed at making the international system less conflict-ridden, their analysis tends to focus less on power differentials, and more on the internal composition of states and the character of international order.

Liberal scholars, such as John M. Owen and Bruce Russett, believe that the greater the number of democratic or liberal states in the international system, the better the chances for peace. Since leaders in democratic states are accountable to the electorate, operate in a system characterised by divisions of power and internal checks and balances, waging wars is a time-consuming and difficult task. As a result, in their interactions with each other, democracies need not fear surprise attacks and are able to form a liberal zone of peace. However, as non-democratic states are not similarly restrained, democracies need to be on their guard against non-democracies, and be prepared to undertake pre-emptive action to foster regime change. Most liberal theorists endorse the proposition that democracies do not fight each other, and support the view that the increasing number of democratic states in the international system has helped to realise Kant's vision of a pacific union (Doyle, 1986; Oneal and Russett, 2001; Owen, 1997; Russett, 1993). Within this pacific union, power transition becomes a relatively "peaceable" affair (Doyle, 2001). Thus, most liberal theorists argue that the scope for conflict is determined not by power differentials, but rather by the internal political arrangement of states: an illiberal state – whether rising or inert – is a source of instability for the international system.

Nevertheless, given all the recent discussions about a rising China, liberal scholars have started paying attention to the implications such shifting power differentials may have on the international system. Ikenberry (2000), for example, admits that liberalism has neglected power asymmetries among states and the challenges to cooperation that they pose. Charles Kupchan, taking note of the contemporary power transition, explains that "rising powers, whether democratic or not, will not obediently take their place within the liberal order erected during the West's watch [...] they will want to recast the international system in ways that advantage their interests and ideological preferences" (2012: 15). In order to preserve the liberal ethos of the present order, Kupchan argues that the Atlantic Alliance needs to be fostered as the bedrock of liberal democracy. To accommodate the interests of rising powers, he advocates the cooperation of the United States and the West in evolving a new set of global rules (within the parameters of the existing order) to everyone's benefit. Both Ikenberry and Kupchan locate the rise of new powers within the framework of the prevailing liberal order, an order that they believe the rising powers will not fundamentally change. As a result, their policy prescriptions are focused largely on further integrating the rising powers into the present liberal order, and making them responsible stakeholders in the existing arrangements. The spectre of a potential conflict, as witnessed in bygone eras, is not manifestly evident in their scholarship.

With respect to the rise of China, Ikenberry argues that power transitions need not always be conflict-ridden and that variations in the outcome of such transitions are dependent on the regime type of the rising power and the character of the prevailing international order. Since the current international order is a liberal hegemonic one, which he describes as being institutionalised, legitimate, open, rule based, and deeply integrated, Ikenberry argues that China, and we can assume India, likely "will seek accommodation and integration with the West" (Ikenberry, 2008: 114). By focusing on the nature of the liberal international order, Ikenberry moves away from the regime change argument advocated by some adherents of the democratic peace thesis. For Ikenberry, the key to averting conflict between rising and falling powers is for the liberal hegemon – the United States – to remain committed to upholding the norms and institutions of the liberal order that it created after the Second World War. As compared to Ikenberry and Kupchan, Nye interprets the rise of the new powers in a more competitive light. Yet he argues strongly against containing China as "Asia has its own internal balance of power" (Nye, 2001). Instead, he maintains that the United States needs to engage China on a "trust but verify" credo. It is notable that Nye's position most clearly takes note of the role of power in the ongoing debate about rising powers by invoking the balance of power thesis. However, having done so, he reverts back to the liberal argument that China is focused on economic development, and that talk of it challenging the present system is far-fetched.

Here, it is important to bear in mind that even when liberal scholars acknowledge the salience of rising powers and power transition in the international system, they are only willing to contemplate the repercussions up to a certain point. Hence, they seem to be united in their view that rising powers will not want to overthrow the existing liberal order, but will instead be looking to shape it to suit their interests. Such a conceptualisation does not allow liberal scholars to envision that countries like China might want to totally overhaul the system; this prevents them from providing policy prescriptions that pay more attention to the competitive and conflict-ridden aspects of international relations. By placing power and power politics at the centre of their analyses, realists provide a wider set of challenges that rising powers can pose to the status quo powers, and thus offer a wider range of recommendations, including engagement and appeasement.

Realism and power politics

Realists, given their belief that shifts in the distribution of power have a direct bearing on the overall stability of the international system, follow the rise and fall of powers with great interest. A principal reason why realists worry about power transitions is that they are the theorists of power politics; the role of power has been, and continues to be, central to any realist theory. Ever since Thucydides theorised the growth of Athenian power and the fear this created for Sparta as the underlying cause of the Peloponnesian War, calculations about power have been at the heart of the realists' analysis of international politics. Realists posit that the acquisition of, and competition over, power is the central feature of politics among nations; yet, beginning with Thucydides, they have provided divergent explanations of the power impulse, provided different criteria for defining and measuring power, and offered diverse policy prescriptions for the management of power (Schmidt, 2005).

There is one point about power on which all realists agree: it is not power alone that matters, but the power that one state has *relative* to another state. The quest for power does not take place in a vacuum, but rather in relation to other actors. Thus, even though states can be conceived as egoists interested in maximising their share of power, their quest takes place in a competitive context, where other states are also interested in maximising their share. While attributing the drive for power to human nature, Hans J. Morgenthau underlined the relational aspect of power when he argued that man's lust for it was manifest in the "desire to maintain the range of one's own person with regard to others, to increase it, or to demonstrate it" (1946: 192). Structural realists argue that states worry about their relative power position because of the security competition that arises when there is no centralised power to help guarantee survival; they do, however, have different views about the degree of competition that exists in the anarchical international system. If one assumes that the logic of anarchy dictates that states should always maximise power, then any rising power will inherently be a risk to the others in the system. Conversely, if one does not assume that power maximisation is always the logical behaviour under anarchy, then power transitions need not be viewed as inherently threatening to the existing international order. Finally, there is also the possibility that the consequences of a rising power cannot be determined solely on the basis of power calculations, and that the interests and identity of the rising state must also be taken into consideration: for both *classical* and *neoclassical* realists, a key determinant in assessing the threat that a rising power poses is whether it is a status quo or revisionist state.

Before proceeding to analyse how the respective schools of realism view rising powers, there is one additional concept that needs to be mentioned: the balance of power (Little, 2007). In theory, the balance of power is the realists' generic answer to the question: what do states usually do when one of them is sharply rising in power relative to the other states? The mechanism of the balance of power is meant to ensure an equilibrium of power in which no single state is in a position to dominate all the others. Accordingly, if the survival of a state or a number of weaker states is threatened by a state that is rising in power, they should each seek to increase their own military capabilities (internal balancing) or join forces by establishing an alliance (external balancing), and preserve their independence by checking the power of the rising state. It is in the pursuit of maintaining a balance of power that some realists advocate preventive war as a means of dealing with rising powers. Whether or not balance of power politics is an efficacious strategy for responding to a rising power is a point of contention among the realist thinkers that we now consider.

Post-war realism

For the realists who rose to prominence after the Second World War, it was self-evident that international politics was a never-ending struggle for power. Having witnessed Nazi Germany's bid for hegemony, and the USSR's dramatic rebuilding efforts after 1945, post-war realists were keenly aware of the profound challenge that rising powers posed to the existing international order. In the aftermath of the two World Wars, this generation recognised the need for peaceful change. Scholars devoted attention to figuring out a proper formula for accommodating shifts in the distribution of power brought about by a rising power that did not entail fighting a major war. In addition to emphasising the role of power in precipitating change, the first generation of realists were keenly aware that the goals of a state, especially a rising power, were a key determinant of the possibilities for peaceful change. For these realists, the key distinction, in terms of state goals, was between *satisfied* and *dissatisfied* powers, or *status quo* and *revisionist* powers (Carr, 1964; Wolfers, 1962). While power politics remained a constant, these scholars argued that the character of the competition and the prospects for international order were largely determined by the dynamic interaction between such status quo and revisionist states.

If another great power war was to be avoided, Carr argued, political change in the form of a satisfactory compromise between power and morality had to be found. The Versailles settlement, according to Carr, was doomed from the start as the power of the liberal states was used vindictively to punish and ostracise Germany under the liberal pretence of a universal harmony of interest. Yet the international community could not prevent the rise of Germany, which was, for Carr, a quintessentially dissatisfied state. Germany's rise in power relative to the satisfied, liberal states necessitated the need for political change, and Carr struggled to find a satisfactory solution to the problem of peaceful change. In 1939, Carr was of the opinion that appeasement – conceptualised as a synthesis of power and morality – was a solution for peaceful change. On the eve of the Second World War, Carr wrote, "the negotiations which led up to the Munich Agreement [...] were the nearest approach in recent years to the settlement of a major international issue by a procedure of peaceful change" (1939: 282).

Largely owing to the fatal outcome of the Munich Agreement, any attempt to deal with rising powers through appeasement has subsequently been discredited. Norrin Ripsman and Jack Levy observe that the "futility of appeasement has acquired the status of a lawlike generalisation" (2008: 148). Yet, in their estimation, appeasement, which they define "as a strategy of sustained, asymmetrical concessions in response to a threat, with the aim of avoiding war, at least in the short term", has been unfairly denigrated as a strategy of statecraft owing to its close affiliation with British and French diplomacy in the 1930s (2008: 154). It is certainly worth recalling that it was the "realist" Carr who championed appeasement as a way of dealing with a rising Germany, although Lucian Ashworth (2002) slightly exaggerates the degree to which early realist thinkers were supporters of the strategy. Morgenthau, for example, regarded appeasement to be "a corrupted policy of compromise" that would inevitably fail to produce a negotiated settlement with a rising power (1955: 60). In order to reach a satisfactory negotiated settlement with the Soviet Union, which he advocated in the early years of the Cold War, Morgenthau emphasised the importance of diplomacy, which he conceptualised as the "promotion of the national interest by peaceful means" (1955: 505). Unlike structural realism, with its highly mechanistic accounts of the balance of power, Morgenthau understood that the proper functioning of a balance of power system was dependent on a "complex set of social, ideational, and material factors" (Little, 2007: 92).

As many have noted, one of the problems with Morgenthau's understanding of the balance of power is that he ascribes a number of different meanings to the concept (Claude, 1962). It is possible to argue, however, that it is the recurring phenomenon of rising powers that leads Morgenthau to conclude that policies aiming to preserve a balance of power are a necessary aspect of international politics. According to Morgenthau, because the goal of the balance of power "is stability plus the preservation of all the elements of the system, the equilibrium must aim at preventing any element from gaining ascendancy over the others" (1955: 157). As a result of the uncertainties that are involved in making accurate calculations about the distribution of power, Morgenthau argues that a state does not actually aim to achieve equality, but rather a preponderance of power. Yet in the event that a single state rose to achieve universal domination, the independence and survival of all the other states would be jeopardised. Thus it is not the desire for equilibrium per se, but the will to survive that compels states to check rising powers. Morgenthau discusses a wide variety of methods, including divide and rule, compensations, armaments, alliances, and preventive war, that can be implemented to achieve an equal distribution of power.

With the onset of the Cold War and a bi-polar distribution of power, Morgenthau grew less confident about the balance of power system. He also became increasingly worried about the rise of the USSR, epitomised by the Soviet atomic test in 1949 and the launch of Sputnik in 1957. The change from a multipolar to a bipolar balance of *terror* meant that the balance of power system had lost much of its flexibility, depriving the other states from playing a role in re-establishing an equilibrium. Moreover, the moral consensus that had previously underpinned the functioning of the balance of power was now destroyed by both nationalistic universalism and the expansion from a European to a world state system. It was in this context that Morgenthau seriously pondered the possibility of achieving a negotiated settlement with a rising USSR. Consistent with his realist ethos, Morgenthau argued that the United States should enter negotiations with the Soviets from a position of strength, and despite the irrationality of the arms race, he recommended an increase in militarily spending and the development of the H-bomb (Cox, 2007; Scheuerman, 2009). A negotiated settlement with the Soviets was not inconceivable for Morgenthau as long as negotiations were based on the vital interests of each side leading to the possibility of what the historian Marc Trachtenberg (1999) described as a "spheres of influence peace".

Scheuerman (2009: 76) explains that critics of realism linked Morgenthau's call for a negotiated settlement to Neville Chamberlain's attempt to appease Nazi Germany; but the type of bargaining Morgenthau had in mind – aiming to preserve American power – was diametrically opposed to the futile type of compromise that he associated with appeasement. If one defines appeasement in terms of a "buying-time strategy" in which the "aim is to diffuse the threat temporarily and avoid war in the short term, thus facilitating balancing over the longer term by buying time to build up one's military power internally or to secure allies against the external threat", then it is possible to view it as a realist policy prescription for dealing with rising powers (Ripsman and Levy, 2008: 156).

Unlike Morgenthau, Kennan dismissed the possibility of reaching any kind of deal with Moscow. Instead, Kennan advocated a "patient but firm and vigilant containment of Russian expansive tendencies" (1984: 119). The type of containment strategy that Kennan envisioned reflected his ambivalence about the nature of Soviet power. While some of the post-war technological and industrial accomplishments of the USSR were impressive, Kennan was astutely aware that the United States was the stronger party. Moreover, in his 1947 *Foreign Affairs* article, Kennan questioned whether the USSR was actually as powerful as many believed. He held out the possibility "that Soviet power, like the capitalist world of its conception, bears within it the seeds of its own decay, and that the sprouting of those seeds is well advanced" (Kennan, 1984: 125). Kennan, like Morgenthau, argued that it was prudent for the United States to get its own affairs in order, and augment its relative power, rather than single-mindedly focus on the apparent increase in USSR's power.

Structural realism: Defensive, offensive, and preponderance

The publication of Kenneth Waltz's *Theory of International Politics* (1979) marked a change in the way realism viewed questions of war and peace. While structural realists concur that changes in the international distribution of power profoundly shape the behaviour of states, they disagree on how states should respond to relative shifts in power, and differ in their policy advice for dealing with rising powers. While acknowledging that power politics is ubiquitous, structural realists emphasise that states need to be rational in their outlook. Hence, in light of the ebb and flow of balance of power politics, states can either adopt non-confrontational, conciliatory strategies or more hard-line, confrontational approaches in dealing with rising powers. The recent rise in power of a number of states relative to the United States has sparked a debate about balance of power politics in a unipolar system along those lines (Brooks and Wohlforth, 2008; Ikenberry, 2002). Interestingly, realists who advocate offshore balancing and retrenchment maintain their faith in the tenets of the balance of power, while advocates of preponderance and hierarchy believe that the logic of the balance of power will be nullified if the dominant power accrues a huge quantity of capabilities: faced with an overwhelming power differential, potential challengers will not balance against but *bandwagon* with the leader.

Given that the core proposition of Waltz's structural realist theory is that "balances of power recurrently form" (Waltz, 1979: 128), one can expect great powers to balance the military power of rising states. The prevalence of balancing behaviour leads Waltz, and defensive realists more generally, to postulate that states seek to maximise *security*, not power. As a result of Waltz's belief that states are strongly inclined to balance against rising powers, they are, in Joseph Grieco's terms, "defensive positionalists" and "will only seek the minimum level of power that is needed to attain and to maintain their security and survival" (1997: 167). Waltz's belief in balance of power politics has led him to be sharply critical of realists, such as William C. Wohlforth, who advocate a hegemonic grand strategy as a means of deterring the ambitions of rising powers. Following the end of the Cold War, Waltz fully expected the "unipolar moment" to be short-lived, as new powers would rise to balance the power of the United States. According to Waltz, such an eventuality cannot be avoided: "for a country to choose not to become a great power is a structural anomaly" (2000: 33). That being the case, the United States' attempt to perpetuate unipolarity and maximise its power is futile, as it seeks to escape a foreordained logic in international politics: the rise of challengers. By seeking to perpetuate unipolarity, the United States will cause secondary great powers to collectively balance against it. Some argue that the United States' ill-advised attempt to perpetuate unipolarity has led to the first stages of a balancing dynamic – "soft balancing" – which refers to "actions [...] that use non-military tools to delay, frustrate and undermine aggressive unilateral U.S. military policies" (Pape, 2005: 10).

Notwithstanding the strong case made by Waltzian realists about the need for the United States to adopt a self-effacing approach, scholars like Wohlforth (1999), advocate a strategy of preponderance. With the United

States being the dominant power since 1991 with no peer competitors – an unprecedented occurrence in the modern international system – proponents of primacy argue that it is imperative that it maintain its overwhelming power differential over its potential challengers (Khalilzad, 1995; Kristol and Kagan, 1996). Parting ways with Waltz's balance of power theory, which predicts that, given the system's status quo bias, a preponderant state will be balanced by others, Wohlforth, argues that the position of the United States in the post-Cold War system is unparalleled. Since states are rational actors, potential challengers in a unipolar system will realise the futility of balancing against the dominant power; thus, they will not balance against but rather bandwagon with it. He justifies the irrelevance of the balance of power logic by arguing that "given the dramatically different power distribution alone, we should expect world politics to work much differently now than in the past" (Wohlforth, 1999: 22). In such a system, the dominant power ought to maintain its power differential so that balancing is not a feasible option for others. To stave off the possibility of getting mired in conflicts not of its own making, the unipole has to take an active interest in others' affairs and "pacify" them. This is achieved by addressing the concerns of the secondary great powers, which leads to the stability of a system, precluding the use of force by the dominant power and the resultant decline in its relative power. It also prevents the rise of new powers and thus helps maintain the status quo.

During the period when the United States was pursuing an explicit strategy of preponderance, India, described as an important "swing state" (Mohan, 2006) and traditionally very critical of US foreign policy, decided to significantly improve its relations with the United States. To the surprise of many, it supported the United States on missile defence, protected US vessels transiting through the Straits of Malacca during Operation Enduring Freedom in Afghanistan, and also voted twice along with the United States against Iran at the International Atomic Energy Agency (Mohan, 2006: 27). Some claim that by re-orienting its strategy, India was demonstrating elements of bandwagoning with the United States (Rudolph and Hoeber, 2006). Despite suggestions that India, along with Russia and China, had sought to "soft balance" against the United States (Paul, 2005), the evidence does not fully support this observation: while the three states did discuss the formation of a "strategic triangle" against US-led NATO policies in the spring of 1999, the initiative did not gain traction. The above points illustrate that there is merit in the primacists' claim that a wide power differential leads to potential challengers to bandwagon, and not balance, with the dominant power.

Offensive realists, who also recognise that the anarchical structure of the international system leads to uneven growth rates in power and the inevitable rise and fall of great powers, argue – against Wohlforth – that the strategy of preponderance is deeply flawed (Layne, 2006; Mearsheimer, 2011). Not only does Mearsheimer conclude that the "stopping power of water" makes it impossible for any state to achieve global hegemony, he also argues that a hegemonic grand strategy is unduly expensive and leads to fighting a series of unnecessary and costly wars. Attempting to inhibit the rise of new powers through a grand strategy of primacy contributes, ironically enough, to "imperial overstretch" – a phenomenon that has led to the decline of previous dominant powers. Moreover, offensive realists argue that the very attempt to achieve preponderance, as witnessed in the behaviour of the United States, will lead other states to engage in activities to restore a balance of power (Layne, 2006).

While the critique of preponderance made by offensive realists is similar to that of Waltzian realists, many among them recommend a strategy of offshore balancing, which is more fine-grained than a global balance of power strategy. Layne explains that offshore balancing is a multipolar strategy that accommodates "the rise of new great powers while simultaneously shifting, or devolving, to Eurasia's major powers the primary responsibility for their own defence" (2006: 160). An offshore balancing grand strategy is aimed at preserving the regionally preponderant position of the United States through either a buck-passing or balancing policy in order to forestall the emergence of a rival regional hegemon. Offensive realists argue that the possibility of a rising state, such as India or China, achieving regional hegemony is a situation that should be avoided. In this regard, Mearsheimer writes, "China cannot rise peacefully, and if it continues its dramatic economic growth over the next few decades, the United States and China are likely to engage in an intense security competition with considerable potential for war" (Mearsheimer, 2005: 47).

The redeeming factor from the perspective of the United States – an existing regional hegemon – is that since all great powers are power-maximisers, they will seek to prevent the emergence of a new regionally dominant power. Thus, it behoves the United States to sit back, pass the buck to established regional powers, and rely on them to prevent the emergence of a new hegemon in their own region, which would represent a threat to US hegemony. If these powers are unable to balance this potential hegemon, and the emergence of a peer competitor seems imminent, the United States can step in and redress the regional balance of power (Mearsheimer, 2001: 140–143). Whereas proponents of preponderance care little about the rivalry that exists between the rising powers by assuming that they will be focused on challenging the dominant power if the power differential reduces, advocates of offshore balancing focus on the competition that ensues among the powers in other regions and its beneficial impact for the standing of the sole regional hegemon. Proponents of offshore balancing also believe that catering to the security and economic needs of rising powers in other regions is dangerous as it nullifies the valuable system maintaining function of the balance of power dynamic. Such a strategy is well suited for a multipolar system where the dominant power can count on similarly positioned potential challengers to balance each other (Layne, 1997: 112).

In light of China's phenomenal rise in recent years, and the potential for its emergence as a regional hegemon, the United States has sought to balance it with India's help. Robert Kaplan (2009) thus calls for a sea-based offshore balancing role for the United States to deny China a monopoly over the Indian Ocean, which he identifies as the next big theatre of great-power rivalry. Aware that the power disparity between India and China is too large for the United States to adopt a hands-off approach in Asia, and thereby follow a buck passing policy, the United States has sought to help India enhance its capabilities both militarily and politically. President Bill Clinton's visit to India in March 2000 is seen as a historic one as it recognised India's standing as a regional power (Rudolph and Hoeber, 2006: 705). The United States was more explicit on this aspect in 2005 when it announced its intention to help India become a "major world power" in the twenty-first century. On the military front, in 2005 the two countries signed a "New Framework for the US–India Defence Relationship". It is noteworthy that while the bulk of India's military hardware has traditionally been of Russian origin, the recent years have witnessed a steady infusion of armaments from America and its close ally, Israel, into the Indian military (Dasgupta and Cohen, 2011).

Taking a leaf out of the offshore balancing manual, Thomas Christensen (2001) points at the critical role the dominant power's offshore allies play in checking the rise of challengers. While they provide yeoman's service by offering bases to the leader, which enables it to project its power and maintain the balance of power, the partners can also aggravate tension and imperil stability by adopting measures that undermine the core interests of other regional powers that are on the rise. For instance, by declaring independence from China, Taiwan – a key ally of the United States in East Asia – can imperil the stability of the region and force the United States to enter into a confrontation with China (Christensen, 2001: 37). As a result, it is necessary for the dominant power to ascertain the core interests of the rising power and follow a policy of reassurance by reining in its allies, and preventing the latter from needlessly endangering the rising power's core concerns.

Another crucial point made by Christensen is that the rising power need not be a peer competitor of the dominant power for it to challenge the latter. Rather, if the rising power develops technology that can hurt the dominant power and raise the cost of its involvement in the politics of that region, the latter's ability to shape the balance of power will be weakened. As a result, the dominant power has to develop capabilities that can deter the rising power from hurting it and its allies at a regional level (Christensen, 2001: 34–36). Contrary to advocates of preponderance, Christensen believes that considerations of relative power may not be the sole determinant in causing a rising power to take on the dominant power and that a dual strategy of deterrence and reassurance can help it maintain the peace and its own standing in the system.

In the ever-changing world of power differentials among states, the hegemon sometimes finds itself losing power at such a rapid rate in relation to its rivals that the loss is referred to as "acute relative decline" (MacDonald and Parent, 2011). While preventive war, as we discuss later, is an option for such a declining power, this policy option carries formidable challenges and risks: even if the system leader ends up winning the war, it is probable that it will be so weakened that its security in the post-war period will be imperilled. Stated otherwise, even winning a preventive war does not buy the dominant power the security it seeks. MacDonald and Parent instead advocate a strategy of "retrenchment", which argues that, faced with a steep decline, the dominant power has to cut down on military spending and reduce its international commitments. The strategy has two dimensions: internal and external. The former consists of reducing military spending and promoting innovation in the military sector to enhance efficiency with the available resources. The external dimension consists of reducing its commitments towards other states and renewing or entering into alliances only where it impinges on its core interests. In certain cases, the declining power may also appease the rising challenger by making asymmetrical concessions (MacDonald and Parent, 2011: 21). While retrenchment has certain similarities with offshore balancing in that it advocates a scaling down of the leader's global footprint, the difference is that it also entails a significant cutback and rationalisation of resources at the domestic level.

Not all structural realists view rising powers with the same degree of trepidation as offensive realists. Building on Waltz's understanding of the international system as relatively benign, defensive realists argue that rising powers can be accommodated. Defensive realists disagree with offensive realists and do not assume that all states are driven to maximise their share of relative power; nor do they assume that all states have revisionist aims. They start from the premise that states, including rising powers, are *status quo security* seekers. Consequently, defensive realists do not recommend adopting hard-line policies to contain rising powers as such policies will inevitably increase tension and fuel insecurity. While recognising that the international system gives rise to the security dilemma, defensive realists such as Charles Glaser argue that it can be mitigated, thus reducing the likelihood of the rise and fall of powers dynamic leading to major war. In addition to geographic distance and the role of nuclear weapons making conquest almost impossible, Glaser argues that "the intensity of the security dilemma also depends on states' beliefs about one another's motives and goals" (2011: 82). The important insight that the security dilemma is variable leads defensive realists to advocate policies that augment, rather than diminish, a rising state's sense of security. In order to foster security and allow for the possibility of achieving cooperation, defensive realists recommend that a dominant power should exercise restraint and accommodate the interests of the rising power. An offensive realist would likely respond that these policies are extremely risky because of the uncertainty that exists about the present and future intentions of rising powers.

Neoclassical realism

A principal limitation of structural realism is that by simply focusing on power differentials, it is unable to predict whether a rising power intends to integrate with the existing system or challenge it. By incorporating unit level variables and looking inside the black box that is the state, neoclassical realists such as Randall Schweller have built theories that can anticipate the foreign policies of specific states. With the help of these "bridging theories" (Christensen, 1996: 6) they ascertain the intentions of a rising power, the impact on its foreign policy, and what this implies for the dominant power in the international system.

Schweller's central contribution is to "bring the revisionist state back in" by examining state intentions, thereby differentiating status quo and revisionist powers (1994: 75); by doing so, he can explain why dominant powers react in varied ways to rising powers. In spite of being a rising power, India, given its moderate streak of revisionism, hardly causes any alarm in Washington, whereas Iran, a less materially capable power but displaying a strong revisionist mind-set, is turning out to be a major foreign policy problem for the United States. The revisionism of a state is not simply a function of its growing capabilities, as structural realism suggests, but is premised on its conviction that the existing international order – predicated on the division of territory, institutional arrangements, governing structures, and norms and values – lacks legitimacy (Schweller, 2006: 28). When faced with a moderately revisionist, risk-averse rising power, the dominant power is advised to adopt a strategy of engagement. By doing so, the rising power will be further socialised into the existing ethos and rules of the international order, to the point where its desire to effect change will be greatly reduced. The dominant power may also resort to appeasing the moderately revisionist rising power, which entails readjusting territories and spheres of influence and making tangible concessions (Schweller, 2006: 37). Not engaging the moderately revisionist power could not only lead to it becoming more revisionist; it could also bandwagon with another rising power that is far more prone to overthrowing the existing order. The dominant power is thus also counselled to undertake a preventive war to avert a threat to the existing system from such an uncompromisingly revisionist rising power.

Schweller posits that the slow shift of the international system from uni- to multipolarity does not imply that the latter system will be more conflict-ridden, as some structural realists predict. The stability of the coming multipolar era will depend on the interests of the great powers, and, especially, which among three roles *China* will adopt – that of a spoiler, that of a supporter, or that of a shirker – in relation to the prevailing order (Schweller and Pu, 2011: 42). Probing further into the black box that is the state, Schweller claims that given its resource crunch and a fragile domestic political environment, as well as its self-image as a "developing" state, China – the most materially preponderant of all the rising powers – will adopt a hedging strategy – based on shirking responsibilities – and will thus not pose a threat to the United States. Thus, for the short to medium term, China might at best challenge the United States from within the confines of the existing order, and use existing institutions and channels to challenge the United States' legitimacy. However, utilising existing institutions to mount "rightful resistance" might end up socialising China ever more with the predominant norms and ethos: Schweller seems to suggest that the engagement model would serve the United States' interests in the years to come.

Given the opprobrium that the engagement model faced after the unsuccessful bid to "appease" Germany in the 1930s, it is noteworthy that it has again been resurrected within realism. In fact, history provides quite a few instances of the dominant power engaging its rising counterpart. David Edelstein points out that while it is a flawed strategy – as it increases the capabilities of the challenger – the propensity of states under anarchy to aim for short-term gains and bow to pressure from domestic groups makes the dominant state eschew a tough stand towards the rising power (2002). According to Edelstein, when faced with a rising challenger, while engagement is not optimal, the possibility of the dominant power adopting such a strategy is high.

In an era where we are entering the "Post-American World" (Zakaria, 2008), marked by the rise of new powers, the United States has had to carefully consider the implications of this rise for its standing in international affairs. Having noted India and China's ability to make common cause against the prevailing system, especially in international trade, it has sought to balance China while engaging India by extending a hand of friendship. This variable strategy has played a role in pitting the two Asian powers against each other regarding regional security matters. Given that the United States' disagreements on security issues are fewer and less severe with India than with China, and in light of India's traditional status as a "moderately revisionist" power (Nayar and Paul, 2003: 90), one understands why Delhi is being courted by the United States.

Aware that India's moderate revisionism has been fuelled by its dissatisfaction with the existing non-proliferation regime and the composition of the UN Security Council, the United States has thus made tangible concessions on the first issue, and a symbolic one on the second. By allowing it to benefit from trade in civilian nuclear energy without having to sign the NPT, the US–India Nuclear Cooperation Approval and Non-proliferation Enhancement Act signed in October 2008 clearly undermined the treaty while further integrating India into the international system. By endorsing India's candidature for the permanent seat at the Security Council during his visit to India in November 2010, President Obama further weakened the foundations of India's revisionism. But recent reports indicating that the United States may impose sanctions against India if it does not reduce its imports of oil from Iran (Rajghatta, 2012) demonstrate that the US–India engagement model is still based on self-interest: when the dominant power is unable to change the policies of the moderately revisionist power, it can switch from dangling the carrot to using the stick.

Power transitions, dynamic differentials, and preventive war

Although Bismarck likened it to committing suicide for fear of death, preventive war has been an option that realists throughout the ages have considered for dealing with a rising power. For both classical and structural realists, who believe in the efficacy of the balance of power for maintaining international order, fighting a war to prevent a shift in the distribution of power in favour of a rising power has often been judged to be a necessary course of action. As Jack Levy notes, preventive war is most commonly defined as a "war fought to forestall an adverse shift in the balance of power between two states" (Levy, 2007: 176). The typical motivations behind preventive war – the anticipation of a negative power shift and the fear of its consequences – are, as A.J.P. Taylor observed, responsible for numerous great power wars in the nineteenth and twentieth century. According to many realists, rising powers represent a clear and present danger to the prevailing international order. For scholars, such as A.F.K. Organski and Robert Gilpin, who accentuate the pacifying effects of hierarchy over anarchy and power asymmetries over equilibrium, rising powers have been identified as the main culprits of major war.

While Organski's power transition theory is not, strictly speaking, a realist theory, it is instructive to briefly review its main tenets, as the theory identifies rising powers that overtake the dominant power by developing at an economically faster rate as the principal reason behind international conflict. The presence of a dominant state sitting on top of a hierarchical system in which there is a clear delineation of power is, according to proponents of power transition theory, a typical phenomenon at both the global and regional levels. Dominant states, which the theory argues are by definition status quo powers, shape the international order by creating institutions and norms of behaviour that foster international stability while at the same time advancing their own interests. The sheer preponderance of power on the part of the dominant state serves to deter conflict and solidifies its interest in maintaining the rules to preserve the status quo. Yet, inevitably, a dominant state and the great powers that support the status quo are challenged by a rising, dissatisfied power that aspires to install itself on top of a new hierarchy, which it believes will better conform to its core interests. Uneven rates of growth – due to industrialisation and demographics – are responsible for the rise and fall in the power of states, but as the distribution of power in the international system approaches parity, power transition theory is clear in its assertion that it is the *rising power* that initiates great power war. Indeed, "the most dangerous condition in the international system occurs when a society at the top of the global hierarchy, with a smaller population that has already achieved sustained economic growth, is passed by a rapidly growing nation with a much larger population" (Tammen et al., 2000: 17–18). Given the enormous size of China and India's populations, and the fast pace of their economic growth, power transition theory points to the probability of a major war resulting from their attainment of parity or superiority: in this manner, the theory has a similar outlook on the future as offensive realists.

Gilpin's hegemonic theory of war shares many of the same assumptions about the destabilising consequences of rising powers with power transition theory. For Gilpin, uneven rates of growth among states are the driving force of international politics. Like Organski, Gilpin rejects the main premise of balance of power theory and argues that a hierarchical system with one powerful state is more stable than a system with several states that are roughly equal in power. In fact, the main contributing factor to great power war, according to Gilpin, is that "over time the power of the subordinate state begins to grow disproportionately, and that the rising state comes into conflict with the dominant or hegemonic state in the system" (Gilpin, 1988: 19). When a rising state approaches parity with a dominant state, the international system enters a period of crisis; eventually, a hegemonic war breaks out, which is finally resolved "in favour of one side and the establishment of a new international system that reflects the emergent distribution of power in the system" (Gilpin, 1988: 19). Gilpin does not specify whether it is the declining or rising power that is responsible for initiating war. His theory is meant to underline Thucydides' point that the differential growth of power in the international system is the main factor leading to war between declining and rising powers. By contrast, Organski's power transition theory does assign responsibility to the rising state for the outbreak of major armed conflict, arguing that it is illogical for the dominant state to initiate war because it would be inimical to breaking the rules and norms that it had established.

Yet according to Dale Copeland's dynamic differentials theory, it makes no rational sense for a rising power to initiate war against a dominant state. Copeland reasons that rising powers can simply wait it out and achieve their objectives peacefully as they maximise their power and surpass the dominant state. It is thus little wonder that China has, for some time, been underlining the peaceful nature of its rise and seeking to dispel talk of it being a challenger to the dominant state. The argument of dynamic differentials theory is that dominant military powers that fear significant decline relative to a rising power can pursue preventive war as a policy option to maintain their position in the international system. Copeland's main thesis is that great powers that anticipate deep and inevitable decline are more likely to initiate major wars, or hard-line policies that increase the risk of war, against rising powers. While sharing many of the same assumptions of structural realism, Copeland includes what he terms a *dynamic differential variable* in his theory: "the simultaneous interaction of the differentials of relative military power between great powers and the expected trend of those differentials, distinguishing between the effects of power changes in bipolarity versus multipolarity" (Copeland, 2000: 15).

When examining the conditions under which a dominant, but declining, power might contemplate preventive war, Copeland considers variations in the types of decline a state might be experiencing, and the effect that polarity has on the decision-making progress. He argues that the prospects of a declining power choosing preventive war to deal with a rising challenger are far greater in bi- rather than in multipolar systems. Finally, Copeland attempts to make his theory relevant to the nuclear age by considering all of the foreign policy options – accommodation/conciliation, containment, crisis initiation, and the initiation of preventive war – that a declining state can implement when dealing with a rising power. Copeland recognises that preventive war among nuclear armed states is not necessarily the most rational course of action and considers alternative policy choices that declining states might consider, even with the knowledge that more hard-line policies run the risk of leading to an inadvertent war.

Conclusion

This chapter has shown that realists, like liberals, are aware of the need to analyse the impact that rising powers will have on international politics. Both realists and liberals highlight the importance of engaging rising powers and accommodating their interests to a considerable extent. Like liberals, realists are aware of the need to eschew reckless confrontational policies towards rising powers like China. Notwithstanding these commonalities, it is also evident that realists have a broader, deeper, and a more fine-grained perspective when it comes to rising powers and are thus able to provide us with a wide range of perspectives and policy recommendations. In a world where there are many rising powers, realists underline the necessity of dealing with each rising power individually, keeping in mind their unique geographical location, their equations with other rising powers, and their political attitudes towards the existing order. To that end, the differing policy recommendations help ensure that dominant powers eschew a "one size fits all" response to rising powers and engage with each of them on the basis of their unique attributes and trajectories. The multitude of realist recommendations is thus indicative of its deep and nuanced understanding of international politics and its continued relevance to providing sage advice to policymakers.

References

Ashworth, L. (2002), "Did the Realist-Idealist Great Debate Really Happen? A Revisionist History of International Relations", *International Relations*, 16(1), 33–51.

Brooks, S. G. and Wohlforth, C. W. (2008), *The World Out of Balance: International Relations and the Challenge of American Primacy*, Princeton, NJ: Princeton University Press.

Carr, E. H. (1939), *The Twenty Years' Crisis, 1919–1939: An Introduction to the Study of International Relations*, London: Macmillan.

Carr, E. H. (1964), *The Twenty Years' Crisis, 1919–1939*, New York: Harper and Row.

Christensen, T. J. (1996), *Useful Adversaries: Grand Strategy, Domestic Mobilization and Sino-American Conflict, 1947–1958*, Princeton, NJ: Princeton University Press.

Christensen, T. J. (2001), "Posing Problems without Catching Up: China's Rise and Challenges for US Security Policy", *International Security*, 25(4), 5–40.

Claude, I. L. (1962), *Power and International Relations*, New York: Random House.

Copeland, D. C. (2000), *The Origins of Major War*, Ithaca: Cornell University Press.

Cox, M. (2007), "Hans J. Morgenthau, Realism, and the Rise and Fall of the Cold War", in M. Williams (ed.) *Realism Reconsidered: Hans J. Morgenthau and International Relations*, Oxford: Oxford University Press.

Dasgupta, S. and Cohen, P.S. (2011), "Arms Sales for India: How Military Trade Could Energize US-Indian Relations", *Foreign Affairs*, 90(2), 22–27.

Doyle, M. W. (1986), "Liberalism and World Politics", *American Political Science Review*, 80(4), 1151–1161.

Doyle, M. W. (2001), "Kant, Liberal Legacies, and Foreign Affairs", in E. M. Brown, M. S. Lynn-Jones and E. S. Miller (eds) *Debating the Democratic Peace*, Cambridge, MA: MIT Press.

Edelstein, D. M. (2002), "Managing Uncertainty: Beliefs about Intentions and the Rise of Great Powers", *Security Studies*, 12(1), 1–40.

Gilpin, R. (1988), "The Theory of Hegemonic War", in I. R. Rotberg and K. T. Rabb (eds) *The Origin and Prevention of Major Wars*, Cambridge: Cambridge University Press.

Glaser, C. (2011), "Will China's Rise Lead to War? Why Realism Does Not Mean Pessimism", *Foreign Affairs*, 90(2), 80–91.

Grieco, J. M. (1997), "Realist International Theory and the Study of World Politics", in W. M. Doyle and G. I. John (eds) *New Thinking in International Relations Theory*, Boulder, CO: Westview Press, 163–201.

Ikenberry, G. J. (2000), *After Victory: Institutions, Strategic Restraint, and the Rebuilding of Order after Major Wars*, Princeton, NJ: Princeton University Press.

Ikenberry, G. J. (ed.) (2002) *America Unrivaled: The Future of the Balance of Power*, Ithaca: Cornell University Press.

Ikenberry, G. J. (2008), "The Rise of China: Power, Institutions, and the Western Order", in S. R. Ross and Z. Feng (eds) *China's Ascent: Power, Security, and the Future of International Politics*, Ithaca: Cornell University Press, 89–114.

Kaplan, R. D. (2009), "Center Stage for the Twenty-first Century: Power Plays in the Indian Ocean", *Foreign Affairs*, 88(2), 16–32.

Kennan, G. F. (1984), *American Diplomacy* (expanded edition), Chicago: University of Chicago Press.

Kennedy, P. (1987), *The Rise and Fall of the Great Powers: Economic Change and Military Conflict from 1500 to 2000*, New York: Vintage Books.

Khalilzad, Z. M. (1995), *From Containment to Global Leadership: America and the World After the Cold War*, Rand.

Kristol, W. and Kagan, R. (1996), "Towards a Reaganite Foreign Policy", *Foreign Affairs* (July/August).

Kupchan, C. (2012), "Grand Strategy: The Four Pillars of the Future", *Democracy: A Journal of Ideas* (23). Available at http://www.democracyjournal.org/23/grand-strategy-the-four-pillars-of-the-future.php?page= all (accessed 25 September 2012).

Layne, C. (1997), "From Preponderance to Offshore Balancing: America's Future Grand Strategy", *International Security*, 22(1), 86–124.

Layne, C. (2006), *The Peace of Illusions: American Grand Strategy from 1940 to the Present*, Ithaca: Cornell University Press.

Levy, J. S. (2007) "Preventive War and the Bush Doctrine: Theoretical Logic and Historical Roots", in A. S. Renshon and P. Suedfeld (eds) *Understanding the Bush Doctrine: Psychology and Strategy in an Age of Terrorism*, London: Routledge.

Little, R. (2007), *The Balance of Power in International Relations: Metaphors, Myths and Models*, Cambridge: Cambridge University Press.

MacDonald, P. K. and Parent, M. J. (2011), "Graceful Decline? The Surprising Success of Great Power Retrenchment", *International Security*, 35(4), 7–44.

Mearsheimer, J. J. (2001), *The Tragedy of Great Power Politics*, New York: W.W. Norton.

Mearsheimer, J. J. (2005), "Clash of the Titans", *Foreign Policy*, 146, 46–49.

Mearsheimer, J. J. (2011), "Imperial by Design", *The National Interest*, 111, 16–34.

Mohan, R. C. (2006), "India and the Balance of Power", *Foreign Affairs*, 85(4), 17–32.

Moravcsik, A. (2008), "Washington Cries Wolf", *Newsweek*, May 31. Available at http://www.princeton.edu/~ amoravcs/chinese.html.

Morgenthau, H. J. (1946), *Scientific Man versus Power Politics*, Chicago: The University of Chicago Press.

Morgenthau, H. J. (1955), *Politics among Nations: The Struggle for Power and Peace*, New York: Alfred A. Knopf.

Nayar, B. R. and Paul, T. V. (2003), *India in the World Order: Searching for Major Power Status*, Cambridge: Cambridge University Press.

Nye, J. S. (2001), "Should China be 'Contained'?" *Project Syndicate*, 4 July. Available at http://www.project-syndicate.org/commentary/should-china-be–contained– (accessed 23 September 2012)

Nye, J. S. (2011), "China's Rise Doesn't Mean War", *Foreign Policy*. Available at http://www.foreignpolicy.com/articles/2011/01/02/unconventional_wisdom?page= 0,3 (accessed 23 September 2012).

Oneal, J. R. and Russett, B. (2001), *Triangulating Peace: Democracy, Interdependence, and International Organizations*, New York: W. W. Norton & Company

Owen IV, J. M. (1997), *Liberal Peace, Liberal War*, Ithaca: Cornell University Press.

Pape, R. A. (2005), "Soft Balancing against the United States", *International Security*, 30(1), 7–45.

Paul, T. V. (2005), "Soft Balancing in the Age of US Primacy", *International Security*, 30(1), 46–71.

Rajghatta, C. (2012), "US Threatens Sanctions against India over Iran Oil", *The Times of India*, 16 March. Available at http://articles.timesofindia.indiatimes.com/2012–03–16/us/31201039_1_iranian-crude-oil-imports-iranian-oil (accessed 18 March 2012).

Ripsman, N. M. and Levy, J. S. (2008), "Wishful Thinking or Buying Time? The Logic of British Appeasement in the 1930s", *International Security*, 33(2), 148–181.

Rudolph, L. I. and Susanne, H. (2006), "The Making of US Foreign Policy for South Asia: Offshore Balancing in Historical Perspective", *Economic and Political Weekly*, 703–709.

Russett, B. M. (1993), *Grasping the Democratic Peace: Principles for a Post-Cold War World*, Princeton, NJ: Princeton University Press.

Scheuerman, W. E. (2009), *Hans Morgenthau: Realism and Beyond*, Cambridge: Polity.

Schmidt, B. C. (2005), "Competing Realist Conceptions of Power", *Millennium: Journal of International Studies*, 33(3), 523–549.

Schweller, R. L. (1994), "Bandwagoning for Profit: Bringing the Revisionist State Back In", *International Security*, 19(1), 72–107.

Schweller, R. L. (2006), *Unanswered Threats: Political Constraints on the Balance of Power*, Princeton, NJ: Princeton University Press.

Schweller, R. L. and Xiaoyu, P. (2011), "After Unipolarity: China's Visions of International Order in an Era of U.S. Decline", *International Security*, 36(1), 41–72.

Tammen, R. L., Kugler, J., Lemke, D., Alsharabati, C., Efird, B. and Organski, A. F. K. (2000), *Power Transitions: Strategies for the 21st Century*, New York: Chatham House.

Trachtenberg, M. (1999) *A Constructed Peace: The Making of the European Settlement, 1945–1963*, Princeton: Princeton University Press.

Waltz, K. N. (1979), *Theory of International Politics*, Reading, MA: Addison-Wesley.

Waltz, K. N. (2000), "Structural Realism after the Cold War", *International Security*, 25(1), 5–41.

Wohlforth, W. C. (1999), "The Stability of a Unipolar World", *International Security*, 24(1), 5–41.

Wolfers, A. (1962), *Discord and Collaboration: Essays on International Politics*, Baltimore: Johns Hopkins University Press.

Zakaria, F. (2008), *The Post American World*, London: Allen Lane.

Part II

Liberalism and American Hegemony

5

The Liberal International Order and Its Discontents

G. John Ikenberry

Introduction

The American-led world system is troubled. Some would argue that it is in crisis.[1] But what sort of crisis is it? Is it a crisis of America's position in the global system or is it a deeper world historical transition in which liberalism and the liberal international order are at risk? Is the American-led "liberal era" ending, or is it transforming into a new sort of liberal order? What would a post-hegemonic liberal order look like? What sort of historical moment is this? Has the "liberal ascendency" of the last 200 years peaked, or is it simply taking new twists and turns? If liberal internationalism as it has been organised in the post-war era is giving way to something new, what is that "something new"? This chapter takes up these questions.

There are lots of observers who see grand changes. Henry Kissinger has argued that he has never seen the world in such "flux" with so few agreed upon rules and norms to guide the flow of change. The National Intelligence Council has published its "Global Trends 2025", arguing that a "return to multipolarity" is the master trend of the coming decades. This movement towards multipolarity will manifest itself in a gradual diffusion of power away from the West, the rise of new power centres, a decay in multilateral institutional governance, and new forms of conflict among great powers and regions (Khanna, 2008; Kupchan, 2003; The National Intelligence Council, 2008; Zakaria, 2009).

Some observers see a new divide between autocratic and liberal-democratic states. The liberal international optimism in the West has given way to worries about coming breakdowns and divides among the great powers. Robert Kagan sees a rise in influence of authoritarian states that are hostile to Western visions of order. Russia and China are the leading edge of the autocratic revival; unlike the old authoritarian states of the last century, they are adaptive to global capitalism, and capable of sustained growth and development. They are able to trade and invest in world markets. Yet, at the same time, they are anti-liberal and hostile to Western democracy. They have, in effect, found a pathway to modernity and development that bypasses liberal democratic practices and institutions; it is only a step away from this analysis to argue that "multiple modernities" exist. The great post-Cold War anticipation of a global liberal revolution has been dashed by the "return of history" (Kagan, 2008; Gat, 2009). Some see China as an emerging rival wielding a non-liberal strategic orientation. Martin Jacques gives a dramatic version of this view. China is emerging as the next global hegemon; it will build a non-liberal, even anti-liberal world order. As a result, the world will have two pathways to modernity. One is the old Western liberal pathway. The other is the authoritarian alternative (Jacques, 2009).

These anticipations of coming struggles with Russia and China see the clash between liberalism and autocracy reinforced by other factors. One is historical grievances. Russia feels disrespected and encroached upon in the decades since the end of the Cold War, and China is an emerging world power that nurses resentments from its century of humiliation. The other is the intensification of competition over energy and resources. This great power competition will reinforce liberal and statist models of economics and security and bring mercantilism back into the centre of world politics.

In the great narratives of this moment, the world is transitioning away from the American-led liberal order. It is a story of the return to multipolarity, the rise of new great powers, and multiple pathways to modernity. The 2008 financial crisis and subsequent world economic downturn – the most severe since the Great Depression – has also been a blow to the American-led system. Unlike past post-war economic crises, this one had its origins in the United States. The repercussions of this economic crisis are complex and still playing out. But it has served to tarnish the American model of liberal capitalism and raised new doubts about the capacities of the United States to act as the global leader n the provision of economic stability and advancement (Lelong and Cohen, 2010; Stiglitz, 2010).

I want to be sceptical of these views. Yes, the American liberal hegemonic order is in crisis. But it is a crisis of authority within the liberal international order and not a crisis of its underlying principles and organisational logic. That is, it is a crisis of the American governance of liberal order and not of liberal order itself. The crisis of liberalism today will ultimately bring forth "more liberalism". This is true if by liberal order we mean an open, rule-based relations system organised around expanding forms of institutionalised cooperation. In this sense, liberal international order can be contrasted with alternative logics of order – blocs, exclusive spheres, and closed geopolitical systems. The future still belongs to the liberal international order.

I argue that the post-Cold War liberal international order is more durable than many think. Russia and China are not its inevitable enemies. A grand alternative does not exist. To put it sharply: the pathway to the future still runs through institutions and relationships created over the last 60 years. American unipolarity will no doubt eventually give way to something new. Power and authority will shift in the global system as they have over the centuries. But rival orders will not emerge – even if new leaders will. In the decades ahead, the United States and Europe and rising states – many of which are in Asia – will have more reasons and not fewer reasons to cooperate in open and rule-based ways.

The rest of the paper is divided into three parts. Firstly, I will talk about the "old order" and highlight its logic and durability. Secondly, I will talk about the sources of crisis. And finally, I will talk about the dilemmas and pathways forward for liberal international order.

American-led liberal international order

Remarkably, we still live in the international order built by the United States and its allies over a half century ago. It is a distinctive type of order, organised around open markets, multilateral institutions, cooperative security, alliance partnership, democratic solidarity, and United States hegemonic leadership. It is an order anchored in large-scale institutions, which include the United Nations, NATO, the Bretton Woods institutions, the World Trade Organisation, alliance partnerships between the United States and Asian partners, and informal governance groupings such at the G-7/8. In the background, the United States played a hegemonic role, providing public goods by supporting open markets and the provisioning of security (Ikenberry, 2001; Patrick, 2009).

This American-led international order was a very specific type of liberal order. It was a liberal *hegemonic* order. The United States did not just encourage an open and rule-based order. It gradually became its hegemonic organiser and manager. The American political system – and its alliances, technology, currency, and markets – became fused to the wider liberal order. In the shadow of the Cold War, the United States became the "owner and operator" of the liberal capitalist political system. The United States supported the rules and institutions of liberal internationalism but it was also given special rights and privileges. It organised and led an extended political system built around multilateral institutions, alliances, strategic partners, and client states. It was an order infused with strategic understandings and hegemonic bargains. The United States provided "services" to other states through the provision of security and its commitment to stability and open markets. In these ways, the United States was more than just a powerful country that *dominated* the global system. It *created* a political order; a hierarchical order with liberal characteristics.

The liberal imagination is vast – and the liberal vision of international order has many facets. From the early nineteenth century through the current era, liberals have articulated a cluster of ideas and aspirations: free trade, multilateralism, collective security, democratic community, progressive change, shared sovereignty, and the rule of law. The post-war American vision was a specific version of liberal international order. It was hegemonic. As noted, it was an arrangement in which the United States actively managed the wider system. The United States and the wider liberal order were organised into a single extended global order. This type of liberal order can be contrasted with earlier liberal political formations. In the nineteenth century, liberal order was manifest in open trade and the gold standard, flourishing in the shadow of British economic and naval mastery. After the First World War, Woodrow Wilson sought to construct a more far-reaching liberal progressive order, organised around the League of Nations. It was a system that did not rely on American hegemony but rather hinged on the cooperation of liberal democracies adhering to open trade and collective security. After the Second World War, Franklin Roosevelt again sought to construct a liberal order organised around great power concert and the United Nations. The rise of the Cold War, the weakness of Europe, and the complexities associated with opening up and managing post-war order brought the United States more directly into the operation and management of the system. In fits and starts, liberal order turned into American liberal hegemonic order (Ikenberry, 2009: 71–87).

This order has also been remarkably successful; it has accomplished a great deal over the last six decades. It provided a framework for the reopening of the world economy after the Second World War, ushering in a "golden age" of growth. It integrated post-war Japan and Germany, who went on to become the second- and third-largest economies in the world, respectively. The Western alliance and the European "project" provided institutional mechanisms to solve Europe's bloodiest geopolitical problem: Franco-German antagonism and the position of Germany within Europe. This was the quiet revolution in post-war world politics. A chronic source of war and political instability was eliminated. The larger Western-based liberal international order also provided an expansive system in which rising and transitioning countries could integrate and join. Over the last 30 years, over 500 million people in countries connected to this liberal order were lifted out of poverty (Jones et al., 2009). The Cold War was also ended peacefully, with countries in eastern Europe and the former Soviet Union integrated into the Western order.

Overall, this American-led arrangement is arguably the most successful international order the world has yet seen. At least this is true if success is defined in terms of wealth creation, physical security, and hope for justice. This order has not solved all the world's problems and it exists in a world with widespread human suffering and rising economic inequality. But in the context of the savage history of world politics over the last centuries, including the world wars of the recent past, it has been an unusually stable and functional system.

The durability of liberal international order

There are also reasons to think that this liberal order will persist, even if it continues to evolve. Firstly, the violent forces that have overthrown international orders in the past do not seem to operate today. We live in the longest period of "great power peace" in modern history. The great powers have not found themselves at war with each other since the guns fell silent in 1945. This non-war outcome is certainly influenced by two realities: nuclear deterrence, which raises the costs of war, and the dominance of democracies, who have found their own pathway to peace. In the past, the great moments of order building came in the aftermath of war when the old order was destroyed. War itself was a ratification of the view that the old order was no longer sustainable. War broke the old order apart, propelled shifts in world power, and opened up the international landscape for new negotiations over the rules and principles of world politics. In the absence of great power war it is harder to clear the ground for new "constitutional" arrangements.

Secondly, this order is also distinctive in its integrative and expansive character. In essence, it is "easy to join and hard to overturn". This follows most fundamentally from the fact that it is a liberal international order – that is, that it is an order that is relatively open and loosely rule based. The order generates participants and stakeholders. Beyond this, there are three reasons why the architectural features of this post-war liberal order reinforce downward and outward integration. One is that the multilateral character of the rules and institutions create opportunities for access and participation. Countries that want to join in can do so. Japan found itself integrating into this order through participation in the trade system and alliance partnership. More recently, China has taken steps to join this order, at least the world trading system. Joining is not costless. Existing members must vote upon membership in institutional bodies, such as the WTO, and states must meet specific requirements. But these bodies are not exclusive or imperial. Secondly, the liberal order is organised around shared leadership and not just the United States. The G-7/8 is an example of a governance organisation that is based on a collective leadership, and the new G-20 grouping has emerged to provide expanded leadership. Finally, the order also provides opportunities for a wide array of states to gain access to the "spoils of modernity". Again, this is not an imperial system in which the riches accrue disproportionately to the centre. States across the system have found ways to integrate into this order and experience economic gains and rapid growth along the way.

Thirdly, rising states do not constitute a bloc that seeks to overturn or reorganise the existing international order. China, India, Russia, Brazil, South Africa – these countries and others all are seeking new roles and more influence within the global system. But they are not a new coalition of states seeking global transformation. All of these states are capitalist and as such are deeply embedded in the world economy. Most of them are democratic and embrace the political principles of the older Western liberal democracies. At the same time, they all have different geopolitical interests. They are as diverse in their orientations as the rest of the world in regard to energy, religion, and ideologies of development. They are not united by a common principled belief in a post-liberal world order. They are all very much inside the existing order and integrated in various ways into existing governance institutions.

Fourthly, the major states in the system – the old great powers and rising states – all have complex alignments of interests. They all are secure in the sense that they are not threatened by other major states. All of them worry about radicalism and failed states. Even in the case of the most fraught relationships – such as the emerging one between the United States and China – there are shared or common interests in global issues related to energy and the environment. These interests are complex. There are lots of ways in which these countries will compete with each other and seek to push "adjustment" to problems onto the other states. But it is precisely the complexity of these shared interests that creates opportunities and incentives to negotiate and cooperate – and, ultimately, to support the open and rule-based frameworks that allow for bargains and agreements to be reached.

Overall, these considerations suggest that the leading states of the world system are travelling along a common pathway to modernity. They are not divided by great ideological clashes or emboldened by the potential gains from great power war. These logics of earlier orders are not salient today. Fascism, communism, and theocratic dictatorships cannot propel you along the modernising pathway. In effect, if you want to be a modern great power you need to join the WTO. The capitalist world economy and the liberal rules and institutions that it supports – and that support it – are foundational to modernisation and progress. The United States and other Western states may rise or fall within the existing global system but the liberal character of that system still provides attractions and benefits to most states within it and on its edges.

Liberal order and the great transformations

Obviously, there are great shifts going on, many of them long in the making. The end of the Cold War triggered a slow-motion transformation in the global system. The American-led liberal order has existed within a larger bipolar Cold War distribution of power. With the collapse of the Soviet Union and the end of Cold War hostilities, this "inside system" became the "outside system". The liberal order was thrown open and exposed to the entire world. This has triggered a variety of complex reactions. New questions were asked about the role of alliances and debates about threats. If the

Cold War alliances were part of the architecture of American-led liberal order, that part of the hegemonic framework was rendered less stable. In addition, new questions about political identity were triggered. Are we "one people"? Is there a "free world"? Does democratic solidarity still matter in the absence of a common enemy? (Ash, 2004)

The end of the Cold War also ushered in problems with Russia. At first, the Western powers and the Russian Federation had found a peaceful settlement of their bipolar rivalry. But the United States and Europe also found themselves encroaching on Russian geopolitical interests. NATO expansion was in part driven by liberal aspirations to expand the club of democracies eastward, to include newly liberalising post-Communist states. But this exercise in liberal expansionism tended to come at the expense of Russia's sensibilities. Other developments also eroded Moscow's relationship with the West. The American withdrawal from the ABM treaty and the failure to go forward with the START II arms control talks signalled a retreat from the vision that American and Soviet leaders articulated at the end of the Cold War. Tensions between the West and Russia have mounted in more recent years over oil and pipeline issues, rights of Russian minorities, borders inherited from the former Soviet Union, and the democratisation of former Soviet republics (Deudney and Ikenberry, 2009–2010: 39–62).

The rise of unipolarity has made American power more controversial and raised the level of uncertainty around the world about the bargains and institutions of liberal order. With the end of the Cold War, America's primacy in the global distribution of capabilities became one of the most salient features of the international system. No other major state has enjoyed such advantages in material capabilities – military, economic, technological, geographical. This unipolar distribution of power is historically unique, and it has ushered in a new set of dynamics that are still working their way through the organisation of world politics. But the rise of unipolarity brings with it a shift in the underlying logic of order and rule in world politics. In a bipolar or multipolar system, powerful states "rule" in the process of leading a coalition of states in balancing against other states. When the system shifts to unipolarity, this logic of rule disappears. Power is no longer based on balancing or equilibrium, but on the predominance of one state. This is new and different, and potentially threatening to weaker and secondary states (Ikenberry et al., 2009: 5).

A more gradual shift in the global system is the unfolding human rights and "responsibility to protect" revolution, resulting in an erosion of the central Westphalian norm of sovereignty over the post-war decades. The international community is seen as having a legitimate interest in what goes on within countries, its growing interest in the domestic governance practices of states driven by considerations of both human rights and security. In consequence, norms of sovereignty are seen as more contingent. Their gradual erosion has created a new "license" for powerful states to intervene in the domestic affairs of weak and troubled states. Over the past few centuries, Westphalian sovereignty has been the single most universal and agreed-upon norm of international politics. It underlies international law, the United Nations, and the great historical movements of anti-colonialism and national self-determination. So when the norm weakens, the consequences are not in the least surprising. But the erosion of state sovereignty norms has not been matched by the rise of new norms and agreements about *how* the international community should make good on human rights and the responsibility to protect. Unresolved disagreements mount regarding the standards of legality and legitimacy that regulate the actions of powerful states acting on behalf of the international community.

The sources of insecurity in world politics have also evolved since the early decades that shaped American liberal hegemony. As noted earlier, the threat to peace is no longer primarily from great powers engaged in security competition. The result has been a shift in the ways in which violence is manifest. In the past, only powerful states were able to gain access to the destructive capabilities that could threaten other societies. Today, it is possible to see technology and the globalisation of the world system as creating opportunities for non-state actors – or transnational gangs – to acquire weapons of mass destruction. As a result, it is now the weakness of states and their inability to enforce law and order within their own societies that provide the most worrisome dangers to the international system.

In contrast to earlier eras, there is no single enemy – or source of violence and insecurity – that frames and reinforces the American-led liberal order. The United States and other states face a diffuse array of threats and challenges. Global warming, health pandemics, nuclear proliferation, jihadist terrorism, energy scarcity – these and other dangers loom on the horizon. Any of these threats could endanger Western lives and liberal ways of life either directly or indirectly by destabilising the global system upon which security and prosperity depend. Pandemics and global warming are not threats wielded by human hands, but their consequences could be equally devastating. Highly infectious disease has the potential to kill millions of people. Global warming threatens to trigger waves of environmental migration, food shortages, further destabilising weak and poor states around the world. The world is also on the cusp of a new round of nuclear proliferation, putting mankind's deadliest weapons in the hands of unstable and hostile states. Terrorist networks offer a new spectre of non-state transnational violence. The point is that none of these threats are, in themselves, so singularly preeminent that they deserve to be the centrepiece of American national security as were anti-fascism and anti-communism in an earlier era.

The master trend behind these diffuse threats is the rise and intensification of "security interdependence". This notion is really a measure of how much a state's national security depends on policies of other actors. If a country is security "independent" it means that it is capable of achieving an acceptable level of security through its own actions. Others can threaten it, but the means for coping with these threats are within its own national hands. This means that the military intentions and capacities of other states are irrelevant to a state's security. This is true either because the potential military threats are too remote and far removed to matter, or because if a foreign power is capable of launching war against the state, it has the capabilities to resist the aggression (Deudney, 2007).

Security interdependence is the opposite circumstance. The state's security depends on the policy and choices of other actors. Security is established by convincing other actors not to attack. During the Cold War, the United States and the Soviet Union were in a situation of supreme security interdependence. Each had nuclear weapons that could destroy the other. It was the logic of deterrence that established the restraints on policy. Each state knew that to launch a nuclear strike on the other would be followed by massive and assured retaliation. States cannot protect themselves or achieve national security without the help of other states. There is no "solution" to the security problem without active cooperation.

Today, more people in more places matter for the security of the states within the old liberal international order. With the growth of transnational and diffuse threats, we are witnessing an explosion in the complexity of security interdependence. What people do and how they live matter in ways that were irrelevant in earlier eras. How people burn energy, provide public health, treat minorities, and enforce rules and treaties count more today than ever before. The result is a rising demand for security cooperation. The demand for universal, cooperative, institutionalised, and rule-based order will grow – and not decline – in the decades ahead.

Trends shaping future liberal international order

In seeking to detect the evolving contours of international order, there are three trends that bear special attention. First is the so-called "return of multipolarity". This is the alleged movement away from American unipolarity to a more decentralised global power structure inhabited by rival great powers. How quickly is this happening and what are its consequences? In tracking this development, it is important to distinguish between three steps towards multipolarity. The first is the simple diffusion of power, a gradual transition in the systemic distribution of power whereby the United States will experience an erosion of its relative advantages in material capabilities. Its share of world GNP in market size and in military capabilities will shrink. A second step towards multipolarity involves not just a redistribution of power but also the rise of new "poles". This entails the emergence of great powers that take on characteristics of a "hub". They have their own security alliances, commercial partners,

political networks, and so forth. A "pole" is manifest not just as a concentration of power but in the way it builds networks and takes on the
role of an organising hub for other states within the larger system. The
third step towards multipolarity would involve not just a diffusion of
power and the rise of new "poles", but also the triggering of balancing
and security competition. This would be a world in which the restraints
and accommodations that the major states have made within the post-war
American-led order would give way to more traditional power balancing.
My point is that it is possible to witness a diffusion of power and not see
the emergence of new "poles", and it is possible to see the rise of new
"poles" without the commencement of great power balance of power politics
(Posen, 2009).

The most important question in this regard is China. Is it emerging as a
geopolitical "pole"? This, in turn, raises specific questions. Is it becoming a
source of attraction? Is it becoming a security provider for states in its region?
What sort of alliance partnerships is it developing, if any? What sorts of
"soft power" characteristics does China project as it rises? Answers to these
questions are not obvious but the way and extent to which China becomes a
"pole" will help shape the character of the next cycle of international order.

The second major trend to watch is the softening or deterioration of political order in key states. This question concerns the stability of political
institutions in late-developing states that have emerged in recent decades
and integrated into the liberal international order. Examples are Brazil,
Mexico, Turkey, and Indonesia. What are the changing political capacities
of these modernising states? Do they face common challenges as middle-
tier states? What will be the consequences for the global system if these
states fall back and experience a decline in their ability to function as stable
democracies?

The third trend to watch is the way and extent to which rising states get
integrated into the existing liberal international order. As I have argued, the
post-war liberal order has been an American-centred and Western-oriented
hegemonic order. The great drama of the next few decades will involve the
choices and strategies of rising states, such as India, China, Brazil, as they
confront this old order.

The analogy might be a big corporation. For over half a century, the liberal international order has been owned and operated by the United States.
It can be called American, Inc. This American-dominated system emerged
out of Cold War circumstances, and the family-owned corporation grew and
prospered. But today, the struggle is to "go public" with the company. Rising countries are seeking a greater role and voice in the global system. The
United States is finding itself in need of turning American Inc. into a pub-
lically traded company. It has to invite new shareholders and add members
to the board of directors. The United States (and Europe) will remain leading members of the board. But their voice and vote will not be what it once

was. The challenge of the liberal international order today is to manage this transition in its ownership and governance.

Conclusions

I want to end where I began by talking about the nature of the "crisis" that besets the American-led liberal international order. My conclusion is that if the "liberal order" is in crisis, it is a crisis of *success* and not a crisis of *failure*. It is not a crisis in the way that some observers have depicted it in the past – by presenting the "liberal project" as an idealist enterprise that cannot take hold in a world of anarchy and power politics. The crisis today is precisely the opposite of this classic charge. That is, the liberal project has succeeded only too well. The global system has boomed under conditions of hegemonic rule. It is expanding and integrating on a global scale and creating economic and security interdependencies well beyond the imagination of its original architects. The crisis today is that the old *hegemonic* foundations of the liberal order are no longer adequate, rather than reflect a failure of the order itself.

In effect, my argument is that this is not an E.H. Carr crisis. Rather it is a Karl Polanyi crisis. An E.H. Carr crisis is a moment when realists can step forward and say liberals had it wrong and that the crisis of their project reveals the enduring truths of self-regarding states and the balance of power. It is a Karl Polanyi crisis, where liberal governance is troubled because dilemmas and long-term shifts in the order can only be solved by rethinking, rebuilding, and extending that liberal order.

Liberal order generates the seeds of its own unmaking, which can only be averted by more liberal order – reformed, updated, and outfitted with a new foundation. This is not a story about the rise and spread of Western liberalism. It is a story of modernity and the global search for universal principles of politics and economics. No region or people own this story. It is a story that is written on a world scale – and it is one of breakthroughs, crises, triumphs, and transformations. The liberal international order is in crisis. But after liberalism there will be more, well, liberalism.

Note

1. This chapter was originally published as an article in *Millennium: Journal of International Studies* 38:3 (2010), pp. 509–521.

References

Ash, T. G.(2004), *Free World: America, Europe, and the Surprising Future of the West*, New York: Random House.

Bradford, L. J. and Cohen, S. S. (2010), *The End of Influence: What Happens When Other Countries Have the Money*, New York: Basic Books.

Deudney, D. (2007), *Bounding Power: Republican Security Theory from the Polis to the Global Village*, Princeton: Princeton University Press.

Deudney, D. and Ikenberry, J. G. (2009–2010), "The Unravelling of the Cold War Settlement", *Survival*, 51(6), 39–62.

Gat, A. (2009), *Victorious and Vulnerable: Why Democracy Won in the 20th Century and How it is Still Imperiled*, New York: Rowman & Littlefield.

Ikenberry, J. G.(2001), *After Victory: Institutions, Strategic Restraint, and the Rebuilding of Order after Major War*, Princeton: Princeton University Press.

Ikenberry, J. G. (2009), "Liberal Internationalism 3.0: America and the Dilemmas of Liberal World Order", *Perspectives on Politics*, 7(1), 71–87.

Ikenberry, J. G., Mastanduno, M and Wohlforth, W. C. (2009) "Introduction: Unipolarity, State Behavior, and Systemic Consequences", *World Politics*, 61(1), 1–27.

Jacques, M. (2009), *When China Rules the World: The End of the Western World and the Birth of a New Global Order*, New York: The Penguin Press.

Jones, B., Pascual, C. and Stedman, S. A. (2009), *Power and Responsibility: Building International Order in an Era of Transnational Threats*, Washington D.C.: Brookings Institution Press.

Kagan, R. (2008), *The Return of History and the End of Dreams*, New York: Knopf.

Khanna, P. (2008), *The Second World: Empires and Influence in the New Global Age*, New York: Random House.

Kupchan, C. (2003), *The End of the American Era: US Foreign Policy and the Geopolitics of the Twenty-First Century*, New York: Knopf.

Patrick, S. (2009), *The Best Laid Plans: The Origins of American Multilateralism and the Dawn of the Cold War*, New York: Rowman & Littlefield.

Posen, B. (2009), "Emerging Multipolarity: Why Should We Care?", *Current History*, 108, 347–352.

Stiglitz, J. (2010), *America, Free Markets, and the Sinking of the World Economy*, New York: Norton.

The National Intelligence Council. (2008), *Global Trends 2025*, Washington, D.C.: The National Intelligence Council.

Zakaria, F (2009), *The Post-American World*, New York: Norton.

6
Power and the Liberal Order

Michael Cox

If international affairs can be defined in terms of decades, then it is common to think of the 1960s as a decade of revolt, the 1970s as an era of global transition, the 1980s as an era when the Cold War came to an end, and the 1990s as a decade of liberal triumph when all sorts of dreams could be dreamed about a world in which a happy marriage between markets, democracy, and a benign American empire would produce an even more robust liberal order. Indeed, the ten years before the beginning of the twenty-first century were decidedly upbeat ones for liberals. With the Cold War a mere memory, globalisation driving all before it, previously closed economic systems opening up, and a new world order taking shape around a series of revamped international institutions, such as the United Nations and the European Union, it really did seem as if Fukuyama's (1992) prediction about the creation of a world in which there was no serious alternative to liberalism had at last come true.

Nowhere was this mood more prevalent perhaps than within the academy itself. Not every writer signed up to the new credo (Robinson, 1996). However, very many did – especially within the field of International Relations (IR). Indeed, IR went through its own form of rediscovery with one influential writer after another informing us that realism had seen its day (Kratochwil, 1993); that the state should no longer be regarded as the main focus of the discipline; that sovereignty belonged to another age; and that it was perfectly reasonable for Western liberal states to intervene into the affairs of other countries if the purpose was to "save strangers" (Wheeler, 2000). Academics of a distinctly liberal persuasion even began to exercise an influence on the policy world. Thus, in the United States, liberal theorists, armed with the latest data, proving democracies did not go to war with another, found a niche for themselves inside the Clinton White House (Cox, 2000). Meanwhile in Britain, Blair assumed office, convinced that liberalism offered a way forward. Indeed, having studied what had happened in the former Yugoslavia – when the West had not intervened at first on the good realist grounds of non-intervention – he came to the very firm conclusion

that something more moral, in a word more liberal, would be more necessary if the West were going to develop a foreign policy better suited to a
globalised world, where the fate of ordinary people in one country (even
those living in faraway places), very directly impinged on the national interests of others. The world may be composed of states, he noted. But at the
end of the day, it was the duty of the more powerful of these to protect the
rights of others and so construct what he hoped would one day emerge – a
true "international community".

If the 1990s marked the high point of liberal aspirations and hopes,
the next ten years seemed to throw the whole liberal project into crisis.
It began with 9/11. Few doubted that the United States would, and indeed
should, respond. Tragically, it responded by employing torture, extraordinary rendition, and abandoning any pretence that it should be constrained
by international law or even the Geneva Convention. The Iraq War only
made things worse. Indeed, by seeking to sell the war in largely liberal
terms (promoting democracy and human rights in Iraq), it led many critics to the not illogical conclusion that liberalism was not simply a set of
decent and acceptable principles designed to make the world a safer and
more prosperous place, but rather a cover story masking a latter-day form of
US empire-building (Cox, 2003, 2004).

The second cause of the crisis was more directly economic and came in
the form of the great financial crash of 2008. This hugely significant event
not only caused untold damage to the Western economic order; it also
undermined that critically important liberal idea that free and unfettered
markets would always and everywhere generate wealth and growth. As one
analyst noted shortly after the crash, it was not just that the crisis on Wall
Street undermined faith in the financial system, making Bankers figures of
hate, while losing millions of ordinary citizens a great deal of money. That
much was self-evident. It was rather that it destroyed the claim made by
the overwhelming majority of economists and the bulk of Western policymakers for generations that market liberalisation was the panacea that
would unlock mankind's full potential and one day bring prosperity to all
(Altman, 2009).

The final challenge came in the rather more traditional form of a rising
state that many had once written off as a proverbial basket-case: namely
communist-led China. Hitherto, liberals had insisted that markets would
always generate pluralism, while freedom was the only firm basis upon
which one would be able to guarantee economic growth. Capitalism, in
other words, required a free society and a free society would be the necessary by-product of capitalism. China undermined this liberal argument at a
stroke. Led by a party whose founders were Marxist and directed by a modern
elite who were decidedly illiberal in outlook, China not only constituted a
problem in terms of the traditional balance of power. It also seemed to undermine the very idea that liberalism represented the wave of the future. A new

order beckoned, and according to some analysts, at least, it was neither going to be Western or liberal (Halper, 2010).

The idea that the last decade of the twentieth century marked the high water mark of liberalism and first ten years of the twenty-first century, its fall, has become an increasingly influential way of thinking about the 20-year period since the end of the Cold War. Book after book, and op-ed piece after op-ed piece, has talked of little else over the past few years. Indeed, the picture now being painted of the West, more generally, and the United States, more particularly, is a decidedly gloomy one. Even some of America's more ardent apologists could hardly contain their Spengler-like gloom. The once mighty empire they opined was going the way of all empires in the past; and as it declined so too would the West as a whole. A crucial corner had been turned. The future looked grim. A new world order beckoned; sadly though, it was unlikely to be Western (Cox, 2007).

Suggesting that the liberal order might not be in crisis is a decidedly unfashionable position to adopt right now. But that is precisely what I wish to do in this chapter. The most direct way of doing this of course would be to point to some fairly self-evident facts: that democracy remains as politically widespread today as it did in the 1990s; that global capitalism continues to function and that globalisation continues apace; and that the American people actually decided to reject many of the policies associated with the Bush administration by electing the most liberal (and the first black) President in the history of the republic. My main argument though does not revolve around demonstrating the empirically obvious, but rather, by making a larger theoretical point – a recognisably realist one – about the relationship between liberal order and the existence of a group of powerful Western states (the most important by far being the United States) all of whom have a very direct interest in upholding and defending this order (Gilpin, 2001). The key question then is not do these states seek to maintain the liberal order – self-evidently they do; but rather, can they retain their hitherto advantageous position in the wider international system? Many now assume they cannot, and indeed have talked at great length of power moving from the liberal West to less liberal East, from democratic American to authoritarian China. But this I believe is yet another myth (Cox, 2012). Indeed, as I will seek to show in what follows, the system of power that brought the world liberalism after the Second World War, and was then reinforced as a result of the end of the Cold War, remains more or less intact today. Battered perhaps. Less self-confident than it was during the halcyon days immediately following the collapse of the USSR. But still retaining enormous staying powers, as I will now seek to show in the remaining part of this chapter.

I have divided the discussion into four sections. In the first section, I deal with the United States and why it may not in fact be in terminal decline as some are now suggesting. In the second section, I look at the liberal Transatlantic relationship and why it remains the axis around which the world still revolves. In the third section, I then deal (albeit very briefly) with China and suggest reasons why it is not about to take over the world. Finally, in the conclusion, I speculate about the future. Here again, I will take the distinctly revisionist view that not only does the West continue to possess structural advantage but that the "rising rest" – far from upsetting the liberal order as some analysts believe they might – are more likely to become important additions to it.

American decline revisited

Let us deal firstly with the wider question as to whether or not the power of the United States and the West are in steep decline as some now seem to be suggesting. Here I think we have to distinguish between recent headlines – all of which appear to be supporting the notion that the last ten years have been "hell" for the West – and some basic economic facts. Some of these undoubtedly point, as LSE economist Danny Quah has argued, to a distinct tilt eastwards (Quah, 2011). But one should not confuse this "tilt" with an irreversible economic decline of the West itself. China may well be consuming twice as much crude steel as the United States, the EU and Japan combined. India may have a modern IT sector, a strong entrepreneurial culture and the richest cricket league in the world. And Brazil's large and growing agricultural, mining, manufacturing, and service sector makes it the dominant economy in Latin America. But the Western economies overall still retain some big structural advantages – none more so than its supposedly beleaguered leader, the United States of America.

Is the US economic star on the wane? Compared to where it was in 1945: most obviously. And in comparative GDP terms: undoubtedly. Nor should we ignore what has become palpably obvious over the past ten years in particular: that a number of significantly large emerging economies have experienced very rapid growth. But this is not the whole story. Others may have taken several leaps forward under conditions of globalisation. But they still have a very long way to go to match the United States, a country we need reminding that still remains remarkably stable and secure, which has the rare privilege of printing the all powerful dollar (still representing over 60 per cent of foreign exchange reserves), and which, because of its sheer dynamism, has been the destination of choice for over 20 million emigrants since 1989. The United States, moreover, sits at the very heart of the wider world economy. Thus, it is, by far and away, the world's biggest source of foreign direct investment (FDI) and the largest recipient of overseas capital (Jackson, 2011). It is also the world's largest trader. Certainly, without the United States importing as much as it does – as much as 8 per cent of China's GDP is exported to the United States each year – not only would the American consumer have a lower standard of living. The world economy simply could not function. The United States may face a unique set of difficulties right now while China and others may be expanding their field of economic operations. But as has recently been suggested, the United States still possesses critical features that give it what Norloff (2010) has called "positional advantages" over all other states. Norloff even challenges the now fashionable view that America's hegemonic burdens are outweighing the benefits. She suggests otherwise: Washington actually reaps more than it pays out in the provision of public goods. Indeed, by maintaining an open market (trade deficits and all) the United States is able to bargain for better commercial deals for American firms by the simple measure of threatening closure (Norloff, 2010).

But it is not just a question of its extraordinarily powerful position in relation to others. Even in simple quantitative terms, the United States is still way ahead of the "rest". GDP is a crude measurement to be sure. But using some recent statistics, the United States would still appear to be over eight times bigger than either Russia or India, over six times bigger than Brazil, and still nearly three times bigger than China. Indeed, the only other part of the world economy which comes anywhere close to matching it is the European Union, an organisation comprising 27 members, including some of the most advanced economies in the world like Germany (IMF, 2010). Indeed, even if you add up all the BRICs together economically – that is to say Brazil, Russia, India, and China – they are still about 40 per cent smaller than the United States. The four moreover are clearly not united; they produce what they do with a combined population nearly eight times larger than the United States, and they all have internal problems such as corruption and a lack of transparency, which do not exist in the United States to anything similar degree. Furthermore, if you were to combine the economic power of the United States with that of its closest Western partner, the European Union, and then set this alongside the BRICs, one discovers that whereas the BRICs account for just over 15 per cent of world GDP, the "West" accounts for nearly 50 per cent – over three times as much in other words (CIA, 2011).

Other economic indicators point to an even greater gap between the United States, the West, and the rest. Take per capita income. In China, life is definitely getting better for the ordinary citizen. But in 2010, average income was still only one-tenth of that found in the West. In India and Brazil, where income is far more unequally distributed, the gap is even greater. The United States is also massively ahead of the emerging economies and the "rest" in terms of global competitiveness. It is certainly true, as recent Davos reports have shown, that the United States has slipped in the world's competitive league table. But it continues to be a highly competitive economy – easily in the top ten alongside its closest political allies in Europe; and it is still a long way ahead of other emerging countries such as China, India, Turkey, and

Brazil. Indeed, of the top 15 competitive countries, all are either identifiably Western or closely allied to the United States; all that is, with the one exception of Hong Kong. China, meanwhile, is ranked 24th; India, 51st; Brazil, 58th; and Russia, 63rd – just one ahead of Uruguay (Schwab, 2010–2011).

Another way of measuring US economic power is to look at its 51 individual states and then compare these to various foreign countries. The Economist did such a survey by matching the GDP equivalent of each American state with that of a sovereign nation. The findings were truly remarkable. Thus Taiwan, with a population of about 23 million, had an economy only 15 per cent bigger than Michigan, even though Michigan only had a population of ten million. Indonesia with a population of over 230 million had an economy only 10 per cent bigger than that of Pennsylvania even though its population (230 million) was 20 times bigger. Turkey's economy, meanwhile, was one-third smaller than that of Florida, Brazil turned out to have an economy just slightly smaller than that of California, while the Russian economy had an economy with more or less the same GDP size as that of Texas; the difference here being that whereas Russia had a population of 140 million, Texas only had 20 million (Loquenzi, 2011).

There are other indicators of national economic strength. One, obviously, is wealth measured by the number of very rich people living in any particular country. Here the headlines always make much of the new class of super-rich in China and India. However, the fact remains that the United States has more millionaires (over five million in all) than the rest of the world put together. There is, in addition, a demographic measurement of national power. Here, we discover that not only are its core numbers all pointing in the right direction – namely upwards – but that the balance in the American population under modern conditions is about as good as it can be (Haas, 2007). Furthermore, though its cities might feel crowded, America is in fact under-populated with enormous room for further population growth. Certainly, when compared with either its peer rivals, its closest allies, and its main competitors, its demographic position looks remarkably secure (Tellis et al., 2010). Americans would also seem to do much more with far less. Indeed, one of the more stunning indicators of US productivity is the simple, but telling fact that with only around 4 per cent of the world's population it still manages to produce something close to around one-quarter of all the world's goods and services.

Then there is the really quite critical issue of Research and Development (R&D). Through innovation, tinkering and the simple act of "borrowing", China and others have certainly managed to narrow the R&D gap somewhat (Durfee and Pomfret, 2011). But while they have done well enough (though by Western standards not that well), the United States continues to lead the field. This was certainly the finding of a detailed RAND study back in 2008. This examined the by then popular – but as it turned out, misguided – view that the United States was losing its competitive edge in science and technology (S&T). The claims were examined and were found to be almost entirely spurious. Indeed, far from falling behind and losing its top ranking, the United States continued to lead the world. In fact, it had not just kept pace with its nearest competitors (again mainly to be found in Europe); it had actually grown faster than all other nations on several measurements. Interestingly, it also continued to benefit enormously from the influx of foreign researchers, who far from being deterred from working in what many now claimed was an environment hostile to outsiders post-9/11, still saw the United States as the cutting-edge centre of S&T, having the best research facilities and of course the more attractive salaries. Significantly, but not coincidentally, of the 10 Nobel prizes awarded in the broad sciences in 2008, eight went to those working in the United States (Galama and Hosek, 2008).

Finally, though much can be said about (and against) the quality of American economic leadership, it is still only the United States and its closest Western allies that really think in leadership terms when it comes to the larger international economy. No doubt their capacity to lead has been badly dented by the economic crisis; and the rise of the rest, as others have pointed out, means the Americans are bound to consult more. However, unlike the rest, it is still only the West – and the United States in particular – that appears to have some sort of positive vision for the world economic order. As Ikenberry has shown, this was first formed in the period after 1945 and has remained remarkably consistent ever since. In fact, so attractive has this "open door" vision been, that even China has been drawn towards it, initially in the 1970s when it opened up diplomatic relations with the United States, then again in the 1990s when it was becoming clear that China had to rejoin the world economy or stagnate, and then finally in 2001 when it formally entered the World Trade Organization (WTO). China may have benefitted as a result. Still, it is surely significant that it was not the United States, which joined a Chinese-created system and then played by its rules. Rather it was to be China that chose to join a world economic order originally created, and in many ways still shaped by rules written by either the United States or its other Western allies (Wade, 2012).

The death of the West?

If the United States remains a far more dominant economic player in the world than some have been suggesting of late, so too is that much under-rated entity known is the Transatlantic economic region. That Asia in general and China in particular are becoming more significant is obvious. But it is one thing to suggest that Asia is growing in economic importance; it is quite another to speak of the Transatlantic area as if it were slipping rapidly into geo-economic obscurity. This ignores many things – most obviously the facts. Indeed, in the rush to prove the existence of an irresistible power shift away from the United States and Europe, these have been in very short supply indeed. Few now seem to pay attention to the fact that the EU and the United States constitute the biggest economic bloc in the world; and that even though trade across the Pacific has been rising fast – largely because of China – trade across the Atlantic still remains huge. Services and foreign investment tell an even more interesting story, however. Consider the bald numbers. Services now make up the bulk of any modern economy, and not surprisingly, trade in services has risen rapidly under conditions of globalisation; but it has risen especially quickly across the Atlantic. Indeed, by 2008, it amounted to around $350 bn, an increase of well over three times since 1995. FDI reveals the same trend. It has climbed steeply since the 1990s; and by 2007, totalled $15.2 trillion. Of this, the bulk (over 65 per cent) went to developed countries, not emerging ones. Moreover, the largest amount was transatlantic, with the largest non-European investors in the EU being the United States ($1.4 trillion in 2007, three times more than the stock of US FDI in the whole of the Asia-Pacific region) and the largest overseas investor in the United States being the EU. Nor should we be so surprised by this. As various studies have shown, the most important determinants shaping the decisions taken by Western companies to invest in other countries is not cheap labour or tax breaks (though sometimes this does make a difference), but rather the size and wealth of the host market, the stability of the country's political system and the predictability of the business climate; and on all these measures, the EU and the United States are vastly more attractive destinations for FDI than most other parts of the world (Whyte, 2009).

But the transatlantic economic region is not just big. It has also been the driver of the world economy since the end of the Second World War. This may of course be changing now, but only to a degree. Possessing as it still does the largest market on earth, the greatest store of wealth, and the bulk of the world's corporations, it is hardly surprising that it exerts the extraordinary pull it does. Indeed, for all the fuss now being made about emerging markets and China, it is easy to forget that they could never have emerged in the first place without the massive stimulus provided by the EU and the United States. Nor should we forget how financially powerful they remain. Indeed, even following the financial crisis, the US and EU financial markets continue to account for well over two-thirds of global banking assets; three- quarters of global financial services; 77 per cent of equity-linked derivatives; more than 70 per cent of all private and public debt securities; almost 80 per cent of all interest- rate derivatives; almost 75 per cent of all new international debt securities; and 70 per cent of all foreign exchange derivatives transactions. Of the global foreign exchange holdings, 92.8 per cent is held in transatlantic currencies, either dollars (62.1 per cent), euros (26.5 per cent), or sterling (4.2 per cent) (Hamilton and Quinlan, 2011).

Taken together, Europe and the United States also possess many other significant assets. They are, for example, home to the overwhelming majority of the world's leading universities. Of the top five, in fact, three are American and two British; within the top 25, only one is Asian (Tokyo University); and within the top 50 only a handful are to be found outside of the United States, Europe, or the English-speaking world more generally. Significantly, no university within the top 100 are Indian, Brazilian, or Russian, and only five are to be found in China (three of these in Hong Kong) (Cox, 2012). This in turn has a massive impact on where students tend to study abroad. It come as no great surprise of course to find out that the bulk of international students choose to study in either North America, western Europe, or some other OECD "western" country, notably English-speaking Australia. Very few on the other hand choose to study in Asia or in any other of the emerging countries' institutions of higher education. Indeed, between them the United States, Canada, the UK, Australia, France, and Germany account for something close to two-thirds of students studying abroad at any one time. The same very unequal pattern is found in terms of the most prestigious business schools. Those most highly rated are found in the advanced Western countries: either the United States, which is home to over 50 per cent of the most highly ranked in the top 100; the United Kingdom which plays host to the best business school in the world (the London Business School); or a few other countries like Canada, Spain, and France. The emerging economies meantime can only boast a handful of the top schools, three in Latin America (though not one in Brazil), two in India, one in South Korea, one in Singapore, and only one in China (in Hong Kong) (*Financial Times*, 2011).

But what about the state of the transatlantic relationship, more generally? Is this not getting worse by the day? Are the Americans not getting bored with Europe; and impatient with NATO? Indeed, has Europe more generally not slipped down America's list of interests? To a minor degree: yes. But again one needs to distinguish between certain shifts in US thinking – shifts that are perhaps making Europe a less privileged partner – and the deeper significance of the relationship itself. Americans might complain at great length about how little their European allies are doing in terms of adding to the net surplus of global security. They worry too about Europe's sluggish recovery from the economic crisis. But that does not mean Europe has become any less important. Thus while the Pentagon might be upset that its NATO allies across the Atlantic are not doing as much they should, it does at least concede that they are at least contributing something. Furthermore, they are doing so within a collective alliance that has stood the test of time, that is in its own way more than just a coalition of the willing, and which has no equivalent anywhere else in the world; and certainly not in Asia. Indeed, having allies one can trust is of huge significance for the United States. The world would certainly be a much lonelier place without them. If nothing else, they give the United States a set of usable friends in another, very important, part of the world. In purely logistical terms they also provide it with a most important forward base. And at crucial times, it adds significantly to what the United States can do. As even those who have sometimes wondered about the Atlantic relationship's durability have conceded, though the relationship is frequently strained, the United States and the Europeans still have more in common than any other group of states in the international system (Cox, 2012). Nor should we be so surprised by this. After all, countries on both continents are composed of democracies, they both work together with reasonable harmony in most international fora, and in spite of some well-advertised differences, their values are more or less the same. In fact, it may well be that they are so alike in so many ways that they sometimes feel a need to stress their differences when these are, in fact, according to one writer, less of an expression of how divided the two are (compared say to the differences between China and the United States), but rather of how similar they happen to be (Baldwin, 2009).

Finally, if we are thinking in terms of relative power, it is important to determine the extent to which the United States and the EU together are still able to shape events, ideas, and values in other parts of the world. The simple headlines all seem to be telling the same downbeat story: that given their many problems and the rise of new centres of power, both are less and less able to influence what is now going on in an ever more complex international system. There is some truth in this of course. But we have to put things into perspective. These two traditional centres of power might now be less able to determine what is happening globally. It would, however, be absurd to suggest that some other state or combination of states will be replacing them any time soon. For one thing, the United States and EU together continue to exercise a great deal of soft power. They also deploy an enormous amount of hard power too – firstly, because of their economic weight, and secondly, because of their military capabilities. Even those European Kantians have more than their fair share of fighter planes, tanks, aircraft carriers, and the like. Indeed, so wedded have analysts become to the idea that Europe has every other kind of power, other than military, that it is very easy to forget that it spends nearly $400 billion per annum on security. China's spending on defence might be on the rise; and countries like Brazil and Russia have sizeable defence sectors. But the Europeans spend far more than the three put together. When this is then combined with US spending, this adds up to well over 70 per cent of the world's total. By comparison, indeed, in 2010 alone, the United States spent close to $700 billion annually on national security; ten times more than its nearest allies, 14 times more than China. Nor is this asymmetry likely to change any time soon. In fact, all future projections show that the United States will be the only major actor in the world capable of global projection for several decades to come. Iraq might have cost the United States dearly; and Afghanistan might cost it more. But neither war will change what has been true since the end of the Cold War and the collapse of the USSR: that there is still only one serious superpower operating in the international system today.

The China challenge

If the Transatlantic relationship at the heart of the old West remains a good deal more robust than recent gloomy analysis has suggested, how are we to evaluate the longer term prospects of the one country that seems to pose the most problems for the West: namely communist-led China? Much ink has been spilt speculating about its future role in international affairs. Some have even predicted that one day it may even be ruling the world from a position of economic supremacy (Jacques, 2009). This though is most unlikely. The Chinese economy may have proven remarkably resilient over the past few years. Its people might be extraordinarily hard working and entrepreneurial. And its economic demand for the world's primary products a God send to the rest of the capitalist world since the great Western downturn of 2008. Still, one has to maintain a sense of proportion.

First, though China's economic rise has been impressive, it still remains what most experts would see as a most incomplete superpower. Materially more powerful than ever, and playing an ever more influential role around the world, it still faces the international system without a very clear idea of what it is doing. Some have talked of China's increasing soft power, and the more alarmist of its growing military prowess. Still, one aircraft carrier and a handful of *Confucious Institutes* do not add up to a forward strategy or a world view. Moreover, the position that it does espouse – the Westphalian notion that states should not interfere into the internal affairs of other states – seems to be particularly ill-suited for dealing with most of the major security challenges facing the world community today (Westad, 2012).

Furthermore, although China has won more than its fair share of grateful friends on continents like Africa because of its economic largesse, there is little indication (yet) that it is wining hearts and minds as well. China might aid and trade in ever-increasing amounts; it can also buy massive amounts of raw materials and oil. But it has proven rather inept when it comes to acquiring true friends. This is in part cultural. It is also linguistic. It is economic too. Take Africa. Here China has made massive economic inroads. But if various reports from around the continent are to be believed, the Chinese are not only regarded as being aloof and distant; among many small African business people they are also seen as being ruthless competitors whose only ambition seems to be to create a monopoly after they have wiped most of the local competition (Alden, 2007).

The very real problems that China is facing on continents like Africa raises a much bigger question concerning its fragility as a would-be superpower in the international system. Here we might identify at least two big problems: one concerns the relationship between its communist superstructure and its increasingly capitalist base. This, it is clear, not only poses a series of long-term problems to which Chinese leaders do not seem too have an easy answer – hence their continued insecurity in spite of their record growth figures. It would also suggest that China's own very unique model combining Stalinist political rule and dynamic state capitalism might work under Chinese conditions but there is little to suggest that it is for export elsewhere. China might attract admiration; it may also command respect. But there is not much to indicate that it is attracting many imitators. Much has been said of late about "the crisis of democracy" and the rise of the authoritarian alternative. But communist parties no longer rule any serious states in the world today – excluding the deeply unattractive North Korea, the fast evolving Cuba, and Vietnam. Nor is the tide of history moving in that direction.

Indeed, in many ways, China remains a most incomplete actor on the world stage. China has only very limited amounts of soft power; it has few major allies worth the name; and even its hard power capabilities are light years behind those of the West in general and the United States, in particular. Furthermore, for a supposed emerging great power with what some claim are hegemonic ambitions, the Chinese themselves appear to be exceedingly modest about what it is they are seeking to achieve internationally and how far they actually want to go in challenging the existing international order. No doubt there may be those in China who want China to confront the West and the United States more forcefully; and there is some evidence to suggest that these voices might be becoming much louder. Even so, what the more influential voices in China (as opposed to the shrillest) seem to be saying is something that they have been repeating for a very long time: namely that China is still a relatively backward country with all sorts of problems that will take it years to address; therefore it is much wiser to keep one's head down, work within the existing global system, and keep on good terms with the United States (JiSi, 2011).

Conclusion

This chapter began with a discussion about the fate of liberalism following the end of the Cold War – first, during the 1990s when it seemed to be driving everything before it, and then again in the decade long period which followed when it appeared to be facing a major crisis. The crisis, I would agree, was real enough. However, it did not (and has not) undermine the foundations of the larger liberal order as some believed it might. Indeed, as in the past, liberalism has proven to be more than capable of withstanding all manner of body blows. This may in large part be because there is no serious alternative to it as an organizing international principle. But as I have tried to argue, underpinning the liberal order is a system of state power; and as long as the liberal West and the United States retain a power advantage – which they most clearly do – then there is every chance that the order they created will persist.

But what about the future? Here we need to display considerable caution given our past failures in getting the future right. But we would not be risking too much in suggesting that the liberal international order still has much life left in it yet. Certainly, any order that could survive the First World War, the Great Depression, and the immediate post-war crisis – and then go on to outlast the communist challenge during the Cold War – has to have something going for it. Nor has it just outlasted its various competitors. Remarkably, it has also proven increasingly attractive even to those who once trod another political path and economic path. Indeed, having joined the Western economic "club" during the 1990s, elites who once proclaimed the virtues of planning having chosen to walk along the non-market road soon discovered that they could wield far more influence (and become a good deal richer) by working within the system than pitting their energies and resources against it. This will not necessarily lead to a fairer or more equal world. Indeed, all the evidence points to the fact that as liberalism has increased its hold and extended its reach into all our lives, the world has become a much more unequal place. No doubt at some point in the future there will be those who will challenge the new liberal consensus in a serious way. But for the time being, it very much looks as if the next few decades of the twenty-first century are going to be liberal – possibly the most liberal – of all time.

References

Alden, C. (2007), *China in Africa: Partner, Competitor or Hegemon?* London: Zed Books.

Altman, R. (2009), "The Great Crash, 2008", *Foreign Affairs*, 88(1), 2–14.

Baldwin, P. (2009), *The Narcissism of Minor Differences: How America and Europe Are Alike*, New York: Oxford University Press.

Cox, M. (2000), "Wilsonianism Resurgent? The Clinton Administration and the Promotion of Democracy", in M. Cox, G. J. Ikenberry and T. Inogucji (eds) *American Democracy Promotion: Impulses, Strategies and Impacts*, Oxford: Oxford University Press, 218–239.

Cox, M. (2003), "The Empire's Back In Town: Or America's Imperial Temptation – Again?" *Millennium*, 32(1), 1–27.

Cox, M. (2004), "Empire, Imperialism and the Bush Doctrine", *Review of International Studies*, 30, 585–608.

Cox, M. (2007), "Is the United States in Decline – Again?" *International Affairs*, 83(4), 643–653.

Cox, M. (2012), "Report's of the West's Demise and East's Rise are Greatly Exaggerated", *Times Higher Education*, 29 (25 October).

Cox, M. (2012), "Power Shifts, Economic Change and the Decline of the West?" *International Relations*, 26(4), 369–388.

Durfee, D. and Pomfret. J. (2011) "China Struggles to Find a Formula for Innovation", *International Herald Tribune* (6 May).

Financial Times. (2011) http://rankings.ft.com/businessschoolrankings/global-mba-rankings- 2011

Fukuyama, F. (1992), *The End of History and the Last Man*, London: Hamish Hamilton.

Galama, T and Hosek. J. (2008), *U.S. Competitiveness in Science and Technology*, Santa Monica: Rand.

Gilpin, R. (2001), *Global Political Economy: Understanding the International Economic Order*, Princeton N.J: Princeton University Press.

Haas, M. L. (2007), "A Geriatric Peace? The Future of U.S. Power in a World of Aging Populations", *International Security*, 32(1), 112–147.

Halper, S. (2010), *The Beijing Consensus; Legitimizing Authoritarianism in Our Time*, New York: Basic Books.

Hamilton, P. S and Quinlan, J. P. (2011), *The Transatlantic Economy*, Washington D.C.: Center for Transatlantic Relations.

International Monetary Fund. (2010), *World Economic Outlook*, Washington D.C.: International Monetary Fund Publication Services.

Jackson, J. (2011), *US Direct Investment Abroad: Trends and Current Issues*, Washington D.C.: Congressional Research Service.

Jacques, M. (2009), *When China Rules the World: The Rise of the Middle Kingdom and the End of the Western World*, London: Penguin Books.

Jisi, W. (2011), "China's Search for a Grand Strategy: A Rising Great Power Finds its Way", *Foreign Affairs* (March/April).

Kratochwil, F. (1993), "The Embarrassment of Changes: Neo-Realism as the Science of Realpolitik without Politics", *Review of International Studies*, 19(1), 63–80.

Loquenzi, G. (2011), "Still Top of the Charts", *Longitude*, 4, 89–91.

Norloff, C. (2010), *America's Global Advantage: US Hegemony and International Cooperation*, Cambridge: Cambridge University Press.

Quah, D. (2011), "The Global Economy's Shifting Centre of Gravity", *Global Policy*, 2(1), 3–9.

Robinson, W. (1996), *Promoting Polyarchy, Globalization, US Intervention and Hegemony*, Cambridge: Cambridge University Press.

Schwab, K. (ed.) (2010–2011), *The Global Competitiveness Report*, Geneva: World Economic Forum.

Tellis, A. J., Marble, T and Tanner, T. (eds) (2010), Asia's Rising Power and America's Continued Purpose. The National Bureau of Asian Research. *http://www.aei.org/docLib/Asia-Pacific-Demographics-Eberstadt-101410.pdf*

Wade, R. (20 October 2012), "The Art of Power Maintenance: How Western States Keep their Lead in Global Organization", Unpublished MS.

Westad, O. A. (2012), *Restless Empire; China and the World Since 1750*, London: The Bodley Head.

Wheeler, N. J. (2000), *Saving Strangers: Humanitarian Intervention in International Society*, Oxford: Oxford University Press.

Whyte, P. (April 2009), *Narrowing the Atlantic: The Way Forward for EU-US Trade and Investment*, London: Centre for European Reform.

World Fact Book. (2011), Washington D.C.: Central Intelligence Agency.

7
American Statecraft in an Era of Domestic Polarisation

Charles A. Kupchan and Peter L. Trubowitz

Throughout the second half of the twentieth century, American foreign policy was guided by the principles of liberal internationalism.[1] Liberal internationalism, which rested on bipartisan political foundations, maintained that US leadership in global affairs should rely on a combination of military power and international partnership. The presidency of George W. Bush, in terms of both its polarising impact on US politics and its assertive unilateralism, appeared to bring the era of liberal internationalism to an end. Most analysts, however, viewed the Bush presidency as an aberration and expected the election of Barack Obama to restore bipartisan support for liberal internationalist principles and values.

Nonetheless, the anticipated "post-partisan" consensus over foreign policy has not materialised during the Obama presidency. Obama's efforts to restore bipartisanship have yielded meagre results. Congress remains deeply divided over foreign policy. Meanwhile, public opinion polls reveal striking gaps between Republican and Democratic voters on issues ranging from the war on terrorism, to Pentagon spending, to the efficacy of international institutions (Jones, 2010a, 2010b; Pew Research Center, 2012). During the 2012 presidential campaign, Mitt Romney adhered closely to the neoconservative playbook, laying out a foreign policy agenda that contrasted sharply with Obama's. And by the time Obama's bid for re-election was getting up to full speed, he had all but abandoned efforts to run as the guardian of bipartisanship.

Why are both bipartisanship and liberal internationalism in such short supply? In this chapter, we argue that the answers to this question lie in the international and domestic circumstances that Obama inherited upon taking office. For the better part of two decades the international and domestic underpinnings of the liberal internationalist compact have been weakening. The liberal internationalist compact was substantive as well as political. Substantively, it entailed a commitment to exercise US power through multilateral partnership. Politically, liberal internationalism drew broad support from regions of a country that had rarely agreed on domestic or foreign policy. Working together, Democrats and Republicans fashioned a bipartisan consensus behind a new type of US engagement in world affairs. Bipartisanship was to prove crucial to the emergence and longevity of a US grand strategy that twinned power and partnership.

Liberal internationalism's rise was the product of both geopolitical and domestic developments. The threats posed by Nazi Germany, Imperial Japan, and the Soviet Union had a dampening effect on partisan politics in the United States. Meanwhile, the fading of ideological divisions in the body politic made it possible for Democrats and Republicans to coalesce around a common strategy. Abroad, the United States used its superior military power to check potential challenges to stability and an open international economy. But at the same time, it turned to multilateral institutions to attract and reassure the partners needed to defeat fascism and communism. At home, the political environment was ripe for the emergence of a "centrist" coalition. The formation of a North–South alliance, the easing of class tensions due to economic growth and rising incomes, political pragmatism, and ideological moderation were the conditions that led Democrats and Republicans alike to forge what Arthur Schlesinger dubbed the "vital centre" (Schlesinger, 1949). Thus began the era of liberal internationalism.

The geopolitical and domestic conditions that sustained liberal internationalism are no longer present. Since the demise of the Soviet Union, Republicans and Democrats have had fewer incentives to adhere to the liberal internationalist compact. Unipolarity has heightened the geopolitical appeal of unilateralism, a trend that even the threat of transnational terrorism has not reversed; it has also loosened the political discipline engendered by the Cold War threat, leaving US foreign policy more vulnerable to growing partisanship at home. Domestic polarisation has dealt a severe blow to the bipartisan compact between power and cooperation. "Red" and "Blue" America disagree about the nature of US international engagement; growing disparities in wealth have reawakened class tensions, and political pragmatism has been losing ground to ideological extremism.

Instead of adhering to the vital centre, the country's elected officials, along with the public, are backing away from the liberal internationalist compact, supporting *either* US power projection *or* international cooperation, but rarely *both*. Most Republicans have abandoned one side of the liberal internationalist compact: multilateralism has received little but contempt on their watch. Meanwhile, the Democrats have neglected the other side: many party stalwarts are uneasy with the assertive use of US power. As the partisan gyre in Washington widened, the political centre narrowed, and support for liberal internationalism diminished. Today, partisanship over foreign policy has reached levels not seen since the Great Depression.

In this chapter, we argue that there is little reason to expect America to rekindle its commitment to liberal internationalism, whose halcyon era is over; the bipartisan compact between power and partnership has been dismantled. If left unattended, the political foundations of US statecraft will continue to disintegrate, exposing the country to the dangers of an erratic and incoherent foreign policy. To avoid this fate, US leaders will have to fashion a new brand of internationalism – one that will necessarily entail less power and less partnership if it is to have a chance of securing broad domestic support. To find a new equilibrium between the nation's commitments abroad and its polarised politics at home, the United States will need a grand strategy that is as selective and judicious as it is purposeful.

Bipartisanship and the rise of the liberal internationalist compact

Scholars and policymakers alike tend to associate liberal internationalism with multilateralism and international institutions. Liberal internationalism does entail a commitment to multilateralism, but it also involves a commitment to the use of military force. Indeed, it was the dual commitment to power projection and international cooperation that distinguished liberal internationalism from earlier strategies.

From the United States' emergence as a great power at the end of the nineteenth century until the 1940s, its political class favoured power or cooperation, but not the two together. Theodore Roosevelt preferred power, taking advantage of a strengthened presidency to pursue an imperialist agenda in Latin America and Asia – but one whose ambition quickly outstripped political support for such expansionism. Woodrow Wilson favoured cooperation, embracing the League of Nations and collective security – but the Senate rejected taking on institutionalised commitments to multilateralism.

Franklin Delano Roosevelt was the first president to blend these two traditions. Franklin Roosevelt's coupling of power and partnership was perhaps most evident in his so-called Great Design – his vision of a cooperative security system in which China, Britain, the Soviet Union, and the United States would form a consortium of great powers to collectively manage the postwar order and put down threats to the peace. Roosevelt dubbed the system the "Four Policemen", envisaging a directorate that resembled the Concert of Europe, which emerged after the defeat of Napoleonic France in 1815. By virtue of its sheer power, the United States would be the first among equals in such a directorate, relying on its primacy to extend its political and economic influence. The Great Design, like the Concert, would embrace a shared set of understandings and norms; territorial issues and political disputes were to be resolved through consultation and compromise. These ideas shaped Roosevelt's diplomacy at the Yalta Conference in 1945, and they found concrete expression in the United Nations and the Bretton Woods system.

Roosevelt's approach to grand strategy was distinguished not just by the marriage of power and cooperation, but also by the exceptional nature of the political support it enjoyed in Washington and the polity at large. Indeed, the rise of liberal internationalism in the United States corresponded with an unprecedented surge in bipartisan cooperation on matters of foreign affairs.[2] As Figure 7.1 illustrates, the politics of foreign policy was deeply partisan prior to the Second World War. In the 1940s bipartisan cooperation increased sharply on foreign policy and, to a lesser extent, on domestic policy. Between the Japanese attack on Pearl Harbour in 1941 and the Tet Offensive in South Vietnam in 1968, members of Congress reached across the aisle nearly three out of every four times they voted on foreign policy legislation. In contrast, bipartisanship occurred about half the time on domestic policy issues. On the basic elements of grand strategy – when military force should be used, the importance of international support, and the role of multilateral institutions – consensus was the norm. Intent on avoiding Wilson's mistakes, his agenda for collective security being deeply partisan, Roosevelt ensured that the United Nations Charter was devoid of provisions that might provoke Republican objections. He also sought to make Republicans stakeholders in his foreign policy by appointing members of the opposition to important foreign policy posts and working closely with Wendell Willkie, the candidate he defeated in the 1940 election, to combat

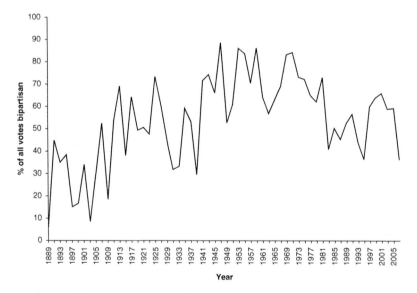

Figure 7.1   Trends in bipartisanship, 1889–2008
Note: Only year of first session in each Congress is labelled.
Source: Voteview.com

isolationism. As Figure 7.1 demonstrates, bipartisan cooperation on foreign policy waned after the Second World War – but only temporarily. It revived with the onset of the Cold War and the rise of the Soviet threat, with Democrats and Republicans closing ranks around the liberal internationalist agenda launched under Roosevelt's watch.

Harry Truman's administration worked closely with lawmakers on Capitol Hill to promote economic recovery, rearmament, and stability in Western Europe. The Marshall Plan and the General Agreement on Tariffs and Trade both enjoyed broad bipartisan support. The United States took the lead in fashioning the North Atlantic Treaty Organisation (NATO) and a host of other alliances, bolstering these pacts with the forward deployment of US troops. A fierce partisan battle over Truman's management of the Korean War did break out during the 82nd Congress (1951–1952), but it was short-lived. As Figure 7.1 makes clear, the bipartisan consensus behind the armistice of 1953 was then to extend until the late 1960s, when it began to be tested by the Vietnam War.

The bipartisanship nurtured by Roosevelt – and sustained by his successors – was intimately linked to the rise of liberal internationalism for three main reasons. Firstly, bipartisanship made possible the political entrepreneurship needed to launch liberal internationalism. A commitment to power and partnership represented a dramatic departure in foreign policy, opening its backers to criticism from the left and right. Secondly, inasmuch as liberal internationalism is both "internationalist" and "liberal", its implementation required broad institutional support, not just strong leadership by the executive branch. The projection of power necessitated that members of Congress were prepared to accept the maintenance of a large military establishment, a sizable defence budget, and the potential sacrifice of US lives in distant missions, three planks that had been long resisted by isolationists and had served as the source of protracted partisan conflict in the past. Thirdly, bipartisanship proved critical to the implementation of liberal internationalism because it provided for constancy and continuity in foreign policy beyond electoral change. During the nineteenth century and the first half of the twentieth, US foreign policy regularly lurched among stark alternatives as control over Congress and the White House changed hands.[3] The coalition of Democrats and Republicans cobbled together by Roosevelt was its political base, and remained so during the Cold War. In this respect, the fortunes of the liberal internationalist compact were directly linked to the strength of the bipartisan centre in US politics, and, as we show in the next section, the international and domestic circumstances that gave rise to it.

The geopolitical sources of liberal internationalism

From the outbreak of the Second World War until the collapse of the Soviet Union, the presence of powerful aggressor states encouraged strong domestic support for a compact between power and cooperation. Even before the United States entered the war, many of the country's leading strategic thinkers (e.g. Isaiah Bowman, Edward Mead Earle, and Nicholas Spykman) had concluded that distance was no longer a reliable guarantee of the nation's security (Bowman, 1928; Earle, 1941; Spykman, 1942). Instead, the United States would have to prevent any single power or group of powers from establishing control over the Eurasian heartland and rimland– the huge landmass extending from Iberia to Siberia. Doing so would require not just the projection of military power, but also the consensual help of allies that shared strategic priorities.

The same intuition about the benefits of linking power and partnership lay at the heart of Truman's strategy of containment. The United States alone did not have sufficient economic and military resources to check the threat posed by Soviet and Chinese expansionism. Allies would be needed to supply the troops needed to balance Soviet and Chinese power and to provide staging areas to deploy US forces across the geographic expanse of Eurasia. Washington also needed a global network of alliances for political reasons – to shore up the Western democracies and their partners in Asia and the Third World by ensuring that these states did not drift towards neutrality or align with the opposing bloc.

Geopolitical and economic imperatives drove the effort to establish a liberal economic order. American elites believed that economic nationalism and mercantilist trade policies had helped set the great powers on the path to the Second World War – hence the need for an open trading system that would benefit all democracies and counter the logic of zero-sum competition. In addition, only if US allies in Europe and Asia enjoyed a speedy and robust economic recovery, would they be able to withstand the military and ideological threat posed by Soviet communism. Justifying economic aid for European recovery on geopolitical rather than humanitarian grounds was key to winning Republican support for the Marshall Plan. The reduction of impediments to trade, the financial institutions fashioned at Bretton Woods, and foreign aid all became central planks of the liberal internationalist agenda.

The Cold War also exercised a disciplining effect on US politics. As during the Second World War, strategic necessity was invoked to tame partisan gamesmanship. By identifying liberal internationalism with anti-communism, Truman and his successors made it politically treacherous for Democrats and Republicans alike to pursue alternative policies. The fear of being labelled soft on communism weaned politicians away from Wilsonianism as well as isolationism. Concurrently, the nuclear era made the potential consequences of recklessness or belligerence unacceptable, keeping politicians from straying too far to the right. When politicians ignored the need for centrism – as did George McGovern on the left and Barry Goldwater on the right – they paid at the polls.

The domestic sources of liberal internationalism

Conditions inside as well as outside the United States were ripe for the onset of an era of bipartisanship. The task of building broad support for liberal internationalism was significantly advanced by profound changes in the country's political landscape that had opened up new opportunities for bipartisan cooperation. Roosevelt occupied the White House at a moment when domestic as well as international circumstances made "going bipartisan" in foreign policy an attractive political strategy for Democrats and Republicans alike (Skowronek, 1997). The convergence of foreign policy interests between the country's northern and southern states and the dampening of ideological differences among elites and the public played important roles in consolidating liberal internationalism.

The North–South alliance

By the mid-1940s, a combination of war, trade, and industrialisation had brought about a major shift in the regional alignments underpinning US foreign policy (Trubowitz, 1998). For decades, the North and South had differed sharply over foreign trade and the size of the military. The Republican North supported a stronger military and protectionist policies towards Europe, invariably running afoul of the Democratic South, which favoured liberalised trade abroad and a smaller federal government at home. By the interwar period, however, rapid industrialisation had transformed the United States into the world's leading economic power. The urban Northeast was the primary beneficiary of the economic expansion. By the time Roosevelt took office in 1933, the Northeast's rising position in the world economy was increasing the region's support for economic openness and giving it a direct interest in the prosperity and stability of Europe, its main export market. After the Depression years, the North was coming to favour a more activist role for the United States in liberalising and stabilising the international system.

As northern support for liberal internationalism increased, so did opportunities for political alliance with the South. Southern elites had their own reasons for backing the liberal internationalist compact. Loyalty to Roosevelt and the Democratic Party certainly played a role. But economic interests were paramount. The South's export of raw materials was still the mainstay of its economy. Southern dependence on international stability and open markets readily translated into support for multilateral institutions such as the United Nations and the Bretton Woods system, which promised to check aggression and prevent the spread of economic nationalism. Meanwhile, military bases and supporting enterprises sprouted throughout the South. A commitment to a foreign policy that combined power and cooperation was now as good for the "martial metropolises" of the South as it was for the urban Northeast.

Converging economic interests were not the only source of the new North–South alliance. The Democratic Party, long based in the South, benefited from the flow of southerners to the North's factories, as well as the party's growing appeal to northern voters. For the first time, the party had a foothold in the North, enabling it to span the Mason-Dixon line. Democrats in the North and South disagreed sharply about civil rights and labour regulation. But they nonetheless found common cause in the fight against economic nationalism, fascism, and communism. This North–South consensus within the Democratic Party paved the way for the sweeping changes in foreign policy orchestrated by Roosevelt and Truman, and then embraced by their successors.

Republicans approached liberal internationalism more tentatively, with the party divided along East–West lines. Dwight Eisenhower (and later Richard Nixon) had to balance the competing interests of the party's eastern wing, which had embraced liberal internationalism, against its western wing in the Great Plains and Mountain West, which had not. This divergence was due in part to western fears of competition from overseas producers of cheap agricultural goods and raw materials. The western wing was also concerned about expenditures on foreign assistance and defence – outlays that bestowed disproportionate benefits on the Northeast and South. Until Ronald Reagan's administration, this intraparty divide compelled Republican leaders to favour liberal internationalism "lite". They looked for ways to limit the cost of maintaining order and openness on the Eurasian landmass by substituting, where possible, allies for arms. Eisenhower presided over the construction of multilateral alliances along the Sino-Soviet perimeter, such as the Southeast Asian Treaty Organisation and the Central Treaty Organisation, while Nixon sought to reduce the costs of containment though various means, including the opening to China, the nurturing of "regional policemen", such as Iran, and arms control with the Soviets.

Republican support for liberal internationalism was thus consistently more qualified than Democratic support. The Republican rank and file was divided over the virtues of free trade, military spending (at least on conventional weapons), and presidential prerogative in making foreign policy. Republicans in the heartland competed with their "Rockefeller" brethren in the East for control of the party's foreign policy agenda. Nonetheless, liberal internationalism had sufficient backing within the Republican Party as a whole to clear the way for a sustainable bipartisan consensus.

The rise of the moderates

The post-Second World War electoral landscape was considerably less polarised than before on regional as well as socio-economic lines – remarkably so, given that class had initially been the principal axis along which the politics of the New Deal was organised. But as V.O. Key explained, and the seminal study *The American Voter* later confirmed, class had declined as the defining feature of political parties after the Second World War (Campbell et al., 1960; Key, 1958: 274). The rapid economic expansion fuelled by the war and the post-war boom were the most important reasons for this change. As it often does, economic growth acted like a political balm, easing the class tensions sparked by the Depression and making it easier for the country's political leaders to find common ground on foreign and domestic policy. Looking back on the period, Walter Dean Burnham (1970: 304) wrote, "The period since 1950 may legitimately be described as one of great confusion in American party politics, a period in which the classic New Deal alignment seems to have evaporated without being replaced by an equally structured ordering of politics".

The narrowing of ideological differences accompanied the decline of region and class as important political dividing lines. Indeed, by the end of the Eisenhower era, the emergence of a pragmatic, moderate centre had prompted Harvard sociologist Daniel Bell (1960) to pronounce "the end of ideology". On Capitol Hill, this development manifested itself in the rise of a "moderate bloc" – a group of lawmakers who were more likely to vote with the opposing party than their own. Conservative Democrats (mostly from the South) regularly aligned with Republicans as part of the so-called Conservative Coalition, while liberal Republicans (mostly from the eastern seaboard) reached out to the left, aligning with northern Democrats. Figure 7.2 reveals the substantial moderate presence in Congress by the 1950s. The unusually centrist character of American politics after the Second World War helped consolidate the bipartisan foreign policy compact between power and cooperation.

Public opinion for the most part tracked elite opinion. On the critical foreign policy question of the era – how to deal with the Soviet Union – Republicans and Democrats generally saw eye to eye. As Figure 7.3 indicates, from the 1948 Berlin Blockade through the escalation of the Vietnam War, Republican and Democratic voters shared much common ground on the appropriate mix of military power and diplomacy needed to counter the Soviet threat. Some years the public was more inclined to support the use of military force; other years, voters preferred greater reliance on negotiation and diplomacy. Nonetheless, partisan affiliation had little impact on preferences; shifts in popular attitudes did not run along party lines.

Moreover, voters from both parties embraced the idea that power, as well as diplomacy, was needed to navigate the geopolitical shoals of superpower rivalry, reflecting the public's willingness to support both defence spending and arms control during the Cold War. Public backing for power projection and collaboration also helped explain why Republican and Democratic administrations alike consistently sought to strike a balance between preventing communist expansion and taking actions that risked triggering a confrontation with the Soviet Union.

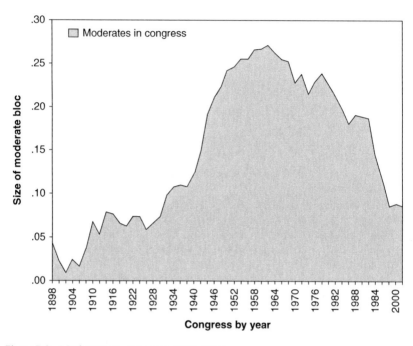

Figure 7.2 Moderates in Congress: 1897–2004
Source: Calculated from Keith Poole and Howard Rosenthal nominate score

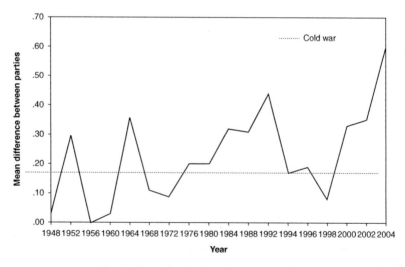

Figure 7.3 Party polarization in the electorate over foreign policy, 1984–2004
Source: National election studies survey data, presidential election years

The demise of the liberal internationalist compact

Despite its impressive political foundations, the liberal internationalist compact did not survive the Cold War's end. Many scholars have chronicled the erosion of liberal internationalism in the United States – and most attribute it to the Bush presidency (see, e.g., Busby and Monten, 2008; Campbell and O'Hanlon, 2006; Daalder and Lindsay, 2003; Fukuyama, 2004; Hart, 2004; Ikenberry, 2004). According to its numerous critics, the Bush administration's sceptical attitude towards international institutions, its belief in the order-producing effects of the assertive use of military force, and its combative approach to neutralising domestic opponents have all taken their toll on liberal internationalism. Although this interpretation is partly correct, the liberal internationalist compact started coming apart well before Bush took office. Indeed, by the 2000 elections, the bipartisan coalition behind liberal internationalism was already in serious disarray.

The roots of liberal internationalism's demise stretch back to the 1970s and the sharp ideological conflicts over foreign policy that emerged during the Vietnam War. While many Americans remained staunch proponents of the militarised containment of Soviet communism, many others began to charge that the United States had fallen prey to errant leadership, exaggerated threats, and the excessive use of power. High levels of defence spending and the extension of Cold War rivalry to the developing world no longer enjoyed steady, bipartisan support. Republicans and Democrats alike continued to back peacetime military deployments in Western Europe and East Asia, and they stood behind an open international economy. But beginning in the 1970s even these fundamental tenets of liberal internationalism were open to challenge on Capitol Hill. Lawmakers on the left tried to curb the use of US military power, while their conservative counterparts looked for ways to reduce the nation's reliance on international institutions and multilateral diplomacy.

The intensification of US–Soviet rivalry during the 1980s bolstered flagging support for the liberal internationalist compact. Liberal internationalism, however, never fully recovered from the political divides produced by the Vietnam War, the Civil Rights movement, and the duress caused by the economic downturn of the 1970s. As Figure 7.1 indicates, despite a temporary increase in the early Reagan years, bipartisanship over foreign policy never returned to the levels of the 1950s and 1960s. The incomplete restoration of bipartisanship in part reflected conflicting judgements about the gravity of the geopolitical risks posed by nuclear parity and the more assertive turn in Soviet foreign policy. But conditions at home had also changed. The Vietnam War left behind the scars of a divided nation: Ronald Reagan was a polarising president; and the North–South alliance of the Roosevelt era was giving way to new tensions between the increasingly Republican South and the increasingly Democratic North.

The liberal internationalist compact, although it began to erode in the 1970s and was only partly repaired in the 1980s, did not meet its demise until the end of the Cold War. Partisan divisions over the Persian Gulf War of 1991 were a harbinger of a widening foreign policy gap between Republicans and Democrats. Partisan differences arose as the war approached; the Senate authorised the use of military force to expel the Iraqi army from Kuwait by only a slim margin – 52–47 – with the vote breaking primarily along party lines. Nonetheless, the norms of liberal internationalism prevailed in terms of both the conduct of the war and public support for it. President George H.W. Bush sought and received the authorisation of the UN Security Council "to use all necessary means [...] to restore international peace and security in the area".[4] More than 70 per cent of the US public supported Operation Desert Storm once it began – in part because the war enjoyed broad international backing. Almost 40 nations contributed ground, sea, or air forces, with foreign countries committing some 200,000 personnel to the conflict. Coalition allies also made significant financial contributions, covering $54 billion of the total cost of $61 billion.

Bush, however, could not translate military success into either re-election or consensus. The partisan divisions that arose in the face of definitive victory in 1991 proved more lasting than the partisanship fuelled by setbacks in Korea some 40 years earlier. As Figure 7.1 shows, bipartisanship dropped significantly during the first half of the 1990s, reaching a post-Second World War low in the 104th Congress (1996–1997). As the Senate minority leader Tom Daschle noted in 1996, "The Cold War exerted a powerful hold on America, and it forced the parties to work together to advance American interests through bipartisan internationalism. [...] The tragedy is that such cooperation increasingly seems an artefact of the past" (Daschle, 1996).

Democrats more regularly identified with one half of the liberal internationalist compact – 'partnership' – while playing down the other – 'power'. The Clinton administration only hesitantly embraced the assertive use of the military. It promptly withdrew from Somalia in 1993 after US personnel suffered fatalities. The Clinton White House also consistently sought to limit the risk to American forces by relying primarily on air power when using force – as in the high-altitude bombing campaign used to drive Yugoslav forces from Kosovo in 1999. Meanwhile, international institutions and treaties fast became marred by partisan conflict, especially after the Republican Party captured control of Congress in 1994. The Clinton administration dragged its feet on signing onto the International Criminal Court and the Kyoto Protocol, but eventually supported US participation in both. Congress, however, was enthusiastic about neither pact. Clinton sent the Comprehensive Test Ban Treaty (CTBT) to the Senate, where Republicans promptly voted it down. He turned to multilateralism to bring peace to Kosovo, but the Republican House refused to pass a resolution endorsing the NATO campaign. Instead, Republicans claimed that the Clinton administration's penchant for multilateralism was compromising US sovereignty. As John Bolton, who would later become undersecretary of state and then UN ambassador in the George W. Bush administration, wrote towards the end of the Clinton administration, "globalists" were imposing "harm and costs to the United States [by] belittling our popular sovereignty and constitutionalism, and restricting both our domestic and our international policy flexibility and power" (Bolton, 2000: 206).

If Clinton tilted towards international partnership, George W. Bush veered towards military power. Secretary of Defence Donald Rumsfeld promised a "revolution" in the country's war-fighting capability and, especially after 9/11, the Pentagon's budget soared. With both the White House and the Congress in Republican hands, Bush gave multilateral cooperation and international institution-building short shrift. Soon after entering office, Bush renounced the Kyoto Protocol, International Criminal Court, and Antiballistic Missile Treaty. He declined offers of NATO involvement in the war against the Taliban in Afghanistan, and then went to war in Iraq without UN authorisation and with only a handful of allies. Through much of his first term, Bush and his top advisers were openly dismissive of international institutions and multilateralism.

President Bush's unilateralism exacerbated partisan tensions at home, as did his governing style. During the 2000 presidential campaign, Bush had promised to govern as "a uniter, not a divider" (Bush, 2000). Once in office, however, he consistently tacked away from the centre, urged by his political advisers to exploit partisan differences. His chief pollster had declared in a memo that the once vaunted centre of US electoral politics had collapsed and political strategies aimed at capturing it would backfire (Edsall, 2006).[5] The underlying logic of the memo was that the most effective policies would be polarising ones – those designed to mobilise the Republican Party's base.

Even after 9/11, with the wars in Afghanistan and Iraq creating a need for national unity, Bush subordinated consensus building to wedge politics. Whereas Roosevelt and his successors sought to foster bipartisanship in foreign policy, the Bush administration used foreign policy as a tool of partisan warfare, especially at election time. In the 2004 presidential election, Bush focused his campaign on the threat of terrorism, charging that the country would "invite disaster" if the Democrats were to win (Alberts, 2004). Vice President Richard Cheney pursued the same critique of the opposition, warning, "If we make the wrong choice [of candidates], then the danger is that we'll get hit again" (quoted in Silva, 2006). Following the election, the Economist (2004) concluded, "America is more bitterly divided than it has been for a generation." The rhetoric continued in the 2006 midterm elections, with Bush insinuating that a Democratic victory means, "The terrorists win and America loses" (Abramowitz, 2006)

Despite the backdrop of 9/11 and the wars that followed, partisanship in US politics intensified. Instead of ushering in an era of revived political cooperation, the terrorist attacks produced only a brief upturn in bipartisanship. During the 108th Congress (2003–2004), voting on foreign policy returned to the pre-9/11 pattern. By the time the Democrats took back the House and Senate in the 2006 mid-terms, the gap had only widened. When the 110th Congress (2007–2008) took its first votes on the Iraq War, only 17 of 201 Republicans in the House joined the Democrats to oppose the surge of US troops into Baghdad. In the Senate, only two Republicans joined the Democrats to approve a resolution calling for a timetable for withdrawal. In contrast, 95 per cent of House and Senate Democrats voted to withdraw US troops in 2008. According to one widely used index, Congress is today more politically fractious and polarised than at any time in the last 100 years.[6]

The Geopolitical sources of liberal internationalism's decline

It is no accident that bipartisanship and liberal internationalism weakened as the Cold War faded into the past. The presence of a nuclear-armed competitor promoted strategic restraint, as did Washington's interest in developing the rules and frameworks needed to sustain cooperation among the Western allies, and recognition of the need to win support at home and abroad for US leadership. Unipolarity provides a very different set of geopolitical and domestic incentives. The absence of a counterpoise has left American power unchecked. During the 1990s, unquestioned primacy and the sense of invulnerability that came with it weakened both sides of the compact between power and partnership. The defence budget shrank; absent the Soviet threat, the country could afford to lighten its load overseas. Unipolarity also meant greater ambivalence towards multilateral engagement. The United States could now shirk off some of the constraining institutional obligations it assumed during the Cold War.

While unipolarity afforded the geopolitical freedom that fuelled neo-isolationist and unilateralist alternatives to liberal internationalism, it also weakened the perceived need for political discipline and bipartisan cooperation. The priority assigned to matters of national security declined and public indifference to foreign policy increased, leaving politicians more free to expose foreign policy to partisan purpose. During the Clinton years, important ambassadorial posts were left vacant because the Republicans refused to confirm the president's nominees. The Senate preferred to vote down the CTBT rather than let the White House withdraw it from consideration. As Republican Senator Chuck Hagel explained, such manoeuvres were fundamentally partisan in nature: "What this is about on the Republican side is a deep dislike and distrust for President Clinton".[7] The public's diminishing interest in matters of state both fuelled and was the product of elite indifference. Media coverage of foreign affairs plunged. The time allocated to international news by the main television networks fell by more than 65 per cent between 1989 and 2000. The space devoted to international news in the mainstream print media experienced a similar decline.[8]

Even with the new sense of threat that emerged after 9/11, unipolarity continued to favour unilateralism. The United States felt strong enough to deal with Islamic extremists on its own, turning down NATO's offer of help in Afghanistan and invading Iraq with only a few allies in tow. The Bush administration and many of its supporters judged traditional allies such as France and Germany as strategic impediments, their opposition to the Iraq war stemming from their desire to contain US power (Kagan, 2003; Mead, 2004). The difficulties that the United States has since encountered in bringing stability to Afghanistan and Iraq have made clear that the Bush administration overestimated both the merits of unilateralism and the utility of superior military force. During his second term, President Bush was more solicitous of allies and more willing to engage in multilateral diplomacy. In 2007, Washington concluded a deal with North Korea to close down its nuclear programme and agreed to negotiate directly with Iran. But these moves represented tactical adjustments in the face of dwindling alternatives, not a return to bipartisanship or the liberal internationalist fold.

Terrorism and the false promise of unity

Many scholars expected the events of 9/11 to restore Washington's enthusiasm for partnership at home and abroad (Fukuyama, 2001; Ikenberry, 2001). As we have shown above, in the immediate aftermath of the attacks, bipartisanship did increase. It had dropped off again by 2003, however, with partisan differences emerging over a range of foreign policy matters. Underlying changes in the US political landscape, which we detail below, were the most potent impediments to the durable reconstitution of a bipartisan centre. But the nature of the new threat – Islamic extremism and transnational terrorism rather than Soviet communism and inter-state war – also stood in the way of the return of the liberal internationalist compact after 9/11.

Unlike the threat posed by an expansionist power, that posed by international terrorism is sporadic and elusive. Many of the most effective countermeasures – law enforcement, intelligence gathering, and covert operations – do not easily lend themselves to consensus building. The greatest successes are unreported non-events: terrorist attacks that are averted or never planned. The country is ostensibly at war, but Americans are not being asked to head to recruiting stations or man production lines. The nation is not collectively involved in the struggle as it was during the Second World War or the Cold War. In these respects, the fight against terrorism does not readily inspire a sense of shared national purpose and sacrifice.

Terrorism has encouraged multilateralism, but only on a limited number of policy items – such as sharing intelligence, cooperating on law enforcement, and freezing the terrorists' sources of financial support. On the central question of military response, terrorism has tended to provoke unilateral retaliation rather than new institutions, multilateral diplomacy, or joint military action. The United States chose to be largely on its own when it invaded Afghanistan and Iraq. Israel has faced terror strikes on its territory for decades, but it has been alone when it responds. The same is true for Britain and its struggle against the Irish Republican Army, and for France and its fight against terrorists from North Africa and the Middle East. This pattern of unilateral response arises from the military requirements of counterterrorist operations. Missions against terrorist networks usually entail special operations and covert action, both of which demand unity of command and close-hold planning.

Historical precedents also suggest that the threat of Islamic extremism may over time lead Americans to raise protective barriers at home rather than to project military power abroad or reinforce multilateral institutions. Terrorism, after all, helped convince Britain and France to retreat from the Middle East and other areas where they were not welcome. And prior to 9/11, it is notable that the United States generally reacted to terrorist attacks on its overseas assets by pulling them out – as in Beirut in 1983, Somalia in 1993, and Yemen in 2000. In the aftermath of the chaos and violence that have wracked Afghanistan and Iraq since the US invasions, Americans may conclude that the best way to guarantee security at home is cordoning the country off from trouble in the Middle East.

Globalisation and international cooperation

Some scholars argue that globalisation provides strong incentives for Democrats and Republicans alike to return to liberal internationalism. According to John Ikenberry, "As global economic interdependence grows, so does the need for multilateral coordination of policies" (Ikenberry, 2003: 540). Combating climate change, advancing global health, and preventing genocide are other challenges that provide Washington good reason to pursue pragmatic collaboration with like-minded states. The US should create "institutions and partnerships that give liberal democracies the collective capacities to protect themselves and solve common problems, both within and alongside existing international institutions" (Ikenberry and Slaughter, 2006: 59).

Interdependence and the growth resulting from foreign trade and investment have helped sustain the United States' enthusiasm for economic openness and its support for multilateral trade and investment regimes. However, globalisation is no guarantee of greater international cooperation. Indeed, as the protectionism and economic nationalism of the interwar period made clear, interdependence can have the opposite effect amid sharp downturns in the international economy. In the United States, the dislocations associated with outsourcing, current account and budget deficits, and higher oil prices have already strengthened protectionist impulses across the political spectrum. As for global warming, the United States has kept its distance from multilateral regimes intended to contain the emission of greenhouse gases. And even if it acted otherwise, collaborative efforts to cut emissions – or, for that matter, find an AIDS vaccine – would not constitute the programmatic investment in institution-building that is central to the liberal internationalist agenda.

The domestic sources of liberal internationalism's decline

Both the rise and demise of liberal internationalism were the product of domestic as well as international circumstances. Indeed, when historians look back on this period, they may well judge domestic developments to be more decisive than geopolitical ones in explaining liberal internationalism's demise. Important shifts inside the United States – predating the collapse of the Soviet empire – have weakened the bipartisan foundations of liberal internationalism and politicised the making of foreign policy.

The return of regional divides

The United States is today experiencing the return of important regional divides; partisan differences are again running along regional lines, making it more difficult to sustain a centrist coalition. Once the core of the Democratic Party, the South is now the Republican Party's main regional power base. At the end of the Second World War, the Democrats "owned" virtually every southern seat in Congress. In the 1970s and 1980s, Republicans made significant gains in the South. By the mid-1990s, they had captured a majority of the South's congressional seats and their hold on the region has only strengthened since.

This Republican drive was actually part of an effective two-pronged "southern strategy" aimed at the West as well as the South. By the time of Bush's 2000 presidential campaign, the party had a virtual lock on the geographic zone that Republican political strategists called the "Big L" – the states stretching from Montana south to Arizona and east to Georgia. Moderate "Rockefeller" Republicans from the Northeast have all but disappeared from the party caucus, paving the way for a conservative takeover. Meanwhile, Democrats in Congress increasingly hail from liberal states in the Northeast and along the Pacific Coast. New England, whose congressional delegations used to be heterogeneous in their partisan composition, has become a Democratic bastion. And as conservative Democrats in the South have gradually lost their seats to Republicans, the Democratic caucus has moved to the left.

From the 1950s to the 1980s, the delegations that states sent to Congress were heterogeneous in their partisan makeup. So were the regional coalitions that formed on Capitol Hill on foreign policy matters. In the last 20 years, congressional delegations have become more politically homogeneous, making it more difficult to build coalitions across partisan and regional divides.

Economic trends have expedited a divergence of interest and outlook across regions and have reinforced the efforts of both parties to secure territorial strongholds. Even before the Berlin Wall came down, higher tax rates, labour costs, and energy prices in the Northeast and Midwest made it harder for elected officials from states in those regions to find common ground on foreign and domestic policy with lawmakers from the South and Mountain West, who had competing economic concerns. The uneven effects of globalisation during the 1990s exacerbated regional economic disparities and tensions. The outsourcing of jobs hit the aging industrial centres of the North especially hard. Well-paying, unionised jobs in manufacturing were the first to be lost as production lines were moved abroad and imports arrived from low-wage economies. Once the leading edge of liberal internationalism, the Northeast and Midwest have been at the forefront of recent efforts to rein in the United States' commitment to free trade. Winning support on Capitol Hill for the liberalisation of foreign trade now depends on the backing of congressional delegations from Red states in the South and Mountain West.

The South and the West have also provided the surest support for foreign policies that put a premium on military power. While some analysts attribute these regional differences to strategic subcultures – southerners are said to be more nationalistic and less willing to accept the constraints on national autonomy – changes in the economic and political geography of military spending and production have also made it harder for politicians from different parts of the country to agree on national security policy. Since the 1970s, Pentagon spending on military procurement and research and development has benefited the South and West at the expense of the Northeast and Midwest, contributing to the decline of the manufacturing sector in the North. In addition, Southern and Western states that make up the so-called gun belt have consistently received a larger share of the resources spent on military bases and personnel.

Demographic developments have also contributed to partisan and regional cleavages. Recent immigration and population movements inside the United States have combined to produce a more politically balkanised country – what demographer William Frey (2003) calls the "two Americas". One America is multiracial and multi-ethnic. It is based in the metropolitan areas along the East and West coasts and in the Great Lakes region, the preferred destinations for many immigrants making their way to US shores from less developed countries. These communities are largely liberal and Democratic. The other America, largely white and from working- or middle-class backgrounds, is also on the move, leaving the multiracial urban centres of the rustbelt and heading to the growing sunbelt economies of the South and Mountain West, where electoral reapportionment magnifies their political weight. These communities are growing more conservative and Republican. As each of the "two Americas" grows more homogeneous, the political gap between them widens, adding to the impediments facing bipartisan cooperation.

Moderates: A dwindling breed

In the 1950s, authoritative voices complained that the absence of substantive differences between the two main political parties was leaving the United States without adequate deliberation and choice. At present, the prevalent worry is that Democrats and Republicans share little, if any, common ground on the main domestic and foreign policy issues, leaving the country divided and adrift. The Council on Foreign Relations saw fit to issue a report calling for urgent efforts to rebuild a bipartisan consensus on foreign policy (Roman, 2005). A group of foreign policy luminaries from both parties founded the Partnership for a Secure America with the primary aim of "recreating the bipartisan centre in American national security and foreign policy".[9] Congress mandated the formation of the Iraq Study Group to forge a policy on Iraq that might enjoy support from both sides of the aisle. As co-chair, James Baker, commented after presenting the report to President Bush, "This is the only bipartisan report that's going to be out there" (Lehrer, 2006).

The concerns of these and similar groups are entirely justified; the political centre in the United States has effectively collapsed. Conservative Democrats and liberal Republicans are a dying breed. The gap between the parties has widened; both are veering away from the ideological commonalities upon which the bipartisan centre was based during the Cold War. Many of the most conservative Democrats in Congress used to be more conservative than the most liberal Republicans. But this overlap has all but disappeared, making it harder to fashion the pragmatic compromises that long sustained liberal internationalism (Stonecash et al., 2003; Theriault, 2006). As Figure 7.2 makes clear, the collapse of the moderates began before the end of the Cold War, but it accelerated in the 1990s, driven by the Republican takeover of Congress and the leadership of House speaker Newt Gingrich. Not since the 1920s have so few lawmakers consistently identified with the political centre. Pragmatism, so vital to liberal internationalism, has given way to ideological extremism.

The Red versus Blue divide both reflects and accelerates this erosion of ideological centrism. As Red America becomes more conservative and Blue America more liberal, the parties that represent these two regions grow further apart ideologically. Congressional redistricting has made matters worse by creating many more safe seats than there were in the past. Partisan gerrymandering to lock up competitive or swing districts has turned into a regularised mechanism for protecting the incumbent party, thereby encouraging ideological conformity and party-line voting. When constituencies tilt heavily towards one party, candidates have little reason to adopt centrist positions to appeal to swing voters and independents. Once lawmakers are in office, the relatively homogenous make-up of their electoral base gives them few incentives to reach out across the aisle. Redistricting has thus diminished the political demand for and the payoffs of bipartisanship.

The sharpening of socio-economic cleavages is contributing to the ideological polarisation in partisan competition. For many Americans, wages have not kept pace with inflation as wealth disparities have increased. Pressure from Americans disadvantaged by globalisation has led some Democratic lawmakers to back away from support for free trade, breaking with the Republicans on this issue and undermining one of the last policy planks of the liberal internationalist compact. Indeed, during the summer of 2007 Congress stripped the White House of "fast track" authority over trade, hampering the administration's ability to secure new free trade agreements. If post-war prosperity was the political balm that soothed ideological clashes over socio-economic issues, the inequities of globalisation are bringing them back to life.

The polarisation of party politics has also been increasingly evident in the public's views of foreign policy. To be sure, the United States' broad engagement in global affairs continues to enjoy substantial support among the public (see Kull and Destler, 1999; Page and Bouton, 2006). Like their elected representatives in Washington, however, voters often sharply disagree about the character of that engagement. One study of public attitudes towards foreign policy reported "an enormous change" to "an American politics that has not only become more divided in partisan and ideological terms on domestic issues but also in the foreign policy arena" (Shapiro and Block-Elkon, 2007: 66). Older political foreign policy divisions are now roiling mass opinion as well.

Republican voters have been, for example, far more willing to invest in military power than Democrats. And as Figure 7.3 indicates, this gap is widening, having more than doubled since the collapse of the Soviet Union. Conflicting funding priorities – guns versus butter – form part of the explanation. Partisan polarisation over Pentagon spending, however, is also driven by diverging public judgements about the relative efficacy of military power versus diplomacy. Republicans increasingly favour military strength over diplomacy to ensure security, while Democrats are moving in the opposite direction. In 1999, 46 per cent of Republicans saw diplomacy as the better option. In contrast, 60 per cent of Democrats favoured diplomacy. This partisan gap has widened as a result of the Iraq War and the war on terrorism (Jacobson, 2007). In the 2004 presidential elections, 66 per cent of Bush voters backed military force as the best way to defeat terrorism compared with 17 per cent of Kerry voters. Among Kerry voters, 76 per cent felt that excessive use of force creates anti-American sentiment and encourages terrorism, with only 25 per cent of Bush voters supporting that position (Pew Research Center, 2005). According to a March 2007 poll, after four years of the United States occupying Iraq, only 24 per cent of Republicans opposed the war, compared with more than 90 per cent of Democrats (Schneider, 2007). This growing public divide did not augur well for grand strategies that seek to combine the use of military force with the building of multilateral institutions.

The Obama presidency: The illusion of liberal internationalism's revival

Obama came to office pledging to reach across the aisle and restore bipartisanship on foreign and domestic policy. He courted George Will, David Brooks, and other conservative commentators. But the pervasive partisan sniping of the Bush years continued. Obama soon realised that the blockage was one of substance, not just style: as the president admitted late in 2009, "What I haven't been able to do in the midst of this [economic] crisis is bring the country together in a way that we had done in the Inauguration. That's what's been lost this year [...] that whole sense of changing how Washington works" (Hackett, 2010).

Evidence backs up the president's own assessment. As Figure 7.1 demonstrates, bipartisan voting on foreign policy has plummeted over the past decade – to its lowest level in the past 60 years. By the end of the Bush presidency, bipartisanship on foreign policy had fallen to lows not experienced since the debilitating battles of the 1930s between internationalists and isolationists. Congressional bipartisanship on foreign policy increased slightly during Obama's first year in office, but the level remained far below the norm during the Cold War. Politics no longer stops at the water's edge.

Party positions on key foreign policy issues provide further evidence of a wide partisan divide. After Obama announced his plans in December 2009 to send additional forces to Afghanistan, Speaker of the House, Nancy Pelosi, spoke for many unhappy Democrats: "I don't think there is a great deal of support for sending more troops to Afghanistan in the country or in Congress" (Schmitt and Sanger, 2009). Many Republicans were also unhappy – but for the opposite reason. They thought the size of the surge was insufficient and criticised Obama for indicating that Washington would begin winding down the war in the summer of 2011 (Jackson, 2009). Although Democrats generally welcomed the administration's revamping of plans for missile defence, House Minority Leader, Republican John Boehner, claimed "scrapping the US missile defence system in Poland and the Czech Republic does little more than empower Russia and Iran at the expense of our allies in Europe" (Baker, 2009). On trade, Republicans are pressing the administration for market-opening policies, while labour unions are pushing Democrats in the opposite direction (Harwood, 2010).

These sharp cleavages tie Obama's hands; the collapse of the bipartisan centre makes it very difficult for him to bring liberal internationalism back to life. He has already had to scale back his goals on climate change, accepting a tentative agreement at Copenhagen in December 2009 because Congress was far from ready for a binding agreement (Eilperin and Faiola, 2009; German, 2009). Treaty-based arms control is a hallmark of the liberal internationalist agenda, but the new Strategic Arms Reduction Treaty (START) was a very hard sell and the CTBT is probably well beyond reach. Ironically, the only foreign policies that are likely to garner bipartisan support are those that the extremes in each party find appealing – most notably, getting tough with China. Such "ends against the middle" coalitions, however, are unusual and unstable; they do not constitute the makings of a bipartisan coalition that could revive liberal internationalism.

A polarised public

Congress may be leading the way when it comes to partisanship, but the public is not far behind. On key foreign policy issues, opinion surveys reveal a wide gap between Democrats and Republicans. Two Gallup polls conducted in February 2010 revealed significantly higher ratings among Democrats than Republicans on the priority of lowering national defence spending (Jones, 2010a), approval rates of the United Nations (Jones, 2010b), public approval of Obama's foreign policy (Newport, 2010), particularly, on Obama's policies towards terrorism, Afghanistan, Iraq, and Iran (Pew Research Center, 2009: 42). The survey data also reveal that public enthusiasm for free trade is sensitive to downturns in the US economy. In April 2008, as the financial crisis was worsening, 61 per cent believed that free trade leads to job losses and 56 per cent that it produces lower wages (Pew Research Center, 2009: 55). As Karl Polanyi and many after him have argued, electorates that feel dislocated and disadvantaged by globalisation may seek to cordon themselves off from the global marketplace, not deepen their attachment to it (Polanyi, 1971; Scheve and Slaughter, 2007).

The American public not only has second thoughts about free trade but also about the scope of the country's global security commitments. The Pew poll from December 2009 revealed that 49 per cent of the public believed that the United States "should mind its own business" – the highest response to that question ever recorded, far surpassing the 32 per cent expressing that attitude in 1972, during the height of opposition to the Vietnam War. The poll also found that 76 per cent of the public think the United States should focus less on international problems and "concentrate more on our own national problems and building up our strength and prosperity here at home" (Pew Research Center, 2009: 3–12). The wars in Iraq and Afghanistan appear to be taking a toll on public support for the burdens of liberal internationalism.

Course correction

The sobering story of Obama's futile efforts to revive bipartisan support for liberal internationalism suggests that the regional and ideological cleavages that have stoked polarisation show little sign of abating; the Red–Blue divide, the income inequalities driven by globalisation, and the ideological homogenisation of the parties all continue to make bipartisanship elusive. Indeed, polarisation has become so deeply etched into the contemporary landscape that it is conceivable that politics in the United States may resemble the pre-Second World War era, when domestic stalemate, inconstancy, and detachment prevailed over both power and partnership (Frieden, 1988; Kindleberger, 1973). To be sure, candidates calling for the United States to rein in its overseas commitments – such as Ron Paul and Dennis Kucinich – have not fared well in recent elections. But in light of US troubles in Afghanistan and Iraq, the widening gap between rich and poor, and stagnant real wages and rising costs for working families, support for strategic disengagement might grow. It should not be surprising that Obama has been facing little resistance, even from Republicans, when it comes to withdrawing from Iraq and Afghanistan. Nor should it be surprising that Obama consistently returned to the theme of "nation-building at home" as he campaigned for re-election.

For now, the most likely outcome is continued partisan wrangling rather than a sharp neo-isolationist turn. But party and ideology have become deeply intertwined, and both have become more rooted in salient regional differences. These trends put Democrats and Republicans on divergent courses. The Democrats, once taking the lead in embracing both assertive military engagement abroad and international institution-building, have increasingly favoured partnership over power. Declining Democratic support for using military force to solve international problems is one barometer of the change. This shift in preferences is not uniform; there are Democratic lawmakers and policy intellectuals who remain committed to Franklin Roosevelt's liberal internationalist formula, but far fewer than during the Cold War.

Meanwhile, the Republicans emphasise military power at the expense of multilateralism. The Republican leadership views international institutions as encroachments on US sovereignty and unnecessary constraints on Washington's freedom of action. The Bush administration's 2002 National Security Strategy, which emphasised "primacy" and "pre-emption" and accorded little weight to multilateralism, was symptomatic of this shift in the party's foreign policy orientation. As he campaigned for the presidency, Romney pledged to increase defence spending – even amid the nation's fiscal crisis. In the wake of the failure in Iraq, it is likely that Republican office-seekers will increasingly distance themselves from the excesses of the Bush administration's foreign policy. Such manoeuvring, however, is unlikely to lead the party back to a sustained embrace of multilateralism.

Under these political circumstances, efforts to rebuild the liberal internationalist centre are unlikely to bear fruit. The United States' deepening polarisation means that its leaders can no longer confidently expect to win strong, bipartisan support for the ambitious mix of power and partnership of the Cold War era. A failure to acknowledge the constraints to liberal internationalism will only strengthen the hands of more extreme voices on the left and the right. The security and welfare of the United States require its continued engagement in global affairs, but trying to resurrect the liberal internationalist consensus to achieve that goal is a prescription for failure.

A wiser course for the United States is to pursue a more discriminating and selective strategy that demands less power and less partnership. As we have argued elsewhere, such a strategy would be based on the following principles (see Kupchan and Trubowitz, 2007). Rather than seek to extend the current range of its global commitments in the absence of domestic support, Washington would encourage others to assume a larger geopolitical role. This approach involves supporting a European Union that can shoulder greater defence burdens – as some of its members did in Libya in 2011. It means greater restraint and resourcefulness in dealing with the regional challenges in Asia posed by China's rise to great power status. It also entails building up regional organisations, such as the Association of Southeast Asian Nations, the Gulf Cooperation Council, and the African Union, so that they can help fill the gap as the United States reduces its geopolitical footprint. Washington would by no means withdraw its forward presence in the strategically important regions of Northeast Asia and the Middle East. But it would shrink the size of its deployments and, especially in the Middle East, gradually move to an offshore posture.

American leaders should also view international partnerships more pragmatically. In an era of partisan polarisation, it is difficult to win congressional approval of international pacts and institutions – as Woodrow Wilson's defeat over the League of Nations made clear. Today, proposals for building grand alliances of democracies and new mechanisms of global governance are likely to find scant domestic support. If the United States is to remain a team player in world politics, and immunise itself against a destructive clash with the many nations still supporting institutionalised multilateralism, presidents will have to rely more on pragmatic partnerships, flexible concerts, and task-specific coalitions. Informal groupings – such as the "contact group" for the Balkans, the Quartet in the Middle East, and the G5+1 coalition seeking to contain Iran's nuclear programme – are fast becoming the most effective vehicles for diplomacy. United States foreign policy must be brought into line with its domestic politics. Selective engagement is best suited to a polarised America.

A strategy of judicious retrenchment would not be the preferred course of neoconservative Republicans or hawkish Democrats, but it would have the political advantage of being less objectionable than the alternatives. Liberal Democrats are more apt to favour retrenchment over strategies that put a premium on the projection of US military power; conservative Republicans would likely prefer it to strategies that substitute institutionalised international partnerships for national strength. Indeed, the same opinion polls that indicate that the United States' appetite for international engagement is diminishing reveal that the inward turn is affecting Republicans and Democrats alike. We are under no illusions; a more discriminating grand strategy will not put an end to partisan differences over foreign policy. But retrenchment does promise to ease the political gridlock on Capitol Hill that would ensue should either party attempt to rebuild the liberal internationalist compact. It is far better for the United States to arrive at a more selective grand strategy that enjoys broad domestic support than to continue drifting towards an intractable polarisation that is a recipe for political stalemate at home and failed leadership abroad. A correction is coming. If the United States is to adapt successfully to today's conditions, its leaders must craft a grand strategy that both meets the country's geopolitical needs and restores the political equilibrium needed to sustain a coherent national strategy.

Notes

1. This chapter draws on Kupchan, C. A. and Trubowitz, P. L. (2007), "Dead Center: The Decline of Liberal Internationalism in the United States", *International Security*, 32(2), 7–44; and Charles A. Kupchan and Peter L. Trubowitz. (2010), "The Illusion of Liberal Internationalism's Revival", *International Security*, 35(1), 95–109.
2. Following common practice, bipartisanship is defined as the extent to which majorities or near majorities of both parties in Congress vote together.
3. For a historical summary of this period, see Kupchan and Trubowitz (2007).
4. Text of the resolution is available at http://www.state.gov/documents/organization/18076.pdf.
5. Matthew Dowd wrote the memo for Bush's chief political adviser, Karl Rove.
6. See http://voteview.com/
7. Quoted in Mitchell (2000).
8. Tyndall Report, as cited in Shaw (2001) and Hall's Magazine Editorial Reports, cited in Hoge (1997).
9. For a description of the organisation and a list of its founding members, see http://www.psaonline.org.

References

Abramowitz, M. (30 October 2006), "Bush Says 'America Loses' under Democrats", *Washington Post*.

Alberts, S. (19 October 2004), "Candidates Address 'Security Moms': Bush Warns Kerry Would 'Invite Disaster' ", *Gazette Montreal*.

America's Angry Election. (3 January 2004), *Economist*.

Baker, P. (17 September 2009), "White House Scraps Bush's Approach to Missile Shield", *New York Times*.

Bell, D. (1960), *The End of Ideology: On the Exhaustion of Political Ideas in the Fifties*, New York: Free Press.

Bolton, J. R. (2000), "Should We Take Global Governance Seriously?" *Chicago Journal of International Law*, 1(2), 205–221.

Bowman, I. (1928), *The New World: Problems in Political Geography*, Yonkers-on-Hudson: World Book.

Burnham, W. D. (1970), *Critical Elections and the Mainsprings of American Politics*, New York: W. W. Norton.

Busby, J. and Monten, J. (2008), "Without Heirs: The Fall of Establishment Internationalism in US Foreign Policy", *Perspectives on Politics*, 6(3), 451–472.

Bush, G. W. (4 August 2000), "Acceptance Speech, Republican National Convention, Philadelphia, Pennsylvania, 3 August 2000", *Washington Post*.

Campbell, A., Converse, P. E., Miller, W. E. and Stokes, D. E. (1960), *The Amerian Voter*, New York: Wiley.

Campbell, K. M. and O'Hanlon, M. E. (2006), *Hard Power: The New Politics of National Security*, New York: Basic Books.

Cnn.com. (13 April 2009), Obama Eases Cuba Travel Restrictions.

Daalder, I. H. and Lindsay, J. M. (2003), *America Unbound: The Bush Revolution in Foreign Policy*, Washington: Brookings.

Daschle, T. (1996). "The Water's Edge", *Foreign Policy* (103), 4–5.

Earle, E. M. (1941), *Against This Torrent*, Princeton: Princeton University Press.

Edsall, T. B. (2006), *Building Red America: The New Conservative Coalition and the Drive for Permanent Power*, New York: Basic Books.

Eilperin, J. and Faiola, A. (19 December 2009), "Climate Deal Falls Short on Key Goals", *Washington Post*.

Frey, W. H. (2003), *Metropolitan Magnets for Domestic and International Migration*, Washington: Brookings.

Frieden, J. A. (1988), "Sectoral Conflict and US Foreign Policy, 1914–1940", *International Organisation*, 42(1), 59–90.

Fukuyama, F. (15–16 September 2001), "The United State", *Financial Times*.

Fukuyama, F. (2004), *America at the Crossroads: Democracy, Power and the Neoconservative Legacy*, New Haven: Yale University Press.

German, B. (18 December 2009), Obama Departs Fractious Copenhagen Talks with Limited Pact. *Hill*. Retrieved from http://thehill.com/homenews/administration/73033-obama-departs-fractious-copenhagen-talks-with-limited-climate-accord

Hackett, L. (25 January 2010), "An Exclusive Interview with the Obamas: Our First Year", *People*, 73(3), 60–65.

Hart, G. (2004), *The Fourth Power: A Grand Strategy for the United States in the Twenty-First Century*, New York: Oxford University Press.

Harwood, J. (2010), "Obama's Balancing Act on Trade", Retrieved from http://thecaucus.blogs.nytimes.com/2010/02/07/obamas-balancing-act-on-trade/.

Hoge, J. F., Jr. (1997), "Foreign News: Who Gives a Damn?" *Columbia Journalism Review*, 36(4), 48–52.

Ikenberry, G. J. (2001), "American Grand Strategy in the Age of Terror", *Survival*, 43(4), 19–34.

Ikenberry, G. J. (2003), "Is American Multilateralism in Decline?" *Perspectives on Politics*, 1(3), 533–550.

Ikenberry, G. J. (2004), "The End of the Neo-Conservative Moment", *Survival*, 46(1), 7–22.

Ikenberry, G. J. and Slaughter, A.-M. (2006), *Forging a World of Liberty under Law: US National Security in the 21st Century*, Princeton: The Woodrow Wilson School of Public and International Affairs, Princeton University.

Jackson, J. (2 December 2009), House Republicans Criticize Obama Timeline. Retrieved from http://www.cbsnews.com/blogs/2009/12/02/politics/politicalhotsheet/entry 5865054.shtml

Jacobson, G. C. (2007), *A Divider, Not a Uniter: George W. Bush and the American People*, New York: Pearson Longman.

Jones, J. M. (18 February 2010a), Americans More Divided on Strength of National Defense. Retrieved from http://www.gallup.com/poll/126101/Americans-Divided-Strength-National-Defense.aspx

Jones, J. M. (19 February 2010b), Americans' Rating of United Nations Improved, But Still Low. Retrieved from http://www.gallup.com/poll/126134/Americans-Rating-United-Nations-Improved-Low.aspx.

Kagan, R. (2003), *Of Paradise and Power: America and Europe in the New World Order*, New York: Alfred A. Knopf.

Key, V. O., Jr. (1958), *Politics, Parties, and Pressure Groups*, New York: Thomas Y. Cromwell.

Kindleberger, C. P. (1973), *A World in Depression, 1929–1939*, Berkeley: University of California Press.

Kull, S. and Destler, I. M. (1999), *Misreading the Public: The Myth of a New Isolationism*, Washington: Brookings.

Kupchan, C. A. and Trubowitz, P. L. (2007). "Grand Strategy for a Divided America", *Foreign Affairs*, 86(4), 71–83.

Lehrer, J. (6 December 2006), Baker, Hamilton Discuss 'New Way Forward' Proposal for Iraq. Retrieved from http://www.pbs.org/newshour/bb/middle_east/july -dec06/bakerhamilton_12-06.html

Mead, W. R. (2004), *Power, Terror, Peace, and War: America's Grand Strategy in a World at Risk*, New York: Alftred A. Knopf.

Mitchell, A. (19 May 2000), "Bush and the G.O.P. Congress", *New York Times*.

Newport, F. (8 February 2010), Obama Approval on Economy Down, on Foreign Affairs Up. Retrieved from http://www.gallup.com/poll/125678/Obama-Approval-Economy-Down-Foreign-Affairs-Up.aspx

Page, B. I. and Bouton, M. M. (2006), *The Foreign Policy Disconnect: What Americans Want from our Leaders but Don't Get*, Chicago: University of Chicago Press.

Pew Research Center. (24 January 2005), Politics and Values in a 51%-48% Nation: National Security More Linked to Party Affiliation. Retrieved from http://people-press.org/reports/display.php3?ReportID=236

Pew Research Center. (3 December 2009), America's Place in the World 2009: An Investigation of Public and Leadership Opinion about International Affairs. Retrieved from http://people-press.org/reports/pdf/569.pdf

Pew Research Center. (23 January 2012), Public Priorities: Deficit Rising, Terrorism Slipping. Retrieved from http://www.people-press.org/2012/01/23/section-2-iran-afghanistan-military-policy-u-s-global-image/

Polanyi, K. (1971), *The Great Transformation: The Political and Economic Origins of Our Times*, Boston: Beacon Press.

Roman, N. E. (2005), *Both Sides of the Aisle: A Call for Bipartisan Foreign Policy*, Washington: Council on Foreign Relations.

Scheve, K. F. and Slaughter, M. J. (2007), "A New Deal for Globalization", *Foreign Affairs*, 86(4), 34–47.

Schlesinger, A. M., Jr. (1949), *The Vital Center*, Boston: Houghton Mifflin.

Schmitt, E.and Sanger, D. E. (11 September 2009), "Obama Faces Doubts from Democrats on Afghanistan", *New York Times*.

Schneider, B. (19 March 2007), Poll: Support for Iraq War Deteriorates. Retrieved from http://www.cnn.com/2007/POLITICS/03/19/iraq.support/index.html

Shapiro, R. Y. and Block-Elkon, Y. (2007), "Political Polarization and the Rational Public", in M. N. Halperin, J. Laurenti, P. Rundlet and S. P. Boyer (eds) *Power and Superpower: Global Leadership and Exceptionalism in the 21st Century*, New York: Century Foundation Press.

Shaw, D. (27 September 2001), "Foreign News Shrinks in Era of Globalization", *Los Angeles Times*.

Silva, M. (18 August 2006), "Cheney Back on the Campaign Trail as GOP's 'Attack Dog' ", *Chicago Tribune*.

Skowronek, S. (1997), *The Politics Presidents Make: Leadership from John Adams to Bill Clinton*, Cambridge: Harvard University Press.

Spykman, N. J. (1942), *America's Strategy in World Politics: The United States and the Balance of Power*, New York: Harcourt, Brace.

Stonecash, J. M., Brewer, M. D. and Mariani, M. D. (2003), *Diverging Parties: Social Change, Realignment and Party Polarisation*, Boulder: Westview.

Theriault, S. M. (2006), "Party Polarization in the US Congress: Member Replacement and Member Adaptation", *Party Politics*, 12(4), 483–503.

Trubowitz, P. L. (1998), *Defining the National Interest: Conflict and Change in American Foreign Policy*, Chicago: University of Chicago Press.

8
Neoconservatism, Neoclassical Realism, and the Narcissism of Small Differences

Jonathan D. Caverley

Does a world after liberalism imply a world after neoconservatism?[1] Realist thinkers would certainly argue this case. Brian Schmidt and Michael Williams (2008: 202) claim that "neoconservatism embraces a liberal theory of international relations", John Mearsheimer (2005) claims that "Neoconservative theory – the Bush doctrine – is essentially Wilsonianism with teeth", and Richard Betts (2010) describes neoconservatives as being "in many ways just liberals in wolves' clothing".

Not coincidentally, these same critics claim that such a move leaves the field of American foreign policy clear of all combatants but realism (Desch, 2007). John Mearsheimer (2005) states that "neoconservatives and realists have fundamentally different views about how the world works and what American foreign policy should look like". Advocates and opponents of the Iraq War, argues Stephen Walt (2005: 29), based their cases on "fundamentally different views about the basic dynamics of interstate relations".

This chapter maintains that such claims are not only wrong, but ironic. The foreign policy tenets of neoconservatism – whether it be Francis Fukuyama's "realistic Wilsonianism", Charles Krauthammer's "democratic realism", or the "democratic globalists" they both attack – are largely motivated by the "Hobbesian" assumptions that underpin the realist tradition: a conflict-prone, anarchic world of sovereign states. Consequently, for neoconservatism and realists alike, power remains the fundamental currency of International Relations (IR) in a dangerous world.

Unlike most self-identified realists, neoconservatives derive an urgent interest in democratisation from these assumptions. However, this chapter argues that a major component behind neoconservatism's urge to spread democracy is the belief in democracy's enervating effects on the creation and use of state power at home and abroad. Consequently, the United States enjoys greater safety among other democracies not only because democracies maintain different foreign policy preferences, but because the resulting distribution of relative power is more favourable to American interests in a competitive, state-centric, and anarchic world. In this chapter, I argue that given these starting assumptions and causal mechanisms, it is not clear that neoclassical realism, the self-identified "foreign policy" wing of realism, offers much of a theoretical alternative.

The remainder of this chapter seeks to accomplish four tasks. Firstly, after establishing the body of work it labels as "neoconservative", and arguing for its treatment as a social scientific theory, the chapter describes the identical starting assumptions shared by neoconservatism and realism. The subsequent section argues that neoconservatism rejects all but one of the liberal mechanisms that reduce international security competition. Thirdly, having isolated attention to regime type as the only feature distinguishing neoconservatism from its realist colleagues, the chapter explores the neoconservative mechanism of democratic weakness. Fourthly, the chapter lays out the considerable overlap between this approach and the recent "neoclassical" attempts to create a realist theory of foreign policy. The conclusion points out flaws jointly shared by neoconservatism and neoclassical realism and suggests why the rest of IR should care.

The case for neoconservatism as a social scientific theory

I am not the first to claim that realism shares a great deal in common with its theoretical antagonist (Alexander, 2007), nor do I argue that neoconservatism and realism are identical. Neoconservatism draws from, and rejects, large swathes of both realism and idealism (Cooper, 2011: 8; Singh, 2009). Rather, by breaking neoconservative thinking down to first principles and comparing them to those of realism, particularly of the neoclassical variety, I find the distinctions less clear. Before examining these first principles, the chapter first states what work it considers neoconservative and makes the case why it should be treated as a social scientific theory.

This chapter reverses the present convention when discussing neoconservatism by focusing on ideas rather than neoconservative policy recommendations or personalities.[2] While the logic informing the invasion of Iraq certainly merits extensive analysis, the Bush administration should not be conflated with neoconservatism any more than the Nixon and Clinton administrations with realist and liberal theory (Vaïsse, 2010). Theory is necessarily prior to policy, and diverse theories can recommend the same policy for very different reasons. Nor does the chapter focus on neoconservatism's normative goals, "like, for example, peace and racial equality", which are shared by most people on the planet (Muravchik, 2007).[3] Instead, I concentrate on the mechanisms (policies) that neoconservative theory posits to achieve these goals.

To show its consistency over time, I include the central works of contemporary neoconservative foreign policy, as well as many writings across Irving Kristol's and Norman Podhoretz's careers that self-consciously refer to neoconservatism and foreign policy. This chapter pays special attention to the "minority reports" of Fukuyama and Jeane Kirkpatrick. Just as examining the writings of various strands of realism allows us to hone in on its central tenets, Fukuyama's (2006: 141) explanation for why "actually existing neoconservatism" has "evolved into something that I can no longer support" is instructive for its own interpretation of neoconservatism's core.[4] Fukuyama based his apparent scepticism of the Iraq invasion on the same assumptions others used to support it.

I conclude this section by acknowledging the difficulties in dragging a collection of writing into a realm its authors evince little desire to enter. Neoconservatism frequently appears to reject the very possibility of a social science of international politics. Irving Kristol ridicules "academic analysts, who will never cease to believe that a foreign policy should be analytically coherent" (Kristol, 1996). Robert Kagan and William Kristol (2000) argue that "the complicated workings of foreign policy and the exceptional position of the United States should guard us against believing that the national interest can be measured in a quasi-scientific fashion". Synthesising such diverse works in order to flesh out and critique a grand theory necessarily leads to simplification, but it remains an essential task if we are to compare explanations and prescriptions of foreign policy.[5]

Living in a realist world

Theory begins with ontology and assumptions, even when tacit. The ones underpinning neoconservatism are familiar to any realist. Randall Schweller (2003: 325) describes three fundamental assumptions that "distinguish realism from all other IR perspectives" and are "common to all realist theories": conflict groups (i.e. states) are the key actors in world politics, power is the fundamental feature of IR, and the essential nature of IR is conflictual. Neoconservatism shares all of these assumptions. The bottom line is, as Joshua Muravchik (1996: 28) observes, "Peace is hard to come by and hard to keep".

Neoconservatism recognises that "in most places, the nation-state remains as strong as ever", and these states are jealous of their sovereignty (Kagan, 2008: 3, 64–66). States interact in an anarchic world; Krauthammer (2003: 12) approvingly cites realism's recognition of "the fundamental fallacy in the whole idea of the international system being modelled on domestic society". Echoing Mearsheimer (2001: 33), he asks, "If someone invades your house, you call the cops. Who do you call if someone invades your country?" Kagan (2003: 75) claims that outside of Europe the "dangerous Hobbesian world still flourishes" (see also Krauthammer, 2009). Again, as with realism, uncertainty of intentions and the shadow of the future loom large, "if history is any guide we are likely to face dangers even within the next decade that we cannot even imagine today" (see also Kagan and Kagan, 2000: 8; Kagan and Kristol, 2000; Podhoretz, 1999: 31). Even when dealing with the threat of non-state actors such as terrorist groups, the target of much of the action are the states that either sponsor or tolerate them.

Since they seek to survive in an uncertain world, states care deeply about their own power and that of other, potentially hostile states. With the possible exception of Europe, all large states, democratic or not, are interested in competing for more power (see also Kagan, 2008; Krauthammer, 2004).[6] Like realism, neoconservatism distinguishes between the great and lesser powers, but anarchy has its effect regardless:

> In an anarchic world small powers always fear they will be victims. Great powers on the other hand, often fear rules that may constrain them more than they do anarchy. In an anarchic world, they rely on their power to provide security and prosperity (Kagan, 2002).

Like their realist cousins, Muravchik's (2007: 135) neoconservatives place their trust in military force and doubt that "economic sanctions or UN intervention or diplomacy, per se, constitute meaningful alternatives". Kagan (2003: 3) argues that "true security and the defence and promotion of a liberal order still depend on the possession and use of military might".

Again, neoconservatism's emphasis on the importance of regime type and the need for a moral foreign policy is not disputed. Rather, the moral concerns are superimposed upon structural forces, that is, the distribution of power.[7]

Scholars are right to point to the spread of democracy and, the free-market and the free-trade economic system as important factors in the maintenance of great-power peace. Where they err is in believing these conditions are either sufficient or self-sustaining. In fact, these are more the consequence of great power peace than the cause (Kagan, 2012).

The master variable underpinning this peace is American power, since,

> International order is not an evolution; it is an imposition. It is the domination of one vision over others – in this case, the domination of liberal principles of economics, domestic politics, and international relations over other, nonliberal principles. It will last only as long as those who imposed it retain the capacity to defend it. This is an uncomfortable reality for liberal internationalists.
>
> (Kagan, 2012)

The next section makes clear that, because of its fixation on power, neoconservatism bears little resemblance to the comprehensive approach to international politics that is liberal internationalism. Kagan (2007) lays out a realist world, where power is the ultimate currency with "global ideological competition" simply "complicating the equation and adding to the stakes" of the "return to the international competition of ambitious nations". That is, ideology is an intervening variable, albeit an important one.

Neoconservatism ain't Wilsonianism

As with realism, liberalism is a rich theoretical treatment that makes it difficult to pin down. Neoconservative writing tends to focus on the aspects of liberal thinking about the international system embodied by Woodrow Wilson. When dealing with contemporary examinations of liberalism, neoconservatives, particularly Robert Kagan, tend to regard John Ikenberry's work as emblematic. This section will do likewise.

Like realism, neoconservatism rejects the Wilsonian and contemporary liberal mechanisms that help to mitigate this competitive realist world. Krauthammer describes neoconservatism's vision of spreading liberal values to other states as "expansive and perhaps utopian. But it ain't Wilsonian" (Krauthammer, 2004). This chapter suggests taking Krauthammer at his word. In terms of foreign policy positions, few labels could be less appropriate for neoconservatism than Wilsonianism – realistic or hard, with boots or with teeth. This chapter does not deny that neoconservatism shares an element at Wilsonian liberalism's core, the international promotion of democratic values. Rather, it points out that this is the only concrete aspect that these two theories have in common.

The differences grow starker still when one compares neoconservatism to contemporary liberal IR theory, which suggests several related mechanisms to undermine the perpetual state of insecurity and competition that typifies a realist world. John Ikenberry (2008: 11–13) identifies six "big ideas" shared by Wilsonianism and modern liberalism. The first four cover various paths to peace: democracy, free trade, international law and international bodies, and collective security. The final two are a progressive optimism about modernity coupled with the need for American global leadership as a "moral agent". Neoconservatism clearly accepts both the importance of democracy as an American national interest and of American moral global leadership, but explicitly rejects the remaining four points of liberalism/Wilsonianism. Indeed, some neoconservative interpretations of Wilsonianism have little to do with any of the ideas above. For Muravchik (1996: 21), Wilsonianism merely "sets a much lower threshold for American involvement abroad, on the theory that early intervention on a small scale may forestall a much heavier commitment later on".

For both realism and neoconservatism, transnational mechanisms have little independent effect on IR. International institutions are epiphenomenal, reflecting the distribution of power, and thus "American hegemony is the only reliable defence against a breakdown of peace and international order" (Kagan and Kristol, 1996: 23). States without a liberal hegemonic protector remain "mired in history, exercising power in the anarchic Hobbesian world where international laws and rules are unreliable" (Kagan, 2003). Fukuyama evinces "scepticism about the legitimacy and effectiveness of international law and institutions to achieve either security or justice" (Fukuyama, 2006: 49). If anything, the democratic predilection for institutions is yet another example of democratic unwillingness to pursue power politics. "Why then this obsession with conventions, protocols, legalisms?", asks Krauthammer (2004), "Their obvious net effect is to temper American power."

Neoconservatism also doubts the pacifying effects of interstate commerce; some neoconservative writings support the spread of free markets, but have little to say on free trade except in the context of alliances and threats. Kagan and Kristol (1996) warn against the "Armand Hammerism" of "blindly 'doing business' with every nation, no matter its regime". Norman Podhoretz (1996) castigates 1980's businessmen for "loving commerce" more than "they loathed communism".[8] As in realism (Gowa, 1994), trade and security are inescapably linked not as a means of preserving peace between rivals but as a form of strengthening alliances; in the context of the American–Japanese trade disputes of the 1980s and 1990s, Muravchik (1996: 202) characterises the view that "security relations with Japan [...] could be sealed off from economic issues" as "either disingenuous or self-delusional". Kagan (2008) rejects the logic of the commercial peace as a "comfortable doctrine of passivity", and, echoing Kenneth Waltz (1979), suggests that economic interdependence is as likely to cause conflict as prevent it. Like Mearsheimer (2001), he mournfully shakes his head at Norman Angell's claims of a commercial peace in the early twentieth century (Kagan, 2012: 47–48).

As with trade, culture and norms are of little relevance at the international level, although they remain a powerful force within states. Neoconservatism evinces strong scepticism regarding the power of the transnational norms championed by liberals; "there is little sense of shared morality and common political principle among the great powers" (Kagan, 2007). Krauthammer (2004) bluntly observes that "moral suasion is a farce", in his explicit rejection of Wilsonianism. Similarly, neoconservatism contains little notion of ideas being used to co-opt potential adversaries in the form of "soft power" (Kagan, 2002). So while neoconservatism understands that ideas matter on the domestic front, and that regime and individual identity are co-constituted, the claim that neoconservatism represents "a systemic constructivist account of IR" is surely wrong (Rapport, 2008). Neoconservatism, like realism, claims that anarchy is always "Hobbesian" unless a hegemon can enforce its preferred order; Europe's Kantian "geopolitical fantasy" would not continue were the United States to withdraw its protection (Kagan, 2003: 57; Mearsheimer, 2001). Indeed, Krauthammer explicitly rejects the liberal dream to "transform the international system from the

Hobbesian universe into a Lockean universe" (Krauthammer, 2004), much less a Kantian one.

Neoconservatism does support "democracy at home and abroad", but given its scepticism of other liberal mechanisms, one suspects the means of causation differs from liberal IR theory.[9] Muravchik cites research claiming that democracies rarely fight each other, but rejects the empirical finding that democracies are as likely to start wars against non-democracies as any other regime because "it flies in the face of common sense [...] The cold war as a whole was a one-sided creation of the Soviet Union, while the United States all along wanted peace". Muravchik lays out the democratic pacifist logic explicitly, "Indeed, in this century, the democracies have several times helped to cause wars by being so pacific that dictators were tempted to overreach" (Muravchik, 1996: 174).

Democratic weakness

As Irving Kristol writes, "in the end the fundamental problem for American democracy is that its foreign policy is democratic" (Kristol, 1996). Neoconservatism is a theory of democratic weakness in a realist world. The type of weakness that concerns neoconservatives is not a lack of economic power; the world's richest states are almost uniformly democratic. Nor is it a lack of military power; most of the world's largest military budgets belong to democratic states.[10] Rather, as this section demonstrates, neoconservatism seeks to point out the debilitating effects of democracy that prevent such a government from spending appropriate levels of its wealth on military power and from employing any military power that it does possess.

Several realists have rightly avoided conflating liberalism and neoconservatism, and instead emphasise the latter's emergence as a reaction to American liberalism (Rapport, 2008; Williams, 2005, 2007). Neoconservatism's origins lie as much in an "ambivalent attitude towards liberal modernisation and the socio-cultural forces that the latter sets forth", as in an enthusiastic resistance to Soviet communism (Drolet, 2007: 248). In linking the international and domestic spheres, neoconservatism advances an expansive conception of the "national interest" as the domestic health of a society, finding a tendency towards self-destructive decadence inherent in liberalism. Unrestrained liberalism becomes, quite literally, an existential threat (Schmidt and Williams, 2008: 211). Because of this dangerous side effect, the democratic state must pursue a "moral" foreign policy, which is "an expression of [citizens'] values, and which they can identify with" (see also Podhoretz, 1999; Schmidt and Williams, 2008: 323).

However, it is not apparent that most neoconservatives, particularly in the contemporary generation, regard foreign policy primarily as a means to ameliorating liberal decadence at home, nor that culture is considered the "defining element of politics" even within a state. According to Kagan

(2003: 83), culture cannot explain recent changes in US foreign policy behaviour, "Americans are no more or less idealistic than they were fifty years ago. It is objective reality that has changed, not the American character". Similarly, in comparing Europe and the United States, "these differences in strategic culture do not spring naturally from the national characters of Americans and Europeans" (Kagan, 2008: 7–8).

However, neoconservative works are just as concerned, if not more so, with the opposite direction of causality – how domestic politics affect a state's ability to compete in a self-help international system. Neoconservatism advocates a "broad, sustaining policy vision", because without it, "the American people will be inclined to withdraw from the world [...] they will seek deeper and deeper cuts in the defence and foreign affairs budgets and gradually decimate the tools of US hegemony" (Kagan and Kristol, 1996: 82; see also Krauthammer, 2003). More succinctly put by Irving Kristol, "in the modern world, a non-ideological politics is a politics disarmed" (Kristol, 1983). Decadence can only be an "existential threat" if society faces an external peril. Like realism, neoconservative foreign policy regards *aussenpolitik* as paramount. Liberal democracy makes states less capable of surviving in the competitive realist world posited by neoconservatism. Democracy weakens states; democratisation is one means of ameliorating this.

A world unsafe for democracy

Liberal publics are cost averse and inwardly focused; "[Americans] have continually searched for a way to reconcile their demand for a certain kind of world and their wish to avoid costs, including the moral costs, of imposing that world on others" (Kagan, 2008: 53). "Americans", observes Krauthammer, "have a healthy aversion to foreign policy" (Krauthammer, 2004). Kagan and Kagan make the point more broadly – "The record of liberal, democratic, commercial nations, no matter how great their strength, in keeping the peace over the long run is abysmal. The absence of an immediate threat permits democracies to focus on domestic comfort" (Kagan and Kagan, 2000: 4). A democracy's responsiveness to voters, neoconservative theory posits, produces unfortunate side effects that include: a perverse welfare state, an inattention to foreign policy, and consequent military decline. This conclusion is in complete opposition to the general finding of liberal IR theorists that democracies tend to pursue exceptionally competent foreign policies.

Neoconservatism acquired its name in part by eschewing mainstream conservatism's disavowal of the welfare state. While generally agnostic on its virtue, neoconservatism accepts that "the welfare state is with us, for better or worse" (Kristol, 1993). This modern welfare state produces some undesirable consequences. Government redistribution erodes economic growth –

itself a crucial element of national clout – but how wealth is redistributed also matters. Irving Kristol seeks a return to an "older, masculine, paternalistic version of the welfare state" to help shore up an economically powerful, militarily strong state well suited for international competition (Kristol, 2000). While the first journal associated with neoconservatism specifically excluded foreign policy, Kristol describes the philosophy underpinning *The Public Interest* as "linking its work in economic and social policy to our national destiny as a world power" (Kristol, 2006).

The liberal welfare state under-invests in military power; voters choose butter over guns and consumption over the death and taxes entailed by military competition. There's much to be said for the decency and relative equality of social democracy. But it comes at a cost: diminished social mobility, higher unemployment, less innovation, less dynamism and creative destruction, less overall growth. This affects the ability to project power (Krauthammer, 2009).

While not as dire as Europe, Kristol and Kagan (1996) fear that "American civilians at home, preoccupied with the distribution of tax breaks and government benefits, will not come to [the military's] support when the going gets tough". Muravchik (1996: 39) claims that "public illusions" of wanting a "balanced budget but resist[ing] increases in taxes or reductions in benefits" are likely to force politicians to cut spending on foreign policy. Kagan and Kristol (1996) describe the American military as "uncomfortable with some of the missions that the new American role requires" (see also Kagan and Kagan, 2000; Kristol, 2003).

Democracy makes states both weaker militarily and less willing to use the remaining power they possess, preferring to use meeker foreign policy tools. "Every [US] administration is attracted to economic sanctions as against military intervention, because although they are ineffectual […] they do give the appearance of attentive action" (Kristol, 1996). In international security competition, democratic states play with a handicap.

On the other hand, non-democratic states do not feel this redistributive, pacifying drag on their military power. Irving Kristol (1997) clearly draws the link:

> In world affairs the poorer nations that are not welfare states, not nearly as risk averse since they have so little to lose, will be (as they are already becoming) the activist countries, the ones that create the crises and set the international agenda.

Unlike democracies, other regime types experience domestic incentives to grow more powerful since "strength and control at home allow Russia to be strong abroad. Strength abroad justifies strong rule at home". In Kagan's description, states like China and Russia have the principal (realist) goal of defending their sovereignty (Kagan, 2008: 55). But he also makes clear that the United States is less worried about this goal because its sovereignty is so obviously assured. In this sense, the promotion of one's values abroad is a luxury good.[11]

Threats to the United States come in the form of ideologies, coupled with material power (Fukuyama, 2006: 29). Muravchik's (1996: 34) citation of Napoleon's maxim, "in warfare, moral factors are three times more important than material ones", shows neoconservatism's approach to ideology as a lens through which state power is focused. Whereas fascism took German industry and focused it into a tight beam of military conquest, democracy takes American wealth and diffuses it, or, worse still, reflects it back within in the form of destructive welfare policies (Kagan and Kagan, 2000). By this reasoning, militant Islam could take materially feeble Middle Eastern states and magnify their impact through terror, "oppression transmuted and deflected by regimes with no legitimacy into virulent, murderous anti-Americanism" (Krauthammer, 2004, see also Muravchik, 2007).[12] Kagan (2007) clearly makes this case when arguing:

> In the Middle East, competition for influence among powers both inside and outside the region has raged for at least two centuries. The rise of Islamic fundamentalism doesn't change this. It only adds a new and threatening dimension to the competition.

The state-centrism that neoconservatism shares with realism precludes focusing on the non-state actor nature of groups like Al Qaeda.[13] In the war against terror, "you win by taking territory" (Krauthammer, 2004).

Often cited as the exception that proves the neoconservative rule, Kirkpatrick's famous denunciation of the Carter administration's focus on human rights promotion actually establishes the proposition that totalitarian regimes are inherently more threatening than authoritarian ones (and that introducing liberal democracy will weaken the state).[14] Robert Kagan deploys this logic while challenging the power political logic of trading with a potential rival when he approvingly quotes Arvind Subramanian (2011: 125):

> China's [trade] surpluses lead to concentrated acquisition of resources in the hands of the state,' which keeps the rulers in power and gives them the ability to project power internationally. (Kagan, 2012)

Kagan uses this calculus to describe Russia, China, Iran, and Syria as roughly equivalent threats (Kagan, 2007). This fundamental link between latent state power and regime type, which as we shall see is accepted by many self-described realists, leads to the very implications to which realists object.

(1) The Pursuit of Pre-eminence, Military Power, and the RMA: Fighting with one arm tied behind their backs, democracies require a lot of power

to compete in a dangerous world. Irving Kristol (1996) compares favourably the United States' prospects to those of ancient Athens, "where a democratic foreign policy led to one disaster after another", but this is only because "Athens was never the great power the United States is today". Krauthammer echoes this analysis when describing "Arab-Islamic totalitarianism" as a far greater threat than Soviet communism:

> Were that the only difference between [the Cold War] and then, our situation would be hopeless. But there is a second difference between now and then: the uniqueness of our power, unrivalled, not just today but ever. That evens the odds. (Krauthammer, 2004, emphasis added)

For a democratic state, only primacy will ensure its safety.

A patriotic culture of "national greatness" is one means of mobilising state resources in a democracy, but neoconservatism does not take chances. Podhoretz (1999) writes of the need to exploit "our superior technology to minimise American casualties while inflicting maximum damage on the enemy, even if innocent civilians might be harmed or killed in the process", in order to compete against "the callous indifference to their own casualties of armies like the Russian and the Chinese". The "revolution in military affairs" (RMA) allows the United States to do more with less and – more importantly – not subject its constituents to undue physical risk (Kagan, 2003: 23).

One can derive neoconservatism's particular zeal for missile defence from this conviction. Missile defence is not designed to counter a nuclear threat per se; Robert Kagan (2000) acknowledges that "even the crazies are unlikely to fire a warhead at the United States". Preventing the homeland from being held hostage will give the United States the political will to use its military abroad. "The sine qua non for a strategy of American global pre-eminence [...] is a missile defence system", write Kagan and Kristol (1996), "only a well-protected America will be capable of deterring – and when necessary moving against – 'rogue' regimes when they rise to challenge regional stability".

This predominance is not only necessary to overcome the democratic handicap but it is the cornerstone on which all other aspects of international order rest. Again, the contention by Kagan (and many other neoconservatives) that the United States has used its power to shape the international order in a liberal fashion, and that any other unipolar regime would do likewise, is not a controversial claim in most fleshed out forms of realism.

By this logic, for a unipolar United States, "the main threat [it] faces comes not from the outside but within –from the temptation to renounce these heavy burdens and allow itself to become weak" (Podhoretz, 1999: 31). Or, as Robert Kagan (2012: 7) puts it more pithily, the United States may be primed for "pre-emptive superpower suicide". "Decline", insists Krauthammer (2009), "is a choice. More than a choice, a temptation. How to resist it?"

(2) Democratisation: Fukuyama (2006: 14) observes that the advocates of transforming Iraq into a Western-style democracy are the same people who question the "dangers of ambitious social engineering". This apparent paradox becomes coherent given this idea of democratic enfeeblement. Democratisation is at once a means of shoring up one's own absolute power. In Waltzian terms, it is a form of internal balancing by mobilising society towards a common goal, but also serves as a means of diminishing the threatening power of other potential rivals. As others have already ably described the former mechanism (Schmidt and Williams, 2008), I will focus on the latter.

Kirkpatrick (1979) points out that because totalitarian states are inherently more threatening, the United States should focus its democratisation efforts there. Her famous essay does not criticise the neoconservative enthusiasm for democratisation; it rather connects it to a grand strategic logic. Because of the military advantage enjoyed by non-democracies, a United States interested in self-preservation should aggressively spread this cost aversion.[15] Muravchik (2007) succinctly states the core (and inherently power political) logic: "The spread of democracy offers an important, peaceful way to weaken our foe. "[16]

(3) Bandwagoning and Democratic Dominoes: Mearsheimer (2005) argues that in a realist world, states balance against potential hegemons. In a neoconservative world, states bandwagon, or at least fail to balance against, the powerful United States. As with the democratic peace, neoconservatism can point to another important empirical finding unaccounted for by neorealism: the utter lack of balancing against the United States.[17] Neoconservatism views bandwagoning with the United States as likely for two reasons.

The first is not hard to understand. Weak states, as they have for time immemorial, "suffer what they must". Bandwagoning is their only option. But an additional neoconservative mechanism for bandwagoning exists given liberalism's inherent enervation of even strong powers. If democracy weakens states, a "democratic domino" theory becomes logical. After all, "a democratising Russia, and even Gorbachev's democratising Soviet Union, took a fairly benign view of NATO" (Kagan, 2008: 61; Muravchik, 1996).

Unlike the neoconservatives, realists were sceptical that the United States would be allowed to enjoy this power for very long. But in a strange way, democratic weakness demands the maintenance of a massive power advantage even as it makes this power less threatening to other states:

[Americans'] very distractedness, their evident desire to hold themselves apart from the world even as they shape it with their power, makes them an often frustrating ally, a confusing adversary, but also a less imposing, less frightening hegemon (Kagan, 2012: 16).

This reluctance to use its vast power makes American hegemony relatively attractive to other countries (Muravchik, 1996: 56).

(4) Preventative War: Neoconservatism's theory of democratic weakness in a realist world creates "closing windows of opportunity" that prime it for pre-emption (Van Evera, 1999). If one believes that decline and disengagement are likely in democracies over time, then rising non-democratic great powers and radicalising weak states will catch up inevitably and perhaps quickly. Given the high likelihood of conflict on worse terms in the future, it makes sense to strike while power is sufficiently imbalanced to give democracies a chance. Plus, both neoconservatism and realism agree that early aggressiveness during a power transition is cheaper; "early intervention on a small scale may forestall a much heavier commitment later on" (Muravchik, 1996: 21; Podhoretz, 1999).

While Dale Copeland claims that such preventative wars occur only under exceptional circumstances, neoconservative logic opens the door to a whole host of justifications for intervention if regime type accelerates these changes in power (Copeland, 2000). This combination of focusing on the mere "possibility of conflict", shared with offensive realism, coupled with a focus on the potentially enervating effects of regime type makes neoconservatism's foreign policy implications so volatile (Brooks, 1997).

Neoconservatism is not an alternative

Democratic enfeeblement is not normally associated with realism. However, the previous section makes clear that the many implications of neoconservatism require a realist world as a necessary condition. Moreover, if many of the current generation of realists are to be believed, examining democracy as a factor in IR should not disqualify neoconservatism from the realist tradition, so long as it is done to study its effect on the generation of international political power. Ironically, even as Williams suggests that Hans Morgenthau "provides a remarkably prescient warning" of neoconservatism's dangerous interpretation of the national interest, the band of self-identified realists who seek to bring a new rigour to Morgenthau's classical realism quite clearly fail to distinguish themselves from neoconservatism (Williams, 2005). Put simply, no element of neoclassical realism logically precludes a neoconservative foreign policy.

Neoclassical realism seeks to correct the flaws of neorealism to the point that Randall Schweller (2003: 347) claims it to be "the only game in town for the current and next generation of realists", because the alternatives are "highly abstract, purely structural-systemic theories". Like neoconservatism, neoclassical realism focuses on foreign policy as much as system-level phenomena (Schweller, 2003: 317). Like neoconservatism, neoclassical realism generally assumes that as a state's international political power waxes and wanes, so too does its efforts to influence other states (Kagan, 2002, 2008; Zakaria, 1998: 43). Like neoconservatism, neoclassical realism incorporates the role of ideas while continuing to give materialist causes their due.

Since the publication of the piece coining the term "neoclassical realism", the number of scholars identifying themselves as such has grown considerably (Rose, 1998). These thinkers have responded to Stephen Walt's criticism that neoclassical realism "tends to incorporate domestic variables in an ad hoc manner", and "has yet to offer a distinct set of explanatory hypotheses of its own" (Walt, 2002: 211). The more recent generation has focused largely on a single factor: "whether state leaders have the power to convert the nation's economic power into military power or to translate the nation's economic and military power into foreign policy actions" (see also Lobell and Ripsman et al., 2009: 44; Taliaferro, 2006: 486). Brian Rathbun (2008: 302) puts it most succinctly: "Power can be used only if it can be mobilised. Two variables are particularly important for this: the state's extractive ability and inspirational capacity". Neoclassical realism does not limit itself to material variables, but even so, "identity and ideology are used primarily as part of self-help" (Rathbun, 2008: 303).[18] Neoconservatism could not agree more.

Despite considering a wide range of domestic-level variables, neoclassical realism has devoted remarkably little attention to regime type. The few exceptions are suggestive, however. Aaron Friedberg (1988) argues that strong, centralised states are better equipped to react to adverse shifts in relative power and "it would not be surprising, therefore, if liberal democracies failed to do particularly well in this regard" (see also Zakaria, 1997).[19] Norrin Ripsman (2009) posits that the ballot box can be a drag on the generation of military power and Colin Dueck (2006) argues that the prospect of elections forces American presidents to fight wars in ways they would prefer not to. Thomas Christensen (1996) describes the American government's need to inflate the threat posed by Communist China to rouse an American public into mobilising sufficient power to counter the "real" Soviet threat.

Schweller, one of the first to embrace the neoclassical label, has derived many of the same conclusions as neoconservatives. In early work (1992), Schweller argues that democracies avoid preventative wars against rising major powers. Although he does not specifically mention democracy, he later finds, like Friedberg, that "the behaviour of weak and incoherent states does not conform to the logic of balance of power theory; they do not systematically balance against external threats or take advantage of opportunities to expand when they can" (Schweller, 2003: 344, 2004). Schweller's recent work (2009) explains ideology as a prerequisite of international power and conquest in the "age of mass politics". In this argument, fascism is the ultimate source of military power, whereas realism and liberalism are insufficient ideological motivators. What separates these arguments from those of neoconservatism is not easy to discern.

Neoclassical realism insists that the competitive international system remains the prime mover of foreign policy. In order to distinguish itself from liberal approaches, neoclassical realism tends to choose a privileged actor to represent the "state" by assuming that "the national security executive [...] is best equipped to perceive systemic constraints and deduce the national interest" (Lobell and Ripsman et al., 2009: 25). This is, to say the least, a heroic assumption on par with the traditional state-as-unitary-actor, but with far more dangerous consequences. The latter assumption merely implies that regime type does not matter; the former suggests that executive autonomy determines "whether states respond to international pressures in a timely and efficient fashion" and is thus the recipe for success in international politics. The Kagans strike a similar theme, "it is not enough, however, to say of a democracy that it could not follow a particular policy because the people did not wish to do so. For the necessary and proper role of leaders is to lead" (Kagan and Kagan, 2000: 43). Whereas Richard Ashley (1984) famously criticised neorealism (and neoliberalism) for its dangerous reification of the state, neoclassical realism reifies a very specific embodiment of the state (i.e. the executive).

The illiberal implications of such a move are clear from extending neoconservative logic; mitigating one's own democratic mechanisms in order to advance them elsewhere becomes reasonable. Irving Kristol (1996) compares American prospects favourably to Athens' fate because "the Athenian version of democracy had far fewer ways of shaping, refining, and even sometimes thwarting popular opinion" than the American one. While many have focused on threats to civil liberties in the Global War on Terror, a more troubling consequence could be attempts to decouple the decision to use force from the voter (Drolet, 2007: 262). An RMA military insulated from the pacifist pressures of a democratic electorate would undermine the democratic pacifism that allows the United States to be viewed as a Kantian peacemaker, triggering the balance of power politics that contrary to structural realist predictions have not yet developed.

Neoclassical realists may defend themselves against this chapter's claims by observing that no one in their ranks has argued for spreading democracy. This chapter asks, "why not"? While both neoconservatism and neoclassical realism focus on domestic aspects of power generation, to date, the latter has generally taken a strikingly non-strategic approach to it. Neoconservatism acknowledges that if domestic factors affect a state's ability to balance against threat or power, a strategic actor should incorporate other states' domestic factors into its geopolitical calculus. Intervening in other states' internal affairs becomes a form of both internal and external balancing (as well as means of shaping others' foreign policy aims).

More than any other aspect of neoconservatism, attention to a state's regime type appears to be a clear violation of the realist tradition, and yet neoclassical realism cannot reject such an implication in its current state. Incorporating what one author (Levy, 1988) has called "as close as anything we have to an empirical law in international relations" is no less reasonable than many of the ad hoc additions of neoclassical realism to its structural antecedent, and considerably more parsimonious than some versions. Lack of enthusiasm for democratisation is not really a logical proposition for neoclassical realists so much as a taboo left over from their ancestors.

Why care?

This chapter has sought to show that neoconservatism takes a realist starting point to justify foreign policies that profoundly differ from those generally considered to be within the realist tradition. But even in policy terms, the differences are not as extreme as one might think. A recent "Teaching and Research in International Politics" (TRIP) survey of American IR scholars (Maliniak et al., 2012) found that self-identified realists were no less likely to have supported the Iraq War than liberals or those who did not choose a paradigm.[20] Perhaps even more surprising, self-identified realists are more inclined to favour a pre-emptive attack on a nuclearising Iran (Maliniak et al., 2012).[21] And of course, like neoconservatives, prominent realists have predicted that the United States is headed towards a more conflictual relationship with China.

Structural realism has long been criticised, not least by neoclassical realists, for being largely incapable of creating a theory of foreign policy. Sebastian Rosato and John Schuessler (2011: 804) present a spare but crystalline version: "balance against other great powers and also against hostile minor powers that inhabit strategically important regions of the world", but have little to say on what power is, how it is generated, and how one defines "hostile". Realists unsatisfied with such stark recommendations will face uncomfortable implications. Once one assumes a conflict-prone, anarchic world of sovereign states and then attempts to bring the domestic "in", little prevents a neoconservative approach to the world. Whereas Rosato and Schuessler counsel restraint against Iran, as the TRIP survey shows, not all self-identified realists agree.

Realists can justifiably claim to have by and large rejected the Iraq War in the debate leading up to the invasion. But the arguments against the war made by structural realists (Mearsheimer and Walt, 2003) focused on the limitations of military power, the history of Saddam Hussein's containment and deterability, the lack of a connection to Al-Qaeda, the power of nationalism, and Iraqi societal divisions. In short, the difference between neoconservatism and neorealism on this issue appears to be a largely empirical question.

Refereeing between the two will require a shift in emphasis in the empirical implications privileged in realist work. Much of realism's competitive theory testing to date focuses on targets – institutions, transnational norms, trade, "soft power" – squarely within neoconservatives' crosshairs. Undermining the claim that democratic voters need a liberal ideology to underpin their security policy would damage the neoconservative case, but many realists assume this to be the case as well (Mearsheimer, 2001: 42). Alexander Downes (2009) finds that regime type makes little difference in wartime performance, although he does not focus on neoconservative arguments that democracies are less adept at fighting rather than more. More directly, Alexander Downes and Jonathan Monten (2013) cast doubt on the advisability of foreign imposed regime change. On the whole, however, little empirical work exists directly comparing the two approaches' arguments.

Many readers of this book may be uninterested in a squabble on the fine-grained differences between these two traditions, neither of which have many representatives in the academy.[22] Those who do not directly share a stake in this debate would be mistaken in ignoring it, however. In essence, this chapter identifies a new "neo–neo" debate, in which the disagreements are even more limited than those between neoliberal institutionalism and neorealism. Ole Wæver (1996) describes the earlier debate as veering beyond the "boundary of boredom". A world in which neoclassical realism and neoconservatism are the two salient policy options for the state that remains by far the world's most powerful will be plenty interesting, even if the science is not.

Ultimately, we must care about these small differences because their policy implications are great. If the parameters of the debate are so limited, we are unlikely to see real change in the behaviour of the United States. While Robert Kagan (2010) expressed disappointment with Obama's failure to recognise the "zero sum" nature of international politics at the beginning of the president's term, Kagan's analysis six months later took a decidedly more charitable turn.[23] At the time he made it, Kagan's (2008) confident prediction that "in 2008, as in almost every election of the past century, American voters will choose between two variations of the same worldview" struck many observers of the McCain-Obama race as implausible. The post-election policies of Barak Obama – the toppling of Libya's dictator by force, the routine use of drone-launched ordnance with little fuss from either the public or Congress, a paucity of efforts to advance free trade, little effort to renew or reform international institutions even in the aftermath of a global financial meltdown, and the quiet shelving of efforts to establish a new global norm of "nuclear zero" – suggest that Kagan was on to something.

Notes

1. Portions of this chapter are taken from Jonathan D. Caverley. (2010), "Power and Democratic Weakness: Neoconservatism and Neoclassical Realism", *Millennium* 38(3), 593–614.

2. Norman Podhoretz's 1999 survey article usefully identifies other "neocon-servatives" whose thinking has remained consistent before and after the Cold War, and acknowledges that they often disagree on policy while sharing a common logic. Norman Podhoretz. (1999), "Strange Bedfellows: A Guide to the New Foreign Policy Debates", *Commentary*, 108(5), 19–31. Interestingly, Podhoretz excludes Krauthammer from the ranks.

3. "Neoconservatives argue that liberal policies – for example, disarmament in the pursuit of peace, or affirmative action in the pursuit of racial equality – undermined those goals rather than advancing them." Joshua Muravchik (2007). "The past, present, and future of neoconservatism", *Commentary*, 124(3), 19–29. On the importance of focusing on neoconservative means, rather than ends, see Christopher J. Fettweis, Dangerous Revisionism: On the Founders, "Neocons" and the Importance of History, *Orbis*, 53(3), 509.

4. Irving Kristol also evinced scepticism over promoting democracy by the sword.

5. Put differently, this chapter errs on the side of extrapolation rather then eso-tericism. See the exchange with Daniel Nexon, "Against Esoteric Readings of Neoconservatvism, or Always Check the Footnotes", 15 June 2011. Duck of Minerva. http://www.whiteoliphaunt.com/duckofminerva/2011/06/against-esoteric-readings-of.html

6. Fukuyama does contrast realism and neoconservatism: "the nature of the regime matters to external behaviour is held much more consistently by neoconservatives than the alternative realist view that all states seek power regardless of regime type", but then acknowledges the "realist dimension" that "power is often necessary to achieve moral purposes". Fukuyama, *America at the Crossroads*, 61–62.

7. Danny Cooper (and others) would disagree, claiming that an obsession with unipolarity stems from an even more visceral desire to spread human rights around the globe. This chapter is unlikely to put this debate to rest, but again that is not its purpose. Cooper, *Neoconservatism and American Foreign Policy*, 11.

8. The phrase is originally George Will's.

9. Benjamin Miller. (2010), "Democracy Promotion: Offensive Liberalism versus the Rest (of IR Theory)", *Millennium*, 38(3), 561–591. For this reason, while Miller's "offensive liberalism" may be a useful analytic category, it does not describe neoconservatism.

10. Neoconservatives square the circle of American unipolarity and liberalism by arguing that the United States' dominance was essentially "accidental". Kagan, "End of Dreams"; Krauthammer "Decline is a Choice".

11. Robert Jervis (2003) makes the same point, although he argues that the United States' pursuit of these luxury goods is due its inability "to place sensible limits on its fears and aspirations". "Understanding the Bush Doctrine", *Political Science Quarterly*, 118(3) , 365–388, 366.

12. Note that Krauthammer regards Islamic terrorism as part of a "larger, and state-based trend, the Arab-Islamic totalitarianism that has threatened us in both its secular and religious forms for the quarter-century since the Khomeini revolution of 1979".

13. Muravchik (2007) states: "A key goal in the larger war against terrorism has been to put an end to state support for terrorists." State-centrism is a criticism that was frequently applied to the Bush Administration's response to the September 11 terror attacks.

14. I acknowledge that tying Kirkpatrick into this chapter's overall argument requires considerable interpolation. Nonetheless, I address her work as a part of this tradition, rather than ignoring it, as do most examinations of neoconservatism.
15. Muravchik recommends not going to war to spread democracy, although "exceptions may occur, especially where the issue of democracy combines with others to make a compelling interest", *Imperative of American Leadership*, 164.
16. To reiterate, Muravchik's "foe" is Islamic terrorism, which he clearly states is a state-based phenomenon.
17. Muravchik (1994) cites Paul Schroeder, "Historical Reality vs. Neo-Realist Theory", *International Security*, 19(1), 108–148. On lack of balancing in the post-Cold War world, see Stephen G. Brooks and William C. Wohlforth. (2008), *World out of Balance: International Relations and the Challenge of American Primacy*, Princeton, NJ: Princeton University Press.
18. Indeed, like neoconservatives, several self-identified neoclassical realists argue that ideology directly affects foreign policy behaviour rather than power mobilisation. Colin Dueck (2006) argues that American strategic culture filters out *realpolitik* policy options. Christopher Layne (2006) argues that liberal economic ideology led to American over-expansion. William Wohlforth (1993) focuses on the perception of power.
19. Whereas Mearsheimer and Walt characterise Friedberg as a neoconservative, Schweller describes Friedberg as a "neoclassical realist". This chapter claims they are both correct. John J. Mearsheimer and Stephen M. Walt. (2007), *The Israel Lobby and US Foreign Policy*, New York: Farrar, Straus and Giroux, 129; Schweller, "The Progressiveness of Neoclassical Realism", 318.
20. Indeed if one did not control for one's political ideology, realists were *more* likely to support the Iraq invasion.
21. They were less enthusiastic about the Libya and Syria interventions, however.
22. Neoconservatives brag of their lack of academic positions, while 16 per cent of TRIP respondents identified themselves as realists, versus 20 per cent each for constructivists and liberals.
23. Robert Kagan, "Obama's 5 Foreign Policy Victories", *Washington Post*, 29 June 2010.

References

Alexander, G. (2007), "International Relations Theory Meets World Politics: The Neoconservative vs. Realism Debate", in S. Renshon and P. Suedfeld (eds) *Understanding the Bush Doctrine*, London: Routledge, 39–62.

Ashley, R. K. (1984), "The Poverty of Neorealism", *International Organization*, 38(2), 225–286.

Betts, R. K. (2010), "Conflict or Cooperation? Three Visions Revisited", *Foreign Affairs*, 89(6), 186–194.

Brooks, S. G. (1997), "Dueling Realisms", *International Organization*, 51(3), 445–477.

Christensen, T. J. (1996), *Useful Adversaries: Grand Strategy, Domestic Mobilization, and Sino-American Conflict, 1947–1958*, Princeton, N.J.: Princeton University Press.

Cooper, D. (2011), *Neoconservatism and American Foreign Policy: A Critical Analysis*, London: Routledge.

Copeland, D. C. (2000), *The Origins of Major War*, Ithaca N.Y.: Cornell University Press.

Desch, M. C. (2007), "America's Liberal Illiberalism: The Ideological Origins of Overreaction in U.S. Foreign Policy", *International Security*, 32(3), 7–43.

Downes, A. B. (2009), "How Smart and Tough are Democracies? Reassessing Theories of Democratic Victory in War", *International Security*, 33(4), 9–51.

Downes, A. B. and Monten, J. (2013). "Freedom by Force: Foreign-Imposed Regime Change and Democratization", *International Security*.

Drolet, J.-F. (2007), "The Visible Hand of Neo-conservative Capitalism", *Millennium*, 35(2), 245–278.

Dueck, C. (2006), *Reluctant Crusaders: Power, Culture, and Change in American Grand Strategy*, Princeton, N.J.: Princeton University Press.

Friedberg, A. L. (1988), *The Weary Titan: Britain and the Experience of Relative Decline, 1895–1905*, Princeton, N.J.: Princeton University Press.

Fukuyama, F. (2006), *America at the Crossroads: Democracy, Power, and the Neoconservative Legacy*, New Haven Conn.: Yale University Press.

Gowa, J. S. (1994), *Allies, Adversaries, and International Trade*, Princeton, N.J.: Princeton University Press.

Ikenberry, G. J. (2008), "Introduction: Woodrow Wilson, the Bush Administration, and the Future of Liberal Internationalism", in G. J. Ikenberry, T. J. Knock, A.-M. Slaughter and T. Smith (eds) *The Crisis of American Foreign Policy: Wilsonianism in the Twenty-first Century*, New York: Princeton University Press, 1–24.

Kagan, R. (21 May 2000), "A Real Case for Missile Defense", *The Washington Post*.

Kagan, R. (2002), "Power and Weakness", *Policy Review* (113), 3–28.

Kagan, R. (2003), *Of Paradise and Power: America and Europe in the New World Order*, New York: Knopf.

Kagan, R. (2007), "End of Dreams, Return of History", *Policy Review* (144), 17–44.

Kagan, R. (2008), "Neocon Nation: Neoconservatism, c.1776", *World Affairs*, 170(4), 13.

Kagan, R. (2008), *The Return of History and the End of Dreams*, New York: Knopf.

Kagan, R. (2010), "Obama's Year One: Contra", *World Affairs*, Retrieved from http://www.worldaffairsjournal.org/article/obamas-year-one-contra

Kagan, R. (2012), *The World America Made*, New York, N.Y.: Knopf.

Kagan, D. and Kagan, F. W. (2000), *While America Sleeps: Self-Delusion, Military Weakness, and the Threat to Peace Today*, New York: St. Martin's Press.

Kagan, R. and Kristol, W. (1996), "Toward a Neo-Reaganite Foreign Policy", *Foreign Affairs*, 75(4), 18–32.

Kagan, R. and Kristol, W. (2000), "Introduction: National Interest and Global Responsibility", in R. Kagan and W. Kristol (eds) *Present Dangers: Crisis and Opportunities in American Foreign and Defense Policy*, New York: Encounter Books, 3–24.

Kirkpatrick, J. J. (1979), "Dictatorships and Double Standards", *Commentary*, 68(5), 34–45.

Krauthammer, C. (2003), "The Unipolar Moment Revisited", *The National Interest* (70), 5–17.

Krauthammer, C. (2004), "Democratic Realism: An American Foreign Policy for a Unipolar World". *2004 Irving Kristol Lecture*, Washington, DC: American Enterprise Institute.

Krauthammer, C. (2004), "In Defense of Democratic Realism", *The National Interest* (77), 15–26.

Krauthammer, C. (19 October 2009), "Decline is a Choice: The New Liberalism and the end of American Ascendancy", *The Weekly Standard*, 15(5), Retrieved from http://www.weeklystandard.com/Content/Public/Articles/000/000/017/056lfnpr.asp

Kristol, I. (1983), *Reflections of a Neoconservative: Looking Back, Looking Ahead*, New York: Basic Books.

Kristol, I. (14 June1993), "A Conservative Welfare State", *Wall Street Journal*.

Kristol, I. (2 August1996), "A Post-Wilsonian Foreign Policy", *Wall Street Journal*.

Kristol, I. (1997), *The Lost Soul of the Welfare State. On the Issues*, Washington, D.C.: American Enterprise Institute.

Kristol, I. (19 October 2000), "The Two Welfare States", *Wall Street Journal*, New York.

Kristol, I. (25 August 2003), "The Neoconservative Persuasion", *The Weekly Standard*, 8(47), Retrieved from http://www.weeklystandard.com/Content/Public/Articles/000/000/003/000tzmlw.asp#

Kristol, I. (8 December 2006), "My Public Interest", *The Weekly Standard*, 12(14), Retrieved from http://www.weeklystandard.com/Content/Public/Articles/000/000/013/064fooiq.asp

Layne, C. (2006), *The Peace of Illusions: American Grand Strategy From 1940 to the Present*, Ithaca: Cornell University Press.

Levy, J. S. (1988), "Domestic Politics of War", *Journal of Interdisciplinary History*, 18, 653–673.

Lobell S. E., Ripsman, N. M. and Taliaferro, J. W. (2009), "Introduction", in S. E. Lobell, N. M. Ripsman and J. W. Taliaferro (eds) *Neoclassical Realism, the State, and Foreign Policy*, Cambridge: Cambridge University Press, 1–41.

Maliniak, D., Peterson, S. and Tierney, M. J. (2012), *TRIP Around the World: Teaching, Research, and Policy Views of International Relations Faculty in 20 Countries*, Williamsburg: VA, Institute for the Theory and Practice of International Relations, College of William and Mary.

Mearsheimer, J. J. (2001), "The Future of the American Pacifier", *Foreign Affairs*, 80(5), 46–61.

Mearsheimer, J. J. (2001), *The Tragedy of Great Power Politics*, New York: Norton.

Mearsheimer, J. J. (2005), "Hans Morgenthau and the Iraq War: Realism versus Neo-Conservatism", *Open Democracy*, Retrieved from http://www.opendemocracy.net/democracy-americanpower/morgenthau_2522.jsp

Mearsheimer, J. J. and Walt, S. M. (2003), "An Unnecessary War", *Foreign Policy*, 134(1), 50–59.

Miller, B. (2010), "Democracy Promotion: Offensive Liberalism versus the Rest (of IR Theory)", *Millennium*, 38(3), 561–591.

Muravchik, J. (1996), *The Imperative of American Leadership: A Challenge to Neo-Isolationism*, Washington, D.C.: The AEI Press.

Muravchik, J. (2007), "The Past, Present, and Future of Neoconservatism", *Commentary*, 124(3), 19–29.

Podhoretz, N. (1996), "Neoconservatism: A Eulogy", Bradley Lecture Series, Washington, DC: American Enterprise Institute.

Podhoretz, N. (1999), "Strange Bedfellows: A Guide to the New Foreign-Policy Debates", *Commentary*, 108(5), 19–31.

Rapport, A. (2008), "Unexpected Affinities? Neoconservatism's Place in IR Theory", *Security Studies*, 17(2), 257–293.

Rathbun, B. (2008), "A Rose by any Other Name: Neoclassical Realism as the Logical and Necessary Extension of Structural Realism", *Security Studies*, 17(2), 294–321.

Ripsman, N. M. (2009), "Neoclassical Realism and Domestic Interest Groups", in S. E. Lobell, N. M. Ripsman and J. W. Taliaferro (eds) *Neoclassical Realism, the State and Foreign Policy*, New York: Cambridge University Press.

Rosato, S. and Schuessler, J. (2011), "A Realist Foreign Policy for the United States", *Perspectives on Politics*, 9(4), 803–819.

Rose, G. (1998), "Neoclassical Realism and Theories of Foreign Policy", *World Politics*, 51(1), 44–72.

Schmidt, B. C. and Williams, M. C. (2008), "The Bush Doctrine and the Iraq War: Neoconservatives versus Realists", *Security Studies*, 17(2), 191–220.

Schweller, R. L. (1992), "Domestic Structure And Preventive War – Are Democracies More Pacific", *World Politics*, 44(2), 235–269.

Schweller, R. L. (2003), "The Progressiveness of Neoclassical Realism", in C. Elman and M. F. Elman (eds) *Progress in International Relations Theory: Appraising the Field*, Cambridge: MIT Press.

Schweller, R. L. (2004), "Unanswered Threats – A Neoclassical Realist Theory of Underbalancing", *International Security*, 29(2), 159–201.

Schweller, R. L. (2009), "Neoclassical Realism and State Mobilization: Expansionist Ideology in the Age of Mass Politics", in S. E. Lobell, N. M. Ripsman and J. W. Taliaferro (eds) *Neoclassical Realism, the State and Foreign Policy*, New York: Cambridge University Press.

Singh, R. (2009), "Neo-Conservatism: Theory and Practice", in I. Paramer, L. Miller and M. Ledwidge (eds) *New Directions in US Foreign Policy*, London: Routledge.

Subramanian, A. (2011), *Eclipse: Living in the Shadow of China's Economic Dominance*, Washington, D.C.: Institute of International Economics.

Taliaferro, J. W. (2006), "State Building for Future Wars: Neoclassical Realism and the Resource-Extractive State", *Security Studies*, 15(3), 464–495.

Van Evera, S. (1999), *Causes of War: Power and the Roots of Conflict*, Ithaca: Cornell University Press.

Vaïsse, J. (2010), *Neoconservatism: The Biography of a Movement*, Cambridge: Harvard University Press.

Wæver, O. (1996), "The Rise and Fall of the Inter-Paradigm Debate", in S. Smith, K. Booth and M. Zalewski (eds) *International Theory: Positivism and Beyond*, Cambridge: Cambridge University Press, 149–185.

Walt, S. M. (2002), "The Enduring Relevance of the Realist Tradition", in I. Katznelson and H. V. Milner (eds) *Political Science: The State of the Discipline*, New York: W.W. Norton.

Walt, S. M. (2005), "The Relationship Between Theory and Policy in International Relations", *Annual Review of Political Science*, 8(1), 23–48.

Waltz, K. N. (1979), *Theory of international politics*, Reading, MA: Addison-Wesley Pub. Co.

Williams, M. C. (2005), "What is the National Interest? The Neoconservative Challenge in IR Theory", *European Journal of International Relations*, 11(3), 307–337.

Williams, M. C. (2007), *Realism Reconsidered: The Legacy of Hans Morgenthau in International Relations*, Oxford; New York: Oxford University Press.

Wohlforth, W. C. (1993), *The Elusive Balance: Power and Perceptions During the Cold War*, Ithaca: Cornell University Press.

Zakaria, F. (1997), "The Rise of Illiberal Democracy", *Foreign Affairs*, 76(6), 22–43.

Zakaria, F. (1998), *From Wealth to Power: The Unusual Origins of America's World Role*, Princeton, NJ: Princeton University Press.

9
The Liberal International Order Reconsidered

Christian Reus-Smit

For many scholars, policymakers, and media commentators, it is self-evident that we live today in a liberal international order and that the big questions concern the durability of this order; its ability, in particular, to survive the rise of non-liberal great powers and the politics of anti-liberal social forces. But what is an international order, and what is the nature of the liberal international order, in particular? One prominent answer is provided by John Ikenberry, who defines an international order as "the 'governing' arrangements among a group of states, including its fundamental rules, principles, and institutions" (2001: 23), and a liberal international order as one that "is open and loosely rule based", creating "a foundation in which states can engage in reciprocity and institutionalised cooperation" (2011: 18). International orders, so understood, are constructed by great powers, and the present liberal order reflects the post-1945 ascendance of the United States.

This chapter takes issue with this understanding of international orders, in general, and the liberal international order, in particular. Nowhere do I deny that an important dimension of an international order is its architecture of institutional rules and practices. Nor that the liberal international order is structured by a distinctive set of such practices, informed as they are by liberal ideals of governance transposed onto the international system. International orders are much more than this, though. They comprise, I shall argue, at least three basic elements: a systemic configuration of institutionalised power and authority (sovereignty, heteronomy, suzerainty, empire, etc.), an architecture of fundamental rules and practices that facilitate coexistence and cooperation between loci of authority, and a framework of constitutional social norms that license both of these. In characterising the liberal international order, Ikenberry focuses solely on the second of these – the liberal architecture of international rules and practices constructed after 1945. He misses, however, two arguably more fundamental features of the contemporary liberal order: universalised state sovereignty, which contrasts with the long-standing conjunction of sovereignty in the core and empire in the periphery; and a justificatory framework that grounds territorial particularism in a form of moral universalism. Together these elements have produced an international order with four often contradictory characteristics: "Millian" sovereignty, liberal proceduralism, embedded cosmopolitanism, and hierarchy without empire.

International orders

Hedley Bull famously defined order as a purposive arrangement of units – books set alphabetically on a shelf, for example. An international order, he continued, is a purposive arrangement of sovereign states, in which the preservation of the society of states, territorial independence, and limiting interstate violence constitute the underlying purposes, and basic institutional practices, such as diplomacy and international law, define the arrangement (Bull, 1995: Chapter 1). Bull contrasted orders such as these with world orders, which encompass not merely states and their institutional practices, but the broader social universe of peoples, institutions, and practices in which they are embedded (1995: 19). Bull's project was to show (contra realism) that international order is not only possible but a recurrent feature of international life, and (contra cosmopolitanism) that world order is an ambition yet to be realised. To the extent that order exists globally, it is the order of the society of sovereign states.

Influential as it is, this understanding of international order is vulnerable to at least two criticisms. Firstly, the "arrangement" of states is defined narrowly in terms of the external institutional practices that condition their interaction. Yet the arrangement that characterises an international order starts with something more fundamental – the organisation of political life into territorially demarcated sovereign states. Not all international orders are structured this way: some are heteronomous, some suzerain, some imperial, and some, a combination of these forms. If we want to understand international orders as purposive arrangements of units, then "arrangement" needs to be conceived broadly to include the nature and constitution of the units themselves. Secondly, in drawing a distinction between international and world orders, and in defining the former in terms of existential state purposes and supporting institutional practices, the role that global social processes have played in the constitution of international orders is occluded. We know, however, that international orders are not generated simply through the external interaction of pre-constituted units; the units themselves emerge out of complex social and political processes. International order, as Bull imagined it, is constituted by world social forces.

Because of these problems, several authors have advanced more expansive conceptions of international order. In a recent book, Andrew Phillips defines international orders "as systemic structures that cohere within culturally and historically specific social imaginaries, and that are composed of an *order-producing* normative complex and its accompanying fundamental institutions. Both an international order's normative complex and its fundamental institutions rest in turn on a permissive *order-enabling* material foundation" (2011: 23–24). The great virtue of this conception is that the fundamental institutions of an international order (which, in the present system, Phillips takes to include both the configuration of sovereign political units and interstate institutional practices) can vary: indeed he compares sovereign, suzerain, and heteronomous international orders. Added to this, Phillips' conception explicitly grounds these institutions in deeper normative complexes and material conditions. The former "confers upon actors a shared collective identity, as well as providing ethical prescriptions to regulate actors' behaviour and a justificatory rationale to stabilise and sustain relations of organised domination", while the latter "sets concrete material constraints on the scope and character of agents' interactions" (Phillips, 2011: 24). Finally, Phillips is clear that international orders – their fundamental institutions and normative and material supports – are embedded within broader social universes: in fact, it is changes in these broader universes that bring about the collapse of international orders (2011: 43–46).

My own view of international orders has much in common with Phillips', though I define their constituent elements differently. International orders are, first of all, *systemic configurations of political authority*. In sovereign orders, political authority is organised into multiple, territorially demarcated political units. Within these units, authority is centralised, exclusive, and bounded. Heteronomous orders, in contrast, have multiple centres of political authority, all with overlapping jurisdictions. Imperial orders, as a third form, organise political authority hierarchically. They are, as Michael Doyle argues, "a system of interaction between two political entities, one of which, the dominant metropolis, exerts political control over the internal and external policy – effective sovereignty – of the other, the subordinate periphery" (1986: 45). Secondly, international orders develop architectures of *fundamental institutional practices* that allow coexistence and cooperation between loci of political authority. Elsewhere I have written at length about why different societies of sovereign states (or sovereign international orders) have developed different fundamental institutions (Reus-Smit, 1999), and Phillips and others have discussed their nature and development in heteronomous and suzerain orders (Phillips, 2011; Zhang and Buzan, 2012). Because I am interested in variations in fundamental institutions across sovereign orders, however, and because I see fundamental institutions as second-order institutional constructions, I do not, like Phillips, class basic organising principles, such as sovereignty and heteronomy, as fundamental institutions. Rather, I include these organising principles in a third constitutive element of international orders: their deep *constitutional structures*.

These ensembles of intersubjective norms and principles license a particular systemic configuration of political authority (by privileging a particular organising principle), define what constitutes legitimate political agency (with reference of hegemonic ideas of the moral purpose the "state", broadly understood), and sanction particular kinds of fundamental institutional practices (in line with an ascendant norm of procedural justice) (Reus-Smit, 1999: 30–33).

Of these three constitutive elements, the last is foundational. Systemic configurations of political authority, such as those comprised of independent sovereign states or the heteronomous ordering of multiple yet overlapping centres of authority, are not distributions of material resources, even if they relate, in important ways, to such distributions. Political authority, as Weber explained, is "the legitimate exercise of imperative control" (1964: 153).[1] Systemic configurations of such political authority are thus system-wide arrangements of legitimate rule, and these configurations ultimately rest on intersubjective understandings (Mattern, 2005). Constitutional structures help sustain this legitimacy: their organising principles license the prevailing spatial configuration of rule, and hegemonic beliefs about the moral purpose of the state justify both this spatial arrangement and the substantive complexion of legitimate political authority. In the Absolutist international order that existed in Europe from the seventeenth to the early nineteenth centuries, for example, intersubjective beliefs about divine right licensed both sovereign territoriality and monarchic rule. In a similar way, constitutional structures also condition the nature of fundamental institutional practices. Systemic norms of procedural justice encourage the adoption and development of particular kinds of institutional practices over others. For instance, the Absolutist idea that legitimate law was the command of a superior authority licensed the development of a distinctive, naturalist conception of international law and a peculiar form of "old" diplomacy.

Ikenberry's order

In the spectrum of conceptions of international order, Ikenberry's is closest to Bull's. Like Bull, he sees international orders as arrangements of states, with "arrangement" defined in terms of prevailing international institutional practices – international orders, he holds, are "the settled rules and arrangements that guide the relations among states" (Ikenberry, 2001: 47). He gives less emphasis to the purposive dimension of international order, but it is there nonetheless. At a minimum, states construct international orders to preserve their own security and establish a stable systemic peace. More ambitiously, "states engaged in order building have also gone beyond this and attempted to establish a wider array of political and economic rules and principles of order" (Ikenberry, 2011: 11).

In this conception, the principal agents constructing and maintaining international orders are great powers. "In every era", Ikenberry argues, "great powers have rise up to build rules and institutions of relations between states, only to see those ordering arrangements eventually break down or transform" (2011: 11). Major projects of order building usually occur after major wars. "The violence of great-power war tears the old order apart. The war strips the rules and arrangements of the pre-war system of its last shreds of legitimacy.... And in the aftermath of war, victors are empowered to organise a new system with rules and arrangements that accord with their interests" (2001: 11–12). For Ikenberry, the distribution of material power among great powers provides the underlying framework of opportunities and constraints in which international orders are constructed, and the interests of predominant powers determine the kinds of international orders established within such frameworks (2011: 35–47).

In both of his major works, Ikenberry distinguishes between three different forms of international order. The first is the familiar balance of power orders emphasised in realist theory. Here order is a simple by-product of the competitive dynamics of the international system: as great powers struggle with one another for security or primacy, a constraining equilibrium is reached. "Order is based on the balancing actions of states – the necessary and inevitable outcome of states seeking to ensure their security in an anarchic system" (2001: 25). The second form of order is hierarchical, as it is "organised around the domination of a powerful state" (2011: 55). The contours of a hierarchical order reflect the interests of the hegemonic power, as well as the military, financial, and technical resources it can draw on to command compliance. "Within a hegemonic order", Ikenberry writes, "rules and rights are established and enforced by the power capabilities of the leading state. Compliance and participation within the order are ultimately ensured by the range of power capabilities available to the hegemon.... Direct coercion is always an option in the enforcement of order, but less direct 'carrots and sticks' also maintain hegemonic control" (2011: 57). The third type of international order is constitutional, in the sense that it is built on rules and institutions that reflect the common interests and consent of principal states. "States enter the international order out of enlightened self-interest, engaging in self-restraint and binding themselves to agreed-upon rules and institutions".

An initial contradiction is already apparent in Ikenberry's understanding of international orders. His definition of an international order is institutional – it is a system of governance that includes "fundamental rules, principles, and institutions" (2001: 23). Yet his first type of order does not fit this definition. There is nothing institutional about it; order, now understood as a precarious peace, is simply an unintended consequence of material competition. It would be different if Ikenberry had followed Bull in seeing the balance of power as an institution – a deliberately engineered equilibrium of forces, such as the Concert of Europe – but this is not the case. One might also ask whether his second form of international order is consistent with his general definition. To be sure, the hegemonic state establishes rules that serve its interests and to which other states must comply. Yet these rules take the form of commands, and other states comply because of the hegemon's capacity to coerce and bribe: rule observance does not rest, to any significant degree, on legitimacy bred of consent or norm internalisation. Only the last of Ikenberry's forms of international order – the "constitutional" form – fits squarely within his definition. At best, one can say that in his typology of forms of international order, Ikenberry slides from one conception of order to another: from order understood as stability or a minimal peace to order as a form of governance; an institutionalised arrangement of states.[2] His balance of power order is an example of the former; his constitutional order, a case of the latter.

This problem aside, how does Ikenberry conceive the liberal international order? In general, he argues that "liberal international order is defined as order that is open and loosely rule-based. Openness is manifest when states trade and exchange on the basis of mutual gain. Rules and institutions operate as mechanism of governance – and they are at least partially autonomous from the exercise of state power. In its ideal form", he contends, "liberal international order creates a foundation in which states can engage in reciprocity and institutionalised cooperation" (Ikenberry, 2011: 18). Liberal orders can vary, though: in the scope of liberal values they seek to realise (from free trade to the promotion of human rights), in their geographical scope (from the Western sphere of international system during the Cold War, to the entire globe thereafter), and, most importantly, in the degree to which they are hierarchically ordered (Ikenberry, 2011: 19–22). The liberal international order has been evolving since the latter part of the nineteenth century, but its most significant elaboration, Ikenberry contends, came after the Second World War. What developed then was a liberal international order that was substantively ambitious, highly institutionalised, and hierarchically ordered. The post-1945 order is a hybrid; it is both constitutional, in the sense in that it comprises an elaborate architecture of agreed upon rules and practices, and hierarchical, because its construction has been driven by the United States, reflected American interests, and depended on the exercise of American power. It has been, Ikenberry concludes, a "liberal hegemonic order", in which the "liberal hegemonic state dominates the order by establishing and maintaining its rules and institutions – but in doing so, it operates to a greater or lesser degree within those rules and institutions" (Ikenberry, 2011: 16).

Ikenberry's understanding of the liberal international order is attractive on several fronts; not the least because of its parsimony and elegance. It captures the architecture of interstate institutional practices that condition relations between states at any particular historical juncture, highlights the significant role that great powers have played in building such architectures, and correctly insists that while the distribution of material power provides the permissive context for order building, it does not determine the kind of order constructed; this derives ultimately from the identities and interests of predominant powers – liberal hegemons construct liberal institutional architectures. Yet from the perspective advanced here, Ikenberry's understanding is as problematic as it is illuminating.

In the end, he presents neither a full account of international orders, in general, nor of the liberal international order, in particular. To begin with, he provides no account of the basic "arrangement" of any international order – the nature of its political units, and how they stand in relation to each other. In this respect, he is vulnerable to the same criticism John Ruggie levelled long ago at Waltz's theory of international politics. Waltz famously identifies three elements of an international system's structure: its organising principle, the functional differentiation of the units, and the distribution of capabilities. Only the first and last of these are seen as variables, however; as states are seen as functionally similar: they all perform the same basic functions. Yet as Ruggie argues, Waltz misunderstands the sociological meaning of "differentiation". He treats it as meaning "sameness" or "difference", where it actually refers to the basis on which units are "separated and segmented" (Ruggie, 1983: 274). When understood in this way, the differentiation of a system's political units becomes a major axis of change and variation: indeed, the principal difference between sovereign, heteronomous, suzerain, and imperial systems is how their units are separated and segmented.

Of course, Ikenberry is not developing a general theory of international politics, as was Waltz. His project is to understand the nature of international orders, and even then, he is primarily concerned with only one: the liberal. This hardly dulls the criticism, though. Historically, a crucial difference between international orders has been how their units have stood in relation to one another: whether they have been legally equal with their jurisdictions territorially bounded; have stood in relations of formal legal and political hierarchy; or have existed within more complex webs of political and legal jurisdiction. Understanding the "arrangement" of "states" within an international order is thus unavoidably about understanding their differentiation or segmentation. More than this, though, the problem relates directly to understanding the nature of the liberal international order itself. Ikenberry takes the world of sovereign states as given and focuses on the development of a liberal architecture of institutional practices within that system. Yet the rise of the liberal international order occurred hand in hand with a reordering of how the international system's political units stood in relation to one another. Until the middle of the nineteenth century, the prevailing configuration of political authority globally was sovereignty in the core and empire in the periphery – sovereignty was not a universal organising principle. The development of the liberal order from the late nineteenth century onward coincides with the gradual proliferation of anti-colonial struggles, and Ikenberry's golden age of the liberal order after 1945 is when the institution of empire is finally delegitimised and sovereignty universalised. I will argue in the following section that these are not just simultaneous developments; they are both part of the liberal international order's complex evolution.

The second problem with Ikenberry's understanding concerns the liberal order's normative and ideational underpinnings. Ultimately, liberalism is a set of ideas about the nature of the individual, society, and the state, and about their appropriate interrelations. And when we talk about a "liberal" international order, we are talking about one that is structured, in significant respects, by such liberal ideas. This begs two questions, though: What is the nature of these liberal ideas? And how, and in what way, did they come to shape the order we now call liberal? At first glance, Ikenberry's answer to the first of these is wide-ranging. Seven ideational commitments are said to have informed post-1945 order building: open markets, economic security, multilateralism, cooperative security, democratic solidarity, human rights and progressive change, and American hegemonic leadership. On closer inspection, however, not all of these get equal billing in Ikenberry's account. He states repeatedly that a liberal international order "is open and loosely rule-based", and that it allows states to "engage in reciprocity and institutionalised cooperation" (Ikenberry, 2011: 18). This understanding has three notable characteristics: it is statist, it stresses openness and reciprocity between states, and it is institutional. Given this, it is not at all surprising that ideational commitments that fit within this broad framework are given special emphasis. Open markets, multilateralism, and cooperative security loom large in Ikenberry's account, as does American hegemonic leadership (on the grounds that the United States is thought to have been singularly important in the construction of the liberal order, that it is an open society, providing opportunities for other states to have "voice" in its decision-making, and that it has exercised authority through international institutions). The liberal ideas that are left out of this schema are those of a more individualist/cosmopolitan nature: in particular, human rights. To be sure, he lists promoting human rights and progressive change as an ambition of wartime and the post-1945 US administrations, and he credits American liberals with the construction of key elements of the international bill of rights, such as the 1948 Universal Declaration. But he argues explicitly that the liberal international order was, until the end of the Cold War, founded on Westphalian notions of sovereignty, and he sees human rights principles complicating this only in upheavals experienced by the international order in the last 20 years (Ikenberry, 2011: 287–290).

This brings me to the third problem with Ikenberry's account: his understanding of agency in the construction of the liberal international order. For him, this is a house that Washington built. He explains, of course, that its construction dates from the late nineteenth century and that Britain played a crucial role in its early development. But he is also clear that the liberal order's golden age occurred after 1945, and in this period, the United States played a singularly important role. Indeed, although Ikenberry acknowledges the willing collaboration of other Western democracies, he comes close to casting the United States as a sole architect and builder. Yet in key areas this sits uncomfortably with the historical record.

The first inconsistency concerns the development of the institutional architecture that has come to characterise the liberal international order. As I have argued elsewhere, the post-1945 period should be seen as more one of mass institutional construction than architectural innovation (Reus-Smit, 1999: 154). This is not to downplay the very real innovations that occurred after the Second World War (in governance of the world economy, and in the human rights regime, for example), but the basic institutional principles of multilateralism and contractual international law that structured these innovations were embraced by the community of states as early at the Hague Conferences of 1899 and 1906. More than this, the Hague Conferences, and later the Versailles Peace Conference, endorsed the idea that the international system should be governed by a universal conference of states, based on the principle of multilateralism, and that there should be an international judicial body interpret international law. In constructing the post-1945 international institutional order, therefore, the United States, in association with other powers, worked within a pre-existing framework of institutional principles. To be sure, from Versailles onward, the United States was a key player in the articulation and mobilisation of these principles, but as we have seen on many an occasion, it has also been an ambivalent, partially committed player.

A second inconsistency relates to the institutional regime established to manage the post-1945 global economy. Few doubt the crucial role played here by the United States. Yet this is not a simple story of American preferences translated into concomitant institutional practices. Indeed, on one reading, the Bretton Woods system of international economic management reflects a hard fought political compromise between Washington's commitment to multilateral free trade and London's emphasis on full employment. A more satisfactory account holds, however, that during the Second World War the leading Western powers reached a consensus on how best to manage the world economy; a consensus that contained a mix of principles that were not reducible to an original set of American preferences. As Ruggie argues in his oft-cited article on "embedded liberalism", "that multilateralism and the quest for domestic stability were coupled and even conditioned by one another reflected the shared legitimacy of a set of social objectives to which the industrial world had moved, unevenly but 'as a single entity'" (1982: 397–398).

With regard, therefore, to both the fundamental institutional practices that came to characterise the liberal international order and the specific institutional arrangements of the post-1945 economic order, agency cannot be reduced to the deft hand of the United States. American power was a vital element, but only when fused with legitimate social purposes that had wider social purchase. It was this unique combination, Ruggie argues, that produce a distinctive configuration of institutionalised political authority that has characterised the liberal order (1982: 382–384).

The problem of agency is even more pronounced, though, when it comes to the more cosmopolitan aspects of the liberal international order; in particular, the development of the international human rights regime. As noted above, Ikenberry has very little to say about this dimension of the liberal order, but has no qualms about assigning almost sole credit to American policymakers and prominent liberals. He writes:

> The notion that the United States wanted to organise the post-war system so as to promote American-held progressive values was evident early in the Second World War. Like Woodrow Wilson before him, Franklin Roosevelt saw American involvement in World War II as part of a grand clash of ideals. Early in the war, he articulated an American commitment to universal human rights, most notably in the Four Freedoms speech and in the promises laid out in the Atlantic Charter in 1941. These commitments were later enshrined in the U.N. Charter in 1945 and in the Universal Declaration of Human Rights adopted by the U.N. General Assembly in December 1948, which launched the post-war human rights revolution. Championed by liberals such as Eleanor Roosevelt and others, the declaration articulated a notion of universal individual rights that deserved to be recognised by the whole of mankind and no simply left to sovereign governments to define and enforce.
>
> (Ikenberry, 2011: 190–191)

The story of the "human rights revolution" is far more complex than this, though, and the role of the United States is less straightforward and flattering. Human rights were among a panoply of concerns pursued by the Roosevelt and Truman Administrations, and they were instrumental in having them included in key documents, such as the Atlantic and United Nations Charters. Furthermore, Eleanor Roosevelt did play a catalytic role in the negotiation of the Universal Declaration. Yet as Mary Ann Glendon explains, the content of the Declaration was the outcome of a unique dialogue among representatives of the world's great cultural and legal traditions, and in significant respects departed from initial American preferences (Glendon, 2002). When we get to the subsequent negotiation of the two International Covenants on Human Rights, the gap between what Washington wanted and the content of the Treaties is even greater.

The United States, along with other prominent Western powers, opposed the right of individuals to petition UN rights bodies directly, but was forced to accept the compromise of the First Optional Protocol to the Covenant on Civil and Political Rights. A similar alliance of Western powers unsuccessfully sought to insert a "federal states" clause into the Treaties, effectively diluting their responsibilities to ensure universal compliance within their jurisdictions. And, perhaps most significantly, the United States sided with Europe's colonial powers to oppose the inclusion of the right to self-determination in the Covenant's. In each of these cases, what came to be the legally binding core of the international human rights regime departed significantly from Washington's preferences, and contrary to common wisdom, newly independent post-colonial states, together with Latin American states, were key agents in its construction (Reus-Smit, 2001).

A reconception

If Ikenberry's account of the liberal international order is problematic, how then should it be conceived? Recall here my earlier account of international orders in general. They are, first and foremost, systemic configurations of political authority. They develop architectures of fundamental institutions that facilitate coexistence and cooperation among loci of authority. And they rest on deep constitutional structures that inform and license both the systemic configuration of authority and the framework of basic institutional practices. To understand the liberal international order – its form and evolution – we thus need to understand the distinctive "liberal" manifestation of each of these three elements. In the following pages, I sketch, firstly, the liberal order's underlying constitutional structure, then, discuss briefly its impact on the nature of fundamental institutional practices. My main concern, however, is with the paired development of the order's peculiar configuration of political authority – universal state sovereignty – and its unique form of institutionalised cosmopolitanism, manifest primarily, though not exclusively, in the international human rights regime.

As noted earlier, constitutional structures are systemic complexes of inter-subjective norms and principles that license particular configurations of authority, define forms of legitimate agency, and sanction certain sorts of fundamental institutional practices. The constitutional structure of the liberal international order is distinctive in several respects.[3] Its organising principle of sovereignty is consistent with that of the preceding Absolutist order, though, as we shall see, when paired with a particular notion of the moral purpose of the state, its practical manifestations have been radically different. This conception of moral purpose defines the role of the legitimate state as the protection of individuals' rights, and the augmentation of their purposes and potentialities.[4] Once the moral purpose of the state is understood in these terms, a particular norm of procedural justice comes to the fore. Such norms do not prescribe substantive principles of justice, only "a correct or fair procedure such that the outcome is likewise correct or fair, whatever it is, providing the procedure has been followed properly" (Rawls, 1973: 86). In liberal polities, and in the liberal international order more generally, the ascendant norm of procedural justice holds that legitimate norms, rules, and principles are authored by those subject to them, or by their duly appointed representatives, and apply equally to all in all like cases. In terms of concrete practices, this favours parliamentary forms of legislation and conceptions of positive law (in which legal obligation is said to derive from consent).

Elsewhere I have explained at length how this constitutional structure conditioned the development of the liberal international order's fundamental institutional practices, and I do no more than summarise the argument here (Reus-Smit, 1999, 1997). During the second half of the nineteenth century, liberal conceptions of legitimate statehood and procedural justice became not only the prevailing measures of political legitimacy and rightful state action, but had a profound effect on the nature of domestic political institutions. As David Thomson observes, "In almost the whole of western and central Europe, parliamentary institutions developed between 1871 and 1914", and during the same period there was a gradual move towards universal suffrage (1962: 323). By the First World War, David Kaiser argues, "Every European government had to maintain a working majority within an elected parliament in order to carry on the essential business of government" (1990: 275–276). Over time, these same liberal norms began to influence institutional developments at the international level. Older "natural" conceptions of international law had already been displaced by notions of "positive" law, in which states are obliged to observe the law of nations not because of fealty to God, but because they had consented. The advent of this new understanding of international law had a profound effect on diplomatic practices. If legitimate international laws were based on the consent of states, and if they were meant to apply equally to all parties, then some mechanism was required to legislate such laws. Not surprisingly, therefore, as we see notions of positive law embraced at the international level, so too do we see the normative and practical ascendance of multilateralism, an institutional practice that "coordinates behaviour among three or more states on the basis of generalised principles of conduct: that is, principles which specify appropriate conduct for a class of actions, without regards to the particularistic interests of the parties or the strategic exigencies that may exist in any specific occurrence" (Ruggie, 1993: 14).. Between 1648 and 1815, European states concluded only 127 multilateral treaties. In the following century, this figure jumped to 817, and thereafter into the thousands (Mostecky, 1965).

Important as this is, the constitutional structure of the liberal international order had an arguably more significant constitutive effect. Mobilised in the anti-colonial struggles of the second half of the twentieth century, its organising principle of sovereignty and legitimating conception of the moral purpose of the state licensed the dismantling of the old systemic configuration of political authority (which conjoined sovereignty in the core with empire abroad) and the construction of the present configuration based on universal state sovereignty. Universal sovereignty – where the territorially demarcated sovereign state is the sole legitimate form of political organisation, and where the system of sovereign states encompasses the entire globe – is an entirely novel configuration of political authority. It is also a distinctively liberal one. There were, of course, strong liberal defences of the old order, in which empire was justified as Europe's civilisational responsibility. The division of the world into sovereign states also stands in tension with other more cosmopolitan aspects of the liberal order. And, undeniably, the global system of sovereign states is populated by many illiberal states, engaged in illiberal practices.

Nevertheless, the current configuration of political authority can be considered liberal in three respects. Firstly, as many scholars have observed, the idea that the international system is, and should be, comprised of independent states, each pursuing their own purposes, and each invoking their sovereign liberties is the liberal conception of society and the individual writ large: states are individuals too! Secondly, and I will return to this below, the oft-heard proposition that sovereignty is cardinal international value because it provides a protective barrier that allows polities to develop their own forms of collective life is a liberal value, expressed most clearly in classical and contemporary liberal defences of the right to non-intervention (from Mill to Walzer). Thirdly, and most importantly, liberal ideals of the moral purpose of the state were deeply implicated it the political struggles that produced this systemic configuration of authority.

Until the twentieth century, two institutions were nested together, jointly shaping the global configuration of political authority: sovereignty in the core, and empire between the core and the periphery. Formal equality and independence, on the one hand, and formal hierarchy and dependence, on the other. Such was the order of things. Only in the second half of the twentieth century was this conjunction of institutions broken, as empire was delegitimised as an acceptable form of rule and sovereignty universalised. Many factors were implicated in this transformation, with the weakening of Europe's imperial powers after two World Wars and the rise of anti-colonial nationalist movements the most commonly cited. But while these factors shed light on the collapse of particular empires, they do not explain the demise of the institution of empire itself, or the rapid and universal nature of post-1945 decolonisation. For this, a normative revolution was required.

This revolution took place within the emergent human rights forums of the United Nations and involved the reformulation and reassertion of the right to self-determination.[5] The norm of self-determination that had emerged out of the Versailles settlement was circumscribed in two ways: it was a right of ethnically defined nations, and only those within Europe. This formulation was fundamentally discredited by the Nazis' genocidal war for a culturally homogenous greater Germany, but it was also decidedly unhelpful to non-European subject peoples, most of whom lived within culturally heterogeneous colonial units. Between 1945 and 1960, post-colonial states who had gained their independence immediately after the Second World War worked within United Nation's human rights bodies to recast and reassert the right to self-determination. Contrary to standard accounts, these states played a key role in the negotiation of the two legally binding International Covenants on human rights, strongly defending the priority of civil and political rights (against the Soviet bloc), and pushing for the Treaties universal application (against the leading imperial powers, backed by the United States). Post-colonial states successfully opposed moves by Britain and France (supported by Australia, Canada, and the United States) to limit the application of the Covenant on Civil and Political rights in "Non-Self-Governing and Trust Territories" and argued against leading Western powers that individuals, in addition to states, should have the right to petition United Nations human rights bodies.

Within this framework of emergent international human rights law, post-colonial states reconstructed the right to self-determination. Their strategy was to graft the latter right to the new human rights principles, arguing that the self-determination of peoples was a necessary prerequisite for the satisfaction of individuals' civil and political rights. In 1951 leading post-colonial states called on the General Assembly to compel the Human Rights Commission to insert an article on self-determination into the two draft covenants, arguing that "No basic rights could be ensured unless this right were ensured" (United Nations, 1952b: 485). In response, the Commission not only inserted the articles but ask the General Assembly to pass a separate resolution encouraging states to uphold the right. Resolution 637 (A) explicitly tied the right to self-determination to individual human rights: "the rights of peoples and nations to self-determination is a prerequisite for the enjoyment of all fundamental human rights" (United Nations, 1952a). These moves were vigorously opposed by leading Western states, including the United States, and intense debate continued throughout the 1950s. A fundamental normative shift occurred during this period, however. In 1960 the United Nations adopted the Declaration on the Granting of Independence to Colonial Countries and Peoples, which declared that "subjection of peoples to alien subjugation, domination, and exploitation constitutes a denial of fundamental human rights" (United Nations, 1960). But where in 1952 most Western states voted en mass against Resolution 637 (A), many now voted in support of Declaration, and the remainder (including Australia, Belgium, France, Portugal, Spain, Britain, and the United States) abstained, unwilling to pay the reputational costs of opposing a measure supported by 90 per cent of member states.

Parallel, therefore, to the construction of the liberal international order's architecture of fundamental institutions, sovereignty was being universalised. And where the first process involved liberal ideas about procedural justice licensing the development of distinctive, multilateral institutional practices, the second saw liberal principles of individual rights and legitimate authority codified in the legal core of the international human rights regime, and used to delegitimise the institution of empire and justify the proliferation of sovereign states. The varied configurations of political agency driving these parallel processes are important to note. While one can plausibly argue that the United States and other industrialised powers played a key role in the construction of the post-1945 architecture of multilateral institutions, they played no such role in the second process. Here the crucial agents were post-colonial states, who not only played a critical – if largely unacknowledged – role in the negotiation of the human rights regime, but also worked to undercut the normative foundations of the institution of empire. In the human rights negotiations leading Western powers sought repeatedly to water down key provisions, and they vigorously and consistently opposed the codification of the right to self-determination.

Millian sovereignty, embedded cosmopolitanism

Over time, these processes produced a liberal international order with four distinctive characteristics: Millian sovereignty, liberal proceduralism, embedded cosmopolitanism, and hierarchy without empire. Not only is this order more complex than Ikenberry claims, but these characteristics stand in dynamic tension, giving the order its all too apparent contradictions.

Not only has sovereignty been universalised in the liberal international order, but it takes a "Millian" quality. John Stuart Mill famously argued that among "civilised" states a strong norm of non-intervention should apply, even when the claimed purpose of intervention is to free a subject people from tyranny. His argument was not, however, the standard one that the mutual recognition of sovereignty and the categorical principle of non-intervention are essential to the preservation of international peace and stability (the position of English School "pluralists" among others). Rather, his argument had to do with the conditions of freedom. If freedom is to mean anything to a people, they must fight for it themselves: "The only test possessing any real value, of a people's having become fit for popular institutions, is that they, or a sufficient portion of them to prevail in the contest, are willing to brave labour and danger for their liberation" (Mill, 1859: 6). At root, this is a claim about the importance of self-determination for the political evolution of a people. Only free from external interference (or assistance) can a people make itself according to its own conception of the good – the classic liberal ideal of self-realisation.

This was, in essence, the argument made by anti-colonialists after 1945. Imperial powers had long argued that they had a sacred duty to raise subject peoples up to a level where they would be able to govern themselves (the idea undergirding the "Trusteeship" system). Anti-colonialists reversed this equation, arguing that self-determination was a prerequisite for the political development of a people. Mill, of course, drew a sharp distinction between relations among "civilised" nations and those between the civilised and the "barbarous". The norm of non-intervention could not, and should not, apply to the latter; as "nations which are still barbarous have not yet got beyond the period during which it is likely to be for their benefit that they should be conquered and held in subjection by [civilised] foreigners" (Mill, 1859: 4). One of the great accomplishments of post-1945 anti-colonialism was to delegitimise not only the institution of empire, but also this explicitly racist division of the world's peoples into civilised and barbarian. All states have since been subsumed into a single category; all endowed with a sovereign right to non-intervention, justified as necessary for their self-determination (qua self-realisation).

The order's second characteristic is liberal proceduralism. On one reading, liberalism is a procedural doctrine. Individuals are said to be animated by their own conceptions of the good, and political institutions are considered legitimate to the extent that they enable such individuals to reach decisions about the distribution of social benefits and burdens that are procedurally "fair". Fathoming what such procedures might be has animated much liberal political philosophy, with Rawls' original position and Habermas' ideal speech situation among the most prominent propositions. In general, though, liberals have considered three principles essential to fair procedures: the equal standing of individuals, consent, and reciprocity (the notion that rules should apply equally to all those subject to them).

As we have seen, as liberal constitutional norms began shaping the institutional architecture of the modern international order, these ideas were expressed in the fundamental institutional practices of multilateralism and contractual international law. In its ideal form, multilateralism involves cooperation between three or more states based on reciprocally binding norms of conduct. And, unsurprisingly, contractual international law is considered the product of state consent. Indeed, in the modern era, consent is considered the principal source of international legal obligation. Today, the huge multiplicity of multilateral institutions embodies and promotes countless substantive values, from biodiversity to nuclear non-proliferation. And many of these values are codified in international legal agreements. Yet it remains the case that the basic institutional practices that have enabled the negotiation and codification of these values are both procedural and liberal in nature.

These two characteristics – Millian sovereignty and liberal proceduralism – are statist: they institutionalise the system of sovereign states, and license a particular set of institutional practices to facilitate interstate cooperation and coexistence. A third characteristic pushes in a different direction, though. The constitutional norms of the liberal international order justify territorial particularism on the grounds of a form of ethical universalism: sovereign states are the sole legitimate form of political organisation, but the moral purpose of the state is to augment the purposes, and protect the basic rights, of individuals. While particular states are responsible for the purposes and rights of the individuals within their borders, the rights in question are considered universal: freedom of conscience, expression, and association, rights to political representation and participation, non-discrimination and equality before the law, physical security, and so on.

Yet while an increasing number of states fulfil this purpose with varying degrees of success, states remain the principal violators of individuals' rights, and often egregiously so. The construction of the international human rights regime has been a response to this; an attempt to create a legally binding regime of international rules to ensure state respect for fundamental human rights. This has been matched by the parallel development of international humanitarian law, and by the development of international judicial mechanisms for the prosecution of crimes against humanity, war crimes, genocide, and acts of aggression. Together these amount to what I term "embedded cosmopolitanism". My claim is not that the system has become cosmopolitan *in toto*; the aforementioned characteristics push against this. The liberal order is distinctive, however, for its increasingly dense and legalised architecture of international human rights norms and attendant practices. Furthermore, this architecture has empowered new forms of national, international, and transnational politics, which now constitutes an important force affecting the nature of polities and the legitimate scope of sovereign authority (see Risse et al., 2013; Sikkink, 2011).

The final characteristic is what I shall term "hierarchy without empire". As emphasised earlier, one of the defining achievements of the latter half of the twentieth century was the delegitimation of the institution of empire. From this point onward, empires, understood as hierarchical systems of rule in which peripheral polities are formally subordinated to a ruling metropolis, have been deemed illegitimate, with the term "empire" assuming a pejorative quality. This does not mean, however, that hierarchy in international relations has disappeared; indeed, its persistence is now the subject of considerable scholarly attention (see Lake, 2009). What much of this scholarship misses, however, is that a fundamental structural condition shapes the expression of hierarchy in the contemporary liberal order: universal state sovereignty. Hierarchy, under such conditions, cannot take the form of empire; it must be more informal, often diffuse, frequently negotiated, and compatible with *de jure* sovereign equality.

Ikenberry makes much of the fact that American hegemony has not been imperial; that it has rested on "political bargains, diffuse reciprocity, the provision of public goods, and mutually agreeable institutions and working relationships" (Ikenberry, 2011: 26). Yet he attributes this largely to the liberal sensibilities of American policymakers: the hegemony of the United State has taken the form it has because enlightened leaders understood that American interests were best served by embedding them within multilateral institutions. But while the liberal identity of the United States shaped the nature of American hegemony in far-reaching ways, that authority evolved in a period of universalising sovereignty which bounded it in significant ways. Furthermore, as we have seen, universalised sovereignty was an achievement of actors other than the United States, with materially weak anti-colonial movements and post-colonial states playing a critical role. Universal sovereignty mandates hierarchy without empire.

Conclusion

International orders are more than the governing institutions and arrangements that exist between sovereign states at a particular moment in history. They are comprehensive social orders, characterised principally by a systemic configuration of power and authority, an architecture of fundamental institutional practices, and a framework of constitutional norms that legitimise both. When understood in this way, the generative forces that produce, reproduce, and transform international orders turn out to be more variegated than Ikenberry and others assume: the designs and practices of great powers are important, but so too is the agency of other actors, often those written out of the conventional international relations script. Only through this more comprehensive understanding of international orders can we grasp the liberal international order in its full, deeply contradictory complexity. In particular, grasping how liberal constitutional ideas about the moral purpose of the state, sovereignty as an organising principle, and legislative notions of procedural justice informed the diverse political projects of anti-colonialism, multilateral governance, and international human rights renders explicable the otherwise disparate faces of the liberal international order – its Millian form of sovereignty, liberal proceduralism, embedded cosmopolitanism, and hierarchy without empire.

Notes

1. It is important to note that Weber distinguished between "power" and "imperative control". The former he defined as "the probability that one actor within a social relationship will be in a position to carry out his own will despite resistance". In contrast, imperative control is "the probability that a command with a given content will be obeyed by a given group of persons". Such control, for Weber, always rests voluntary compliance, a necessary source of which is legitimacy. See Weber (1964: 152, 324–329).

2. Drawing on earlier writings by Bull and Jon Elster, Andrew Hurrell describes this as a difference between order as fact and order as value. See Hurrell (2007: 2).
3. My discussion here is necessarily brief, but is a summary of the more detailed account I provide in Reus-Smit 1999: Chapters 2 and 6. There I refer to the constitutional structure of "modern" international society. I regard, however, this structure to be "liberal" in essence, and I because I consider international orders to be social formations, I treat international order and society as synonymous.
4. In a similar vein, Phillips defines the modern conception of legitimate statehood in terms of "Popular eudemonism, human emancipation, and the augmentation of collective and individual capacities for self-determination" (Phillips, 2011: 31).
5. The following discussion draws on a more detailed account in Reus-Smit (2011: 232–236).

References

Bull, H. (1995), *The Anarchical Society*, London: Macmillan.
Doyle, M. (1986), *Empires*, Ithaca NY: Cornell University Press.
Glendon, M. A. (2002), *A World Made New: Eleanor Roosevelt and the Universal Declaration of Human Rights*. New York: Random House.
Hurrell, A. (2007), *On Global Order: Power, Values, and the Constitution of International Society*, Oxford: Oxford University Press.
Ikenberry, G. I. (2001), *After Victory*, Princeton NJ: Princeton University Press.
Ikenberry, G. I. (2011), *Liberal Leviathan*, Princeton NJ: Princeton University Press.
Kaiser, D. (1990), *Politics and War: European Conflict from Philip II to Hitler*, Cambridge MA: Harvard University Press.
Lake, D. A. (2009), *Hierarchy in International Relations*, Ithaca: Cornell University Press.
Mattern, J. B. (2005), *Ordering International Politics: Identity, Crisis and Representational Force*. New York NY: Routledge.
Mill, J. S. (1859), "A Few Words on Non-Intervention", *Foreign Policy Perspectives* (8) (http://www.libertarian.co.uk/lapubs/forep/forep008.pdf) p.6. Accessed 5 May 2012.
Mostecky, V. (1965), *Index of Multilateral Treaties: A Chronological List of Multi-Party International Agreements from the Sixteenth Century through 1963*, Cambridge MA: Harvard Law School Library.
Phillips, A. (2011), *War, Religion, and Empire: The Transformation of International Orders*, Cambridge: Cambridge University Press.
Rawls, J. (1973), *Theory of Justice*, Oxford: Oxford University Press.
Reus-Smit, C. (1997), "The Constitutional Structure of International Society and the Nature of Fundamental Institutions", *International Organization*, 51(4), 555–589.
Reus-Smit, C. (1999), *The Moral Purpose of the State*, Princeton NJ: Princeton University Press.
Reus-Smit, C. (2001), "Human Rights and the Social Construction of Sovereignty", *Review of International Studies*, 27(4), 519–538.
Reus-Smit, C. (2011), "Struggles for Individual Rights and the Expansion of the International System", *International Organization*, 65(2), 232–236.
Risse, T., Ropp, S. and Sikkink, K. (eds) (2013), *From Commitment to Compliance: The Persistent Power of Human Rights*, Cambridge: Cambridge University Press.
Ruggie, J. G. (1982), "International Regimes, Transactions, and Change: Embedded Liberalism in the Post-war Economic Order", *International Organization*, 36(2), 379–415.
Ruggie, J. G. (1983), "Continuity and Transformation", *World Politics*, 35(2), 261–285.

Ruggie, J. G. (1993), "Multilateralism: The Anatomy of an Institution", in J. G. Ruggie (ed.) *Multilateralism Matters: The Theory and Practice of an Institutional Form*, New York: Columbia University Press.

Sikkink, K. (2011), *The Justice Cascade: How Human Rights Prosecutions Are Changing World Politics*, New York: Norton.

Thomson, D. (1962), *Europe Since Napoleon*, London: Longmans.

United Nations. (1952a), United Nations 1952a Document A/RES/637 (VII), Preamble, 16 December 1952.

United Nations. (1952b), *Yearbook of the United Nations 1951*, New York: Office of Public Information.

United Nations. (1960), United Nations Document A/RES/1514 (XV), Art.1, 14, December 1960.

Weber, M. (1964), *The Theory of Social and Economic Organization*, New York: Free Press.

Zhang, Y. and Buzan, B. (2012), "The Tributary System as International Society in Theory and Practice" (Unpublished manuscript).

Part III

The Diffusion of Liberalism

10
The Paradox of Liberalism in a Globalising World

Philip G. Cerny

Introduction

Liberalism inherently involves a profound paradox that has shaped its trajectory in the modern world over more than two centuries and is ever more relevant in a new century of what has come to be called globalisation.[1] Understanding this paradox is increasingly applicable in an international political economy dominated by financial crises, austerity, and the shrinking of the welfare state – not to mention the challenges of multiculturalism, democratisation, the changing face of the use of force and violence, and the proliferation of transnational governance processes and webs of power. The late twentieth and early twenty-first centuries have been characterised by a fundamental restructuring of liberalism itself, but the outcome of this shift is yet to be determined, shaped as it will be by multilayered, cross-cutting political processes and the as yet embryonic political action of key strategically situated groups.

This chapter will first examine the historical and philosophical problematics underlying the liberal paradox; I will then analyse the economic challenges facing contemporary liberalism, especially in the globalising financial sector; this will be followed by a brief survey of the other challenges mentioned above; and finally, I will set out four possible scenarios for the development of liberalism in world politics in the foreseeable future. Unlike Immanuel Wallerstein (1995), who entitled a book *After Liberalism*, I do not see liberalism as a 200-year phase that ended in 1989 with the fall of the Berlin Wall, nor do I see a homogeneous American-style liberalism as the hegemonic legacy of the "end of history" (Fukuyama, 1992). Rather, I see liberalism as an evolving concept, characterised by fundamental, underlying endogenous tensions that can lead in different directions at different times, depending on the ideational, material, and socio-political circumstances of the epoch. And the time, as the twenty-first century unfolds, is ripe for the reconstruction of liberalism in new, diverse forms – not its demise.

The liberal paradox in theory

The fundamental ideational ground for liberalism is the shift of the basic unit of political, social, and economic action from various corporate or organic categories, groups and hierarchies – tribe, caste, race and ethnicity, religious hierarchies, kinship and familism, hereditary aristocracy and monarchy, and so on – to the individual or "autonomous person" (Comaroff and Comaroff, 2012). It represents a shift from *Gemeinschaft* – usually mistranslated as "community" but really meaning what Laslett (1965) called the "subsumption" of the individual in an organic or holistic macro-social category – to *Gesellschaft* (Tönnies, 1887/2003), or a society composed of individual parts and an assembled range of micro- and meso-level groups, themselves also made up of individuals acting in concert. Liberalism's origins in Enlightenment thought and its various manifestations in modern history thus paradoxically contain the roots of both individualism and collective action – of personal autonomy and shared sociality – and its very evolution has embodied the immensely dynamic and productive tension between those two otherwise ostensibly polar conceptions of social, economic, and political life in the making of the modern world.

This dynamic tension was rooted, in particular, in the Scottish Enlightenment (Herman, 2001; cf. Foucault, 2008). It has involved an ongoing, uneven, and problematic process of navigating between, on the one hand, the concept of the individual as the basic unit of human life and, on the other hand, the rootedness of those individuals in multi-level social relations which, rather than being imposed authoritatively from the top down, are themselves produced by the ongoing interaction of individuals and their micro-social and meso-social groups from the bottom-up. This dynamic interaction, in turn, enables the development of both socio-political cohesion at the macro-social level and the economic growth that makes that cohesion possible. As Foucault has pointed out, for today's neoliberals in particular, "there is only one true and fundamental social policy: economic growth" (Foucault, 2008: 144). In this process, liberalism generates not only the emergence and political power of leaders and leadership groups and processes – and of social, economic, and political brokers who attempt to orchestrate this process of navigating between the personal and the social; it also underlies the appearance of popular movements and groups of followers who band together or are banded together to use their collective power either to maintain and embed social stasis and continuity or to promote and shape change.

It is these social, economic, and political actors who, most importantly, structure the process of navigating and reconciling the tension inherent in the liberal paradox – a process sometimes called "structuration" (Cerny, 2010: 87–97). In more concrete political and economic terms, this process has been embodied in the trajectories of both liberal democracy and liberal capitalism. It is a process in continual evolution and frequent upheaval, as these complex, interacting imperatives of autonomous personhood, social bonds, and the general economic growth that enables their reconciliation in particular circumstances – the "growing pie" – clash and reconcile. It is intrinsic to the very concept of modernity itself – or what have been called "the antinomies of modernity", involving inherent tensions and contradictions. These tensions and contradictions are played out through complex processes such as political conflict, coalition-building, institution-building, the intrinsic economic struggle yet umbilical co-dependence of labour and capital, the clash of cultures, the invention of tradition, and the evolution of polycultural biopolitics (Comaroff and Comaroff, 2012)[2] in comprising the system of world politics as a whole.

This is all problematic enough in the domestic context of modern nation-states, where discovering and pursuing the balance between individual rights and the public interest or common good is at the heart of liberal democracy and the secular if uneven decline of authoritarianism over the past three centuries. In economics, it is similarly at the core of the relationship and ongoing debates, mainly within national economies, between free markets, on the one hand, and government regulation and intervention – the key *social* functions of capitalism, along with the welfare state and the promotion of national identity – on the other. And in sociological terms, it concerns the extent to which the "nation" (as represented in and by nation-states) – "national culture societies" (Znaniecki, 1952/1973) and "imagined communities" (Anderson, 1991) – can claim *a priori* loyalty and identity over competing and cross-cutting group or community bonds from localistic familism to religious and ethnic identities to migratory diasporas and even "global tribes" (Kotkin, 1992). Since the British, American, and French revolutions and democratic transitions from the seventeenth to the twentieth centuries, and in philosophical terms since the Enlightenment, liberalism in its more individualistic, atomistic manifestation has been in everyday conflict and competition with its more holistic social democratic form. When President Barack Obama recently said of even small businesses "you didn't build that", he meant you didn't build that *on your own*, but as a part of a dialectical social and economic process linking individual and group effort to such classic public functions as providing social stability, infrastructure, and the basic conditions for economic activity.

The result has been the emergence and consolidation at the domestic level of alternative national varieties of liberalism. The best known of these can be seen in the contrasting ways the word "liberalism" is manifested, on the one hand, in American public discourse, where it is seen as a centre-left, progressive, almost social democratic standpoint, and, on the other, in its Continental European version, where it generally retains a strong right-wing orientation that prioritises the private over the public. In both cases, however, concepts such as personal freedom and liberty – after all, the etymological origin of the word liberalism itself – and such things as an emphasis on rights – whether rights to social justice and equal opportunity, in the centre-left version, or property rights and limits on government, in the right-wing version – are central to seeing the socio-political superstructure of liberal societies as representing a collection of persons and not the intrinsic top down authority of an *a priori* social, metaphysical, or political hierarchy.

Liberalism and the nation-state

Nevertheless, whether one looks at politics, economy, or society, "modernity" – or "modernities", in both liberal and illiberal or authoritarian varieties – has been rooted in and dependent upon the emergence and development of one predominant structural site for attempting to reconcile those tensions in practice and to create institutionalised mechanisms for regularising and stabilising the balancing and navigating process characteristic of the liberal paradox – the "sovereign" nation-state (Spruyt, 1994). National "political systems" have been established and entrenched at various levels, mainly in the so-called "developed" world, not only through imposition from above and revolutions from below, but also through international wars. Modern warfare, in particular, identified by Clausewitz as the core of nation-building - and especially the two World Wars and the Cold War of the twentieth century - have entrenched national security and military systems in national societies. These top-down "command systems" have been seen to represent the common good in its most solidaristic manifestation of defending the territorial integrity of the nation-state – even legitimising the possibility of nuclear "mutually assured destruction" (MAD) – on the one hand, while at the same time protecting liberal domestic political systems at home and eventually undermining authoritarian systems abroad through international wars for democracy, on the other.

At a second level, probably the most "internationalist" dimension of modernity until the middle of the twentieth century, formal imperialism, was succeeded through the decolonisation process in the developing world not by more flexible, multi-level institutions and social structures, which were believed to suffer from the centrifugal risks of such forces as tribalism, but instead by "nation-building" (Bendix, 1964) and "new states". Despite endemic instability in many postcolonial states – complex rebellions and cross-border ethnic or quasi-ethnic conflict, enclave politics from local autonomism and tribalism to piracy, state failures, and the frequent breakdown of liberal and democratic experiments – the goal of former colonial powers and "liberation" elites alike, both democratic and authoritarian, was to try to copy the Euro-American nation-state path to development. "Nation-building", as noted above, has thus always been an artificial exercise, but it has been the predominant goal of virtually all of these conflicting groups. And at a third level, it should be remembered that the "embedded liberal" international regime established after the Second World War was imposed through the political and economic power of liberal nation-states under American hegemony (Ruggie, 1982). In effect, liberalism in the modern world has been the creation of the nation-state-based "international system" and has depended on the structure and dynamics of that system for its expansion and development (Moravcsik, 1997).

However, that structural dependency has also been under continual challenge throughout modern history. In the first place, political liberalism and liberal democracy have appealed to and been rooted in individualistic, subnational, cross-national, and universalistic values from the beginning, as both imperialism (and postcolonialism) at the international level and cultural diversity and fragile, artificial nation-building at the socio-political level have shown (Cerny, 2010: ch. 10). Nation-states and broad power shifts in the international system may have been the vehicles for the transmission – and frequently the imposition – of liberal national political and social systems on an empirical level. However, in recent decades liberal values have also become increasingly widespread and deeply embedded in the so-called "global village", especially through the spread of modern media (McLuhan, 1964) and the more recent rapid development of information and communications technology. The future, I would argue, is less and less in the hands of national elites and more and more in those of a growing and complex, multi-level range of groups. This is especially true of what have been labelled the "new middle classes", among others – a process first identified at the ancient city-state level by Aristotle and typified recently by the Arab Spring. As Robert Kaplan has written: "these activities will be framed more and more by a global civilisation, the product of a new [internationalised] bourgeoisie" (Kaplan, 2010: 323). And as Steven Pinker (2011) argues, the spread of Enlightenment values such as individualism, liberty, rights, and the rule of law may well be the dominant variable in the dramatic decline of violent conflict in the world, especially since the mid-twentieth century. The emergence of a post-national *raison du monde* or globalising – neo-Foucauldian? – "governmentality" (Cerny, 2010) is increasingly coexisting with, wrestling with, and progressively undermining the *raison d'État* that has long dominated our paradigmatic understanding of both domestic and international politics (Foucault, 2008).

Particularly significant for this transformation – although obscured by the national and state-centric paradigms of modern social science – has been the fact, already noted, that this is not an entirely new phenomenon. National economies and national polities have always been enmeshed in transnational and global webs, whether through imperial imposition and integration, the economics of "comparative advantage", or the existence and spread of cross-cutting markets and production systems. Such globalising (and so-called "glocalising") economic trends have accelerated dramatically since the middle of the twentieth century. Markets are not, of course, intrinsically national by nature. They can exist on any scale, whether global or local or regional, and the creation of national markets, while crucial in the shift from the local to wider scales in the development of capitalism – as exemplified in the title and theme of Eugen Weber's *Peasants Into Frenchmen* (1976) – is likely to have been merely a staging post in the transition to an increasingly globalised or at least "transnationalised" international political economy. With the continued innovation and spread of new technologies – the main source of economic development and productivity improvement throughout modern history, but especially in terms of late twentieth century developments in information and communications technology and flexible production systems – and with the relative insulation of the larger emerging market economies (the so-called BRICs: Brazil, Russia, India, and China, along with occasional others) from the current global financial crisis, secular global economic and financial integration may pause but is likely to continue in the medium to long term. Former US President Bill Clinton has recently written, "borders have become more like nets than walls" (*TIME Magazine*, 21 September 2012). But people and animals quickly get tangled up in nets, and the more they struggle, the more they get caught up in them.

Thus globalisation is not only the biggest challenge to liberalism in world politics, but also, paradoxically, its biggest opportunity. The main point of this chapter is that liberalism is not an inherently state-centric phenomenon. As noted above, it is rooted in the concept of autonomous personhood and non-state groups formed by individuals cooperating at least relatively freely, whether through pluralistic interaction, democratic political processes, or economic markets. In this case, the sovereign state – despite having been historically and structurally prioritised as both a dominant "arena of collective action" domestically and the source of "credible commitments" among states since the end of the Middle Ages (Spruyt, 1994) – is in principle a potentially transient epiphenomenon, just one structured action field (Crozier and Friedberg, 1977) among others.

Therefore, while the study of International Relations (IR), as traditionally conceived, makes states the fount of liberalism, nevertheless liberalism can – and is indeed increasingly likely to – chip away at and even fragment both domestic state-centrism and the structural hegemony of the states system itself. As I will argue below, liberalism is leading to a more wide-ranging but embryonic and uneven diffusion of governance. This process can be seen along several developmental dimensions, each of which can be potentially both stabilising and destabilising in a world of increasingly "durable disorder" (Minc, 1993). I will look in the next section primarily at one of these, that of complex economic interdependence. This is, in the last analysis, a situation in which "multiple equilibria" – what economists call alternative relatively stable future outcomes – are not only possible but at the core of political cooperation and conflict in the twenty-first century world. In the final section I will set out four potential scenarios for the future of liberalism and world politics. Liberalism is a work in progress in a globalising world.

Economic interdependence and the liberal paradox

What is central to the liberal paradox today, then, is that liberalism is inherently a source of both the disempowerment of some groups and actors and the empowerment of others, of both instability and stability, and of both degeneration and progress in human society. In this context, the key is not found merely in a kind of predestined structure of a fully globalised world as some sort of "end state", but rather lies in the way history is shaped by how actors act, react, and interact in facing a range of challenges in diverse, complex issue-areas. In a globalising world, liberalism in its "modern" manifestation as a state-centric phenomenon is challenged by several interacting broad trends. They all involve dimensions of what has been called "complex interdependence" (Keohane and Nye, 1977/2000), a structural transformation that is evolving all the time. Complex interdependence involves the emergence and consolidation of linkages and networks that include not merely credible interstate commitments, although, as noted above, those have been crucial in the historical processes leading to globalisation and the spread of liberalism, but also, even more importantly, a diverse and growing range of cross-border forms of collective action. These include, most critically, non-state, cross-cutting – "below the state" – and supranational – "above the state" – interactive processes. The main dimension addressed in this section is economic interdependence, the spread of markets and production systems across borders. This is what many social scientists mean by "globalisation", which why I use this term advisedly in this chapter.

Probably the most commented on dimension of the liberal paradox is therefore found in the economic realm. The liberal paradox in economics lies in the relationship between markets – in the ideal type sense of cumulative but decentralised individual decisions to buy or sell commodities – and governments or "governance", that is, the way such processes are organised and institutionalised.[3] This sort of economic liberalism has often been described, especially in the light of history from the mid-nineteenth to the mid-twentieth centuries, as a set of alternatives along a scale ranging from pure decentralised free markets, on the one hand, to top-down "command economies" represented by the "totalitarian" extremes of fascism, Nazism, and Soviet Communism, on the other. In the context of liberalism, however, given the role of cumulative personhood in the way social bonds are portrayed in the liberal tradition generally, the scale instead runs from the same sort of ideal type free market, on the one hand, to a regulated market or "social market" economy, in which market transactions are paradoxically enabled and optimised by strong collective rule-making and enforcement, on the other (Bonefeld 2013).

In the former case, Hayek's vision of markets was one where efficiency and productivity could only be maximised by permitting the untrammelled working of what he famously called a "spontaneous ('grown') order" – as distinct from an "organised ('made') order" (Hayek, 1989). This market system was, crucially, stabilised by the automatic workings of the price mechanism – or what late twentieth-century "efficient market" economists called the collective "Mr Market", operating through an all-encompassing rationality where all relevant information is available and integrated into each individual's decision-making process in buying and selling goods and assets (Fox, 2009). The best of all possible worlds was at one level therefore an extremely decentralised one, but ironically at the same time one in which the sum total of individual decisions created a collective optimum.

On the other hand, theorists like Keynes saw markets as inherently potentially unstable, requiring collective rules and regulatory mechanisms to counteract potential *irrationality* deriving from "animal spirits" (Akerlof and Shiller, 2009) and suboptimal mechanisms like casinos, "beauty contests", and so-called "asymmetric information" or the ability of certain market actors to corner the market by controlling access to key facts otherwise crucial for other market actors to make rational decisions. Governments in this second version were inherently, but paradoxically, needed to make the market work well – or indeed *at all* – rather than preventing it from doing so. This has been described since the 1930s as "saving capitalism from the capitalists" (Cerny, 2011). Indeed, liberalism, as I have described it in this chapter, is inherently *both* a "spontaneous" order and a "made" order. The difference between Hayek and Keynes, and between free market and regulated market theorists generally, is that the latter see Hayekian spontaneity as unstable, unpredictable, and controllable by rent-seeking market actors who are able to distort those markets to their advantage – and thus potentially highly counterproductive – rather than self-regulating and optimising. However, Keynesians and the like also see the very purpose of regulation as being to *enable and incentivise* market actors to act in ways that maximise spontaneity, stability, and rational decision-making.

At the core of this problematic of liberal capitalism, of reconciling individual market behaviour with overall growth and prosperity in a virtuous circle or "positive sum game", has been the notion of competition. Competition among economic actors forces them, in theory, to act in rational and efficient ways, keeping costs and prices down in order to compete with other providers, ensuring that competitive new entrants keep existing firms on their toes, stimulating technological innovation and the continued development of new products and production methods, and producing profits that would then be invested in keeping the process moving forward in a virtuous circle, thereby generating continuing economic growth and prosperity – if such perpetual growth would indeed be physically possible. Thus, competition was the dynamic process of interaction that made capitalism work. However, competition cannot be taken for granted. The history of capitalism is littered with examples of what in economic theory is called "rent-seeking" and "opportunism", where economic actors are seen as essentially engaging in oligopolistic and monopolistic behaviour. It is, indeed, rational for market actors, once they have begun to be successful at competition, to plan to put their erstwhile competitors out of business rather than to continue to hew to the rigours of active competing. This permits them to make guaranteed "excess profits" at the expense not only of the consumer but also of other existing or potential competitors who are unable to counteract the "first mover advantages" held by the original winners. In other words, the dynamics of competition themselves often ironically undermine its efficient operation.

Furthermore, perhaps more important than this sort of individual anti-competitive behaviour is that certain kinds of production and distribution processes are actually more efficiently pursued by hierarchically organised firms – firms, in the terms used in institutional economics, usually found in sectors characterised by "specific assets", that is, technological economies of scale and/or high transactions costs (Williamson, 1975, 1985). In either case, public regulation is required to restrict structurally embedded monopoly and cartel behaviour and the excess profits they produce, in both the public and private sectors – even when those firms need to be preserved and enabled for them to fulfil their basic functions of producing those inherently hierarchically governed "club goods" or cartel goods that are essential to economic growth and prosperity, from commercial aircraft and transport infrastructure to energy production and, some would argue, even banking and finance (Cerny, 2013d).

In other words, the preservation and promotion of competition itself requires pro-market or pro-competitive regulation (Cerny, 1991). Production and efficiency in key sectors depend on government regulation in order to play the efficient market game in the first place. This economic liberal paradox, that markets are not "self-regulating" (Polanyi, 1944), does not mean that they need to be replaced by hierarchical forms of economic organisation such as command planning, national monopolies or "national champions", or indeed by public ownership. Rather, it means that they only work well in the context of the kind of regulation and interventionism that encourages and promotes market-like behaviour through the enforcement of property rights, antitrust regulation, basic structural or "design" regulation of key infrastructure sectors such as finance – upon which the rest of the economy depends for investment and the efficient allocation of capital from investors to producers – as well as the prevention of fraud and the like. A strong legal system, coherent regulatory system, and an understanding of the requirements of pro-competitive regulation, sometimes seen as a contradiction in terms, are crucial here.

This role in the modern world, and especially in the developed capitalist economies, has been vested in the liberal state in its diverse varieties. Indeed, it has been argued that what is called "extensive development" requires stronger command-style state interventionism, while "intensive development" requires the kind of pro-market, pro-competitive regulation and intervention discussed above. On the one hand, extensive development means finding and bringing in new resources and factors of capital (land, labour, physical capital such as factories and infrastructure, and financial capital) to underdeveloped economies. That is how Germany developed at the end of the nineteenth century – what Barrington Moore called the "modernisation revolution from above" (Moore, 1966). This analysis has been widely applied to the Soviet model (Gregory and Stuart, 1997), to the Japanese "developmental state" (Johnson, 1982), and to the kind of "authoritarian liberalism" or "state capitalism" supposedly characteristic of Chinese development and the "Beijing Consensus" (Bremmer, 2010). But the drawbacks of overly authoritarian forms of supposed liberalism are obviously similar to those of top-down monopolistic behaviour – corruption, over-bureaucratisation and a vicious circle of inefficiency and often state authoritarianism to keep the system going.

On the other hand, pro-market regulation and intervention – regulation and intervention designed not to take economic activities out of the market, but rather to enable markets to work more efficiently – may be needed, especially in particular sectors, as stated above, in order to promote what has been called, in contrast, "intensive development". Intensive development is said to occur mainly after the sort of extensive development described above. As Adam Smith wrote, "to improve land, like all other commercial projects, requires exact attention to small savings and small gains". Intensive development means continually improving the micro-economic efficiency, competitiveness, and profitability of industry – even to the extent of engaging in what Joseph Schumpeter called the "creative destruction" of old capital and technology to make way for the latest cutting-edge production, financing, and marketing methods. Profits need to be made from market efficiency and expansion and not from rents.[4]

Modern liberal capitalist states have therefore evolved through a process of navigating between more direct forms of intervention, on the one hand, and what has been called "arm's length" or more indirect forms of market enabling and market-promoting regulation, on the other. However, as many analysts have argued, this has usually been a process of trial and error. New regulations are introduced mainly as the result of crises, whether crises in particular sectors like railways or nuclear energy, or the more general and dangerous crises of the system itself, as in the various responses to the Great Depression other major financial crises in modern history (Reinhart and Rogoff, 2009). In between crises, there tends to be a longer term, uneven erosion of regulatory restraints and the revival of both theoretical and practical claims for market "liberalisation" and deregulation, that is the lifting of even pro-market government controls. This has particularly been the case in the "neoliberal" era since the 1970s, as noted below (Stedman Jones, 2012). The liberal paradox is thus always in flux.

Liberalism and globalisation: The evolution of neoliberalism

In this situation, the main driver of the liberal paradox over recent decades has been globalisation. Economic globalisation, broadly speaking, involves several elements. The first has been the post-Second World War opening of the international economic system through the expansion of free trade and capital flows. A second has been technological change and, as noted above, the internationalisation of production systems especially through flexible production – the so-called Second Industrial Revolution – and financial innovation. A third has been a broad-based shift in politics away from the post-war welfare state and towards government policies aimed at increasing the international competitiveness of economic activities. As I have argued elsewhere, the liberal – or "neoliberal" – state is more and more a "Competition State" (Cerny, 1997, 2000, 2010: ch. 8). An effective Competition State requires the state to integrate the domestic economy into a rapidly changing world economy and to promote the global competitiveness of its domestic economic sectors. This often, again paradoxically, means virtually disarming the state's capacity for direct intervention in and control of the economy and a shift towards a so-called "regulatory state" (Jordana and Levi-Faur, 2004; Moran, 2003).

In this context, a phenomenon like "outsourcing", for example, is merely the tip of the iceberg. The key challenge facing not only nation-states but also embryonic and uneven processes of "global governance" is to expand and strengthen mechanisms of indirect regulation rather than direct intervention in ways that tackle and channel the liberal paradox more consistently across borders. States themselves, and state actors, often lack the policy capacity to do this by themselves. As the recent global financial crisis demonstrates, the capacity of bricolage-based international regimes like the Financial Stability Board or the International Organisation of Securities Commissions – that is, regimes that are set up to deal with particular problems and sectors, rather than overarching, holistic, state-like authority structures – to coordinate regulatory change is extremely limited, more akin to well-intentioned persuasion than to concrete policy change.

Probably the most important factor in attempting to reconcile the market versus regulatory hierarchy dilemma at the core of the liberal paradox in a globalising world therefore is not the crystallisation and consolidation of formal cooperation or "global governance" institutions and processes, but found rather in the spread of ideas, in particular the evolution of the concept of "neoliberalism". Neoliberalism is indeed the twenty-first-century version of the liberal paradox. Neoliberalism, as I have argued elsewhere, is a complex package of different policy priorities: tackling inflation in order to prevent 1970s-style crises of stagflation, especially through monetary policy, what I have called "embedded financial orthodoxy" (Cerny, 1994); opening borders to international capital flows, free trade and production systems, often (appropriately) called "liberalisation"; transitioning from the welfare state to the Competition State in regulatory and fiscal policy; privatising previously publicly organised production sectors and services, especially nationalised industries but also infrastructure and indeed welfare provision, not only directly but involving new forms of so-called "public/private partnerships", such as the Private Finance Initiative in the United Kingdom for the private financing of public services; promoting the flexibilisation of labour markets (which means, in particular, reducing the role of trade unions); and the like (Cerny, 2010: ch. 7). Ironically, too, a key aspect of the liberal paradox is that such policy shifts also require some sorts of mechanisms for what has been widely called "compensating losers", which means the restructuring of the welfare state itself in ways that target those specific groups that have been disadvantaged by globalisation and technological change rather than spending on universal benefits. Indeed, welfare spending has hardly gone down in liberal states, but its structure has changed significantly (Clayton and Pontusson, 1998).

Not all political and state actors have bought the whole neoliberal package, and the recent global financial crisis has strengthened pockets of resistance to some of its parts. However, politics in most countries increasingly revolves around the conflict between resisting neoliberal policies in order to preserve either social values or entrenched positions (or both), on the one hand, and attempting to capture the benefits of globalisation by internalising neoliberal prescriptions, on the other (Soederberg et al., 2005). At the same time, alternatives to neoliberalism have also been ineffectual and often incoherent. For most observers and policymakers, however, what I have described as diverse dimensions of neoliberalism constitute component parts of a coherent package (Harvey, 2005).

Nevertheless, in a globalising world these dimensions are increasingly fungible in practice, especially in the context of financial crisis, thereby increasing the opportunities for actors to influence and shape outcomes. Insulated domestic political solutions are more and more impossible to design in an open, interdependent world. It is not only multinational corporations that must increasingly define their interests in transnational fashion, but also a growing number of small businesses dependent on some combination of exports, imported inputs, investment from markets and institutions themselves dependent on globalised circuits of capital, changing consumer preferences and the like, that pressure institutions and policymakers to pursue neoliberal policies. Traditional sectional (or "material") interest groups such as businesses, trade associations, and even trade unions (Evans, 2007) now seek to develop active, organised cross-border networks. Both sectional interest groups, on the one hand, and cause groups and social movements are also increasingly associating through non-governmental organisations and so-called "global civil society" to pursue their wider goals (Edwards, 2004).

The most effective sectional interest groups and value groups or social movements in this emerging world are those that can proactively articulate their activities on what I have called a "multi-nodal" basis (Cerny, 2009), that is on and across diverse, cross-cutting levels of political processes. Contemporary liberal politics thus entails not only a process of both choosing between different varieties of neoliberalism in a state-centric world, but also attempting to innovate creatively within a more complex, multilayered, and transnational neoliberal playing field. In turn, conceptions of how to improve welfare have partly shifted to the transnational level too – what I have elsewhere called the emergence of a kind of embryonic "social neoliberalism", especially in some emerging economies like Brazil (Cerny, 2010: ch. 7). Linking trade opening to environmental and labour standards gives additional leverage to a kind of extraterritorial social policy too.

The stress put by neoliberalism on arms' length regulation has actually helped increase the demand for, and supply of, regulation across the world by redefining regulation as a transnationally indispensable requirement. Demands for stricter and more accountable international rules and procedures for corporate governance, accounting standards, bond rating agencies, private mediation and arbitration procedures, antitrust regulation and the like are reshaping government–business relations. In this context, the ongoing global financial crisis in particular, not merely its post-2007 manifestation but in the perspective of multiple financial crises around the world since the 1970s, is restructuring financial governance and public policy generally across borders through imitation and policy transfer (Evans, 2005) – rather than through formal institution-building – in ways that are only starting to crystallise. While this process has up to now mainly involved transfers among states, it is also leading pressures for more complex transnational responses. This process of evolution and reinvention is leading to the spread of increasingly distinctive varieties of neoliberalism at multiple levels. The paradox of neoliberalism "after liberalism" is therefore a dual one – not simply the tension between traditional state-centric liberalism and this embryonic transnational neoliberalism, but also that neoliberalism itself embodies that very same kind of tension in an unevenly globalising world.

Political and social dimensions of the liberal paradox: A brief survey

However, the liberal paradox can be seen to characterise a range of other crucial issue-areas, not just the economic. In this section, I will refer briefly to four other such issue-areas, although there is no space to address them in detail. The first is the rapid development of complex, transnational socio-cultural networks, rooted in information and communications technology, migration and other forms of human movement, and multiculturalism – better labelled as "polyculturalism" or "policulturalism" (to emphasise the political dimension too: Comaroff and Comaroff 2012: ch. 3) – and characterised by increasing but uneven socio-political pluralism – and neopluralism (Cerny, 2010). "Polyculturalism" involves the interaction, overlapping, and partial mixing of cultures, and all the social schizophrenia and conflict that can involve – in contrast to what might be called "mono-multiculturalism", that is the mere peaceful coexistence of different hierarchically organised and imposed cultural bonds and identities.

In other words, one major dimension of nation-state wholeness and legitimacy, the sharing and homogenisation of "national" social and cultural bonds, is becoming increasingly problematic in a world where subnational and transnational bonds are being revived, reinvented, and spread through migration and new communications technologies, but no longer can live in isolation. Nationalism today, for example, can mean many things – above, below, and/or across borders – and, ironically, the nation-state's monopoly of nationalism itself is being challenged not only in terms of individuals' and groups' action frameworks but also in terms of the basic legitimacy of political institutions and processes. We live in a world of increasing multi-level nationalisms and polycultural identities. In this context, new forms of liberalism are possible, below, above, and cutting across borders.

A second dimension, partly linked with polyculturalism, is the spread of Enlightenment values, from human rights to ideological pluralism to democratisation to liberalism itself. Liberalism is, of course, the main Enlightenment value, and the liberal paradox is at its core. Both polyculturalism and the spread of Enlightenment values have, however, also developed alongside religious, nationalist, and subnationalist backlashes, some of which reject liberalism altogether, as with religious fundamentalism and terrorism. Polyculturalism and global value shift are increasingly challenging the ideological claim of the "modern" nation-state to social and indeed ideological unity – and primacy – and to its ostensible monopoly of overarching and holistic social bonds, what might be called the *"Gemeinschaft* mirage"*, where the "imagined" becomes "imaginary".

At the same time, however, these backlashes are not so much a fore-shadowing of a world of increasingly violent conflict, despite the Bush administration's ideological promotion of the notion of an ongoing "Global

War on Terror", but rather an ironic reflection of the increasing overall hegemony of Enlightenment values and liberalism. More and more groups are seeing their own security and interests – sometimes even after ostensible defeat in violent conflict – as wrapped up in acquiescing to and even positive acceptance of relatively peaceful intercommunal toleration. There seems to be a dialectical interaction at work here, wherein the exhaustion of inconclusive conflict and resistance – along with what in the Vietnam War era was called the "body bag syndrome" – leads to an acceptance of pluralism and even democratisation. This is especially the case where economic growth comes to be more and more widely perceived as the main enabler of future prosperity and socio-economic mobility – what IR scholars call "absolute gains" – in contrast to the zero-sum games of winners and losers seeking "relative gains". Pinker (2011), in particular, regards the spread of Enlightenment values as the key driver of the dramatic reduction of violence in the world, as represented in the next dimension of the liberal paradox. Therefore this is not merely an ideational trend, but a socially embedded one too. The convergence of values, especially in the emergence of a globalising new middle class in the developing world, is key not only for the growing pressure for democratisation and liberalisation in domestic and political terms, but also to the third dimension, what Joshua Goldstein (2011) has called "winning the war on war" and Pinker (2011) the realisation of Abraham Lincoln's "better angels of our nature".

This third dimension, then, is the transformation of the use of force and violence themselves – the often overlooked dramatic reduction of the number of conflicts, both interstate and civil, going on in the world and the huge drop in the number of deaths of both soldiers and civilians in violent conflict since the late twentieth century. It involves a shift from the modern trend towards increasing destruction and potential annihilation at the interstate level – from the "total war" of the two World Wars and the threat of nuclear annihilation in the Cold War – to "small wars", low-level conflict including ethnic and religious backlashes as well as terrorism, alongside the spread of international (mainly United Nations) peacekeeping (Goldstein, 2011), and the uneven transnationalisation of what Max Weber called "legitimate violence", which he regarded as the core of the development of the nation-state. This transformation has been called "from warriors to police" (Marlantes, 2011), that is from taking sides and seeking to suppress "enemies" to enforcing a general, legitimised rule of law.

Central elements in this trend are the so-called "civilianisation" of security – the long-term reduction of military spending, of the maintenance of maximum readiness for all-out war, and of institutional autonomy of the military itself – and the shift of a range of issue-areas from those that are seen to be characterised by what have been called "existential threats" to the nation-state – the traditional conception of "security" – towards what Ole Wæver has called "desecuritisation" (Buzan and de Wilde, 1998:

207–209; cf. Pinker, 2011 and Cerny, 2013a). Sheehan (2008) documents the transition, for example, of Europe – once the main crucible of modern nation-state-centric warfare since the decline of feudalism – from a group of states whose main *raison d'être* was often being able to engage relatively successfully in escalating forms of warfare with each other into what he calls "civilian states" since the end of the Second World War. Desecuritised, civilian states pave the way for the transformation of liberalism and the liberal paradox from the nation-state to the international, transnational and eventually global levels in a multi-level, multi-nodal structuration process.

The final trend involves the rather piecemeal spread of transnational and international institutions, regimes and other political processes, including the patchy development of what have been called "global governance" and "global civil society" (Cerny, 2010: ch. 9). There is no space to go into this trend in any detail, but taken together, the five processes surveyed here – especially economic interdependence – enmesh states in transnational "webs of power" characterised not by states traditionally seen as "vertical", territorially defined "containers" (Brenner et al., 2003), but instead by an increasingly diverse range of cross-cutting issue-areas, social networks, and economic sectors (Cerny, 2010). These processes are sometimes referred to as one of the forms of "functional differentiation" (as distinct from the "segmental" differentiation of holistic nation-states, tribes, and cultures) that characterise complex modern, or postmodern, society (Albert et al., 2013; Cerny, 2013b). World politics thus becomes a more intricate and fluid structure in which states are just one level or form of structured interaction, among others – a multi-level, multi-nodal playing field ranging from the global to the local (so-called "glocalisation"), with multifarious and unevenly developing circuits of power (Foucault, 1980) and arenas of collective action in between and cutting across boundaries (Cerny, 2012).

In this context, globalisation and what has been called "liberal internationalism",[5] while challenging the pathways by which liberalism spreads through national statecraft, also create new pathways that are, I believe, more profoundly faithful to the traditions of Enlightenment liberalism and the pluralisation of social orders than states or the "realist" interstate system could ever be. At one level, the twenty-first century therefore holds out the promise of transcending the limitations of the states system in as yet embryonic but potentially transformative ways, while nevertheless also leading to potential sources of future instability and entropy as well as constructive development at another level. The interaction of these two pathways – of stabilisation and progress, on the one hand, and destabilisation and conflict between different visions of liberalism – represents the reincarnation of the original liberal paradox at world level.

This interaction furthermore implies a diffusion of governance in world politics – an uneven seeping away of the capacity not only of particular strong or hegemonic states but indeed, more importantly, of the states system itself, to be at the "wheel of control" (Griffith, 1989) – and the increasing power and influence of globalising markets, ostensibly self-regulating networks, cross-border social bonds, and transnationally inter-connected interest groups. Whether this will lead to a more holistic tran-sition to a new, more open, and healthily pluralistic global society or – more likely – to a "new medievalism" of unevenly developed, competing institutions and socio-political processes on overlapping and diverse juris-dictions and playing fields (Cerny, 1998) is still to be determined. Given the existence, however, of multiple equilibria or alternative possible out-comes, it will not be shaped primarily through structural determinism, given the potential malleability of international structures, but rather through political, social, and economic action – the competition and conflict of strategically situated social, political, and economic *actors* in shaping those structures themselves – as has been the case with regard to the liberal paradox throughout modern times.

From polyculturalism to Enlightenment values to the drop in violent con-flict to global governance and to complex economic interdependence, the crucial shift tying them all together is the increasing hegemony of liberal-ism as a fluid, multidimensional, and transnational phenomenon. But that hegemony is not a unidimensional straight line. It is a process of structura-tion and evolution, underlain by a fundamental, ongoing tension between individualism and cumulative collective action and provision, and between autonomous personhood and shared sociality. Not just each generation, but people within each generation, are confronted on a daily basis by this paradox, and must navigate its ongoing tensions on both a short- and a long-term basis. This process is, as I said earlier, at root a question of jug-gling what to many are contradictory ideas, understandings, aims and action frameworks. But progress in the modern world, whether social, economic, or political, has been shaped by that navigation process and its outcomes in specific historical circumstances.

Throughout most of modern history until the last half of the twentieth century and the beginning of the twenty- first century, the reconciliation of those tendencies – always tentative and provisional – has, in the wider historical context, involved the emergence, consolidation, and hegemony of the nation-state and the states system as the action field or set of are-nas within which the liberal paradox has been given shape and alternative varieties of liberalism developed. Today, however, given the increasingly open and nebulous character of systemic transformation in the twenty-first century, this will involve the possibility of new kinds of multiple equilibria, and only through a continuing de facto process of structuration will a new structural pattern – or patterns – crystallise and consolidate. I have argued that the shape of the future will depend on the way strategically situated agents of all kinds shape that process, whether consciously or unwittingly.

The future of the liberal paradox can therefore take several alternative directions.

Liberalism in a globalising world: Future scenarios

The first scenario suggests that the structural developments outlined above do *not* entail a fundamental structural shift in the international system. From this perspective, globalising pressures merely trigger a range of *adaptive* or "reinforcive" behaviours (Avelino 2012: 71–72; Cerny 2010: 87–90) on the part of strategically situated actors in light of each of the trends discussed above. Such actors are still significantly constrained in their capacity to form effective transformative networks cutting across those categories and/or consciously choose (or are overdetermined) to try to maintain or reinforce the role of the nation-state and the states system in shaping the kind of liberalism that prevails. In such circumstances, it is likely that the key to understanding the future of liberalism (however limited) will most likely rest with traditional political agents – politicians and bureaucrats whose power and legitimacy are rooted in the existing order. Such actors, enmeshed in and, perhaps more importantly, legitimised by their roles in the deeply embedded nation-states system, are likely to react to pressures for change by increasing the adaptive capacity of, for example, national-level regulation, the continued promotion of national cultural homogeneity and assimilation (or subordination) of minorities – including, in particular, attempts to restrict immigration – the reinforcement of national security regimes and traditional forms of foreign policy, and existing types of international cooperation, especially "intergovernmental" regimes that have nation-states as their core members, along with pressure on other domestic and international actors to adapt as well.

At the same time, state-centric policy approaches – whether concerning issues of environmental change, financial regulation and crisis, macroeconomic policy, or social policy – will either permit emerging global challenges to be more or less effectively managed or at least provide sufficient "band-aids" to prevent them spiralling out of control. These approaches include proponents of a wide range of ostensibly diverse concepts, such as the "Beijing Consensus", and a turn to "authoritarian liberalism" or "state capitalism" (Bremmer, 2010) in economic and development policy. This is what Hirst and Thompson (1999) called an "inter-national" approach, as distinct from a global or transnational one. It also characterises the main responses to the recent global financial crisis, with national regulatory regimes struggling to reform their national financial systems, as with the Dodd-Frank Act in the United States (Acharya et al., 2010).

I suggest that this approach has already been largely undermined by globalisation and transnationalisation. However, some, even many, of the most influential transnational interest groups – especially, but not exclusively, business groups – may also prefer this outcome. It would allow them to expand their levers of control over key aspects of the globalisation process itself, for example entrenching even further the clout of international financial market actors through lobbying and regulatory avoidance, getting around whatever fragmented new rules are adopted. This would lead to a growing de facto "privatisation of [international] governance" itself (Lake, 1999), while maintaining the ideological façade of democratic or developmentalist legitimacy and keeping domestic constituencies under control. Thus the liberal paradox would be not only partially addressed but also circumvented, its more social dimensions ironically evaded and manipulated by state-centric and private sector rent-seeking actors and incremental structuration processes.

A second alternative scenario might be based on the predominance of transnational social movements and their ability to shape the agendas of other actors both within and cutting across states. Such movements or value groups are often thought to be at the cutting edge of the promotion of more transnational and global liberal values (Tarrow, 2005). Their impact is frequently seen to be potentially "innovative" and/or "transformative" rather than adaptive or reinforcive (Avelino, 2012: 73–74; Cerny, 2010: 89–90). Two linked hypotheses can again be raised here: on the one hand, the development of a "global civil society", based on transnational liberal norms and values, despite the limitations suggested earlier; and on the other hand, the emergence of a genuine cross-cutting pluralism. Held (1995), for example, has suggested some mixture of analogous developments might well lead to the emergence of a transnational "cosmopolitan democracy". It might especially be the case that, should transnational social movements prove to be the predominant institutional entrepreneurs of a transnational structuration process, then a more complex, supranational process of "mainstreaming" might well provide the glue for some form of de facto democratisation-without-the-state (Cerny, 2010: ch. 10). Such an outcome, however, is unlikely.

Therefore this remains a "rosy scenario", an idealised state of affairs, which it might be unwise to expect. On the one hand, the crystallisation of a widening and deepening globalising rationality – a *raison du monde* rooted in Enlightenment values – is likely to strengthen such value groups and permit them to increase their competitive and bargaining clout in a transnational liberalising process. At the same time, the influence of such groups is likely to be highly variable across different issue areas. For example, the experience of the Occupy movement in the wake of the global financial crisis has remained marginal despite the ability of a number of national Occupy groups to mobilise salient protest movements, in New York and London in particular. Occupy has increasingly suffered from protest fatigue and fragmentation and has not been able to influence policymaking in any lasting way. In this case, there is clearly a clash within liberalism – characteristic of the liberal paradox – between actors representing social dimensions of liberalism, on the one hand, and more powerful groups representing transnationally linked financial markets and firms as well as state actors in regulatory institutions – what Lindblom (1977) referred to as the "privileged position of business" in the policymaking process. This is particularly relevant to the third scenario.

Thirdly, then, the dominant image of transnationalisation and globalisation today, as suggested earlier, is still that of economic and business globalisation. Economic agents, through the transnational expansion of both markets and hierarchical (firm) structures and institutions, increasingly shape a range of key outcomes in terms of the allocation of both resources and values. Neoliberal ideology presents such developments as inevitable; in Mrs. Thatcher's famous phrase: "There is no alternative" (TINA). Should transnational social movements prove more peripheral to the structuration process than a Polanyian "double movement" might suggest, and should political actors and the state increasingly act as promoters of globalisation and enforcement, as in the Competition State, then the governance structures of the twenty-first century international system will be likely to reflect in a more direct and instrumental way than outlined in the first scenario the priorities of international capital. Without a world government or set of effective "inter-national" (cooperative interstate) governance mechanisms, private economic regimes such as internationalised financial markets and associations of transnationally active firms, large and small, are likely to shape the international system through their ability to channel investment flows and set cross-border prices for both capital and physical assets as well (Cerny, 2013d). In this sense, the shape of the governance structures of such a system will merely mimic the structures of capital, ensuring that the sort of liberalism that emerges is one that is dominated by markets and market actors rather than regulation or transnational social justice.

This raises a number of issues. In the first place, it has been suggested that capital cannot directly control society. Capitalists are concerned first and foremost with competing with each other, not with policing the system (which can eat up profits). Furthermore, there is no collective mechanism, no "ideal collective capitalist" to regulate the system in the interests of capital *as a whole*, other than the state (Holloway and Picciotto, 1978). Nevertheless, indirect forms of control, for example through Gramscian cultural hegemony, may be more important at transnational level than the state per se (especially in its limited guise as a "nation-state"). Stephen Gill (1990, 2003), among others, sees the Trilateral Commission, the World Economic Forum (Davos) and other formal and informal networks among transnationally linked businessmen and their social and political allies as bearers of such an hegemony – the "Post-modern Prince" (Gill, 2012).

Furthermore, it may be possible to hypothesise that, should transnational capital take a relatively holistic hegemonic form, then the international system of the twenty-first century will represent an even more truly economically liberal – or, indeed, neoliberal – capitalist society in a way that no capitalist state has ever been able to. Markets, as noted earlier, can be of any scale, and global markets are at the forefront of the globalisation process. Private-sector-based mechanisms of control at a transnational level may indeed replace the state as what Marx called a "committee of the whole bourgeoisie". In this case, capitalists and a "transnational capitalist class" (van der Pijl, 2012) may be – and indeed may already be – the key innovative and transformative actors in a globalising world.

However, the crystallisation of other forms of international capital can also be envisaged, reflecting an unequal distribution of power or representation rather than monistic class domination, for example among different economic sectors. For example, in the 1970s what essentially were cartels of hierarchically organised multinational corporations were thought by many on both sides of the political divide to be the form that international capital would take in the future. But in the world of dramatic international capital movements, especially since the 1980s, it is more often the financial markets which might be seen as exercising a "sectoral hegemony" over the international system (Cerny, 1994). In either case, however, any significant transfer of power or system control from political agents (*via* states) to economic agents would represent a fundamental change in the nature of governance, giving economic actors much greater control over the way the liberal paradox is navigated and reconciled in practice.

A final scenario, which I have explored elsewhere (Cerny, 1998), is that exogenous pressures on the nation-state/states system, interacting with and exacerbating the tensions within that system, will cause that system to erode and weaken in key ways, but without providing enough in the way of structural resources to *any* category of agents (or combination of categories) to effectively shape the overarching transnational structuration process in a systematic way. In other words, no group or group of groups will be at the steering wheel of change in the international system, and competition between different groups will in turn undermine the capacity of any one of them to determine the sort of liberalism that emerges. In such circumstances, the outcome might be what has been called "neomedievalism" or an "archipelago" form of liberalism: a fluid, multilayered structure of overlapping and competing institutions, characterised by cultural flux, multiple, and shifting identities and loyalties in a complex and uneven transnational multiculturalism, and uneven competition between economic actors and state actors – with different "niches" at different levels for groups to focus their energies on. The medieval world was not a world of chaos; as noted above, it was a world of "durable disorder" (Minc, 1993).

Unless some coherent group of institutional entrepreneurs emerges to control and direct how the liberal paradox evolves, then the medieval analogy may provide a better guide to understanding the international system in the twenty-first century than previous models involving states and the states system, or some sort of homogenous globalisation, both domestically and internationally. There is no reason in principle, after all, why diverse forms of liberalism have to be tidy and logically coherent. The nation-state as such, and in particular the national industrial welfare state of the Second Industrial Revolution, especially in terms of compensating losers, is likely to be caught up in such wider, more complex webs, leading to increased uncertainty and possible disorder. At the same time, however, cross-cutting neopluralist networks of economic, political, and social agents would lead to an increase in the influence and power wielded by transnationally linked institutional entrepreneurs, some of whom will certainly attempt to transcend the limits of adaptive behaviour and develop new institutional strategies to for transforming and reconstructing liberalism and neoliberalism in this fluid, globalising world.

In each of these scenarios, then, we can see either an incremental or a much more rapid feedback process, based on actors' evolving strategies, behaviours, and discourses, leading to a ratcheting up of the globalisation process itself and the relative capacity of different actors to pursue their visions of liberalism and, today, neoliberalism. Therefore the shape that process takes in the future will differ depending on which actors – and coalitions of actors – develop the most influence and power to manipulate and mould particular outcomes within and across a range of critical issue-areas – what Avelino (2012: 86) calls their "transition potential". The way different kinds of actors perceive opportunities, mobilise resources, and exercise power and influence through individual and group action and coalition-building can lead to either adaptive/reforcive outcomes or innovative/transformative change, depending on the intersection of structural preconditions on the one hand and actor orientations and behaviour on the other – the process of structuration. Structural changes by themselves are ambiguous and amorphous in their ramifications not only for short-term events but also for long-term transformations; they can lead to a range of alternative outcomes.

Therefore, it is crucial that we analyse the future of liberalism through competing paradigms, narratives, and discourses. It involves conscious actors, whether individuals or groups, who can interpret and manipulate structural changes, alternative pathways and opportunities creatively and proactively; change and refine their strategies; negotiate, bargain, build coalitions, and mobilise their power resources in ongoing interactions with other actors; and – both in winning and losing – affect and shape medium- and long-term outcomes. The liberal paradox is a complex phenomenon that must be understood in its historical, structural, and conjunctural complexity. In particular, transnational social movements are likely to bump up against powerful transnational economic interest groups in influencing policy responses to systemic events like the global financial crisis in shaping the future of liberalism. However, by restoring political action and process to centre stage – and focusing on the process of navigation between the autonomous person and collective action in a rapidly changing and fluid global environment – understanding the liberal paradox provides an analytically effective way to conceptualise the restructuring of liberalism in the world of the twenty-first century and beyond.

Notes

1. This chapter began as a keynote address to the conference of the Central and East European International Studies Association, St. Petersburg, Russia, 3 September 2009. Other earlier versions were also delivered to a colloquium at Kenyon College, Ohio, USA, 19 October 2010, and to the Distinguished Senior Scholar panel, International Political Economy Section, International Studies Association, Montreal, Canada, 18 March 2011. I would like to thank Werner Bonefeld, Renee Marlin-Bennett, Louis Pauly, Neil Robinson, Gita Subrahmanyam, and the editors for their comments on an earlier draft.
2. That is, the interaction of multiple, overlapping, and interacting cultural identities.
3. I am using the term "governance" in its original sense of the word, as a set of less formal processes of collective decision-making, rather than a hierarchical structure of formal institutions (Cerny, 2013c).
4. Rents are, by definition, profits made over and above what they would be in an efficient, competitive marketplace; extensive rent-seeking is at the core of opportunistic and monopolistic behaviour.
5. Whether the hegemonic provision of international public goods such as free trade and an international monetary system, Wilsonian democratisation, humanitarian interventionism, or the development of international and regional institutions and regimes.

References

Acharya, V. V., Cooley, T. F., Richardson, M. P. and Walter, I. (eds) (2010), *Regulating Wall Street: The Dodd-Frank Act and the New Architecture of Global Finance*, Hoboken, New Jersey: Wiley.

Akerlof, G. A. and Shiller, R. J. (2009), *Animal Spirits: How Human Psychology Drives the Economy, and Why It Matters for Global Capitalism*, Princeton, New Jersey: Princeton University Press.

Albert, M., Buzan, B. and Zürn, M. (eds) (2013), *Bringing Sociology to International Relations: World Politics as Differentiation Theory*, Cambridge: Cambridge University Press.

Anderson, B. (1991), *Imagined Communities: Reflections on the Origin and Spread of Nationalism*, London: Verso.

Avelino, F. (2012), *Power in Transition: Empowering Discourses on Sustainability Transitions*, Rotterdam: Dutch Research Institute for Transitions, Erasmus University.

Bendix, R. (1964), *Nation-Building and Citizenship*, Garden City, New York: Anchor Books.

Bonefeld, W. (2013),On the Strong Liberal State: Beyond Berghahn and Young", *New Political Economy*, Retrieved from http://dx.doi.org/10.1080/13563467.2012.753046

Bremmer, I. (2010), *The End of the Free Market: Who Wins the War Between States and Corporations?* New York: Portfolio.

Brenner, N., Jessop, B., Jones, M. and MacLeod, G. (eds) (2003), *State/Space: A Reader*, Oxford: Blackwell.

Buzan, B., Wæver, O. and Wilde, J. (1998). *Security: A New Framework for Analysis*, Boulder, Colorado: Lynne Rienner.

Cerny, P. G. (1991), "The Limits of Deregulation: Transnational Interpenetration and Policy Change", *European Journal of Political Research*, 19(2 & 3) (March/April), 173–196.

Cerny, P. G. (1994), "The Infrastructure of the Infrastructure? Toward 'Embedded Financial Orthodoxy' in the International Political Economy", in B. Gills and R. Palan (eds) *Transcending the State-Global Divide: The Neostructuralist Agenda in International Relations*, Boulder, Colorado: Lynne Reinner, 223–249.

Cerny, P. G. (1997), "Paradoxes of the Competition State: The Dynamics of Political Globalization", *Government and Opposition*, 32(2) (Spring), 251–274.

Cerny, P. G. (1998), "Neomedievalism, Civil Wars and the New Security Dilemma: Globalization as Durable Disorder", *Civil Wars*, 1(1) (Spring), 36–64.

Cerny, P. G. (2000), "Restructuring the Political Arena: Globalization and the Paradoxes of the Competition State", in D. R. Germain (ed.) *Globalization and Its Critics: Perspectives from Political Economy*, London: Macmillan, 117–138.

Cerny, P. G. (2009), "Multi-Nodal Politics: Globalisation Is What Actors Make of It", *Review of International Studies*, 35(2) (April), 421–449.

Cerny, P. G. (2010), *Rethinking World Politics: A Theory of Transnational Neopluralism*, New York: Oxford University Press.

Cerny, P. G. (2011), "Saving Capitalism from the Capitalists? Financial Regulation After the Crash", *St. Antony's International Review*, 7(1) (March), 11–29.

Cerny, P. G. (2012), "Globalization and the Transformation of Power", in M. Haugaard and K. Ryan (eds) *Political Power: The State of the Art*, Barbara Budrich: Leverkusen Opladen for the International Political Science Association, Research Committee No. 36, Political Power, 187–215.

Cerny, P. G. (2013a), "From Warriors to Police? *Raison du monde* and the Transformation of Security in the 21st Century", paper presented to the Workshop on Non-Traditional Security, Queen Mary University of London, 7–8 March.

Cerny, P. G. (2013b), "Functional Differentiation, Globalisation and the New Transnational Neopluralism", in M. Albert, B. Buzan and M. Zürn (eds) *Bringing Sociology to International Relations: World Politics as Differentiation Theory* Cambridge: Cambridge University Press, in press.

Cerny, P. G. (2013c), "Transnational Neopluralism and the Process of Governance", in J. A. Payne and N. Phillips (eds) *The International Political Economy of Governance*, Cheltenham, Glos. and Northampton, MA: Edward Elgar.

Cerny, P. G. (2013d), "Is Financial Regulation a Public Good?" Article in Preparation for a Special Issue of *Critical Policy Studies*.

Clayton, R. and Pontusson, J. (1998), "Welfare State Retrenchment Revisited: Entitlement Cuts, Public Sector Restructuring, and Inegalitarian Trends in Advanced Capitalist Societies", *World Politics*, 51(1) (October), 67–98.

Comaroff, J. and Comaroff, J. L. (2012), *Theory from the South: Or, How Euro-America Is Evolving Toward Africa*, Boulder, Colorado: Paradigm Publishers.

Crozier, M. and Friedberg, E. (1977), *L'Acteur et le système: les contraintes de l'action collective*, Paris: Éditions du Seuil.

Edwards, M. (2004), *Civil Society*, Cambridge and Malden, MA: Polity Press.

Evans, M. G. (2005), *Policy Transfer in Global Perspective*, London: Ashgate.

Evans, P. (2007), "Is it Labor's Turn to Globalize? 21st Century Challenges and Opportunities", paper presented to the Democracy and Development Seminar, Princeton Institute for International and Regional Studies (24 October).

Foucault, M. (1980), *Power/Knowledge: Selected Interviews and Other Writings, 1972–1977*, edited by Colin Gordon, New York: Longman.

Foucault, M. (2008), *The Birth of Biopolitics: Lectures at the Collège de France, 1978–1979*, translated by Graham Burchell, London: Palgrave Macmillan; French edition 2004.

Fox, J. (2009), *The Myth of the Rational Market: A History of Risk, Reward, and Delusion on Wall Street*, New York: HarperBusiness.

Fukuyama, F. (1992), *The End of History and the Last Man*, Glencoe, Illinois: Free Press.

Gill, S. (1990), *American Hegemony and the Trilateral Commission*, Cambridge: Cambridge University Press.

Gill, S. (2003), *Power and Resistance in the New World Order*, London: Palgrave Macmillan.

Gill, S. (2012), "Towards a Radical Concept of Praxis: Imperial 'Common Sense' Versus the Post-modern Prince", *Millennium: Journal of International Studies*, 40(3) (Autumn) 505–524.

Goldstein, J. S. (2011), *Winning the War on War: The Decline of Armed Conflict Worldwide*, New York: Dutton.

Gregory, P. R. and Stuart, R. C. (1997), *Russian and Soviet Economic Performance and Structure*, 6th edition, Boston: Addison-Wesley.

Griffith, N. (1989), *"It's a Hard Life Wherever You Go"*, *Storms*, Nashville, Tennessee: MCA Records.

Harvey, D. (2005), *A Brief History of Neoliberalism*, Oxford: Oxford University Press.

Hayek, F. A. Von. (1989), "Spontaneous ('Grown') Order and Organized ('Made') Order", in N. Modlovsky (ed.) *Order – With or Without Design?* London: Centre for Research into Communist Economies, 101–123.

Held, D. (1995), *Democracy and the Global Order: From the Modern State to Cosmopolitan Governance*, Cambridge: Polity Press.

Herman, A. (2001), *The Scottish Enlightenment: The Scots' Invention of the Modern World*, London: Fourth Estate.

Hirst, P. and Thompson, G. (1999), *Globalization in Question: The International Political Economy and the Possibilities of Governance*, 2nd edition, Cambridge: Polity Press.

Holloway, J. and Picciotto, S. (eds) (1978), *State and Capital: A Marxist Debate*, London: Edward Arnold.

Johnson, C. (1982), *M.I.T.I. and the Japanese Miracle: The Growth of Industrial Policy, 1925–1975*, Stanford: Stanford University Press.

Jordana, J, and Levi-Faur, D. (eds) (2004), *The Politics of Regulation: Institutions and Regulatory Reforms for the Age of Governance*, Cheltenham, Glos. and Northampton, MA: Edward Elgar.

Kaplan, R. D. (2010), *Monsoon: The Indian Ocean and the Future of American Power*, New York: Random House.

Keohane, R. O. and Nye, J. S. Jr. (1977/2000), *Power and Interdependence*, 3rd edition, New York: Longman.

Kotkin, J. (1992), *Tribes: How Race, Religion and Identity Determine Success in the New Global Economy*, New York: Random House.

Lake, D. A. (1999), "Global Governance: A Relational Contracting Approach", in A. Prakash and A. J. Hart (eds) *Globalization and Governance*, London: Routledge, 31–53.

Laslett, P. (1965), *The World We Have Lost*, London: Methuen.

Lindblom, C. E. (1977), *Politics and Markets : The World's Political-Economic Systems*, New York: Basic Books.

Marlantes, K. (2011), *What It Is Like to Go to War*, New York: Atlantic Monthly Press.

McLuhan, M. (1964), *Understanding Media: The Extensions of Man*, New York: McGraw Hill.

Minc, A. (1993), *Le nouveau Moyen Âge*, Paris: Gallimard.

Moore, B. Jr. (1966), *Social Origins of Dictatorship and Democracy: Lord and Peasant in the Making of the Modern World*, Boston: Beacon Press.

Moran, M. (2003), *The British Regulatory State: High Modernism and Hyper-Innovation*, Oxford: Oxford University Press.

Moravcsik, A. (1997), "A Liberal Theory of International Politics", *International Organization*, 51(4) (Autumn), 513–553.

Pijl, K. (2012), *The Making of an Atlantic Ruling Class*, 2nd edition, London: Verso.

Pinker, S. (2011), *The Better Angels of Our Nature: The Decline of Violence in History and Its Causes*, New York: Viking Penguin.

Polanyi, K. (1944), *The Great Transformation: The Political and Economic Origins of Our Time*, Boston: Beacon Press.

Reinhart, C. M. and Rogoff, K. S. (2009), *This Time Is Different: Eight Centuries of Financial Folly*, Princeton, New Jersey: Princeton University Press.

Ruggie, J. G. (1982), "International Regimes, Transactions, and Change: Embedded Liberalism in the Post-war Economic Order", in D. S. Krasner (ed.) *International Regimes* Ithaca, NY: Cornell University Press, 195–231.

Sheehan, J. J. (2008), *Where Have All the Soldiers Gone? The Transformation of Modern Europe*, Boston: Houghton Mifflin.

Soederberg, S., Menz, G. and Cerny, P. G. (eds) (2005), *Internalizing Globalization: The Rise of Neoliberalism and the Erosion of National Varieties of Capitalism*, London and New York: Palgrave Macmillan.

Spruyt, H. (1994), *The Sovereign State and Its Competitors: An Analysis of Systems Change*, Princeton, NJ: Princeton University Press.

Stedman, J. D. (2012), *Masters of the Universe: Hayek, Friedman, and the Birth of Neoliberal Politics*, Princeton, New Jersey: Princeton University Press.

Tarrow, S. (2005), *The New Transnational Activism*, Cambridge: Cambridge University Press.

Tönnies, F. (1887/2003), *Community and Society [Gemeinschaft und Gesellschaft]*, Mineola, N.Y.: Dover Publications, originally published 1887.

Wallerstein, I. (1995), *After Liberalism*, New York: New Press.

Weber, E. (1976), *Peasants Into Frenchmen: Modernization of Rural France, 1870–1914*, Stanford, California: Stanford University Press.

Williamson, O. E. (1975), *Markets and Hierarchies*, New York: Free Press.

Williamson, O. E. (1985), *The Economic Institutions of Capitalism*, New York: Free Press.

Znaniecki, F. (1952/1973), *Modern Nationalities: A Sociological Study*, Westport, Conn.: Greenwood Press.

11
Debating China's Rise in China

Ren Xiao

In 2006, the 12-part TV documentary series "Rising Powers" (*daquo jueqi*) was airing in China. This popular television programme portrayed the conditions that gave rise to other modern great powers in history (Portugal, Spain, Holland, France, Great Britain, Germany, Russia, the USSR, Japan, and the United States); it attracted much attention at home and abroad. What constituted the background was the lively ongoing debate on China's possible "peaceful rise". Four years later, it was widely reported that China surpassed Japan and became the world's second-largest economy. Even though Beijing usually intends to keep a low profile in terms of national comprehensive power, China's official white paper states its total economic output reached $5.88 trillion in 2010, more than 16 times that of 1978 when China started to reform, and amounted to 9.3 per cent of the world's total from 1.8 per cent in 1978 (The State Council Information Office, 2011a). Undoubtedly, China is rising. A heated debate has emerged over the impact and implications of China's rise. This chapter first analyses China's options for the liberal domestic and international policies that have contributed to its growth, and then elaborates on the debate within China on its own ascent and accompanying views on China's self-identification. This chapter also discusses whether China's "peaceful rise" doctrine accommodates its military modernisation drive, before coming to its conclusion.

The rise of a liberal China?

China has now been undergoing profound changes over at least the past three decades. The (re)emergence of a major power such as China will inevitably have a tremendous impact on the world, given the country's sheer size and population. While the global financial crisis has proved to be a

---

This chapter partially draws on my essay "China's Possible New Path", *East Asian Policy* July/September 2010.

serious setback for the liberal international order – because of the growth of protectionism, the stalled Doha Round of multilateral trade negotiations, discredited "market fundamentalism", and the bankruptcy of so-called "neo-liberalism", defined as the "one-size-fits-all" kind of "Washington Consensus" – it may also have become a turning point for the rise to prominence of the emerging powers, represented by the so-called BRIC nations,[1] including China. The change to a more multipolar world now seems more apparent, and China's rise has accelerated this trend. As Western countries have been struggling with their crises, China has been relatively more successful in combating the global crisis and has maintained robust economic growth, and thus served as a key growth engine to save the world economy from a greater recession. These trends have prompted discussions and debates about the possible emergence of the "China (development) model".

For a leading Chinese philosopher, the implications of the "China model" for the world are that there is not only one feasible mode of development; in fact, there are alternative developmental patterns. Every nation must have a clear understanding of its own national situation, first, and, meanwhile, refer to other countries' experiences in a learning process; they should conduct dialogues on an equal footing (Chinanews.com, 2011). According to others, there is no such thing as a "China model".[2] China's hyper growth over the past three decades has proved that the market economy is the fundamental way towards an increase in individual freedom and wealth. If it is reversed, freedom and wealth throughout society are also undone, whether in China or in other countries. But, regardless of whether a distinct "China model" exists and to which extent it can be positively evaluated, a fundamental and fascinating development may have been the recent emergence of a liberal China.

According to G. John Ikenberry (2010), a liberal order encompasses "an open, rule-based system organised around expanding forms of institutionalised cooperation". In this sense, a liberal international order can be contrasted with alternative logics of order – blocs, exclusive spheres, and closed geopolitical systems. For James Kurth (2011), liberal internationalism as we have known it over the past generation or two has included several interrelated but distinct elements: (1) liberal democracy in politics; (2) free markets in economics; (3) an open society with respect to borders and culture, and (4) multilateral diplomacy in international affairs. I use these stipulations as overall criteria to evaluate changes and trends in China.

Liberal-democratic development

Within this first element, according to *The Oxford Paperback Dictionary* (1994: 461), "liberal" means "tolerant, open-minded, especially in religion and politics". It moreover refers to the protection of private property and the guaranteeing of individual rights. In 2004, China instituted an amendment to its constitution which introduced important new articles, stipulating that "legitimate private properties cannot be deprived" and that "the state protects the citizens' private property right and the right to inheritance". Incorporating this seemingly obvious content into the constitution was actually not a minor development. It was the logical political reflection of the market economy's consolidation in China. A market economy is based on transactions, and the conduct of transactions is premised on the safety of property. Thus, a market economy inherently requires that citizens' private property rights are guaranteed and clarified in the constitution, the highest legal authority. Though one has to admit that the protection of individual rights in China is far from perfect, it is safe to say the country is moving in the right direction.

Also, a Chinese-style democracy is developing in China, for example at the grassroots level (Ogden, 2002), and it will further unfold in the future. Its features include wider political participation, an inclusive political process that accommodates inputs from different quarters of Chinese society, and collective political leadership with regular turnover based on term limits (see also Liu and Chen, 2012). Deputies elected to the People's Congresses at different levels participate more proactively these days in deliberations on public affairs. Members of the Chinese People's Political Consultative Conference (CPPCC) can gradually have their voices heard at various levels and have bills put on the legislative agenda. Undoubtedly, these evolving institutional arrangements in China will inevitably bear "Chinese characteristics". This is a monumental issue, which is beyond the scope of this chapter. Below I will analyse the three other elements highlighted by Kurth in turn.

Free market

The reform era in China has been a period marked by the dissolving of the command economy, and the growth of a market economy. Accompanying this was a theoretical evolution that culminated in 1992, when the Chinese leadership decided that establishing a "socialist market economy system" should become the new strategic objective of China's reform and opening. A market economy inherently requires removing all kinds of out-of-date regulations that constrain the free flow of people, capital, information, and labour; that is exactly what has happened in Chinese society.

A milestone in this regard was China's entry into the World Trade Organisation (WTO) in December 2001, after a long, strenuous, 15-year journey of negotiation. By the time of the tenth anniversary of China's membership, WTO entry had led to several profound changes. Firstly, China's average tariff level was lowered from 15.3 per cent to 9.8 per cent. Secondly, considerable non-tariff barriers, such as subsidies and favourable export treatments had been removed. Thirdly, China had opened up over 100 service trade sectors. Fourthly, there had been governmental behavioural changes.

Previously, government agencies at different levels had often resorted to the notorious "red-headed documents" (*hongtou wenjian*) to exercise, often inefficiently, the management of economic activities. Each year they issued numerous documents of this kind. This is no longer valid. Nowadays, WTO rules for openness and transparency have to be observed, treating Chinese and foreign firms – state-owned or private – on an equal footing. Accordingly, China has undergone the large-scale enactment of over 3,000 clearing laws and regulations (2011: 2).

Through a learning process involving the application of market rules and the establishment of a stable, transparent, and predictable trading system, the business environment in China has become much more open. By implanting the WTO principles of non-discrimination, transparency, and fair play in China's economic system, market consciousness, the spirit of the rule of law, and the idea of intellectual property rights have been established. In a word, with WTO membership, China has decided to play by the WTO rules, and it has experienced a role change from being a new member to an active participant and accelerator. Over ten years ago, when the difficult and hard-headed bilateral negotiations were still ongoing, people in China called this WTO membership business "dancing with the wolves". After all, dancing has to be conducted in line with the rules, and this is exactly the case in the world trading system.[3] According to Long Yongtu, onetime Chief Chinese Negotiator for WTO Accession, because of China's WTO membership and its commitment to observing its rules and opening up markets, the external environment of Chinese development has greatly improved. It is generally believed that a nation, however powerful, does not pose a threat as long as it accepts and observes rules. Committed to solving trade and other disputes within the WTO, China has avoided direct confrontations with other nations (Long, 2011).

In addition to the WTO, China has been actively pursuing free trade agreements, bilaterally and regionally. China has already concluded seven bilateral FTAs, with ASEAN, Peru, Pakistan, Chile, New Zealand, Singapore, and Costa Rica. Five more FTAs are under negotiation, with the Gulf Cooperation Council (GCC), Australia, Iceland, Norway, and the South African Customs Union (SACU). In terms of overseas direct investment (ODI) volume, according to the United Nations Conference on Trade and Development (UNCTAD), China climbed up the world rankings to fifth-largest outbound direct investor in 2010 (Ding and Zhou, 2011: 7). Today, China is the largest exporter, second-largest importer, and the largest holder of foreign currency reserves.

A more open society

Together with reform, opening-up is the other driving force that has characterised China's evolution throughout the past generation or so. This is a two-dimensional process, involving both *internal* and *external* openings.

Internally, a market economy requires a freer flow of labour as a resource endowment. The freer flow of people has led to the relaxation of the *hukou* (household registration) system in China. Set up in 1958, the *hukou* system was meant to control the movement of people between urban and rural areas. Under the system, one's job opportunity, daily food supply, schooling of children, and the availability of housing were all related to his/her *hukou*. Without *hukou*, one could hardly obtain anything. Thus, under that system, people were tied to the *hukou* and the place they lived, and it was very difficult, if not totally impossible, for them to move to other places based on their own will. The system contains a rigid rural–urban division that excluded and discriminated against rural residents – the majority of the Chinese population. Throughout the reform period, as China is becoming an increasingly dynamic country, the *hukou* system, while still enduring, has loosened (Yin, 2011). As a result, hundreds of millions of farmers have moved into urban areas to become new workers. Clearly, more freedom is fundamentally reshaping many people's lives and has brewed creativity, vitality, and dynamism in Chinese society.

The loosening of the *hukou* system and its impact are just one example[4]; even more impressive is China's opening to the outside world. An increasingly large number of Chinese nationals are going abroad for travel, work, study, or to visit their families. In 2009, the number of people who travelled abroad reached 47.66 million, a growth of 4 per cent from the previous year. The number of tourist destinations increased to 139. In 2010, the total number of people entering and leaving through Chinese immigration reached 382 million, up 9.8 per cent from the previous year. Equally, China receives an increasing number of foreign visitors. In 2010, 52.11 million foreigners passed Chinese immigration, a 19.2 per cent growth from the previous year.[5] According to World Tourism Organisation forecasts, by 2015, both the numbers of Chinese tourists going abroad and external tourists coming into China will reach 100 million.[6]

As China is opening up further, foreign direct investment has continued to flow in, bringing China into the global production system. As a result of the deepening of economic globalisation, China is increasingly embedded in the global division of labour. In the past 30 years, China has utilised a total of US$903.8 billion of overseas investment and approved the establishment of over 670,000 overseas-funded enterprises. Almost all of the world's top 500 companies have invested in China (Wu, 2010). In turn, since joining the WTO in 2001, China has, on average, imported commodities worth US$687 billion each year and created about 14 million job opportunities in other countries and regions (ibid.). According to Pascal Lamy (2011: 11), "China is now the world's second largest importer and imports have risen nearly six times to $1.4 trillion since the WTO accession. The Chinese market has become one of the most important in the world for many exporting nations, including the United States and Brazil".

Multilateral diplomacy

Once self-identified as the "centre of the world revolution", today's China is committed to the existing international order. It has joined most of the key international covenants, treaties, and organisations. As a party to over 300 international treaties and a member of more than 130 inter-governmental organisations or regimes, China has taken an active part in international cooperation, from nuclear non-proliferation to mitigating global climate change. Seeing multilateral forums as an "important arena",[7] China's multilateral diplomacy takes three main forms.

Firstly, China has proactively engaged in developing regional multilateral organisations or mechanisms. Amidst the Asian financial crisis, China, together with Japan and South Korea, joined hands with ASEAN (the Association of Southeast Asian Nations), creating the ASEAN plus Three process of East Asian cooperation; they have since formed a web of cooperation mechanisms in a range of functional areas and at various levels. China and the ten-member ASEAN have also created a free trade area for a mutually beneficial, freer flow of goods, people, capital, and mutual investment. As a result, China–ASEAN trade amounted to $35.3billion in 2000 and soared to nearly $293 billion in 2010. The annual value of ASEAN–China trade is expected to reach $500 billion by the end of 2015 (Kwang, 2011: 24).

Building on their interaction within the ASEAN plus three grouping, China, Japan, and South Korea have also initiated trilateral cooperation. This has become institutionalised through annual summits held on a rotating basis. Recently, they have also set up a trilateral cooperation secretariat in Seoul.[8] Meanwhile, the "Shanghai Five" has developed into the Shanghai Cooperation Organisation, which includes China, Russia, Kazakhstan, Kyrgyzstan, Tajikistan, and Uzbekistan as member states, and operates a secretariat in Beijing. China has played a prominent role in facilitating its development (see Hu, 2005). Furthermore, China was instrumental in the Six-Party process on Korean denuclearisation and crisis prevention, acting as the chair of the Six-Party Talks since 2003; this has been an ad hoc regional security mechanism to manage a specific security issue that has significant regional implications.

Secondly, China has been involved in efforts to strengthen global institutions, especially the United Nations (UN). Beijing puts much emphasis on the UN's efficient performance and continued authority. Among the five permanent members of the Security Council, China has sent more peacekeeping troops than any other power to trouble spots throughout the world. In recent years, China has considerably increased its share of UN dues. Since 2000, its percentage in these dues has kept growing: from 0.995 per cent that year to 1.54 per cent in 2001, 2.053 per cent in 2004, 2.667 per cent in 2007, and 3.189 per cent in 2010, with each time's growth rate exceeding 0.5 per cent. Thus, it has increased more than twofold since 2000. Yet China's actual contribution is not limited to the growth of its payments to the UN's regular budget. Each year, the whole UN system needs a budget of $12 billion, and peacekeeping operations are expensive: from 2009 to 2010, the peacekeeping budget was as high as $7.75 billion. According to the burden-sharing principle of international peacekeeping, China, as one of the permanent five of the UN Security Council, bears 3.2375 per cent of total peacekeeping costs, amounting to about $250 million. In 2010, the four categories of China's remittances to the UN added up to over $300 million; those of 2011 are estimated to reach $400 million.[9] It is likely that China's contribution to the UN will continue to grow.

Thirdly, China has been positive towards other mechanisms for global dialogue or coordination. Since 2003, China has, for example, participated in the G8 outreach dialogues with five major developing countries: Brazil, China, India, Mexico, and South Africa. Against the backdrop of the 2008 global financial crisis, the G20 summit came into existence; it is seen as the "premium platform of global economic cooperation".[10] The group includes all the major developing countries; within it, they can work with the developed powers on a more equal footing, one of the main reasons China attaches so much importance to it. As a founding member, a shaping force, and a core participant in this new mechanism for global economic governance, China sees the G20 as an institutional recognition of its major power status as well as of its crucial role. Beijing also lays emphasis on the grouping of BRICS (Brazil, Russia, India, China, and now also South Africa) states. It has also participated in larger, inter-regional forums such as the Asia–Europe Meeting (ASEM) and the Forum on East Asia–Latin America Cooperation, as well as the Forum on China–Africa Cooperation, which it has itself orchestrated.

Based on the above, it can be argued that in its adherence to the free market, free trade, a more open society, and multilateral diplomacy, China meets the criteria for being considered a proponent of the liberal world order. Undoubtedly, the emergence of a major power such as China has potentially great significance for global economics and politics. How does China view its own growth and role in the world? This has given rise to a lively debate in the country.

From "peaceful rise" to "peaceful development"

As China continues to move into the centre of the world stage, its peaceful rise/peaceful development theory, far from being in "demise" – as some American analysts (Glaser and Medeiros, 2007) claim – will prove to be a profound intellectual move forward, potentially significant for the future of China and the world because of its most fundamental foreign policy implications. This has much to do with the current Chinese leadership's policy thinking.

In December 2002, Mr Zheng Bijian, Chairman of the China Reform Forum (CRF – a newly founded research group) and former Executive Vice-President of the Central Party School, led a CRF delegation on a visit to the United States. During the trip, Zheng met and spoke extensively with leading American strategists, including former National Security Advisors Henry Kissinger, Zbigniew Brzezinski, Brent Scowcroft, and Samuel Berger, as well as the serving Assistant to the President for National Security Affairs, Condoleezza Rice. The impression Zheng gained was that, while the American strategists had both positive and negative views of China's rise, their worries outweighed their positive evaluations. Both the "China threat" and the "China collapse" thesis were fairly widespread at the time. Upon his return, Zheng prepared and submitted a report to the top Chinese leadership in which he suggested that research into what he called a "new path of China's peaceful rise" be quickly organised and conducted.[11]

A month later, Hu Jintao, the new CCP General Secretary, offered his full support for the research project on China's "peaceful rise". Soon, the Central Party School was assigned to coordinate research work, and Zheng was asked to lead the efforts. The top leadership readily embraced the idea and encouraged the project. With this official endorsement, Zheng began to publicise the notion and sell it to wider audiences, at venues like the Bo'ao Forum for Asia. Thereafter, the "peaceful rise" thesis quickly emerged as a conspicuous topic, attracting much attention at home and abroad. President Hu and Premier Wen Jiabao subsequently adopted the term "peaceful rise" and incorporated it into their most important speeches. It also quickly became a hot research topic in the Chinese social sciences.

The "peaceful rise" thesis became not only popular, but also controversial. The Ministry of Foreign Affairs (MOFA) was reluctant to use the word "rise" (*jue qi*), out of concern that use of that term might be inconsistent with the then-current guideline of keeping a low profile in world affairs. Quite a few retired ambassadors voiced their opposition to the use of "peaceful rise", specifically reacting to the use of the word "rise". These critics took full advantage of the latitude afforded by their positions to voice their opinions. Two main criticisms arose. The first consisted of objections to the concept itself: advocates of this view argued statements that China had already risen were premature, owing to China's uneven and unbalanced development.[12] It was one matter for other countries to talk about China's rise, but it was quite another for China to play up its own rise, they argued. Using a term like "peaceful development" would sound more modest and emphasise China's desire to maintain a low profile in international politics. The second criticism was bureaucratic-procedural. To those in the MOFA system, foreign affairs were considered MOFA's exclusive territory; a theory that had emerged from outside this system was not looked upon kindly.

Aware of these different opinions, the leadership chose the prudent path and opted to use a more modest wording: "taking a path of peaceful development". Meanwhile, the "peaceful rise" project proceeded in parallel. After the 2005 Bo'ao Forum in April, Zheng again submitted his report to the top leadership, adding his speech at Bo'ao as a supplement. Soon after, Hu offered supportive remarks, stating that "it was necessary to deepen the studies in 'China's peaceful rise' ". Despite the aforementioned differences, as late as in early June 2005, Zheng had had the opportunity to talk with Hu and other top leaders. Hu and Premier Wen once again provided their support for the project, thus greatly encouraging Zheng. Later that month, Zheng again led a delegation on a visit to the United States. The agenda included a meeting with then Secretary of State Rice, the third time they had met since 2002. The successful visit helped pave the way for President Hu's own visit to Washington in September of that year.

The peaceful rise/peaceful development discourse, and the debate over the emerging philosophy of Chinese domestic and foreign policies, culminated in the October 2007 Seventeenth Party Congress Report (Hu, 2007), in which one section was devoted to the need to "unswervingly take the path of peaceful development". Although the thesis had been reiterated and elaborated previously, the inclusion of the formulation in a Party Congress Report was of particular importance. These reports are issued only once every five years and enjoy higher authority and respect than any other document in the country. The inclusion of the phrase "peaceful development" illustrates the consensus of China's leadership on the term; though disagreements remain, they are more rhetorical than substantive. Why would the ascent of the "peaceful rise" thesis prove to be a significant development in China? The crucial reason is that it suggests a changing way of thinking regarding the path that China should take. Moreover, "peaceful rise" is not just a statement of intent; it also has the potential to become a new philosophy in China's domestic and foreign policy.

The change from "peaceful rise" to "peaceful development" occurred because the latter was more widely acceptable to all quarters in China, and thus less controversial. After all, China was increasingly becoming a pluralistic society in which very different views could emerge. The compromise indicated this change was actually not the "demise" of "peaceful rise", but rather a rhetorical variation designed to moderate the tone and soothe those critics.[13] As so often happens, the change was the result of a compromise. What really mattered was the adoption of that thought as a new principle, embedded into China's foreign policy doctrine through the expression of "taking a path of peaceful development". Theoretically, peaceful rise was possible, as also concluded by Barry Buzan (2010).

However, unsurprisingly, all kinds of – often radically opposing – commentaries on China's rise have not receded; on the contrary, they are continuing to emerge. The need to bring them together has led to a new white paper on

China's Peaceful Development. In 2005, when China's first white paper on the road towards peaceful development was published, the country ranked as the sixth-largest economy in the world. At a surprising speed, China quickly surpassed Japan and became the second largest in 2010. Making strides in its advance towards great power status at such a rapid pace has inevitably aroused all kinds of further reactions, be they praise, admiration, uneasiness, scepticism, and fear, all combining to create a complex situation. The widely used "China threat" thesis (*zhongguo weixie lun*) could no longer grasp these nuances. The "China's responsibility" thesis was becoming more popular. Meanwhile, a picture of an "assertive China" was being painted, out of whatever motivation. While many countries wanted to jump on the bandwagon of China's rapid economic growth, they were often wary of China's rise as well. A love–hate ambivalence was widespread; the status of China and its relations were questions that continued to occupy the minds of many an observer.

In such a context, China felt it necessary and even compelling to respond to the questions raised both in and outside the country. To tell the rest of the world what kind of developmental path China was taking and would be taking in the future, and also to educate its own people, China published the "China's Peaceful Development" white paper, the second of its kind, six years after the original one, in September 2011. The white paper argues against the logic that a rising power was bound to seek hegemony, and states that China has broken away from that traditional pattern. The paper highlights that the experiences of the past decades have proved the correctness of the strategy of peaceful development, from which there is no reason to deviate. In particular, the "peaceful development" thesis has the six following components:

- In the first place, *scientific development*, which puts people first and promotes comprehensive, balanced, and sustainable development.
- Secondly, *independent development*, which requires that China must act in keeping with its national conditions and carry out reform and innovation for economic and social development through its own efforts. It must not shift problems and difficulties onto other countries.
- Thirdly, *open development*. China has learned from its history that it cannot develop itself with its door closed. Executing reforms and opening up are basic policies: China both carries out domestic reforms and opens itself to the outside world; it both pursues independent development and takes part in economic globalisation.
- Fourthly, *peaceful development*. The Chinese people have learned the value of peace and the pressing need for development. They understand that only peace can allow them to live and work in prosperity and contentment and that only development can provide them with a decent standard of living.

- Fifthly, *cooperative development*: China seeks to establish and develop different cooperative relationships with other countries and works with them to solve major problems that affect world economic development, as well as human survival and progress.
- Finally, *common development*. Only when the common development of all countries is realised and more people share the fruits of development, can world peace and stability have a solid foundation and be effectively guaranteed, and can development be sustainable in all countries (The State Council Information Office, 2011a).

The White Paper is the most recent effort to answer questions as to what China wants and what kind of world China hopes to see. While it is basically a statement of benign intentions, the key is to convince others that China is sincere. Some voices within policy circles have stated that to make others believe that China is indeed taking a path towards peaceful development, China itself should genuinely believe the peaceful development doctrine first. The question then becomes whether the peaceful development doctrine can effectively guide China's concrete domestic and foreign policies. Herein lies the real challenge: if benign statements cannot convince the outside sceptics in the short run, China has to prove through its behaviour that it honours its own words by actually taking the path of peaceful development. In this context, one important question arises: how does a rising China perceive its role and status in the world today?

Debating China's self-identity

Inevitably, any pursuit of peaceful development is closely related to China's self-identification: its perceptions on what kind of power it is and what kind of role it should play in the world. After three decades of successful development during which great changes have taken place, what kind of power is China today? This question on self-identity has recently been bothering and plaguing Beijing, which continues to search for a satisfying answer. In November 2009, a nation-wide academic conference was held in the capital with the participation of representatives from leading institutions, specifically aiming at exploring "the international repositioning of contemporary China" (Wu, 2009). Appeals were made for greater efforts to define China's own international role more proactively with respect to both rhetoric and behaviour (Gao, 2010).

As was discussed in the 2009 conference, a rising power may play a number of possible roles. The question of whether China is a challenger repeatedly came up. In reality, the Chinese leadership has often been reminded not to become a challenger to the current number one great power, nor to try to overthrow the existing international system,[14] which could be disastrous for the challenger. Is China a free rider? This depends on how "free rider" is defined. If China ever was a "free rider", the question is when. After the 1989 political turmoil in Beijing, Western countries imposed various sanctions upon China. Soon after, China encountered new and enormous difficulties during WTO entry negotiations, as Western countries further raised the bar. Thus, the preceding period – in the 1980s – was the only possible period for China to "free ride" on the West. No matter whether that is true, in any case, China is no longer a free rider today in whatever sense of the term. Less controversial are China's participation in most of the international institutions or regional cooperative arrangements, and China's role as a builder of the international order in various areas, through its part in UN-sponsored operations (e.g. peacekeeping, anti-piracy, or nuclear non-proliferation), trading regimes, and regional trade or security groupings.

Undoubtedly, China is in transition. It is undergoing a rapid transformation from a relatively backward to a more modernised country, and from a lower-level living standard to a generally well-off society. Despite having become the world's second-largest economy, China is not yet affluent, with a number of contradictions or problems to be overcome. Given the constant changes in the country, the boundaries distinguishing developing from developed status are becoming increasingly blurred.

This massive transition, profound and complex in nature, has given rise to China's multiple identifications. Earlier on, China might have been seen as part of the Third World, and later as a regional power with global implications in terms of its influence. More recently, a number of adjectives have been added to China to describe the country: developing, socialist (though this meaning is becoming more difficult to detect), emerging, and rising. Some quarters in China still have a victim complex emerging from the "century of humiliation" it experienced, leading to sometimes overly sensitive reactions to external criticisms. But in reality, today's China is no longer the "sick man of East Asia", but, rather, a very different country standing on a new starting point. Its decisions or options may have a considerable impact upon the rest of the world. Against this backdrop, it is widely believed that China needs to better define its desired role in the world; thus far, different answers have been given in China.

Answer number one: China is an emerging, major developing power. This argument posits that, on the one hand, China's economic magnitude and the significant growth of its power status have been recognised by the international community; on the other hand, China's level of development has not yet reached that of a medium developed country. China's per capita GDP was just about $3,000 in 2008, still far below the world average of $7,119.[15] According to the World Bank's criteria, per capita consumption is less than $1.25 per day, there are still 250 million people living in poverty in China, putting the country in second place in terms of their absolute number. China still has a long way to go to modernise its society (Yang, 2009).[16] Others say that current conditions make it impossible to ignore the difficulties and hardships in the processes leading towards developed nation status (Tang, 2006: 54). It can only be reasonable and practical to identify China's responsibility in the world in accordance with its status as a developing country (Ouyang, 2010).

Answer number two: China stands on a new threshold. With China's comprehensive national power rapidly growing, it is manifesting some features that distinguish it from normal developing countries. China's self-identification as a developing country can no longer be widely acknowledged in the international community (Zhao, 2009: 5). The growth of China's national power has already reached a critical point (*lin jie dian*). Since the 2008 outbreak of the global financial crisis, there has been a further elevation of both its hard and soft power, as China has been playing the role of economic powerhouse to help draw the world economy out of trouble (Huang, 2010). China has become the largest emerging market in the developing world, a new driving force of the global economy, and is changing from a regional power to a great power with global influence, awareness, and responsibility (Wang, 2009).

Answer number three: China should act as a harmonious force in the world, based on the central tenets of traditional Chinese thought and their long-time persistence in international interactions. There are two messages this repositioning may convey to others, and that the outside world can also expect hearing from China. For one thing, harmony is what the world desires, and China is willing to contribute its wisdom and power for the building or shaping of a new global system; for another, a harmonious force rejects the traditional logic of a struggle for power, turns to cooperation instead of confrontation, and cherishes equality instead of pure power mechanisms. This ought to be part of China's pursuit for international values (Chen, 2009).

There is still *a fourth answer*, which advocates that China should act as a "free-rider", defined very differently from its traditional usage, as free-riding on the world's fundamental trends. This, by and large, encompasses multi-dimensional progress, combined with deep and extensive engagement in the globalisation process (Tang, 2006: fn. 7). In fact, this is not a true free-riding argument but, rather, a plea for being an active and autonomous participant in global politics, economics, and development.

Throughout the debate, what is prominent in the Chinese discourse is a continuing self-identification as a developing country. This is an interesting phenomenon, and there are reasons for this key form of self-identification. Firstly, many people recognise that, in terms of its level of development, China's per capita income is still low. Secondly, China sees itself as part of the developing world by inertia. Yet herein lies an inherent contradiction. Since becoming a medium-developed country by the mid-century has been set as China's strategic goal, Beijing will consequently deviate from this status as a developing country; to date, no direct answer has been given to this inconsistency. Thirdly, there is a political consideration, a need to align China with the developing countries and win their support. This line of thinking is reflected in the expression "developing countries are the foundation", which is one of the principles guiding China's foreign relations. Some proponents of this line have even been so radical as to state that "China is forever a developing country".

Finally, there is the practical advantage to being treated as a developing country, for example in the WTO. The Doha Round of trade negotiations has been ongoing for over ten years, and its fate is relevant for the future of the world's multilateral trading system. The negotiations are important for China, this being the first time it is participating in the making of world trading rules. For Sun Zhenyu (2011: 122–123), China's first ambassador to the WTO, the Doha Round is stalled largely because of US domestic politics. Washington has put forward satisfying US demands for market access as the condition for completing the Doha Round of negotiations, and this has inevitably been opposed and resisted by the emerging economies and developing countries. China should stand with the developing countries, bring the appeals of the vast developing members to attention in the negotiations, and strive for negotiation outcomes truly favourable to their development.

When looking at the same country, putting emphasis on either aggregate or average national power leads to different interpretations: either that China enjoys high world status in aggregate terms, or that it needs to keep a low profile in per capita terms. In fact, both ways coexist, and they are the two faces of China. This will likely continue into the future. That the country maintains a number of characteristics of a developing country is a fairly widely held view in China, and hence, for some time, it won't be able to completely break away from that characterisation. However, as China is continuing to change and rise, the boundaries are gradually blurred. It is likely Beijing will cautiously reposition and gradually adjust itself between these multiple identities in terms of its global role. After all, China is both adapting and shaping the new global reality.

Peaceful rise versus military modernisation?

Does China's peaceful rise/development discourse matter? We know that rhetoric can be shallow, and thus somewhat bereft of meaning. However, it can also point to the direction of or create real constraints for policy-making. If a discourse is emphasised over and over again, it is possible for people to become bound to it through expectations. Westerners tend to doubt rhetoric, but it can also be an important phase of policy construction. Still, people may come up with questions. In spite of the "peaceful rise" discourse, China's military modernisation continues. Are the two developments contradictory? This question is worth careful consideration and examination.

Basically, "peaceful rise" has two key connotations: rise through peaceful means and rise for peaceful purposes. In other words, the rise occurs not through exercising violence or waging war, but rather by aiming to wage peace. Thus, peaceful rise by definition does not preclude defence modernisation, while military modernisation does not disprove peaceful rise either, while logically remaining an inherent component of a "rise". Without defence modernisation, a "rise" would probably not be genuine. The October 2009 parade in Beijing – on the occasion of the 60th anniversary of the PRC – could be seen as a review of progress regarding defence modernisation. As usual, there are different interpretations of China's military changes, on both capability and intention. It would not be surprising if outsiders retained uneasiness or concern. However, observers should consider that as China rises to a great power status, it becoming a militarily more powerful state is simply a matter of time. Normally, a power's military prowess will grow to a level equivalent to its economic and technological advancement. In the case of China, two particular motives are driving military modernisation: the persistence of the Taiwan issue and the spread of Beijing's overseas interests.

When Mr Ma Ying-Jeou won the Taiwan election in March 2008, people felt somewhat relieved that the cross-Taiwan Straits relationship was brought back on track. With the resumption of talks and the full realisation of three links – direct travel, commercial relations, and mail services – cross-strait tensions have decreased. However, Chinese analysts widely believe that the basic political configuration in Taiwan – "blue camp vs. green camp" – essentially remains unchanged. The blue camp's performance in the 2009 local elections disappointed the mainland's observers and policymakers and cautioned them not to overestimate the achievements thus far, which seem limited and not irreversible. Thus, the People's Liberation Army (PLA) has to remain well prepared for a worst-case scenario and be ready to win a conflict should Taiwanese pro-independence groups move in a "dangerous" direction. Only when the PLA has the will and capability to do so, can a war be eventually avoided. In order to make deterrence work, one has to convince others that one's will and capability are real, that one is not a toothless paper tiger – quite on the contrary.

The second major demand comes from the rapid spread of China's overseas interests, which have already become ubiquitous and wide-ranging. This spread has followed a three-phased "going-out" process. Firstly, there was the obvious "going-out" of Chinese visitors and tourists. Not long thereafter, a "going-out" of Chinese enterprises followed, to engage in trade, construction, and so forth. Of more fundamental significance is the "going-out" of Chinese capital, a strategy of investment which has experienced some setbacks but will nonetheless certainly continue. In fact, the presence of

China and its interests can be increasingly felt all over the world, including in African, Latin American, and South Pacific countries, let alone China's immediate neighbourhood: the recent start of construction of a pipeline connecting the Myanmar port of Kyaukphyu with China's Southwest is but one example. These developments have added to the burden of China's security, because the stable provision and shipment of oil and gas have to be assured, and the safety of sea-lanes protected.

In that regard, China is unfortunate as it borders as many as 14 countries, more than any other nation in the world. In addition, several other countries across the seas can be added to this already long list. The vast landmass, complex borders, and long coastlines require China to maintain considerable armed forces. In fact, there are many other tasks emanating from the multi-purpose nature of the PLA. Similarly to the military forces of other countries, the PLA has been engaged in operations such as disaster relief, international peace-keeping, anti-piracy naval patrols, and other tasks. When earthquakes devastated parts of Sichuan Province in 2008, disaster relief operations would not have been successful without the PLA's large-scale involvement.

Looking around the world, every nation is taking steps to modernise its military. China is no exception. To some extent, understandably, this upsets some foreign observers. For an accurate grasp of the nature of China's military, three fundamental facts can be discerned and should be borne in mind. Firstly, in terms of Chinese civil–military relations, there has been institutionalised and solidified civilian control of the military. The "gun" is firmly under the control of civilian leaders, whose thinking matters more for the role of PLA, not the other way around. There is no reason why this situation should not continue into the future.

The second fact is that peace is very much established as a value now and is actively pursued, as embodied in the principle of "independent foreign policy in favour of peace". After quite a few rounds of debates in the 1980s and 1990s, the Chinese leadership and policy community have come very close to the conclusion that the current era *is* an one of peace and development. This is a fundamental judgement of crucial importance to the formulation of China's domestic and international policies. This judgement has experienced challenges over time, especially when major events occurred and shocked the population. Prominent ones include the difficulties China encountered throughout the GATT/WTO membership negotiations, the 1999 NATO bombing of the Chinese embassy in Belgrade, and the mid-air collision between American and Chinese aircraft off Hainan Island in 2001, to name just a few. However, this judgement has survived these and other turbulences, and it still holds today. Experience has clearly taught China that lasting economic development can only be achieved in a stable and peaceful environment. China therefore has every reason not to disrupt, but to strive for such an external environment.

Thirdly, an analysis of intentions is much more important than a focus on China's military capabilities. The flawed argument that history repeats itself and major powers inevitably fight each other is fatalistic; it doesn't hold. Taking into account the circumstances of the early twenty-first century, there is no reason for an emerging power to take the path of military expansion, out of its own national interests. Clearly, there is little desire in China to challenge US power and global status. As Joshua S. Goldstein points out, "a military conflict (particularly with its biggest customer and debtor) would impede China's global trading posture and endanger its prosperity. Since Chairman Mao's death, China has been hands-down the most peaceful great power of its time. For all the recent concern about a newly assertive Chinese navy in disputed international waters, China's military hasn't fired a single shot in battle in 25 years" (Goldstein, 2011). Moreover, China's history of being bullied enables a habitual sympathetic understanding other peoples' wishes and feelings. Nonetheless, Beijing has every reason to defend its own interests, and to request others to respect those – and particularly its core – interests.

More recently, China has been called upon to share responsibility in global affairs and help provide for public goods, something from which it should not and cannot escape. Chinese armed forces will become involved in more military operations beyond war, in this context, such as the recent operations in the Gulf of Aden, off Somalia. "The PLA's going out to fight piracy and terrorism is to a large extent safeguarding international security, and is an embodiment of shouldering international responsibility" (Cheng, 2007). Several years ago, when an earthquake-induced tsunami had struck and devastated the Indian Ocean rim countries, China engaged in disaster relief operations while at the same time being painfully aware of the deficiency of its capability to rapidly project substantial military personnel and deliver supplies, as the United States was able to do in just a few days. A more successful role from the PLA could be seen in 2008, during the disaster relief operations in response to the earthquake in Sichuan province. Overall, the PLA will play a larger and legitimate part in global military-related affairs. That is a justifiable role, which by no means implies an expansionist and threatening stance. Otherwise, it would lead to an undesirable situation in opposition to China's own interests, a situation its peaceful development doctrine inhibits. China's overall defensive posture and growing role in world affairs are the key to an accurate understanding of the path it is taking, both in the present and in the future.

Conclusion

Looking at China's recent international behaviour, numerous actions or policies aimed at power balancing can be discerned, especially regarding the constraining of United States' moves to wage war against Iraq in 2002–2003, or to impose sanctions on Myanmar in 2007, and Syria in 2011. In that sense, it can be argued that China has adopted realist, balance of power policies, and that it is thus a realist power. However, China has actively sought to join the WTO and remains an adamant supporter of the global free trade regime. Within the multilateral trade regime, China has evolved from learning the rules of the game – familiarising itself with them – to applying the rules, and even participating in rule-making: it is, in fact, becoming a mature member in the multilateral trade system. In East Asia, China has become deeply involved in the regional web of free trade arrangements. Trying to be prudent, it is careful not to seek a "maximisation of interest", but instead attempts to care about others' preferences and tries to share economic development and prosperity with other Asian countries. It is even prepared to give more and retrieve less (*duo yu shao qu*) in its relations with neighbouring countries: giving more is aimed at winning the hearts and minds of its neighbours, not to increase material power. These actions defy John Mearsheimer's (2001) offensive realist arguments. Based on China's choice of policies directed towards the free market, free trade, an opening up of society, and multilateral diplomacy, I tend to argue that the rise of China is, to a large extent, the rise of a liberal China.

The famous fable of four blind men touching the elephant recounts how each of the four men was able to reach part of the big animal, consequently coming up with different descriptions. The man who reached the nose described the elephant as a tube. The second, who reached the ear, compared the elephant with a fan. The third said it was like a wall, whereas the last equated it to a tree-trunk. Each was partly correct, at best. China's foreign policy exhibits a mixture of realist and liberal elements or approaches. After all, in practice, definitions of foreign policy and strategy are never clear-cut. No single paradigm can adequately explain the behaviours of a complex great power like China. This tells us that, very often, what a researcher describes can be the partial truth, if not a distorted one. Different elements can be discerned in the debates regarding China's possible peaceful rise, and its self-identifications. China is in profound transition. So are its clashing ideas and thoughts; and all are relevant to informing a new research agenda.

Notes

1. This term was coined by Jim O'Neil of Goldman Sachs and refers to Brazil, Russia, India, China, and South Africa.
2. For example, Chen Zhiwu, a professor at Yale University School of Management.
3. For an excellent overview, see Sun (2011). Sun was the first Chinese Ambassador to the World Trade Organisation.
4. Fei-Ling Wang (2011) argues that a key reason why Chinese economic development – especially its export-led growth – has been so impressive is because of its *hukou* system, a powerful institution of organising and managing people, China's most important and plentiful resource.

5. *Xinhua News Agency*, 12 January 2011.
6. *Xinhua News Agency*, 12 October 2009.
7. This is the term used by China's Ministry of Foreign Affairs.
8. For a detailed study, see Xiao (2009).
9. *China Youth Daily*, 22 October 2011.
10. Leaders' Statement: The Pittsburgh Summit, 24–25 September 2009.
11. The report is dated 30 December 2002. See Zheng (2006).
12. This author gained that impression during various conference discussions.
13. The critics include quite a few retired Chinese Ambassadors, who were pretty vocal at the time. The discussions at the highest level of Chinese leadership eventually decided the change of the wording.
14. For example, Shi (2000).
15. According to China's National Statistic Bureau, in 2010, China's GDP was close to 40 trillion, its per capita GDP over $4,000.
16. According to Le (2011), the number of people who are living below the poverty line is 150 million, taking the UN's standard of one US dollar a day.

References

Buzan, B. (2010), "China in International Society: Is 'Peaceful Rise' Possible?" *The Chinese Journal of International Politics*, 3, 5–36.
Chen, Y. (3 December 2009), "Zhongguo de guoji dingwei: 'hexie liliang' " (China's International Positioning: 'A Harmonious Force'), *Zhongguo shehui kexue bao* (*Chinese Social Sciences Today*), 5.
Cheng, Y. (6 July 2007), "Zhongguo jundui you zeren zouchuqu" (China's PLA has a Responsibility to go out), *Huanqiu shibao* (*Global Times*), 11.
Chinanews.com (2011), "Interview with Yi Junqing, Director of the Central Compilation and Translation Bureau", available at http://www.chinanews.com/gn/2011/03-03/2881172.shtml.
Ding Q. and Zhou S. (29 July 2011), "China in Top Five of Global ODI Table", *China Daily Asia Weekly*.
Gao, Z. (14 September 2010), "Zhongguo juese dingwei de neiwai zhi bian" (The Internal and External Identification of China's Role), available at http://theory.people.com.cn/GB/12718529.html.
Glaser, B. S. and Medeiros, E. S. (2007), "The Changing Ecology of Foreign Policy-Making in China: The Ascension and Demise of the Theory of 'Peaceful Rise' ", *The China Quarterly*, 190, 291–310.
Goldstein, J. S. (2011), "World Peace Could Be Closer Than You Think", *Foreign Policy* (September/October), 53–56.
Hu, R.W. (2005), "China's Central Asia Policy: Making Sense of the Shanghai Cooperation Organization", in B. Rumer (ed.) *Central Asia at the End of the Transition*, Armonk, NY and London: M.E. Sharpe.
Hu, J. (2007), *Report to the Seventeenth Party Congress*, Beijing: Renmin Chubanshe.
Huang, R. (16 November 2010), "Zhongguo guoji juese dingwei fangshi" (Ways of Identifying China's International Role), *Wen Hui Bao* (Wenhui Daily), 7.
Ikenberry, G. J. (2010), "The Liberal International Order and its Discontents", *Millennium: Journal of International Studies*, 38(3), 509–521.
Kurth, J. (2011), "The New Liberalism in Global Politics: From Internationalism to Transnationalism", available at http://fpri.org/enotes/201103.kurth.transnationalism.html.

Kwang, M. (9 September 2011), "Changing Equations", *China Daily Asia Weekly*, 24.

Lamy, P. (16 December 2011), "China's Accession to WTO Worth Celebrating", *China Daily Asia Weekly*, 11.

Le, Y. (1 July 2011), "Different Kind of Exceptionalism", *China Daily Asia Weekly*, 1.

Liu, Y. and Chen, D. (2012), "Why China Will Democratize", *The Washington Quarterly*, 35(1), 41–63.

Long, Y. (2011), *"Zhongguo rushi de hexin liyi ji fazhanzhong cunzai de wenti"* (The Core interests of China's Joining the WTO and the Existing Issues), *Guoji jingji pinglun* (*International Economic Review*), 95(5), 14–21.

Mearsheimer, J. J. (2001), *The Tragedy of Great Power Politics*, New York: W.W. Norton.

"Minister of Commerce Chen Deming spoke at the World Economic Forum" (29 January 2011), *Renmin ribao* (*People's Daily, Overseas Edition*).

Ogden, S. (2002), *The Inklings of Democracy in China*, Cambridge: Harvard University Press.

Ouyang, K. (5 January 2010), "Zai jidang jibian de shijie geju zhong tisheng 'zhongguo zijue'" (Promoting the "China Self-Consciousness" in a Turbulent World), *Chinese Social Sciences Today*.

Shi, Y. (2000), "Dangjin he weilai shijie zhengzhi de jiben wenti" (The Fundamental Issues of Current and Future World Politics), *Taipingyang xuebao* (*The Pacific Journal*) (2).

Sun, Z. (2011) "Zhongguo rushi shi zhounian zhiji de huigu yu zhanwang" (China's Ten Years in the WTO: Retrospect and Prospect), *Guoji jingji pinglun* (*International Economic Review*), 94(4), 114–123.

Tang, Y. (2006), *"Zhongguo guoji juese fenxi"* (An Analysis of China's International Role), *Xiandai guoji guanxi* (*Contemporary International Relations*) (10).

The Oxford Paperback Dictionary (1994), 4th edition, Oxford: Oxford University Press.

The State Council Information Office. (2011a), *China's Peaceful Development*, available at http://www.scio.gov.cn/zfbps/ndhf/2011/index.htm.

Wang, Y. (1 July 2009), *"Rongru: zhongguo yu shijie guanxi de lishixing bianhua"* (Integration: The Historical Changes in China's Relations with the World), *Zhongguo shehui kexue bao* (*Chinese Social Sciences Today*), B12.

Wang, F. (24 October 2011), "A Success Tough to Duplicate: The Chinese Hukou System", *Fair Observer*, available at http://fairobserver.com/articles/success-tough-duplicate-chinese-hukou-system.

Wu, B. (2010), "China's Development and China-US Relations: Address by H.E. Wu Bangguo, Chairman of the Standing Committee of the National People's Congress of the People's Republic of China, Washington, DC, 10 September 2009", in *China's Foreign Affairs*, Beijing: World Affairs Press.

Wu, L. (2009), "'Dangdai zhongguo de guoji dingwei' xueshu yantaohui zongshu" (The International Repositioning of Contemporary China: A Conference Report), *Xiandai guoji guanxi* (*Contemporary International Relations*), (12).

Xiao, R. (2009), "Between Adapting and Shaping: China's Role in Asian Regional Cooperation", *Journal of Contemporary China*, 18(59), 303–320.

Yang, C. (3 December 2009), "Wo dui zhongguo guoji dingwei de renshi" (How I Perceive China's International Positioning), *Zhongguo shehui kexue bao* (*Chinese Social Sciences Today*), 5.

Yin, P. (28 April 2011), "Breaking the Bondage", *Beijing Review*.

Zhao, K. (3 December 2009), "Zhongguo mianlin guoji dingwei de chongxin xuanze" (China is Facing to Re-opt for an International Positioning), *Zhongguo shehui kexue bao* (*Chinese Social Sciences Today*).

Zheng, B. (2006), "Jianyi jiu 'zhongguo heping jueqi fazhan daolu' zhankai yanjiu" (A Proposal for Conducting Studies in the "Development Path of China's Peaceful Rise"), in B. Zheng (ed.) *Sikao de licheng* (*The Passage of Thinking*), Beijing: Zhonggong Zhongyang Dangxiao Chubanshe (Central Party School Press).

12
The Export of Liberalism to Russia

Margot Light

Introduction

Throughout the nineteenth century, Russia was governed by autocratic rulers who suppressed revolutionary ideas imported from the West. Nevertheless, the Russian intelligentsia was familiar with a variety of political ideas, including conservative, constitutionalist, liberal, and revolutionary theories. Liberalism, for example, was an important component of the debate between Westernisers and Slavophiles. They argued about the best political arrangements for Russia; Westernisers believed that Russia should adopt Western liberal ideals and institutions, while Slavophiles thought that they should be rejected in favour of Russian values based on the virtues of the peasant "obschina" (commune) (Walicki, 1980). However, only after the 1905 Revolution did liberal political parties emerge, most notably, the more progressive Constitutional Democratic Party (KADETS) and the more conservative Union of October 17 (Octobrists).

In the wake of the 1905 Revolution and Russia's defeat in the Russo-Japanese War later that year, Tsar Nicholas II issued the October manifesto granting personal inviolability, freedom of conscience, speech, assembly and association, and a Duma (parliament) elected on a popular franchise to approve all future laws. The first two Dumas, dominated by the Kadets, were deemed to be too radical and were dissolved after a few months each. The Octobrists held the majority of the seats in the third Duma, elected in November 1907, which served a full five-year term. They were the second largest party in the fourth Duma, in which conservatives of various parties held the majority. During the February 1917 Revolution, a group of Duma members formed the Provisional Committee, which later formed the Provisional Government. The Octobrist party was disbanded in March 1917, while the Kadet Party was banned by the Bolsheviks in November 1917. It was only when the dissident movement began in the 1970s that liberal ideas again began to circulate in the Soviet Union, albeit among a very small minority of the population. Until the Gorbachev reforms, therefore, "there existed only an intellectual reflection on liberal values and a brief experience with party-building and political struggle" (Walicki, 1980).

As a political programme, contemporary Russian liberalism developed from tentative beginnings in the mid-1980s when Mikhail Gorbachev became General Secretary of the Communist Party of the Soviet Union (CPSU), to subsequently become the dominant opposition to the CPSU by the beginning of the 1990s and the leading political force in the newly independent Russian Republic in 1992. By 2003, however, although liberals retained a few seats in the Duma (Russia's lower house of parliament), it was no longer deemed to be a political programme appropriate for Russia. In the 2007 election, liberals were completely excluded from the Duma. In its neoliberal *economic* form, however, liberalism has been rather more durable. It was the dominant economic ideology in the West when the Soviet Union collapsed. When President Boris Yeltsin asked Western economists for advice about the Russian economy at the beginning of the 1990s, therefore, they naturally suggested neoliberal economic reforms. Although the state has retaken control over some significant sections of the economy, it is still the principal form of economic arrangement in Russia.

This chapter examines why liberalism has failed to take root in Russia. Various explanations have been offered for this failure. Some, for example, blame the Mongol conquest, which separated Russia from European developments in the thirteenth and fourteenth centuries. Others argue that the principles of the Russian Orthodox Church are inimical to liberalism, while for still others, the legacies of totalitarianism and communism are responsible.[1] I argue that, although past historical epochs and events may indeed have an effect on Russian political culture, the main reasons for the failure are more recent. They are to be found, firstly, in the nature of the reforms undertaken in the 1990s and the consequences of those reforms for the majority of the Russian people and, secondly, in the mistakes that were made in the democracy promotion programmes launched by the United States and the European Union (EU) during those years: the failure of liberalism to take root can be explained by an exclusive emphasis on neoliberal economic reforms, the determination to prevent – even if this required adopting undemocratic means – the Communists from winning elections, and a failure to promote robust liberal-democratic institutions. There is, consequently, nothing inevitable about the failure of liberalism in Russia.[2]

In developing my argument, I shall begin with a brief account of the rise and decline of liberalism in the 1980s and 1990s. The second section describes the neoliberal economic reforms implemented in Russia in the early 1990s and examines their economic and social consequences. I then turn to the problems that arose in promoting democracy in Russia and the rise and demise of liberalism in Russian foreign policy. The final section examines the retreat from liberalism and neoliberalism under President Vladimir Putin. In the conclusion, I consider whether the public demonstrations against the results of the 2011 parliamentary elections herald the revival of liberalism in Russia.

The re-emergence of liberalism in the 1980s–1990s

The echoes of the nineteenth century debate between Westernisers and Slavophiles could be heard clearly in the discussions that were held in the late 1980s and 1990s about Russia's future. Since "the historical tendency in Russian liberal thought [was] to emphasise the social dimension of an individual, viewing him as being formed, attaining his freedom, and achieving his goals within the community", when Russian liberalism began to re-emerge in 1985, it contained "a distinct 'communitarian' (or 'social') emphasis" (Timofeyev, 2004: 54).[3]

In fact, there were three distinct phases in this re-emergence. In the first phase, from 1985 to 1987, liberal ideas were tentative and often offered within a broader Marxist–Leninist framework. This is partly because political analysts had discovered that they could now safely debate new ideas without provoking the wrath of Party ideologues, as long as they found some convenient reference in one of Lenin's numerous writings. But it was also due to Gorbachev's initial intention to revitalise and rejuvenate Soviet socialism through the introduction of his programmes of Perestroika (rebuilding) and Glasnost' (openness or transparency): as a result, when considering how to revitalise the economy, prominent reformers confined themselves to the socialist paradigm and thought about the individual's relationship to society. For example, one of the most prominent economic reformers, Tat'yana Zaslavskaya, began by arguing that the problem of the Soviet economic system was that it stifled individual creativity by destroying the link between the interests of the individual and those of society (Zaslavskaya, 1986). In considering what kind of economic structure was necessary to revive the economy, reformist economists in the early perestroika period called not for the freedom of the individual, but for the autonomy of the enterprise from the bureaucracy, with more attention being paid to the demands of consumers. Individual energy was to be contained within a *collective* framework, both to guard against the danger of excessive individualism and to advance the common goals of society.

Glasnost', however, allowed reformers within the intelligentsia to push the limits of possible themes for discussion ever wider. When Gorbachev added democratisation to his reform programme in 1988, the debate shifted in a more traditional liberal direction, leading to the second phase in the development of liberal ideas, which lasted from 1988 to 1989. At the Nineteenth Party Conference in June/July 1988, Gorbachev announced the goal of transferring the duties hitherto performed by the Communist Party back to the state and government bodies to which they constitutionally belonged. He furthermore aimed to liberalise the electoral system and to separate legislative, executive, and judicial powers. Empowered by these dramatic plans, public debate turned towards the core issue of liberalism: the achievement of *individual* political and economic freedom. Some liberals began to look at the issue of private ownership of property as a guarantee of economic independence, others went so far as to call for a free market.[4] They also considered how the irreversibility of the economic and ideological reforms could be assured and called for the rejuvenation of civil society and legal guarantees to safeguard civil rights, economic freedoms, and democratic procedures.[5] By the time of the March 1989 elections to the Congress of People's Deputies, most liberals supported the immediate introduction of democracy, seeing it as the best way both to constrain the state and to nurture an active civil society.

The first two phases of the emergence of liberalism arose from the widening of Gorbachev's reform programme; the third phase, however, was encouraged by events outside the Soviet Union. Russian liberals were emboldened by the wave of anti-Communist revolutions that occurred, with Gorbachev's acquiescence, in eastern Europe in 1989–1990. They began to organise themselves into *Russian* (not Soviet) political parties and movements, and strove to acquire political power in their own right so as to implement their own conception of reforms. In January 1990, they established an electoral bloc – "Democratic Russia" – which called for "freedom, democracy, human rights, a multiparty system, free elections, and a market economy"[6]: the bloc's programme was both a commitment to the main principles of Western liberalism and a general anti-totalitarian statement.

"Democratic Russia" was very successful during the March 1990 Russian parliamentary elections, winning a plurality of the votes cast. The bloc then backed the election of Boris Yeltsin as chairman of the Supreme Soviet (White, 1993: 59). This was, however, its last political success. The fact that "Democratic Russia" was a coalition of various political interests representing several ideological strands, ranging from reformist socialism, through social democracy, to the advocacy of a radical free market, immediately turned out to be a weakness. Once this broad-based electoral bloc had achieved political power, the consensus among its members started unravelling: they began to elaborate different strategies for economic and political reforms, which were predicated on distinct (and often dissimilar) notions about the place of the individual in society, the desirable type of market system and the optimal kind of political structure. As a result, "while retaining their general commitment to democracy and a market-based economy ... two rival perspectives [emerged]: the first adhering to a social liberal (or social-democratic) perspective; the second advocating radical free-market liberalism" (Timofeyev, 2004: 84). The latter group, most notably the economist Yegor Gaidar, increasingly looked to Western neoliberals – in particular, monetarist economists and "new right" politicians – in support of their proposals. The social-liberal and social democratic strands of Russian liberalism, most prominently the economist Grigory Yavlinsky, also supported the transition to a market system; but they advocated a gradual approach that would alleviate its effects on the population.

Throughout 1991, Democratic Russia attempted to unite the democrats in the Russian Supreme Soviet under its broad programme. Its success in getting Yeltsin elected as the first president in Russian history with a popular mandate was also its last. Although it had a significant share of the seats in the legislature, it failed to create sufficient support for his reforms. In the aftermath of the failed October 1991 coup, Democratic Russia began to fragment as many of its constituent groups began to leave the organisation. By December 1991, there were ten different liberal parties and political movements, with none of them enjoying sufficient popular support to provide a commanding majority in the Russian parliament.[7] Democratic Russia ceased to be an important political force in the Russian Federation despite its instrumental role in establishing a new liberal coalition, Russia's Democratic Choice, which became the most influential liberal-democratic organisation in the December 1993 elections.

Russia's neoliberal economic reforms

Russia's constitution did not require the government to reflect the composition of parliament. When Russia became an independent country after the Soviet Union disintegrated in December 1991, Yeltsin thus had no difficulty in giving the management of the Russian economy to the free-market neoliberals, led by Yegor Gaidar. The hardships caused by their policies eventually led to both liberalism and democracy being discredited in the eyes of the Russian public.

On 2 January 1992, prices were deregulated across Russia, causing them to immediately increase by an average of 250 per cent throughout the country. By the end of December, prices were rising at an annualised rate of 2,318 per cent (Reddaway and Glinski, 2001: 249). To institutionalise the free market, a decree issued on 29 January 1992 empowered anyone to sell anything without requiring a permit. Russia's streets immediately became full of traders, many of them educated professionals whose incomes and savings had been wiped out by hyperinflation and who were reduced to selling their possessions for a pittance. Reddaway and Glinski point out that when the German middle class hawked its belongings in the hyperinflation of 1923, it was recognised as a tragedy. In 1992 in Russia it was hailed as "the coming of the market and 'an efficient allocation of goods' " (Reddaway and Glinski, 2001: 247).[8] Unemployment – illegal in the Soviet Union – became commonplace, real wages plummeted and were often paid several months late and in kind, if they were paid at all. Pensions, far too small to cope with the massive price increases, were also paid late.

The programme to privatise state-owned enterprises started in July 1992. It was intended to be a mass privatisation scheme – vouchers with a nominal value of 10,000 roubles each would be issued to all permanent residents, enabling them to buy shares in firms or companies, either directly or through investment funds. Vouchers could also be sold or given away, but they could not be used to purchase commodities. Although about 100,000 enterprises had changed their form of ownership by the time the scheme came to an end in June 1994, the programme did not, as Yeltsin intended, create millions of property owners. One problem was that the value of the vouchers was set before price deregulation led to hyperinflation: by the time the first auction took place in December 1992, inflation was rampant and the vouchers were worth very little. A second problem was that large numbers of people were defrauded – they put their vouchers into pyramid schemes and investment companies, which collapsed and vanished. Thirdly, many Russians had lost all their savings and their jobs; or if they still held on to their jobs, they simply remained unpaid. Desperate, they were forced to sell their vouchers at face value in order to buy necessities. In short, while Yeltsin claimed that privatisation laid the foundations of Russia's new economy, ordinary Russians coined the word *prikhvatizatziya* – a combination of the Russian word for "grab" and the Russianised English word *privatizatsiya* (privatisation), producing the equivalent of "grabification" – to describe what they really thought of the process (White, 2000: 124–128).

There *were* a few people who benefitted from the economic reforms. A number of new businessmen with close ties to government gained access to subsidised government credits. They leveraged this money and their personal relations with officials who had been put in charge of privatisation to acquire control over Russia's most prized assets. In the most notorious scheme – the "loans for shares" scheme – a handful of well-connected businessmen loaned money to the Russian state to assist Yeltsin's election bid in 1996 in exchange for stakes in major Russian companies. When the state could not repay the money, the businessmen gained control of those companies at knockdown prices. At the same time, they also acquired a great deal of political power, becoming known as *oligarchs* (McFaul, 2007).

Most ordinary Russians, however, suffered very severely from the economic reform programme. So did the Russian economy. According to official Russian statistics, gross domestic product (GDP) slumped almost 36 per cent in the ten years from 1991 to 2001, industrial production plummeted 46 per cent, and agricultural output dropped 39 per cent. Compared with the beginning of 1992, the population's real income had decreased 52 per cent by 2000. The government's dependence on foreign loans increased, to the point that Russia's foreign debt reached US $130 billion in 1996, more than half its annual GDP.[9] The economy improved slightly in 1997 but then plunged again in August 1998 when Russia defaulted on its international debts and the rouble dropped sharply against the dollar. Between then and the December 1999 elections, more than two-thirds of the population experienced a decline in living standards, and about a third were living below subsistence levels.

The collapse of the economy had profound effects on Russian society. For example, government spending on healthcare fell dramatically, with disastrous consequences for public health; the resulting fall in life expectancy and rise in infant mortality contributed to a demographic crisis which Russia had already begun to experience before the disintegration of the USSR. There was an alarming rise in crime, and Russia developed one of the worst homicide rates in the world. Corruption became rampant. In the 2000 Corruption Perceptions Index, Russia was listed 82nd out of 90 countries; despite repeated official anti-corruption campaigns, Russia had moved down the list to 154th out of 178 states by 2010.[10]

In short, the neoliberal economic reforms undertaken in the 1990s were extremely difficult processes in Russia. The hardships caused ordinary people to feel humiliated, to lose faith in politics, to intensely dislike the oligarchs who made a great deal of money out of the transition and to resent Western countries, particularly the United States, which provided the models, the advisers, and the loans for the 1990s transition.

Promoting Russian democracy

When communism collapsed, exporting democracy to former socialist states became a high priority goal for many Western governments. USAID's Democracy Initiative aimed to foster competitive political systems, strengthen the rule of law and respect for human rights, invigorate civil society, and promote greater accountability of political institutions and ethical standards in government. The democracy component of the EU's PHARE and TACIS programmes, on the other hand, endeavoured "to contribute to the consolidation of pluralist democratic procedures and practices as well the rule of law", supporting "the acquisition of and application of knowledge and techniques of parliamentary practice and organisation" and "transferring expertise and technical skills about democratic practices and the rule of law" (European Commission, 1998; United States Agency for International Development, 1990). However, in practice, for both the United States and the EU simple economic self-interest sometimes took precedence over fostering democracy. Moreover, both devoted far more funding towards supporting the establishment of market economies than towards strengthening democracy. Thus, for example, funding for the democracy programme was only about 1 per cent of the whole PHARE and TACIS budget during 1992–1997. Moreover, neither the EU's democracy programme nor USAID were concerned with *economic* democracy: ensuring the provision of equal benefits to the population from the goods and services generated by society was not considered important.

In fact, Western governments seemed to believe that if the economic systems of the former socialist states became market economies, democracy would naturally follow, ignoring the fact that many of these countries possessed neither the institutional structures nor the legal basis to promote and consolidate democracy or, for that matter, to underpin the desired economic changes.[11] To be fair, the tasks were daunting: everything was important and everything needed to be done at once. But the emphasis on economic reform tended to distract from the even more pressing need to develop democratic institutions and processes. Furthermore, the consequences of economic reform frequently *undermined* democracy.

As we have seen, the economic reforms concentrated on macroeconomic restructuring and privatisation, ignoring the fact that, as Stiglitz points out, "norms, social institutions, social capital, and trust play critical roles" in the success of a market economy (Stiglitz, 1999: 8). Neither the economic reformers themselves nor their Western advisors seemed aware that political and democratic measures were required to establish the norms, social institutions, social capital, and trust that would make a market economy work. Moreover, concentrating on establishing a market economy at the expense of other aspects of reform appeared to confuse means with ends; these ends were not the market economy itself, but "the improvement of living standards and the establishment of the foundations of sustainable, equitable, and democratic development" that the market economy was intended to produce (Stiglitz, 1999: 3). In fact, as we have seen, far from improving, living standards fell catastrophically, while rapid privatisation allowed the accumulation of property and vast wealth in few hands and opened the door to widespread corruption.

Nor did the reformers understand that *economic* decisions have *political* consequences; voters, for example, are unlikely to cast their ballots for those who support the macroeconomic programmes that impoverish them. Moreover, the corruption that accompanied the reform process (and which seemed to be condoned by Western donors) disillusioned people still further and undermined any support that they could be expected to give to the process. And it was not just their belief in *economic* reform that was affected: since the latter was inspired by the same countries that were exporting *democracy*, confidence in Western models – both economic and democratic – was severely undermined.

The consequences of economic reform were not the only problem complicating the consolidation of democracy in Russia. Western tolerance of blatantly undemocratic practices – ironically undertaken in the name of defending democracy – brought democracy itself into disrepute. The response of Western leaders to President Yeltsin's suspension and dismissal of the Russian Supreme Soviet in September/October 1993 and his subsequent bombardment of its headquarters, the Russian White House (with many deputies still present inside) was the most dramatic example of this tolerance.[12]

Moreover, Western leaders seem to be victims of the "electoralist fallacy": they were happy to legitimise elections as relatively free and fair, even when the regimes that came to power were far from democratic (Hughes, 2000: 28). In Russia in particular, Western governments apparently deemed the prevention of electoral victories by communists or extreme nationalists more important than the establishment of democracy, fearing that if the former regained power, they would abolish future elections and overturn the market reforms. Throughout the 1990s Russian parliamentary and presidential elections were marked by various types of deliberate falsification. Time and again, however, election observers representing Western governments and international organisations declared elections "largely free and fair", simply because they brought to power leaders that were believed to be a bulwark against a communist revival.[13] By condoning the falsification of election results, endemic corruption and the use of undemocratic means in the name of establishing democracy, Western governments and their advisers discredited their own liberal credentials and, more importantly, brought democracy itself into disrepute in the eyes of the very people they wanted to convert.

Russians were also disillusioned about democracy because of the constant political conflict it seemed to produce. Although the 1993 constitution gave predominant political power to the head of state, there was constant strife between the Duma, the lower house of parliament, and the president, his administration and his government throughout the 1990s. Relations between the president and his government were also chronically strained – there were five different prime ministers in Russia between March 1998 (when long-serving premier Viktor Chernomyrdin was dismissed) and August 1999 (when security chief Vladimir Putin became Prime Minister, simultaneously becoming Yeltsin's designated successor). The central government became weaker and weaker between 1993 and 2000, and many Russians came to believe that unless power was returned to the centre, the Russian Federation would disintegrate just like the Soviet Union a decade before.

Russian foreign policy

Western policymakers also believed that exporting democracy would serve their own national security interests. After the end of the Cold War, they became enthusiastic proponents of the democratic peace proposition, previously of interest primarily to academics. Since this proposition posits that peace will prevail in relations between democratic states, converting non-democratic states to democracy would, it was thought, enhance the prospects for international peace. Indeed, the democratisation of the former socialist states seemed to suggest the possibility of a new peaceful liberal international order.[14]

At first, Russian foreign policy appeared to confirm this possibility. Immediately before and after the establishment of an independent Russian state in December 1991, "Liberal Westernisers" controlled the Ministry of Foreign Affair and pro-Western views prevailed in the public discussion of Russian foreign policy. By February 1992, however, differences of opinion had begun to appear among liberal Westernisers about how to define Russia's national interests and what policy to pursue to achieve them. Those who proposed a more independent policy vis-à-vis the West and a more integrationist stance towards the other successor states began to gain the ascendancy. By the spring of 1993, a consensus had begun to emerge about the principles that should underlie Russian foreign policy, and it was the views of the latter group of "pragmatic nationalists" that prevailed. In part, this reflected the general disillusion with Western economic liberalism and democratisation, but pragmatic nationalist views also seemed a more credible foreign policy stance in response to events in the outside world.

The external environment proved far less sympathetic to Russia than liberal Westernisers had expected, and the results of their early pro-Western policies were disappointing. They were shocked to discover, for example, that the much-vaunted free market did not necessarily mean that Russia would have free access to the few markets where its goods enjoyed comparative advantage. There was also a strong sense in Moscow that the West did not understand, or refused to take seriously, Russia's security interests. This was demonstrated by the planned eastward extension of NATO, the refusal to consider Russia's proposals to turn the CSCE into an effective security organisation, the failure to appreciate why the CFE provisions no longer reflected Russia's urgent defence requirements, and, perhaps most importantly, by the lack of sympathy shown by the West to the threats to Russian security posed by the conflicts in the near abroad. They also resented Western attitudes of triumphalism and the tendency to believe that Russia had lost the Cold War and that the United States had won it (Russians believed that the Cold War ended because the Soviet Union ceased to prosecute it). Many liberal Westernisers, therefore, changed their views and began to advocate a more assertive foreign policy. This simply meant, however, that they adopted the standard realist view one might expect the foreign policy elite to hold in any country.[15]

The retreat from liberalism and neoliberalism

When Yeltsin resigned as president at the end of 1999, Prime Minister Putin became acting president, as stipulated by the constitution. In March 2000 he was duly elected president in the first round of the ballot with 52.9 per cent of the vote.[16] The general disillusion with democracy and the decline in the economy and its effect on ordinary Russians made it easy for Putin to embark on a political programme designed to recentralise power and restore law and order. To construct a strong state (or, in Putin's terminology, re-establish the "power vertical"), the president created a strong political party whose only political programme was to support the president, and ensured that it won a majority of seats in the Duma. He also changed the composition of the upper house, the Federal Council, so that it no longer consisted of the governors/presidents[17] and the heads of the legislatures of the federal units; instead, two deputies were appointed to represent each of the federal units. Finally, Putin established seven federal districts encompassing the 89 federal units, each presided over by a governor general representing the president and ensuring the implementation of central laws across the country.

Apart from the extremely vicious war in Chechnya that had begun in 1999 and showed few signs of subsiding,[18] centrifugal tendencies in the Russian Federation seemed to diminish as a result of these measures. But not content with strengthening state institutions, Putin also embarked on a series of moves that represented a significant retreat from democracy. For example, he clamped down on the electronic media critical of the government, in particular by forcing two prominent oligarchs, Vladimir Gusinsky and Boris Berezovsky, to relinquish ownership of their media holdings to companies controlled by the Kremlin – thereby, in effect, re-establishing state control of television.[19] Putin made it clear to other oligarchs that if they wanted to keep their wealth, they had to desist from interfering in politics. When Mikhail Khodorkovsky refused to submit to this warning, he was arrested on charges of fraud and tax evasion in October 2003; in May 2005 he was sentenced to nine years' imprisonment.[20]

In September 2004, terrorists took control of a school in Beslan, a town in North Ossetia and held pupils, teachers, and a number of parents hostage. In the bloody shootout between the terrorists and security forces that brought the crisis to an end, 334 civilians were killed, 186 of them children, and hundreds more wounded. In the wake of the tragedy, President Putin used the incident as a pretext to further erode Russian democracy. Firstly, he abolished the popular election of the governors/presidents of Russia's federal units. From then on, they would be nominated by the president and their "election" would simply be confirmed by the regional legislature. Secondly, he changed the electoral system: whereas previously half the Duma deputies had been elected on the basis of proportional representation and the other half by single-mandate constituencies, in future elections the entire Duma would be elected on the basis of proportional representation alone. At the same time, Putin raised the threshold for parties to be represented in the Duma from 5 to 7 per cent. This effectively prevented smaller political groupings from gaining any seats. In 2003, for example, 100 of the 450 Duma seats were won by independents or candidates representing minor – including liberal – parties. In 2007 only 4 of the 11 parties that were allowed to contest the election gained seats in the Duma, none of them liberal: liberals were completely excluded from the legislature.

Putin certainly fulfilled his goal of creating a "power vertical". But in the process, he reduced the political choices available to Russian citizens, made it more difficult for a plurality of opinions to be heard, and reduced the possibility of the political opposition influencing Russian policy. Apart from the legislative and electoral changes, he also took measures to check the activities of non-governmental organisations (NGOs), in particular complicating the operations of foreign and local foreign-funded NGOs. Independent political action was increasingly subject to repression, opposition or even alternative views became harder to express, and human rights activists and journalists found themselves at extreme risk.[21]

The changes in policy towards NGOs were caused by a determination to prevent Western intervention in Russia's domestic politics. Putin was convinced that the "colour revolutions" in Georgia, Ukraine, and Kyrgyzstan during 2003–2005 had been instigated and sponsored by the West, and he believed that the United States and the EU harboured intentions to bring about similar changes in Russia. Russian policymakers objected to political intervention in their country's domestic politics, but they were also anxious about growing Western influence in neighbouring states. However much they objected to peaceful "democratising" interventions, they were far more vehemently opposed to military intervention, whether it was intended for humanitarian purposes or to bring about regime change. Even before Putin became president, Russia had opposed NATO's intervention against Serbia in the Kosovo crisis in 1999. Putin's objections, for example to the war against Iraq in 2003, were far more forceful. In a speech that seemed to epitomise a new foreign policy assertiveness and Russia's objections to liberal interventionism, Putin attacked the "almost uncontained hyper-use of force – military force – in international relations" at the 2007 Munich Conference on Security Policy, in robust terms.

There was little opposition to these moves from the majority of the Russian population. People were relieved that the constant political conflict had ended. They thought that the new assertive foreign policy made other countries recognise Russia as a great power deserving of respect. They also believed that Putin's policies were working, in particular because of a rapid improvement in the economic situation. A combination of the effects of devaluation during the catastrophic 1998 economic crash and high oil prices made Russia's annual economic performance during 2000 the best since the disintegration of the Soviet Union. From then on, the economy continued improving. GDP, for example, increased year by year, growing a record 8.5 per cent in 2007. Real incomes grew by 10 per cent (World Bank, 2012). Since economic growth began in the year that Putin was elected president, many people ascribed the improved economic performance to his skill. In fact, the most significant factor contributing to Russia's economic performance was the rise in world crude oil prices from a low of around $10 a barrel in December 1998 to around $33 a barrel in September 2000, and nearly $80 a barrel in 2008. Natural resources still constituted around 80 per cent of Russian exports, and oil and gas accounted for 55 per cent of all exports. As much as 37 per cent of Russia's budget revenues were provided by taxes on oil and gas.

However, Russia's revival depended on the state being able to collect those taxes. President Putin appeared committed to a market economy and initiated legislation to improve market conditions and increase tax revenue.[22] But a number of economic developments since 2003 cast doubts on his commitment to a liberal economy. Among others, following Khodorkovsky's arrest in 2003, his oil firm Yukos was dismembered and one of its most important assets, Yuganskneftegaz, was acquired by the state-owned Rosneft. When Roman Abramovich sold Sibneft, Russia's fifth-largest oil firm, to Gazprom, the 51 per cent state-owned gas monopoly, it seemed that although Putin might not intend to renationalise the entire economy, he was certainly determined to return those assets which he and his supporters deemed to be of strategic value to state control.

Like the retreat from democracy, these moves caused consternation and alarm abroad, among Western governments, commentators, and potential investors. But they proved to be very popular in Russia, where there was little sympathy for oligarchs and great resentment of privatisation. In a 2007 survey conducted by the independent Levada polling organisation, 64 per cent of those questioned said they would vote for a party promising "to strengthen the role of the government in the economy", while 53 per cent said they would vote for a party promising to establish order even at the cost of "restricting some democratic freedoms".[23] Most Russians, it seemed, preferred "managed democracy" to democratisation and liberalism.

An overwhelming majority of 70 per cent of Russian voters elected Dmitry Medvedev as the third president of the Russian Federation in March 2008 simply because he was Putin's chosen successor. Medvedev's first act as president was to announce that once inaugurated, he would nominate Vladimir Putin as Prime Minister of Russia. The way in which this political succession was staged seemed to epitomise the "managed democracy" into which Putin had turned Russia. It also seemed to indicate that although, for the most part, neoliberalism still reigned in the economic sphere, as a *political* programme liberalism had been completely defeated.

Conclusion

This chapter has argued that there is nothing inevitable about the failure of liberalism to take root in Russia: the Russians' disillusion, their apparent welcoming of Putin's retreat from democracy to "managed democracy", and their rejection of liberal internationalism was caused by particular policies, their consequences for the majority of people, the speed at which change occurred, and the condoning of undemocratic processes in the name of defending democracy. But Putin had no alternative ideology to offer, and neither did anyone else. "Managed" or "sovereign" democracy is not a potential alternative to liberalism, but simply, as Beate Jahn suggests, liberalism, albeit in a different incarnation. Russia has no grand alternative to the liberal order to offer.

Events in 2011 suddenly seemed to suggest that some Russian people were perhaps not satisfied with the particular shift in register of liberal theory and practice represented by Putin's "managed democracy". In fact, disillusion had begun a few years earlier, when the 2008 global economic crisis hit Russia harder than any other emerging economy. In 2009, Russian GDP shrank by 7.8 per cent, unemployment rose, and the financial surplus Russia had built up in the good years disappeared into propping up the rouble. Although the crisis was caused by external events – and Putin was quick to blame the United States for causing it – the economic skill of the Russian government could seemingly not protect the Russian economy. Putin's standing in the polls remained high, but he no longer seemed unassailable.

Then, in September 2011, Putin and Medvedev announced that the latter would stand down at the end of his first presidential term and Putin would run for re-election as Russian president in March 2012; at the same time they stated that Medvedev would be appointed prime minister after the presidential election. In other words, the 2008 election scenario was to be played in reverse, a step too far in "managed democracy" for many Russians. At Putin's subsequent public appearance at a martial arts event in November, he was booed by the crowd, an unprecedented experience for him.[24]

Parliamentary elections took place in December 2011 and produced two surprises. Firstly, although the "party of power", United Russia, won a plurality of votes, it gained only 49.32 per cent of the vote, almost 15 per cent lower than its result in 2007. This election was clearly the least efficiently managed since 1999, judging by the lowest results for the "party of power" since that year. In addition, the election produced a second unwelcome surprise for the Kremlin in the form of large public demonstrations, with crowds objecting to the falsifications that had occurred during the election. Although the protests were by no means large enough to produce the kind of change witnessed in Tunisia or Egypt during the spring of 2011, they were larger than any demonstrations held in Russia since the coming to power of Putin. Moreover, although the largest rallies were held in Moscow, there were smaller protests in a number of other cities. Despite arrests, the demonstrations were repeated, with the promise that they would continue until the March presidential elections. A variety of public figures, including the Patriarch of the Russian Orthodox Church, demanded either that the parliamentary elections should be rerun or that the authorities should at least agree to a dialogue with the protestors. Both Putin and Medvedev rejected a rerun, but they did offer some political reforms in response to the protests: for example, restoring the popular election of governors and installing surveillance cameras in all polling booths as a measure against fraud during the presidential election. They were duly installed, and in those cases where they caught some obvious examples of ballot stuffing, the results were immediately invalidated.

The demonstrators quite soon began to add other demands to their protests at electoral falsifications. They insisted on the annulment of election results, the resignation of the head of the electoral commission and the establishment of an official investigation into voter fraud. They also demanded freedom for political prisoners (by which they meant people arrested for protesting), the registration of opposition parties, and new and better legislation on parties and elections, aimed at ensuring greater participation and more democratic and open elections.

Liberalism may not have been entirely defeated in Russia after all. According to Mikhail Prokhorov, an extremely rich oligarch who announced in December 2011 that he would stand in the upcoming presidential elections, Russia now has "a generation of Russians with an idea of why democracy and liberalism are values that belong to all of us .... The era of 'managed democracy' is over".[25] There is a strong suspicion in Russia that Prokhorov's candidacy for the presidency was, in fact, arranged by the Kremlin so as to provide a credible opponent for Putin to defeat – in other words, that he was a willing accomplice in yet another device of "managed democracy". That may well be the case, and it is certainly true that Putin was re-elected in the first round and the demonstrations appear have petered out. But this does not necessarily mean that Prokhorov is wrong about young Russians. In fact, more and more of them may come to demand the democracy and liberalism that are rightfully theirs.

Notes

1. See, for example, Sorgin (2003) and Narochnitskaya (2003).
2. See, for example, McFaul (2007).
3. I draw extensively in this section from this excellent – and unique – account of Russian liberalism.
4. On ownership, see Popov (1988), and for an early call for the establishment of a free market, see Petrakov (1988).
5. See, for example, Ambartsumov (1988).
6. For the programme of Democratic Russia, see *Russkaya Mysl'*, 2 February 1990. For a discussion of the establishment of Democratic Russia, see Weigle (2000: 155–156).
7. A table setting out the main features of their programmes can be found in Weigle (2000: 160–161).

8. They are quoting Anders Åslund, one of the most enthusiastic Western neoliberal economic advisers.
9. *Russian Economic Trends,* March, April 1999, cited in Reddaway and Glinski (2001) and see Trading Economics (2012).
10. See table 4.4 in White (2011: 154). Wedel (1999) argues that a small group of Western advisers did more than simply condone corruption; they assisted it and some of them used their advisory role for private gain.
11. For a more detailed discussion of the problems involved in exporting democracy, see Light (2001: 79–92).
12. For an account of the coup and a detailed analysis of the events that led up to it, see Reddaway and Glinski (2001: 370–434).
13. See, for example, the difference between the critical election reports produced by the European Institute the Media in the 1990s (they can be found at http://www.media-politics.com/eimreports.htm) and those produced by the OSCE Parliamentary Assembly (they can be found at http://www.oscepa.org/election-observation/2-uncategorised/411-election-observation).
14. See, for example, President Clinton's State of the Union speech (New York Times, 26 January 1994).
15. Comparing foreign policy statements by President Yeltsin and Foreign Minister Kozyrev in 1991 to those made in 1993 illustrates how far the views of prominent liberal Westernisers changed. For a more detailed account of the changes in Russian foreign policy thinking, see Light (1996).
16. The management of the presidential succession in 2000 is a vivid example of how little Russia had moved along the spectrum from democratisation to consolidated democracy. See White (2011: 82–85, 94–95).
17. Some of the federal units are known as national republics and they have elected presidents; other federal units are administrative areas headed by governors.
18. For an excellent analysis of the Chechen wars, see Hughes (2007).
19. Gusinsky and Berezovsky were both forced into exile. See White (2011: 172–173).
20. In 2010 he was tried on additional charges and sentenced to an additional thirteen and a half years. See White (2011: 173–174).
21. On the excessive executive powers of the Russian authorities, the poor state of countervailing forces, and Russia's dismal human rights record, see White (2011: 338–355).
22. For a lively account of Putin's economic programme, see Roxburgh (2012: 46–56).
23. The poll results were published in RFE/RL *Newsline*, 13 November 2007.
24. *Financial Times,* 21 November 2011.
25. *The Guardian,* 12 January 2012.

References

Ambartsumov, Y. (1988), "O Putyakh Sovershestvoniya Politicheskoy Sistemy Sotsializma", in Y. Afanas'ev (ed.) *Inogo ne Dano*, Moscow: Progress Publishers.
European Commission. (1998), Final Report: Evaluation of the PHARE and TACIS Democracy Programme (1992–1997). Available at http://ec.europa.eu/europeaid/how/evaluation/evaluation_reports/reports/cards/951432_en.pdf
Hughes, J. (2000), "Transition Models and Democratisation in Russia", in M. Bowker and C. Ross (eds) *Russia after the Cold War*, London: Longman.
Hughes, J. (2007), *Chechnya: From Nationalism to Jihad*, Philadelphia: University of Pennsylvania Press.

Light, M. (1996), "Foreign Policy Thinking", in N. Malcolm, A. Pravda, R. Allison and M. Light (eds) *Internal Factors in Russian Foreign Policy*, Oxford: Clarendon Press, 33–100.

Light, M. (2001), "The Export of Democracy", in K. Smith and M. Light (eds) *Ethics and Foreign Policy*, Cambridge: Cambridge University Press, 75–92.

McFaul, M. (March/April 2007), "Liberal Is as Liberal Does", *The American Interest*, 83–89.

Narochnitskaya, N. (2003), "Evropa 'Staraya' i Evropa 'Novaya' ", *Mezhdunarodnaya Zhizn'*(4), 45–63.

New York Times. (26 January 1994), "State of the Union; Excerpts from President Clinton's Message on the State of the Union".

Petrakov, N. (1988), "Tovar i Rynok", *Ogonek*, 34.

Popov, G. (1988), "Pobeseduem v Dukhe Glasnosti", *Ogonek*, 33.

Reddaway, P. and Glinski, D. (2001). *The Tragedy of Russia's Reforms: Market Bolshevism against Democracy*, Washington: United States Institute of Peace Press.

Roxburgh, A. (2012), *The Strongman: Vladimir Putin and the Struggle for Russia*, London: I. B. Tauris.

Sorgin, V. (2003), "The Contemporary Russian Transformation", in M. Siefert (ed.) *Extending the Borders of Russian History: Essays in Honor of Alfred J. Rieber*, Budapest: Central European University Press.

Stiglitz, J. E. (1999), "Whither Reform? Ten Years of Transition", Keynote Address, World Bank Annual Conference on Development Economics, Washington, D.C., 28–30 April. Available at http://siteresources.worldbank.org/INTABCDEWASHINGTON1999/Resources/stiglitz.pdf

Timofeyev, I. V. (2004), "The Development of Russian Liberal Thought since 1985", in A. Brown (ed.) *The Demise of Marxism-Leninism in Russia*. Basingstoke: Palgrave-Macmillan, 51–118.

Trading Economics. (2012), Russia GDP Per Capita. Retrieved 27 January 2012, from http://www.tradingeconomics.com/russia/gdp-per-capita

United States Agency for International Development. (1990), *The Democracy Initiative*. Washington: USAID.

Walicki, A. (1980), *A History of Russian Thought from the Enlightenment to Marxism*, Oxford: Clarendon Press.

Wedel, J. (1999), "Rigging the U.S.-Russian Relationship: Harvard, Chubais and the Transidentity Game", *Demokratizatsiya: The Journal of Post-Soviet Democratization*, 7(4), 469–500.

Weigle, M. A. (2000), *Russia's Liberal Project*, Philadelphia: Pennsylvania University Press.

White, S. (1993), *After Gorbachev*, Cambridge: Cambridge University Press.

White, S. (2000), *Russia's New Politics: the Management of a Postcommunist Society*, Cambridge: Cambridge University Press.

White, S. (2011), *Understanding Russian Politics*, Cambridge: Cambridge University Press.

World Bank. (2012), GDP Growth (annual %). Retrieved 11 January 2012, from http://data.worldbank.org/indicator/NY.GDP.MKTP.KD.ZG

Zaslavskaya, T. Y. (1986), "Chelovecheskiy Faktor Razvitiya Ekonomiki i Sotsial'naya Sprevedlost' ", *Kommunist*, 13, 61–73.

13
Liberal Theory and European Integration

Frank Schimmelfennig

Introduction

Liberal Intergovernmentalism (LI) has established itself as the "baseline theory" for explaining the big decisions in European integration. It is also the only integration theory that has the adjective "liberal" in its name. It is, however, a truncated liberal theory. Whereas LI starts from "neoliberal institutionalism" and includes domestic politics in its account of European integration – as any liberal theory should – it builds mainly on a single variant of liberal theory: commercial liberalism. As a consequence, LI neglects important facets of European integration that derive from the nature of the European Union (EU) as a liberal community. Fundamental developments and outcomes in European integration are difficult to explain, unless the role of liberal values, norms, and identities are properly theorised.

In this chapter, I therefore propose to move beyond the limitations of commercial LI. I formulate building blocks and hypotheses of a theory of liberal community that applies a different variant of liberalism to European integration: ideational liberalism. A liberal international community is a community of liberal states governed by liberal norms such as peace, multilateralism, and democracy, and based on a post-national, civic identity. Ideational liberalism argues that liberal norms shape the constitutional developments of liberal community organisations and override economic interests and material bargaining power.

In order to substantiate this argument, I present three brief case studies on Eastern enlargement, parliamentarisation, and differentiated monetary integration. They represent three different dimensions of integration (enlargement, institutional deepening, and policy integration) and thus help making a general argument about European integration. They have clear economic and power implications for the member states and should thus be hard cases for an ideational approach, and easy cases for LI. They are, however, puzzling for LI and commercial liberalism and can be better explained by norms and identities.

In the second section, I briefly review the main assumptions and expectations of LI. In the third section, I show that it cannot fully explain major events and processes in European integration (Eastern enlargement, the legislative powers of the European Parliament (EP), and differentiated integration in the Eurozone) because of its exclusive orientation towards commercial liberalism. In the fourth section, I therefore present elements of a theory of liberal international community. The fifth section shows how this theory can be applied to explain those outcomes of European integration that commercial LI does not account for. The sixth section concludes the chapter.

Liberal intergovernmentalism

Following the "relance Européenne" – epitomised by the internal market programme and the decision to create a monetary union – the 1990s saw a new wave of theorising on European integration. In essence, the theories of the 1990s revived the debate of the 1960s between neofunctionalism and intergovernmentalism. Whereas "supranationalism" drew inspiration from a slightly reformulated neofunctionalism, Andrew Moravcsik married intergovernmentalist assumptions about the centrality of the state and the national interest in European integration with liberal insights on the relevance of domestic politics and international institutions (Moravcsik, 1993, 1998). Against the neofunctionalist claim that powerful supranational organisations and institutions push integration beyond the preferences and control of governments by joining forces with interest groups, shaping negotiations, and gradually expanding their own competencies, LI maintains that the (major) member states remain in control of the process. Supranational organisations are their instruments, designed to ensure the credible commitment of all members to the rules of integration.

LI has arguably become the "baseline theory" for explaining treaty-making and treaty-revision in European integration (Moravcsik and Schimmelfennig, 2009). Even though not everyone necessarily agrees with LI, it is widely accepted as a parsimonious theoretical starting point that European integration scholars engage with and use as a baseline for exploring alternative explanations (see, for instance, Parsons, 2002; Schimmelfennig, 2001). In addition, it is the only integration theory with an explicit reference to the liberal theory of International Relations (IR), to which Moravcsik has also made an important general contribution (Moravcsik, 1997).

LI is based on "neoliberal institutionalism" in IR (Keohane, 1984; Keohane and Nye, 1977). In line with the *liberal* component of this IR theory, LI assumes that a state's foreign policy results from a domestic policy process and reflects the issue-specific interests of dominant domestic groups. In line with its *institutionalist* component, LI emphasises the relevance of international institutions for facilitating and stabilising cooperation between states.

Moravcsik proposes a three-stage analysis of European integration: domestic politics generates national preferences; intergovernmental negotiations produce substantive bargains; and, after agreement has been reached on substance, further international negotiations on the choice of institutions lead to decisions to pool and delegate state competencies. In its most condensed form, Moravcsik's argument is that

> EU integration can best be understood as a series of rational choices made by national leaders. These choices responded to constraints and opportunities stemming from the *economic interests of powerful domestic constituents*, the *relative power of each state* in the international system, and the role of institutions in bolstering the *credibility of interstate commitments*.
>
> (Moravcsik, 1998: 18, italics added)

Preference formation. In contrast to traditional realist intergovernmentalism, LI follows a liberal theory of foreign policy preference formation. Liberalism as a theory of foreign policy assumes that governmental preferences vary between policy issues and reflect the interests and power of societal groups (intermediated by domestic political institutions). Because European integration has focused on economic policies, state preferences have also been predominantly economic. While general demand for European integration results from interdependence – the pressure to cooperate for mutual benefit in an expanding and "globalising" international economy – concrete integration preferences emerge primarily from "the commercial interests of powerful economic producers" (Moravcsik, 1998: 3). As a consequence, governments pursue integration as "a means to secure commercial advantages for producer groups, subject to regulatory and budgetary constraints" (Moravcsik, 1998: 38). Depending on how competitive these powerful producers are on the European market, states demand either the opening and deregulation of markets or protectionist policies.

Interstate bargaining. The most relevant negotiation processes in European integration are processes of intergovernmental bargaining concerning the distribution of gains from cooperation. Because the costs and benefits of any cooperative arrangement are likely to differ across the member states, the national preferences of the member states usually diverge; and because integration decisions often have binding and substantial material consequences for governments and market actors, the stakes are high. Negotiations therefore consist of hard bargaining. The outcomes of interstate bargaining reflect the relative bargaining power of states, which derives from asymmetrical interdependence. As a liberal theory, LI also theorises the effects of domestic politics on intergovernmental negotiations (Moravcsik, 1993: 514–517). These are captured by the metaphor of the "two-level game" (Putnam, 1988). One implication

is that governments, which are heavily constrained by domestic interests, can obtain a negotiation outcome that is close to their ideal
point because they can credibly threaten their negotiating partners with
non-ratification (aka "Schelling's paradox of weakness").

Institutional choice. LI starts from a functional theory of institutions: states
    establish international institutions because they help them deal with
    fundamental problems of international cooperation (Keohane, 1984).
    The extent to which governments are willing to centralise decision-
    making and delegate more extensive powers of monitoring and com-
    pliance to supranational organisations depends on the enforcement
    problems inherent in cooperation and the stakes involved. The more a
    government benefits from a cooperative agreement, and the higher the
    risks of non-compliance by other governments, the higher is its readi-
    ness to cede competences to the EU to prevent potential losers from
    revising the policy (Moravcsik, 1998: 9, 486–487).

In sum, LI is in essence a materialist and functionalist theory of integration: material, predominantly economic, interdependence prompts states
to integrate in order to reap stable and high benefits from cooperation.
The main liberal element in this theory consists in explaining state preferences and bargaining power by the economic interests of powerful domestic
groups. Among the three variants of liberalism that Moravcsik distinguished elsewhere – ideational, commercial, and republican liberalism –
LI relies almost exclusively on the commercial variant (Moravcsik, 1997:
528–530).

"Identity-based preferences" highlighted by ideational liberalism, which
pertain to ideas about the "scope of the 'nation' ", "particular institutions",
or the "nature of legitimate socioeconomic regulation and redistribution",
only come up as a residual category in LI. They are irrelevant unless economic interests are too weak, or economic consequences too uncertain, to
shape state preferences. In Moravcsik's words, domestic economic interests
most clearly shape state preferences, the "more intense, certain, and institu-
tionally represented and organised" they are (Moravcsik, 1998: 36). Likewise,
a state's institutional preferences in European integration depend on how
certain or strong their welfare implications are. Otherwise, there is room for
ideological attitudes to shape state preferences and behaviour (Moravcsik,
1998: 486–489; Moravcsik and Nicolaïdis, 1999: 61).

There is nothing inherently wrong with basing a theory of European
integration on just one variant of liberal theory. To the contrary, integration theory would be particularly powerful if we could explain the major
integration outcomes with a narrow set of societal and state preferences.
Commercial liberalism becomes problematic, however, if it misses an important part of what is going on in European integration and fails to explain
major events and processes. In the next section, I argue that this is the case.

Puzzles for commercial liberalism

European integration since the 1990s has been characterised by three important developments that LI struggles to explain: enlargement, parliamentarisation, and differentiation.

Enlargement

Enlargement is a major source of growth in European integration. In the past 40 years, the EU has grown from an organisation of six to an organisation of soon-to-be 28 member states. On the basis of commercial liberalism, LI explains many developments in enlargement well. Britain decided to join when the Common Market became more important for the British economy than the Commonwealth (Moravcsik, 1998: 164–176). The remaining Western European non-members sought closer integration at the beginning of the 1990s when they performed worse than the European Community (EC) and experienced a dramatic increase in outward investment. Joining the internal market offered the prospect of increasing competitiveness and decreased the threat of a relocation of investment. The desire of the Central and Eastern European countries (CEECs) to join is also well explained by LI: the CEECs were highly dependent on trade with and investments from the EU, and poorer than the member states. They therefore stood to gain from full access to the internal market, subsidies from the EU budget, and decision-making power in the integrated institutions.

The member states, however, had few material incentives to admit the CEECs. Firstly, the latters' economic and trade relevance for most member states was low. Secondly, the prospect of their accession raised concerns about trade-related and budgetary competition. In particular, the poorer member states, which specialised in the same industries and were the major beneficiaries of the EC budget, opposed any commitment to enlargement in the early 1990s. Moravcsik and Vachudova (2003) argue that the costs of Eastern enlargement are modest enough to prevent severe distributional problems for the old member states. If that was the case, however, why did most member states try to block enlargement in the early 1990s? Thirdly, the association agreements that the EC had concluded with the CEECs constituted an efficient institutional solution from the Community perspective. They liberalised economic exchange between the EU and its associates, thus creating opportunities for welfare gains, while at the same time protecting poorer EU members and non-competitive producers from trade-related and budgetary competition. Finally, the CEECs depended much more on the EU than the other way around and did not have the bargaining power to put pressure on the EU to admit them. The constellation of commercial preferences and bargaining power would thus have predicted association rather than accession (Schimmelfennig, 2001: 49–58). The fact that the EU started accession negotiations with 10 CEECs in 1997 and 1999 and admitted these countries in 2004 and 2007 in its biggest enlargement round ever, is therefore puzzling for LI.

Parliamentarisation

Parliamentarisation is one of the most remarkable institutional developments in European integration. Under the 1957 Treaties of Rome, the Parliamentary Assembly (as it was called then) was composed of delegates from national parliaments and only had a consultative role in legislation. Starting with the cooperation procedure of the Single European Act (SEA) in 1986, the legislative powers of the EP were gradually expanded. The Treaty of Maastricht introduced co-decision, which puts the EP on an equal footing with the Council in deciding legislation. Following the Treaty of Lisbon, co-decision is now the "ordinary legislative procedure".

For LI, parliamentarisation is, again, a puzzling development (Rittberger and Schimmelfennig, 2006: 1151–1155). LI assumes that governments are the dominant actors in European integration, design European integration according to their welfare interests, and seek to remain in control of the integration process. Why then would governments decide to redistribute decision-making power away from them? As described above, the main reasons why governments delegate competencies to supranational organisations have to do with efficiency and credibility. Co-decision does not fit this picture, however. It complicates the legislative process by introducing another veto player and additional readings; it reduces decision-making speed (Golub, 1999; Schulz and König, 2000); and it provides no instruments for improving member state compliance.

In their analysis of the reform of the co-decision procedure at the Amsterdam Treaty negotiations, Moravcsik and Nicolaïdis (1999) claim that partisan calculations paved the way for empowering the EP: a centre-left majority among the governments strengthened a parliament that was also dominated by centre-left parties at the time. This argument is hard to defend on instrumental grounds, however, because "second-order" elections to the EP tend to favour those parties that are in the opposition in the member states. According to Simon Hix, "by strengthening the EP's power, the centre-left governments increased the likelihood of centre-right policies at the European level. Hence, Moravcsik and Nicolaïdis' explanation only holds if it includes the assumption that the governments negotiating the Treaty of Amsterdam made a major miscalculation" (Hix, 2002: 269).

Differentiated integration

Eastern enlargement and parliamentarisation represent major trends in the "widening" and "deepening" of European integration since the 1990s. In addition, however, European integration has been characterised by increasing differentiation, that is, variation in the territorial validity of EU rules (Leuffen et al., 2012). On the basis of commercial liberal assumptions,

LI is able to explain many processes and outcomes in differentiated integration. For instance, the new member states were initially excluded from the Euro and Schengen zones for efficiency reasons. The old member states had doubts about their capacity to maintain macroeconomic stability and to secure the external EU border, and they were able to impose exclusion due to their superior bargaining power in the accession process. In addition, the fact that some new member states have worked hard to meet the conditions for adopting the euro, while others have not, can be attributed to different economic interests having to do with size and interdependence (Johnson, 2008). The smaller and more trade-dependent new member states – the Baltic countries, Slovakia, and Slovenia – had a strong interest in pegging their currencies to the euro to gain international economic credibility and facilitate trade. By contrast, the larger and less trade-dependent new member states – the Czech Republic, Hungary, and Poland – worried more strongly about the potentially growth-inhibiting and inflationary risks of a pegged exchange rate.

On the other hand, however, LI struggles to explain why some of the older members have refused to adopt the euro. Denmark and Sweden are small and highly trade-dependent economies, too. They conduct roughly 70–75 per cent of their foreign trade with the rest of the EU and should therefore have had a similar interest in joining the Eurozone as the smaller new member states. Furthermore, the macroeconomic policy preferences of the opt-out countries do not deviate from the German model on which monetary union is built. Indeed, their preferences were more in line with Germany's, and had been so for a longer time, than those of many of the (southern) Euro countries. Finally, whereas British opposition against EMU can be partly attributed to a lack of economic convergence with the rest of the EU, neither Denmark nor Sweden would have had major difficulties in meeting the convergence criteria. It is further puzzling from an intergovernmentalist perspective that the Danish krone is firmly pegged to the euro despite Denmark's opt-out from monetary union.

In sum, LI has problems to account for many important developments in European integration. In the remainder of the chapter, I argue that this has to do with its theoretical roots in a specific strand of liberal theory: commercial liberalism. In order to come to grips with the unexplained developments, LI needs a broader basis in liberal theory that includes ideational liberalism.

Liberal community and European integration

In the perspective of ideational liberalism, international and regional organisations, such as the EU, are not simply functional institutions for managing interdependence and stabilising cooperation. They represent international communities with distinct identities, values, and norms. For a liberal theory of regional integration, it matters most whether such identities, values, and norms are liberal or not. The international dissemination and institutional-isation of liberal ideas strengthens liberal community, and the strength of liberal community strengthens liberal regional integration.

Liberal community

Liberal international communities are defined by two core characteristics. They are made up of liberal states, and they establish a liberal order among these liberal states. In other words, a liberal international community is both a community of *liberal* states and a *liberal* community of states.

Liberal human rights are the core values of a liberal international community. They are the "constitutive values that define legitimate statehood and rightful state action" in the domestic as well as in the international realm (Reus-Smit, 1997: 558). In the domestic realm, the liberal principles of social and political order – social pluralism, the rule of law, democratic political participation and representation, private property, and a market-based economy – are derived from, and justified by, these liberal human rights. Article 2 of the Treaty on European Union (TEU) embodies the value foundation of the EU as a liberal community. The Union is founded on the values of respect for human dignity, freedom, democracy, equality, the rule of law, and respect for human rights, including the rights of persons belonging to minorities. These values are common to the member states in a society in which pluralism, non-discrimination, tolerance, justice, solidarity, and equality between women and men prevail.

In addition, liberal states transfer their domestic political norms to the international realm (Risse-Kappen, 1995a: 33). The "democratic peace" is rooted in those domestic norms of liberal-democratic states that require political conflicts to be managed and resolved without violence and on the basis of constitutional procedures (Risse-Kappen, 1995b). Multilateralism, that is, the coordination of "relations among three or more states on the basis of generalised principles of conduct" (Ruggie, 1993: 11) corresponds to the basic liberal idea of procedural justice, "the legislative codification of formal, reciprocally binding social rules" among the members of society (Reus-Smit, 1997: 577). It also follows the "principle that social rules should be authored by those subject to them" (Reus-Smit, 1997: 578). Multilateral organisations in the Western international order have the effect of security and economic "co-binding". Liberal states "attempt to tie another down by locking each other into institutions that mutually constrain one another" (Deudney and Ikenberry, 1999: 182–183). Co-binding corresponds to and is facilitated by the internal structure of liberal states whose domestic autonomy is constrained by the separation of powers and systems of checks and balances. Finally, to the extent that international organisations acquire policymaking authority that limits and constrains the sovereignty of the state, they come under pressure to introduce the same institutions of vertical and horizontal accountability that characterise the liberal state.

In the course of European integration, the community members have not only established a stable democratic peace among themselves but also a unique multilateral and legal order. The density and strength of the generalised rules governing the relations between the EU members as well as their delegation and pooling of sovereignty are unparalleled by other multilateral organisations. According to William Wallace, the "intensive multilateralism" involving government officials of the member states at all levels of the bureaucracy in negotiations on a quasi-permanent basis is the "most distinctive governmental characteristic of this regional system" (1999: 206). European law is enforced by an independent supranational court, the European Court of Justice, whose decisions are binding upon the member governments.

Finally, the collective identity of a liberal international community is post-national or civic (Cederman, 2001; Deudney and Ikenberry, 1999: 192–194). Civic identities are based on shared values and norms but do not possess any primordial quality rooted in natural or "naturalised" cultural characteristics. In the words of Jürgen Habermas, post-nationalism "dissolves the historical symbiosis of republicanism and nationalism" and is not dependent on "a mental rootedness in the 'nation' as a pre-political community of fate" (Habermas, 1998: 116–17; my translation). A liberal collective identity is thus a thin identity. It is compatible with various ethnic or religious identities that are being "muted and diluted to the point where [they] tend to be semi-private in character" (Deudney and Ikenberry, 1999: 194) and with a pluralistic authority structure that combines regional, national, and supranational competencies. Its cultural content is limited to *political* culture; ethnic nationalism is replaced with "constitutional patriotism".

These assumptions about the collective identity of a liberal community are corroborated both at the level of basic treaty rules of the EU and at the level of public opinion. At the institutional level, the EU defines its collective identity as a civic identity based on liberal social and political norms (see Article 2 TEU quoted above). It respects the "rich cultural and linguistic diversity" of the EU (Article 3, TEU) and the member states' "national identities" (Article 4, TEU). At the same time, Article 1 of the TEU commits the member states to "ever closer union among the peoples of Europe" and to conferring competences to the union to attain common objectives. Thus, whereas the EU does not stipulate a European identity that ought to replace the national identities of its member states and societies, these national identities need to be both liberal and non-exclusive. Exclusive political nationalism that is inimical to the sharing and delegation of sovereignty and prevents empathy with other liberal nations is hard to reconcile with a liberal international community and limits regional integration.

Research on public opinion in the EU shows that the EU not only cannot, but also need not rely on a "pan-national" (Cederman, 2001) identity of its citizens (Risse, 2010). Not more than a small minority of member state citizens feel predominantly or exclusively attached to Europe or the EU rather than their nation of origin. But "some attachment" to Europe is enough for supporting the EU. Only individuals with exclusive national identities are predominantly opposed to European integration (Hooghe and Marks, 2005).

Hypotheses about regional integration

The main distinction between LI based on commercial liberalism and a theory of liberal community based on ideational liberalism is ontological. Whereas LI is based on a materialist, economic ontology, the theory of liberal community starts from an intersubjectivist or idealist ontology according to which social ideas such as values, norms, and identities matter for social processes and outcomes. On the other hand, the theory of liberal community does not necessarily reject the focus of LI on state or governmental actors, or its assumption of (bounded) rationality and domestic political constraints. Governments may well be both relevant and rational actors, but they act on the basis of ideational preferences and/or in a community environment, in which identities, values, and norms empower or constrain their actions.

Conceiving of the EU as a liberal community organisation leads to several hypotheses that deviate from commercial liberalism and LI. I limit myself here to those hypotheses that are relevant for the three puzzles for LI. Firstly, non-liberal states are excluded from membership in the EU. Conversely, all liberal European states are entitled to membership in the EU if they so desire. In contrast to commercial liberalism, ideational liberalism claims that it is sufficient for states to be liberal (and to be part of the defined region) to become a member of a liberal regional organisation. This holds even if their admission produces net costs for the organisation or individual old member states. In cases of conflict between material (economic) interests and liberal community norms, the norm of liberal membership overrides the economic interests and the superior bargaining power of the member states (Schimmelfennig, 2001).

Secondly, if the transfer of competencies from the state to the EU undermines national liberal and democratic institutions, these institutions (or the functions they perform) are recreated at the supranational level. Whereas commercial liberalism is only concerned with the efficiency of supranational institutions, ideational liberalism claims that they must also be legitimate from a liberal-democratic point of view. This also holds if legitimacy reduces efficiency. Accordingly, the disempowerment of national parliaments and national systems of human rights protection as a result of supranational centralisation leads to the empowerment of the EP and human rights protection in the EU (Rittberger and Schimmelfennig, 2006).

Finally, the extent of supranational centralisation depends on the strength of post-national relative to (exclusive) national identities. At the individual level, exclusive national identities are the strongest predictor of opposition to European integration (Hooghe and Marks, 2005). At the country level, states with high numbers of "exclusive nationalists" are potentially more likely to oppose and opt out of (deeper) European integration. Whether this potential is realised and constrains integration depends on the strength of right-wing populist parties and on institutional rules (such as mandatory referendums and other high thresholds for constitutional change) that accord these parties or the Euro-sceptic electorates veto power (Hooghe and Marks, 2008: 18). According to this perspective, differentiated integration divides countries with more or less post-national identities, and is most likely to occur in policies that affect the core powers of the state and most clearly put in question its sovereignty. Again, this also holds if supranational centralisation was economically efficient.

In sum, the theory of liberal community argues that ideational factors trump economic interests or material bargaining power when community identities, values, and norms are at stake. There is no assumption that such ideational factors produce invariably more integration than economic factors. At times, liberal norms may bring about a larger or more deeply integrated EU than economic interests or bargaining power. On the other hand, however, identities and norms may also prevent steps towards integration that appear functionally efficient.

Enlargement, parliamentarisation, and differentiation in a liberal community perspective

On the basis of these ideational expectations, I will now revisit the developments and outcomes of European integration left unexplained by LI. I seek to show that Eastern enlargement and parliamentarisation are in line with liberal norms, and that variation in liberal international identity explains the opt-outs from monetary integration and other policies.

Eastern enlargement

According to the EU treaty and in line with the expectations of liberal community, any European state that subscribes to the liberal values of the EU may apply to become a member state (Article 49, TEU). The CEECs and their supporters in the EU invoked this membership norm to overcome the reluctance of those member states that feared the costs of enlargement and to commit the EU formally to Eastern enlargement. They framed enlargement as an issue of community identity and argued that it ought not to be seen and decided from the vantage point of national interests and material cost-benefit calculations. They invoked the principles of liberal community, pointed to their achievements in adopting these principles, and predicted dire consequences for the democratic consolidation of Eastern Europe should membership be denied. In addition, they demanded that the community organisations stick to their past promises and practices of enlargement to democratic European countries and accused reticent member states of acting inconsistently and betraying the fundamental values and norms of their own community (Schimmelfennig, 2001: 68–72).

This framing and shaming made it very difficult for the member states to reject enlargement on legitimate grounds. Together with their main supporters – the European Commission, Germany, and Britain – the Eastern European countries were thus able to commit the EC to offering membership to liberal Eastern European countries at the Copenhagen European Council of 1993 under conditions (the "Copenhagen criteria") that were predominantly based on liberal norms of Community membership – rather than economic cost-benefit criteria. Subsequently, the EU has invited those countries that met the liberal criteria to accession negotiations. In addition, those countries that consolidated democracy earlier were also invited earlier to the negotiating table (Schimmelfennig, 2001: 61).

Parliamentarisation

In line with the expectations of the theory of liberal community, the empowerment of the EP was triggered by steps of further supranational integration that threatened to undermine core liberal norms at the national level.

Before they launched the internal market programme in the mid-1980s, the EC member states decided all legal acts by de facto unanimity. This was a result of the Luxembourg Compromise that ended France's boycott against a proposed move towards qualified majority voting (QMV) in 1966. Twenty years later, however, the member states agreed on QMV as a necessary reform to increase the speed of EC decision-making in the internal market and to overcome opposition to market-enhancing regulation by individual member states. The rationale for moving from unanimity to QMV was thus based on commercial interest and efficiency. The governments initially did not plan to increase the legislative powers of the EP, which would have reduced their own power as well as their legislative efficiency.

Yet, QMV implied the possibility of overruling individual national governments and parliaments. It thus undermined the indirect democratic legitimacy of the Community, which was based on the principle that each member "demos" was represented at the European level by a democratically elected and controlled government, and could not be forced to implement laws to which its government had not consented. This democracy deficit was criticised by members of parliament in national parliaments as well as in the EP who demanded that the loss of indirect democratic legitimacy needed to be compensated by expanding the legislative competences of an organisation invested with direct democratic legitimacy: the EP (Rittberger, 2005: 150–152).

The reaction of the member governments to these demands revealed a split that can be attributed to the relative strength of national identity. Whereas the majority of (integration-friendly) governments acquiesced to the demands of the parliamentarians, Denmark and the United Kingdom, the member states with the most Euro-sceptic populations, opposed the empowerment of the EP as a solution to the legitimacy deficit (Rittberger, 2005: 163, 165). Rather, Denmark, in particular, championed the empowerment of the national parliament in European affairs. In the end, a compromise was reached: the "cooperation procedure".

This case shows how the efficiency-based deepening of supranational integration undermined liberal political norms at the national level and generated (successful) demand for compensation in order to uphold the liberal-democratic legitimacy of regional integration. After all, democratic accountability (including the parliamentary accountability of governments) is a shared norm in the community. It also shows, however, how variation in national identity leads to conflicting preferences on whether the compensation should be located at the national or the supranational level.

In the two decades following the Single European Act, the norm that QMV in the Council must be complemented by co-decision has become firmly institutionalised (Goetze and Rittberger, 2010). The Constitutional Convention that prepared the current TEU stipulated that the functioning of the EU should be founded on "representative democracy" and cleared the decision-making process of the EU of all violations of this norm – including in the area of agricultural and fisheries policy, in which vested interests had sought to retain QMV without co-decision (Roederer-Rynning and Schimmelfennig, 2012).

Differentiated integration

The opt-outs from monetary union, the most important integration project of the EU, are mainly identity based. Britain, Denmark, and Sweden have consistently shown high levels of public Euro-scepticism. Survey data from the *Eurobarometer* reveal a comparatively high percentage of exclusive national identities, weak support for further European integration, and a comparatively negative image of the EU.[1] This Euro-scepticism has been boosted by high domestic ratification hurdles. In Denmark and Sweden, for instance, it took popular referendums for the mass-level identity-based opposition to the euro to assert itself against euro-friendly elites. Even though the British government has rejected supranational monetary integration from the very start, it has also constrained its room for manoeuvre by the promise to hold a referendum should it want to introduce the euro. By contrast, the German constitution does not provide for treaty ratification by popular referendum. As a result, popular majorities against the euro have not been able to assert themselves against the pro-euro mainstream parties. Comparatively Euro-sceptic identities, together with domestic institutions that made it possible for them to constrain government policies, have forced governments (at least in Denmark and Sweden) to abandon integration policies they considered to be in their economic interest.

The most Euro-sceptic countries of the EU are also the most important demanders for opt-outs from EU treaty provisions beyond monetary union. Among the old member states of the EU, the United Kingdom is by far the one with most opt-outs, followed by Denmark and Sweden. In contrast, the fact that Ireland also has a high number of opt-outs is a result of its decision to follow Britain in remaining outside the Schengen area of free travel. It was motivated by Ireland's predominant interest in maintain the Common Travel Area with Britain and not an effect of exclusive national identity. In addition, differentiation is strongest in policies that affect core state powers and issues that are likely to mobilise exclusive national identities: external and domestic security; visa, immigration, and asylum policies; the protection of individual rights; and judicial policies (Schimmelfennig and Winzen, 2012). In sum, the member states with strongly national identities seek to opt out of integration in sovereignty and identity-sensitive policy areas.

Conclusions

This chapter has dealt with liberalism in the theory of regional and European integration. I have argued that LI, the most established liberal theory of European integration, is based on only one variant of liberalism in IR theory: commercial liberalism. This truncated liberalism cannot explain many relevant developments and outcomes in European integration, which are better captured by a theory of liberal community based on ideational liberalism. In this chapter, I defined liberal community, derived hypothetical expectations about integration in a liberal community, and sought to show that they can explain the puzzles of commercial liberalism.

The aim of this chapter is not to replace one truncated version of liberalism with another. I do not claim that ideational liberalism provides a comprehensive explanation of regional integration or a more encompassing one than commercial liberalism or LI. Rather, both variants of liberalism are relevant for explaining European integration. The challenge is to provide the scope conditions for each variant.

As described above, Moravcsik suggests that commercial liberalism explains integration best when the economic consequences of integration decisions are clear and certain, and when economic interests are well organised; otherwise, there is room for ideological preferences and norms to gain the upper hand. This scope condition may be too facile: after all, the opponents of enlargement and parliamentary co-decision were motivated by negative economic consequences of which they were – rightly or wrongly – persuaded. The case of differentiated monetary integration shows that strong national identities may trump economic interests – regardless of how well defined or well organised they are.

I suggest that the nature of the issues is decisive. Some issues mobilise identities, values, and norms more than others. Constitutional issues (rather than secondary institutional issues or regulatory and distributive issues) are most likely to involve questions of community identity, values and norms, and demand a principled response that overrides economic cost-benefit calculations and constrains the use of material bargaining power. All issues analysed here – community membership, political accountability, and the supranationalisation of core state powers – are such constitutional issues. Decisions on constitutional issues of regional order are certainly not everyday issues in the EU, but they are too important to be neglected by a narrow reading of liberal theory.

As a final consideration, how does the current crisis in the EU affect liberal community and the adequacy of ideational liberalism as an explanatory theory? For one, the debt and euro crises are not the constitutional issues that ideational liberalism focuses on, but a set of issues that commercial liberalism and LI are well suited to analyze. The crisis reveals conflicting preferences among the Eurozone countries that have mainly to do with their material positions. Those member states that have come under strong pressure from financial markets are predictably in favour of a European solution involving, for instance, the communitarisation of debt via euro-bonds, or "quantitative easing" by the European Central Bank. In contrast, the member states with sustainable debt levels and weak financial market pressures are reluctant to pay for what they see as profligate Eurozone countries. We can also clearly see the impact of bargaining power. Even though Germany's macroeconomic preferences constitute the minority view in the Eurozone and beyond, the German government can impose its austerity policy on the entire zone because it is the pivotal country for guaranteeing the stability of the common currency and for any European bail-out scheme for highly indebted member states. The new institutions of the Eurozone follow German preferences as well.

In addition, there is a threat that the crisis may undermine core liberal community features of the EU. Firstly, crisis management bypasses or silences democratic institutions. Obviously, democracy has been suspended in Greece, but new intergovernmental institutions in the EU – such as the fiscal pact – also sideline the EP. Secondly, the crisis seems to nurture exclusive nationalism both in the debtor and the indebted countries. Thirdly, the EU's self-absorption with internal problems may make it less willing to respond positively to liberal-democratic transitions beyond its borders.

There are, however, opposite signals as well. The EP is fighting for including the fiscal pact into the Community framework and having a say in its decisions. If the fiscal pact will be integrated into the EU a few years after coming into force, it will be very hard to resist the parliamentarisation that has gripped other policies in the past as well. Amidst the turmoil of the

euro crisis, the EU has decided to admit Croatia, to start accession negotiations with Montenegro, and to offer Serbia candidate status. Finally, the crisis
reproduces established patterns of differentiated integration rather than creating new cleavages. That Britain and the Czech Republic have decided to
stay out of the fiscal pact is not surprising. It is rather more surprising that
comparatively Euro-sceptic and non-Euro countries such as Denmark and
Sweden may be willing to join the fiscal pact. In sum, it remains an open
question whether the consequences of the debt and Euro crises will change
the liberal community character of the EU and the explanatory power of
ideational liberalism for constitutional issues in European integration.

Note

1. See Eurobarometer surveys at http://ec.europa.eu/public_opinion/index_en.htm.

References

Cederman, L. (2001). "Political Boundaries and Identity Tradeoffs", in L. Cederman
    (ed.) *Constructing Europe's Identity. The External Dimension*, Boulder: Lynne Rienner,
    1–32.
Deudney, D. and Ikenberry, G. J. (1999), "The Nature and Source of Liberal Interna-
    tional Order", *Review of International Studies*, 25(2), 179–196.
Goetze, S. and Rittberger, B. (2010), "A Matter of Habit? The Sociological Founda-
    tions of Empowering the European Parliament", *Comparative European Politics*, 8(1),
    37–54.
Golub, J. (1999), "In the Shadow of the Vote? Decisionmaking in the European
    Community", *International Organization*, 53(4), 737–768.
Habermas, J. (1998), *Die postnationale Konstellation: Politische Essays*, Frankfurt:
    Suhrkamp.
Hix, S. (2002), "Constitutional Agenda-setting through Discretion in Rule Interpreta-
    tion: Why the European Parliament Won at Amsterdam", *British Journal of Political
    Science*, 32(2), 259–280.
Hooghe, L. and Marks, M. (2005), "Calculation, Community, and Cues: Public
    Opinion on European Integration", *European Union Politics*, 6(4), 421–445.
Hooghe, L. and Marks, G. (2008), "A Postfunctionalist Theory of European Integration:
    From Permissive Consensus to Constraining Dissensus", *British Journal of Political
    Science*, 39(1), 1–23.
Johnson, J. (2008). "The Remains of Conditionality: The Faltering Enlargement of the
    Euro Zone", *Journal of European Public Policy*, 15(6), 826–841.
Keohane, R. (1984), *After Hegemony. Cooperation and Discord in the World Political
    Economy*, Princeton: Princeton University Press.
Keohane, R. and Nye, S. J. (1977), *Power and Interdependence: World Politics in Transition*,
    New York: Harper Collins.
Leuffen, D., Rittberger, B. and Schimmelfennig, F. (2012), *Differentiated Integration.
    Explaining Variation in the European Union*, Basingstoke: Palgrave.
Moravcsik, A. (1993), "Preferences and Power in the European Community. A Liberal
    Intergovernmentalist Approach", *Journal of Common Market Studies*, 31(4), 473–524.

Moravcsik, A. (1997), "Taking Preferences Seriously: A Liberal Theory of International Politics", *International Organization*, 51(4) 513–553.

Moravcsik, A. (1998), *The Choice for Europe: Social Purpose and State Power from Messina to Maastricht*, Ithaca, NY: Cornell University Press.

Moravcsik, A. and Nicolaidis, K. (1999), "Explaining the Treaty of Amsterdam: Interests, Influence, Institutions", *Journal of Common Market Studies*, 37(1), 59–85.

Moravcsik, A. and Schimmelfennig, F. (2009), "Liberal Intergovernmentalism", in A. Wiener and T. Diez (eds) *European Integration Theory*, 2nd edition, Oxford: Oxford University Press, 67–87.

Moravcsik, A. and Vachudova, M. (2003), "National Interests, State Power, EU Enlargement", *East European Politics and Societies*, 17(1), 42–57.

Parsons, C. (2002), "Showing Ideas as Causes. The Origins of the European Union", *International Organization*, 56(1), 47–84.

Putnam, R. D. (1988), "Diplomacy and Domestic Politics: The Logic of Two-Level Games", *International Organization*, 42(3), 427–460.

Reus-Smit, C. (1997), "The Constitutional Structure of International Society and the Nature of Fundamental Institutions", *International Organization*, 51(4), 555–589.

Risse, T. (2010), *A Community of Europeans? Transnational Identities and Public Spheres*, Ithaca, NY: Cornell University Press.

Risse-Kappen, T. (1995a), *Cooperation among Democracies. The European Influence on U.S. Foreign Policy*, Princeton, NJ: Princeton University Press.

Risse-Kappen, T. (1995b), "Democratic Peace – Warlike Democracies? A Social Constructivist Interpretation of the Liberal Argument", *European Journal of International Relations*, 1(4), 491–517.

Rittberger, B. (2005), *Building Europe's Parliament. Democratic Representation beyond the Nation-State*, Oxford: Oxford University Press.

Rittberger, B. and Schimmelfennig, F. (2006), "Explaining the Constitutionalization of the European Union", *Journal of European Public Policy*, 13(8), 1148–1167.

Roederer-Rynning, C. and Schimmelfennig, F. (2012), "Bringing Codecision to Agriculture: A Hard Case of Parliamentarization", *Journal of European Public Policy*, 19(7), 951–968.

Ruggie, J. G. (1993), "Multilateralism: The Anatomy of an Institution", in J. G. Ruggie (ed.) *Multilateralism Matters. The Theory and Praxis of an Institutional Form*, New York: Columbia University Press, 3–47.

Schimmelfennig, F. (2001), "The Community Trap: Liberal Norms, Rhetorical Action, and the Eastern Enlargement of the European Union", *International Organization*, 55(1), 47–80.

Schimmelfennig, F. and Winzen, T. (2012), "Instrumental and Constitutional Differentiation in European Integration", Paper, Swiss Political Science Association.

Schulz, H. and König, T. (2000), "Institutional Reform and Decision-making Efficiency in the European Union", *American Journal of Political Science*, 44(4), 653–666.

14
Beyond Liberalism? Reflections from the Middle East

Louise Fawcett

The Middle East stands out as a particularly interesting, if challenging arena for testing some of the questions explored in this volume. Firstly, because the region, with few exceptions, is widely seen as having had a relatively limited experience with liberalism; secondly, because it has resisted the import of liberalism, and thirdly – like some other emerging world regions – because it appears to offer a challenge to certain assumptions about liberalism as a universal project.

Given this assumed lack of experience, the "Arab Spring" came as a surprise to many Western analysts. Before its onset, Arab authoritarianism was seen to be firmly entrenched, and the prospects for promoting liberalism and democratisation limited. Writing in 2002, Laurence Whitehead explains that while liberal democracy and constitutionalism are "familiar traditions with century long histories in Europe and the Americas, in Asia and Africa they arrived more recently, whereas in much of the Middle East democratisation may be harder to imagine" (Whitehead, 2002: 190). And John Grey, writing some years after the onset of the Iraq War in 2003, commented starkly: "liberal democracy cannot be established in most of the countries of the modern Middle East [...] there is a choice between secular despotism and Islamic rule" (Grey, 2007: 146). Whether the policies of Western powers were seen as part of the problem or the solution – a question to be explored here – the region was widely regarded as either *before* or *beyond* liberalism.

The popular reform movements that commenced late in 2010 served to unseat some of these assumptions. At the time of writing (late 2012), three previously illiberal Arab regimes (in Tunisia, Egypt, and Libya) had fallen; one (in Yemen) had peacefully relinquished power; several more had been obliged to undertake significant reforms; and Syria remained in a state of civil war. The nature and direction of the protests that swept much of the region showed that liberal thinking in a broad sense was very much alive, and that it did not depend, at least not directly, on Western agency. Indeed, the use of the term "Arab Awakening" by Arabs themselves suggested continuity with a more liberal past, recalling popular reform movements initiated over a century ago (Antonius, 1938). Yet, at the same time, as events progressed, it became clear that the diverse demands of the reformers and the responses of new regimes would probably defy any universal or common logic of liberalism, revealing its problematic and contested nature when placed in a global context (Hovden and Keene, 2006: 6–7). For some, the region offers a foretaste of a new world order after liberalism's perceived failure, at least as a Western project; for others, it suggests the need for its rebranding, or at least for a more flexible interpretation of its nature and content in the light of a shifting global balance of power and ideologies.

In order to contribute to the wider debates explored in this volume, this chapter probes the historical record for a better understanding of the Middle East's experience of liberalism. It challenges certain ahistorical and simplifying assumptions about the region's "illiberal" past and seeks to construct an alternative narrative based around critical liberal or liberalising episodes.[1] Commencing in the late Ottoman period, through the period of quasi-sovereignty following the First World War, then independence, the Cold War and after, such episodes left important traces and opened up pathways for future development. This process was by no means continuous: there have been many false starts and reversals. At the time of writing, for example, the road to greater political pluralism in Egypt promised by the Arab Spring was again under challenge. Liberalism, like the democracy with which it is associated – in the Middle East or anywhere else – does not move forward in a seamless or linear way; rather, its progress is punctuated by crisis, retrenchment, reform and renewal (Capoccia and Ziblatt, 2010: 934). Writing about the wider prospects for democracy, Nazih Ayubi (1995: 397) has argued that "the analysis becomes more rewarding if one does not look for democracy as a final product and end result, but rather considers democratisation, or better still liberalisation, as an ongoing process pointing in the direction of pluralism or polyarchy". Such analysis makes the events of the Arab Spring comprehensible.

Against this background – one of stunted or interrupted liberalism – this chapter then examines the relevance and appropriateness of some of the dominant "universal" pretensions of liberalism – those largely advocated and practiced by Western liberal democracies – in the light of the regional experience. Here it suggests that while both Muslim and non-Muslim Arab (and Iranian and Turkish) liberals have undoubtedly embraced the language of liberalism and pluralism – as seminal works on Arabic and Islamic thought by Albert Hourani (1962) and Hamid Enayat (1982) have shown – it is also the case that any modern Middle Eastern reading of liberalism will look different in some important aspects (Ramadan, 2012). These differences, it is argued here, relate to timing – the region's first embrace of liberalism came relatively late; culture – there was and is a tension between certain universal logics of liberalism and local cultures and practices; and, finally, external factors – which have had contradictory push–pull effects, at once promoting and inhibiting liberalisation. In this regard, again, the Middle East is by no means unique – other states and regions have embraced liberalism at different times and in different ways – though it has been perhaps unusual in the longevity of authoritarianism and persistence of illiberal practices. In order to appreciate the nature of the process, it is important not to "fix" liberalism but to embrace the more dynamic stance as advocated by Chantal Mouffe. Her critique of John Rawls's demands for a "reasonable pluralism" are grounded in the idea that it is ultimately too exclusive and fails to make room for what she calls a more inclusive "real pluralism" (Mouffe, 2005: 231). It may be that the very success of liberalism may come depend on its malleability, and the Middle East is an excellent arena to test this.

In discussing liberalism in the contemporary Middle East, in this chapter, a connection is made between liberalism, liberalisation, and democracy, while acknowledging that each have different qualities and character (Bobbio, 2006: 1). While liberalism may be properly located in a discussion of individual rights and freedoms which place limits on the state, it is also located in forms of democratic or constitutional government, incorporating those "mechanisms which characterise a rights based state [and] are intended to guard the individual against abuses of power" (Bobbio, 2006: 15). Writing from an International Relations perspective, John Owen characterises the liberal state as one enjoying freedom of discussion and regular competitive elections (Owen, 1997: 3). Much of the discussion regarding the illiberal nature of regional regimes and even of the region itself has been linked to the widely observed democratic deficit. However, in tracking liberalism's regional roots, the aim is not to uncover any budding liberal or democratic utopia but to make a connection between the development of liberal traditions – liberalisation – and the evidence and further possibilities of liberal and democratic transformation. And, like liberalism, democracy is not an end-state, representing a fixed position on a scale, but a protracted process (Capoccia and Ziblatt, 2010: 940). As Nancy Bermeo elegantly describes it: "A new democracy is more like a collage than a canvas. It will not emerge all of a piece but rather bit by bit, with each component part shaped at different times, by different hands" (Bermeo, 2010: 1120). Even if most states of the region cannot yet be described as "new democracies", it may be that the elements of liberal and democratic change are indeed slowly emerging. But it is also likely – and evidence has already shown this – that these new democracies will differ in important ways from the old.

To track and analyse these processes of change, this chapter is organised into three sections. The first examines the region's past, isolating liberal pathways and episodes over the "long twentieth century"; the second looks at how, and with what consequences, external actors have sought to influence processes of democratisation and liberalisation in the region, particularly since the events of 11 September 2001; a final section, drawing on past events and present experiences, considers some liberal futures.

Elements of a liberal past

As suggested above, there are a series of linked liberalising episodes to explore in the region's history.[2] The latest, post-Cold War episode of democratisation was seen as a limited one from a comparative "Third Wave" perspective (Huntington, 1991); yet now, it has merged into the dramatic events surrounding the rise of popular reform movements in the Arab world, which has seen regimes tumble amid huge clamour for radical change. This clamour is not the result of sophisticated efforts by Western states to orchestrate demands for change in order to weaken and thereby control regional politics, as some have claimed (Mirghani, 2012); the Arab uprisings took the West by surprise, their initial responses were hesitant and clumsy. Rather, they are the result of bottom-up processes, drawing on accumulated experience and growing popular frustration, fed partly by international events such as the Iraq War and its consequences and partly by the effects of globalisation, including the revolution in communications and technology, which has played an important part in transforming Middle Eastern societies (Lynch, 2005).

This reconstruction of the liberal moments experienced in the region starts in the mid-nineteenth century, though any attempt to fix a starting point is somewhat artificial. If at the heart of liberalism lies the question of "establishing peaceful coexistence among peoples with different conceptions of the good" (Mouffe, 2005: 222), then there was already much that was liberal in the long-standing arrangements for coexistence between different subject peoples of the Ottoman Empire, including a significant measure of religious freedom and provincial autonomy (Hourani, 1961: 74). However, it was the Tanzimat (or "regulations") stage of the Ottoman reform movement, which initiated the two great reforming edicts of 1839 and 1856 (Yapp, 1987: 108–114), and culminated in the first Ottoman constitution of 1876, which sought to grant equal rights and liberties to all the empire's subjects and sowed the early seeds of representative government. Influenced by Europe, it was just one of a number of experiments with the idea, if not the practice, of constitutional government in and around the empire (Ibrahim, 2004: 37–39). Tunisia – the spark that lit the Arab Spring – was the first Arab province to acquire a constitution in 1860, the work of a group of young Westernisers who, during the reign of Ahmad Bey, sought to limit the Ottoman Sultan's power. Similarly, in Egypt, liberal reformers called upon the viceroy Khedive Ismail to decree a constitution in 1866, an example that was also followed, unsuccessfully, in Iraq in 1869. Some years later, a group of Egyptian officers, led by Urabi Pasha, called for the election of a Chamber of Deputies and for further constitutional reforms. Iran witnessed its constitutional revolution or "mushrutiyat" between 1905 and 1909, a movement that involved widespread popular participation and resulted in the drafting of a constitution, which granted significant press and other freedoms (Abrahamian, 1969; Browne, 2005).

This early liberal moment was short-lived. The first Ottoman constitution was suspended; its restoration in 1908 was brief, as entry (and defeat) in the First World War heralded the very empire's demise. Those of Tunisia and Egypt were soon overturned, and that of Iran often disregarded under the new dynasty established by the Pahlavis. However, liberalism had not simply died. Nor was it a simple façade, a mere "parody of what happened in Europe" in Elie Kedourie's (1974: 2) words. The late Ottoman period – characterised by increased reformist activity, the budding of civil society, the rise of constitutionalism and the granting of press and other freedoms – was to leave enduring traces and inform future developments (Brown, 2005: 26). Within the empire, Ottoman reforms had revealed a new balance of power between the people, the palace, and the Porte. The first deputies chosen for the newly elected assembly showed "an amazing degree of independent thought and constructive criticism of government" (Davidson, 1968: 107–108). Thus, it has been argued that some of the early "prerequisites" for democratic governance already existed by the early twentieth century (Ibrahim, 2004: 40).

A second liberal moment closely followed the breakup of the Ottoman Empire and the creation of separate successor states as part of the post-war settlement. Many of these states – particularly the so-called mandates of Iraq, Palestine, Transjordan, Syria, and Lebanon – came under new forms of colonial tutelage. The ideas of US President Woodrow Wilson regarding the self-determination of peoples may have figured little in such arrangements, to the disappointment of Arabs, Kurds, and other nationalities, yet such forms were not necessarily or wholly illiberal. Regulated and ultimately limited by the Covenant of the League of Nations, they were, as Elizabeth Monroe (1963: 71) described them, "a cross between liberalism and adherence to war aims". Many bore the distinctive hallmarks of Western European practice, modelled on the governments and administrative arrangements of Britain and France. Yet, this was a *problem* for second-generation liberals. Arab elites and institutions, notwithstanding some democratic credentials, were too closely identified with their colonial masters and with external meddling (Ibrahim, 2004: 40–41). The new Iraqi state, crafted from three former Ottoman provinces, saw the installation of a hereditary constitutional monarchy. Its Ottoman-modelled constitution, incorporating the principle of popular sovereignty, produced a parliament that was – on paper at least – "as powerful as any that has existed in the Arab world" (Brown, 2002: 45); yet it was nonetheless subject to the constraints of the mandate and, as such, unpopular. So were France's attempts to impose its administrative structures in Syria, though in Lebanon the confessional system, with political power allocated among the country's different religious communities, initially showed promise. Egypt's ambitious experiment in guided constitutional government after 1923 proved highly unstable (Maghraoui, 2006). Against a backdrop of growing nationalism – which Britain failed to control – the country saw seven general elections in the space of 15 years, with no single parliament surviving its full term (Vatikiotis, 1991: 273–297).

This era of partial sovereignty, which ended after the Second World War for many new states, did not provide durable foundations for the growth of liberalism. Independent Turkey had an uncertain constitutional trajectory under Kemal Ataturk and his successors, who sought to crush cultural pluralism – most visibly in the case of the Kurds – in the pursuit of a common national identity, though the foundations for the modern state were laid (Zurcher, 1998: 176–180). In Saudi Arabia, under the leadership of Ibn Saud, independence saw the persistence of traditional rule and only the rudiments of a government apparatus. For the mandates and protectorates, the time frame was short, and the circumstances – domestic and external – mostly unpropitious. Nationalism provided a formula for freedom from imperial rule but did not otherwise follow a liberal path: many states started independence with constitutional government, but populist coups brought forward radical regimes that cut short the liberal experiments introduced by external powers. Here, a few cases suffice to reveal the overall pattern. The Egyptian monarchy was overthrown by a military coup led by Nasser in 1952; a series of further coups followed in Iraq and Syria despite, in the latter case, the conditions of "exceptional freedom" which prevailed in the 1954 elections. Where monarchies survived, traditional forms of rule continued, with the partial exception of Jordan, which enjoyed a period of constitutional government from 1952 to 1957. Overall, the new social contracts that were forged saw the postponement or marginalisation of liberal politics (Ibrahim, 1995: 6). A rather different course of events occurred in Iran, though the outcome was similar. Mohammad Reza Shah's pro-Western regime was briefly challenged in the early 1950s by the actions of the popular reformist politician Mohammed Mossadeq, who led a national front coalition calling for oil nationalisation but also a return of constitutional government (Katouzian, 1999). Mossadeq's ousting, in a coup orchestrated by the United States and Britain, secured the Shah's position as virtual dictator and thwarted any possibilities of constitutional revival, at least in the medium term.

This marginalisation of liberal politics – though not unique to the Middle East – prevailed through much of the Cold War period. The reasons for this were numerous and complex. If the suspension of the liberal experiment at independence can be understood through its brevity and shallow roots, its association with Western colonialism, the humiliation of the Arab defeat against Israel in 1948 and the attractions of populist-nationalist politics, its prolongation owed much to the effects of the Cold War balance of power, and the security provided to incumbent regimes by foreign powers and, increasingly, oil rents (Salamé, 1994: 14–15). There were still some liberal turns, notably the growth of multipartism in North Africa. In Egypt, for example, regime change after Nasser's death heralded a period of limited liberalisation under Anwar Sadat, which included a new economic policy, *intifah*, and a return to multiparty politics. The 1971 Constitution duly emphasised individual liberty, freedom of speech, and the rule of law (Owen, 1995: 185). But the reformist spirit was contained. In monarchies and republics alike, autocrats proved effective at making limited concessions while consolidating their position. The political opposition to incumbent regimes that did emerge often took on an Islamic form, rejecting secular nationalism and Western liberalism alike.

The Iranian Revolution of 1979 proved to be an extreme manifestation of this. Despite evidence of early pluralism – the revolution had many liberal fellow travellers – its direction, within a highly sensitive regional and international environment, soon diminished the prospects of a more liberal Islamic republic. While some social and economic inequalities were addressed, individual freedoms, particularly where the rights of women and minorities were concerned, regressed and political pluralism remained limited. Further, in providing some inspiration to other Islamic groups and movements, the creation of an Islamic Republic in Iran fostered Western (and also regional) fears of an expansionist Islam and justified continued support of incumbent authoritarians, a view that would be further encouraged by the tactics of extremist Islamic groups pursuing violence against Western targets.

Another important factor restraining the development of liberal politics in this period was war. Though war has been identified as the engine of liberal change, the festering and unresolved nature of the Arab–Israel conflict and the continuing cycle of wars – civil and international – merely served to justify authoritarianism, militarism and external interference, slowing down any prospects for democratic renewal (Waterbury, 1994: 26–27).

These stop-start features of interrupted liberalisation and authoritarian resilience – with the latter more prevalent – persisted until the end of the Cold War and beyond. Up to the late 1980s, however, as a number of commentators remarked, there was little that was exceptional in political terms about the Middle East from a wider developing country perspective (Waterbury, 1994: 25). Roger Owen (2004: 19) compares the Middle East with other areas where "ambivalent commitments to pluralism and parliamentarianism also tended to give way to military or one-party rule".

The end of the Cold War, however, appeared to usher in a new era of liberal hope and promise. And the Middle East was not exempt from democracy's contagion effects. From the late 1980s onwards, against a backdrop of widespread economic and bureaucratic mismanagement, political stagnation, and corruption, parts of the region saw demands for change. Limited democratisation, including increased electoral competition and multiparty activity, occurred in a number of states (Ayubi, 1995: 396–397).

Throughout North Africa, there were signs of authoritarian erosion and constitutional strengthening. Egypt's Constitutional Court demonstrated a new activism and independence. In Tunisia, President Bourguiba was ousted in a coup in 1987 and his successor, Ben Ali, called for political rejuvenation, constitutionalism, and respect for human rights (Ayubi, 1995: 418). In Lebanon a reformed consociational democracy was restored after the Ta'if Accord of 1989, with the country holding its first parliamentary elections for nearly 20 years. The reunification of Yemen in 1990 brought with it a new constitution guaranteeing a multiparty system, voting rights to all citizens, and equality before the law. Jordan saw a revival of a multiparty system and the removal of press and other restrictions.

External intervention, in the Gulf War of 1990–1991, also prompted changes and demands for democratisation, particularly in the Gulf region itself. Resistance to the Iraqi invasion had seen a proliferation of civil society groups in Kuwait; its aftermath saw a revival and strengthening of parliamentary activity, not only there but in Qatar and Bahrain as well (Ayubi, 1995, 428–429). In Saudi Arabia, the ruling family agreed to the establishment of a Consultative Council in 1992. In Iran, the election, in 1997, of the reformist president Muhammad Khatami was heralded as a "reopening of constitutional politics", characterised by greater liberalism at home coupled with his advocacy of a "dialogue of civilisations" abroad (Arjomand, 2000: 324). These were all-important political openings heralding further changes. No less significant were parallel advances in Arab–Israel relations, with the 1993 Oslo accords promising a new era of regional cooperation. Israel's Foreign Minister, Shimon Peres, wrote how "peace between Israel and its Arab neighbours will create the environment for a basic reorganisation of Middle Eastern institutions" (Peres and Noar, 1993: 62).

Despite some initially promising developments on the domestic and regional fronts, the "new" Middle East of which Peres spoke was not immediately forthcoming. By the end of the decade, the Oslo Peace Process and one of its principal architects – Israeli Prime Minister Yitzhak Rabin – were dead. Events in the wider region continued to defy any expectations of the "New World Order" outlined by President George Bush at the time of the Gulf War. In words that sound hopelessly unrealistic in the light of subsequent events, he spoke of "an era – freer from the threat of terror, stronger in the pursuit of justice and more secure in the quest for peace" (Bush, 1990). The overall consequences of liberalisation and democratisation were quite limited, characterised not only by small advances, but also by reversals. In Algeria, following the electoral victory of the Islamic Salvation Front in late 1991, the electoral process was cancelled by the army, initiating a cycle of violence and a remobilisation of the authoritarian state to crush Islamic opposition (Entelis, 1997: x); in Tunisia also, Ben Ali sought to curtail the effects of liberalisation by suppressing the activities of the Islamic al-Nahda Party and human rights groups. Some states remained stubbornly outside the democratising wave: "To speak about democratisation in Iraq … seems almost to border on the ridiculous" (Ayubi, 1995: 424).

Given the limits to liberalisation described above, particularly when viewed from a comparative perspective, it is unsurprising that the Middle East, with few exceptions, came to be seen as something of an early twenty-first-century anomaly (Diamond, 2010: 93). The challenges to authoritarianism had been largely overcome. The demise, around the turn of the century, of an older generation of Arab leaders – in Syria, Jordan, Bahrain, and Morocco – saw relatively smooth father-to-son successions. Though not immune to the forces of globalisation, these new leaders, building on established structures of centralised and personalised leadership with extensive patronage networks, advocated continuity over change (Owen, 2012). Rather than being identified as part of any global liberalising trend, the fragile post-Cold War revivals described above were seen as mere islands in an authoritarian sea. Reinforcing such perceptions of exceptionalism were the words and deeds of Islamic extremist groups that took centre stage. Most evident through, but by no means limited to the attacks against the United States, the United Kingdom, and Spain between 2001 and 2007, such acts reinforced earlier preconceptions about the threatening and inherent illiberalism of Islam (Hunter, 2009: xix). Even if Islamic terrorism and groups such as Al Qaeda were supported by a tiny minority, their actions coloured the Muslim world, stoking Western hostility and Islamic sensibility. However hard Western liberals tried to disaggregate Islam, the overall effect of extremism was to de-legitimise its liberal potential. And Muslim peoples turned away from a muscular and intrusive Western liberalism that dehumanised Islam and conflated it with terror. Incumbent regimes, or so it seemed, could justify illiberal practices on the grounds of "the terrorist threat" (an argument also used in the Arab Spring) making much of the notion that authoritarian order was preferable to the Islamic alternative. This was not a healthy environment for moderates to thrive in.

The nature and extent of the problems facing the region at the turn of the century were subject to increasingly rigorous scrutiny following the inauguration of a series of *Arab Human Development Reports*. Produced by independent Arab experts under UNDP auspices, the first report, published in 2002, noted how popular demands for greater freedom and democracy remained unfulfilled. While acknowledging some achievements to date, it highlighted institutional weaknesses and the persistence of powerful executives as a barrier to change. Three key shortfalls in human development were identified – freedom, the position of women, and access to knowledge – all of which demanded urgent attention.

"Political participation in Arab countries remains weak, as manifested in the lack of genuine representative democracy and restrictions on liberties.

At the same time, people's aspirations for more freedom and greater partici-pation in decision-making have grown, fuelled by rising incomes, education, and information flows. The mismatch between aspirations and their fulfil-ment has in some cases led to alienation and its offspring – apathy and discontent. Remedying this state of affairs must be a priority for national leaderships" (UNDP, 2002: 9).

Liberalism from above? 9/11 and beyond

Expressions of alienation, popular apathy, and discontent took many forms and targeted regional regimes and the Western powers alike. Multiple terrorist attacks against (mostly) Western targets and the later Arab upris-ings are two dramatic examples. But it was Western shock and outrage at being made the target of Islamic extremism, matched by fears about pos-sible linkages between radical groups and incumbent regimes, which had the most immediate and profound impact on the liberal project. Though a range of different policies were advocated, they converged on the desir-ability of political reform or regime change. Both the United States and its European allies in the European Union had paid lip service to the idea of reform, as displayed by the different programmes and projects they supported in the wider region, of which the Euro–Mediterranean Part-nership (the Barcelona Process) initiated in 1995 is one example. Such programmes, which hitherto had had few significant results, were now to be reinforced: in 2003, the United States unveiled its Middle East Part-nership Initiative and in 2004, the European Union laid out its European Neighbourhood Policy. In both cases, the intention was to address demo-cratic and human rights deficits through engagement, in the words of President George W Bush with "a forward strategy of freedom" (Bush, 2003).

Despite the rhetorical ambition of these projects, the Western promotion of political reform ultimately took second place to security. More than any-thing else, it was the desire for regional security and a favourable balance of power for Western interests, not liberalism per se, that drove policy, most notably in the Iraqi intervention of 2003; the same logic would likely drive any intervention in Iran, should such an intervention occur. This fact alone suggests how the image of liberalism can be tarnished by ill-judged attempts at its export.

The Iraqi case was blatantly one of reform from above: in removing and remaking the Iraqi regime, in neutralising its actual or imagined nuclear potential and links to terrorism, the aim was to build a new democracy and in doing so to promote the regime as a model of liberalism and good gover-nance as a democratic beacon for the region (Fawcett, 2011: 41–43). It was, of course, simultaneously designed to improve Middle East–West relations and bring the region, via Iraq, into the liberal zone of peace.

It is striking in hindsight how none of these objectives were achieved. In the short term, the intervention brought more conflict and instability to the region. The effect of regime change in Iraq was not to significantly liberalise opinion but to radicalise opposition to the West and pro-Western regimes. This was evidenced by the increase of sectarianism and *jihadism*. These, in turn, became a motive for de-liberalisation by incumbent leaderships, fearful for their security and survival. The region was destabilised from within by such radicalism, and by the new balance of power resulting from the fall of Iraq, one which temporarily favoured regional actors such as Syria and Iran. It was destabilised from without by the effects of the intervention itself, and by subsequent efforts by Western powers to reset relations with the Arab world, efforts that were soon to be further interrupted by the events surrounding the Arab Spring.

The Iraq War, which in retrospect stands out as the apogee of liberal interventionism and overstretch – with profound and still unfolding consequences for the Middle East and North Africa –nevertheless offers a salutary lesson (Kitchen and Cox, 2011: 65–84). As the country descended into a destructive civil war, the possibilities of a new Iraq offering a model – a source of regional emulation – seemed increasingly remote, giving superficial credence to the view expressed by John Grey at the start of this chapter about the inherent incompatibility between liberal democracy and the Middle East. Such a view echoes that of an older generation of scholars, such as Elie Kedourie, for whom "there is nothing in the political traditions of the Arab world – which are the political traditions of Islam – which might make familiar, or indeed intelligible, the organising ideas of constitutionalism and representative government" (Kedourie, 1992: 5–6).

Such absolute positions are misplaced. A retrospective view, as advanced here, does not support them or the assumptions that underpin them. Firstly, any pro-democracy intervention in Iraq was bound to be a hazardous affair, with democratisation in the short term more likely to increase the risks of war rather than promote a liberal peace (Mansfield and Snyder, 1995: 36). Its failure, though undoubtedly a setback, does not signal a regional failure of liberalism, rather a failure of the Western effort both to "fix" liberalism and export it. Secondly, as discussed further below, the continued insistence on Arab or Islamic illiberalism is the result of an ahistorical and stilted generalisation, which privileges a focus on certain facts and interpretations of liberalism and Islam, and reveals ignorance of others. It is fed by Western fears and perceptions of the "Islamic Threat", and backed up regime rhetoric. It ignores the region's encounters with liberalisation, and the diversity of regional experience and practice. It also ignores, for example, moderation shown by those Islamist parties that have participated successfully in parliamentary elections in Turkey, Morocco, and Bahrain. It ignores the reformist potential that had been discerned in the Muslim Brotherhood in Egypt (Rutherford, 2008). As the brother of the movement's founder, Hasan al

Banna, has himself suggested, Islamic movements and parties could eventually evolve into a variant of the Christian Democratic parties that have been prevalent Western Europe (Ibrahim, 2004: 43).

The Turkish case, in particular, is interesting. Since the turn of the twenty-first century, there has been a process of democratic and institutional strengthening, which facilitated the advent to power of the Islamist Justice and Development Party (AKP). In the 2002–2003 and subsequent elections (the party secured its third consecutive victory in 2011) the AKP has shown pragmatism and respect for the rules of democratic government. Indeed, the very pragmatism shown by the AKP has led some to use the term "post-Islamic" to describe Turkey's integration of Islam into the political mainstream – a term that has also been used to describe political trends in both Iran and Egypt (Bayat, 2007). While the Iranian example is less immediately compelling – the installation of the conservative President Mahmoud Ahmadinejad in 2005 appeared to offer a stark contrast to the liberal stance of his predecessor Khatami – the continuing demands from within Iran for greater pluralism are indicative of widespread social movements pushing for a similar reformist trajectory. It should be recalled that Iran had its own spring, the "Green Movement", following the controversial elections in 2009, which secured Ahmadinejad a second presidential term.

Finally, and again with the benefit of hindsight, in certain ways the Iraq War did encourage a questioning and resistance to authority that had previously been muted by a combination of co-optation and coercion of opposition and civil society – though not in the manner intended. The humiliation of a repressive dictator, even if externally driven, was inspirational. It undermined assumptions about Arabs and authority, displacing the idea that authoritarianism was untouchable. So while scholars continued to speculate about the resilience of authoritarianism (Schlumberger, 2007: 1–6), the seeds of further discontent were already being sown across the region. Indeed, the years preceding the Arab uprisings were characterised by widespread, if disconnected social and political unrest: strikes in Egypt, ethnic strife in Lebanon, and pro-democracy movements in Iran, fed by the new media and the wider effects of globalisation. The full extent of this discontent and its implications were only fully revealed at the end of a deeply troubled decade with the start of the Arab uprisings.

Towards a more liberal future?

It is against this backdrop and these debates that the events of the Arab Spring should be understood. Triggered by the desperate act of a Tunisian street vendor at the end of 2010, the popular reform movements that swept the Arab world (one year after the crushing of Iran's pro-democracy Green Movement) issued a challenge to widely held assumptions about authoritarian resilience, making the liberal project look possible in ways that many had previously thought unlikely. With demands for pluralism and democratisation writ large, the Arab Spring was quickly likened to the momentous events of 1989 in Eastern Europe.

At first, there was an initial euphoria about democracy's new turn among Western liberals. The mostly non-Islamic content of the early uprisings and the absence of anti-Western rhetoric was occasion for quiet celebration. Yet, when Islamic parties looked set to be the beneficiaries of the popular reform movements the mood changed. While events in the Arab World did indeed question long held assumptions about the region's political character, the final outcome remains uncertain. Scholars have been quick to point out the different political conditions that prevailed in eastern Europe, suggesting that democratisation in the Middle East faces more significant challenges. The Arab Spring, unlike the events of 1989, did not follow the end of foreign occupation and control, nor did it take place under a protective Western umbrella (Springborg, 2011: 5–12).

However, in contrasting these different conditions, it is important to return to the origins and antecedents of the Arab uprisings, and not to lose sight of the wider and longer term picture. With the opening up of the electoral system, Islamic parties were potentially well placed to win because of their longevity and existing institutional structures (Hamid, 2011: 68). How innovative such parties will be in embracing liberalism remains to be seen; certainly, it will be hard to quieten the widespread calls for human dignity and freedom. Rather than heralding a return of illiberalism, however, the success of Islamic parties could be understood as part of a broad and ongoing if interrupted trend towards greater liberalism and respect for democratic procedures.

In Tunisia, elections in 2011 saw the victory of the moderate Al-Nahda party, which promised to retain the country's secular nature. The results from Egypt's elections in mid-2012 saw a victory for the Muslim Brotherhood led by Mohammed Morsi, with similar promises of moderation. Such developments are troubling for some, raising questions about the nature and direction of the liberal project in different settings. However, just as the post-1989 liberal legacy has been a troubled one in states such as Russia, it is likely that its new trajectory in the Middle East will also be bumpy, suggesting there are many roads to liberalism and democracy, which do not all start and end in the same place. We should not expect any quick democratic closure.

Undoubtedly, one of the biggest challenges from a Western perspective will be to embrace "non-Western" interpretations of liberalism, something that has hitherto posed a challenge, particularly where Islamic groups and parties are concerned. The West's reading of Islam will continue to sit uncomfortably with its liberal project, given the preference for a secular liberalism in which "religion is expelled from politics" (Hurd, 2011: 5). Katerina Dalacoura points to three core objections when attempting to reconcile Islam with one central aspect of liberalism: human rights. These are freedom of conscience, the position of women, and the position of non-Muslims in Muslim society. In each of these three areas, she demonstrates that the "contradictions between Islamic law, traditionally conceived, and the principles of equality and freedom of conscience are glossed over rather than resolved" (Dalacoura, 2002: 225). Post-revolutionary Iran provides an example of this. The argument is clearly made, but as with the critique of Rawls noted above, just as there is the danger of "fixing liberalism", so there is the danger of "fixing Islam". There is no single Islam, rather a plurality of voices and opinions of which "traditional Islam" is just one. Tariq Ramadan has alluded to this in *Islam and the Arab Awakening* (2012). Fixing Islam today recalls earlier orientalist understandings of the Arab world, and Western liberals need to guard against the re-orientalisation of perceptions of the Middle East in the light of Islamist revivalism. Only prolonged experience of and exposure to more moderate Islamist trends will shift such perceptions.

To refute such essentialist categories, it is helpful to draw once more on past scholarship and analysis, to acknowledge that liberalism in the Middle East implies not only the sharing and borrowing of Western models, but also their adaptation. As already noted, for many Arab and non-Arab scholars, there is no necessary contradiction between liberal thought and the region's Islamic culture. The possibilities of coexistence are revealed in Albert Hourani's work on Arabic thought and liberalism (Hourani, 1962). Other writers such as Ernest Gellner have pointed to Islam's flexibility, suggesting how "under modern conditions its capacity to be a more abstract faith presiding over an anonymous community of equal believers could reassert itself" (Gellner, 1983: 41–46). While mainly Western intellectuals have focused on radical interpretations of Shari'a law, others have sought to uncover from Islamic sources "the duties, limits and procedures of governance" and to reveal the "democratic temper of Islam" (Enayat, 1982: 120). This point seems particularly apposite when considering the possibility of a more enduring marriage between Islamist and liberal ideas in the new Arab world, or the wider possibilities of innovation in Islam (Kamrava, 2011). In a more modern vein, writers such as Asef Bayat have referred to a post-Islamist trend, where a new political space has opened up where "pious sensibilities are able to incorporate a democratic ethos" (Bayat, 2009).

Turkey is a state that many analysts have fastened upon to illustrate the possibilities of coexistence between Islam, liberalism, and democratic governance. Turkey offers a bridge between Islam and the West, both historically and geographically. And, contrary to widespread perceptions about contemporary Iran, there is a strong tradition of reformism within Shi'a Islam, both pre- and post-revolution, which could yet reveal a new, more liberal turn (Hunter, 2009 : 84–86). Though it is still too early to test the outcome of recent events, the Tunisian elections in 2011 and political developments elsewhere have brought victory to moderate rather than radical Islamists. Al Qaida, a group on which much attention was focused following the 9/11 bombings, is not popular – its leader is now dead – and Islamist parties have shown prudence and restraint in the political arena. Developments in Egypt at the end of 2012, where president Morsi attempted to grant himself additional powers by curbing the role of the judiciary, show that it is too early to speculate about the region's long-term political future. However, given the level of popular resistance, the case of Egypt also shows that it is unlikely to return to an authoritarian past or foster a brand of Islamic despotism. What is clear and inescapable about recent events is that there is a "new language of politics" in the Middle East, which represents above all a fusion of different ideas (Ansary, 2012: 12). In light of the region's past and present experiences, it is likely that any embrace of liberalism will differ in its nature and timing from that that familiarly associated with western Europe, discrediting any attempts crudely to export Western liberal values to the Middle East.

Conclusion

This chapter has sought to qualify the claim that the Middle East's political history should be seen as inherently hostile to democracy and liberalism, or that, seen through the lens of this region, liberalism has failed. It has provided evidence of a liberal past by focusing on critical episodes in a story of interrupted liberalism. These connected, if punctuated episodes – part of a liberal "collage" – provide an important framework for understanding the region's past and present political trajectory. This framework links the slow growth of liberalism and the long-standing democratic deficit to hostile domestic and international conditions: to embedded authoritarianism and personalised rule, to external influence, and to ultimately half-hearted attempts at democracy promotion. However, democracy and liberalism are far from being alien concepts, and pessimism about the region's liberal future is largely unfounded, resting on two related yet ultimately shaky assumptions. Firstly, that the widespread demands for greater representation and political reform will, as in the past, prove fragile and even reversible given the previously shallow and contested roots of liberalisation and the resilience of authoritarianism. Secondly, that the region's limited past and present experience with liberalism appears to represent at best a challenge, at worst a fundamental incompatibility with dominant "universal" interpretations, suggesting that the region is indeed beyond liberalism.

Both assumptions have been challenged here. There is evidently a history of liberalism in the Arab world, and while it is not much divorced from the familiar story of Western liberalism, it has its own distinctive qualities. The surprise of the Arab Spring is less surprising when considered from an historical perspective. Rediscovering the routes, trajectories and liberal possibilities in the region's past has been one aim of this chapter. However, the more liberal moment the region is currently experiencing will not map crudely onto any known experiences. This does not mean that it is "beyond liberalism"; rather that there are many roads to liberalism. Hence, another aim of this chapter has been to test, from a Middle Eastern perspective, the very assumptions lurking behind the notion of liberalism itself. For if the Arab Spring refutes exceptionalism, it also has demonstrated that the political future of Middle East will need to reflect and accommodate the region's history and culture, of which Islam is a central part. And importantly, "the modernisation of Islam", as Mouffe has claimed, will not take place "through Westernization", but on its own terms (Mouffe, 2005: 231).

There is no doubt that the processes of liberalisation in the Middle East have been slow and beset by reversals, but there is nothing in the region's history or culture that suggests it is beyond liberalism or substantially different from other regions that have experienced protracted transitions to democracy. Such assumptions rest on an essentialist and simplifying view of Middle East politics and society, which hark back to the earlier formulas that were so roundly challenged by Edward Said's orientalist critique. The experience of the Middle East today reinforces the point that there is no neat liberal formula or single liberal canvas. In this sense, while the region shows that we may have moved beyond a single dominant narrative of liberalism and crude attempts at exporting it, we have not moved beyond liberalism itself.

Notes

1. References to the region's illiberal history abound, but for a notable example see Kedourie (1974).
2. Parts of this section draw on Fawcett (2008: 116–136).

References

Abrahamian, E. (1969), "The Crowd in the Persian Revolution", *Iranian Studies*, 2(4), 128–150.

Ansary, A. F. (2012), "The Languages of the Arab Revolutions", *Journal of Democracy*, 23(2), 5–18.

Antonius, G. (1938), *The Arab Awakening*, London: Taylor and Francis.

Arjomand, S. A. (2000), "Authority in Shi'ism and Constitutional Developments in the Islamic Republic of Iran", in W. Ende and R. Brunner (eds) *The Shia in Modern Times. Religious Culture and Political History*, Leiden: Brill.

Ayubi, N. (1995), *Overstating the Arab State. Politics and Society in the Middle East*, London: I.B. Tauris.

Bayat, A. (2007), *Making Islam Democratic. Social Movements and the Post-Islamist Turn*, Stanford: Stanford University Press.

Bayat, A. (2009), "Democracy and the Muslim world. The post-Islamist Turn", *Open Democracy* (6 March).

Bermeo, N. (2010), "Interest, Inequality and Illusion in the Choice for Fair Elections", *Comparative Political Studies*, 43(8/9).

Bobbio, N. (2006), *Liberalism and Democracy*, London: Verso.

Brown, N. J. (2002), *Constitutions in a Non-Constitutional World*, New York: SUNY Press.

Browne, E. G. (2005), *The Persian Revolution 1905–1909*, London: Frank Cass.

Bush, G. H. W. (1990), "Address before a Joint Session of the Congress on the Persian Gulf Crisis and the Federal Budget Deficit", 11 September.

Bush, G.W. (2003), "Remarks by George W Bush at the Twentieth Anniversary of the National Endowment for Democracy", available at http://www.ned.org/node/658.

Capoccia, G. and Ziblatt, D. (2010), "The Historical Turn in Democratization Studies. A New Agenda for Europe and Beyond", *Comparative Political Studies*, 43(8–9), 931–968.

Davidson, R. H. (1968), "Advent of the Principle of Representation in the Government of the Ottoman Empire", in W.R. Polk and R.L. Chambers (eds) *The Beginnings of Modernization in the Middle East: The Nineteenth Century*, Chicago: University of Chicago Press, 96–108.

Delacoura, K. (2002), "International Human Rights Norms in Egypt and Tunisia", in E. Hovden and E. Keene (eds) *The Globalization of Liberalism*, Basingstoke: Palgrave, 218–241.

Diamond, L. (2010), "Why Are There No Arab Democracies?" *Journal of Democracy*, 21(1), 93–104.

Enayat, H. (1982), *Modern Islamic Political Thought*, London: MacMillan.

Entelis, J. P. (1997), *Islam, Democracy and the State in North Africa*, Bloomington: Indiana University Press.

Fawcett, L. (2008), "Neither Traditional nor Modern: Constitutionalism in the Ottoman Empire and Its Successor States", *Journal of Modern European History*, 6, 116–136.

Fawcett, L. (2011), "Regional Order in the Middle East", in A. Acharya and H. Katsumata (eds) *Beyond Iraq. The Future of World Order*, Singapore: World Scientific Publishing, 35–64.

Gellner, E. (1983), *Nations and Nationalism*, New York: Ithaca.

Grey, J. (2007), *Black Mass. Apocalyptic Religion and the Death of Utopia*, London: Penguin.

Hamid, S. (2011), "Arab Islamist Parties: Losing on Purpose?" *Journal of Democracy*, 22(1), 68–80.

Hourani, A. (1961), *A Vision of History. Near Eastern and Other Essays*, Beirut: Khayats.

Hourani, A. (1962), *Arabic Thought in the Liberal Age 1798–1939*, Cambridge: Cambridge University Press.

Hovden, E. and Keene, E. (2006), *The Globalization of Liberalism*, New York: Palgrave.

Hunter, S. T. (ed.) (2009), *Reformist Voices of Islam*, New York: ME Sharpe.

Huntington, S. P. (1991), *The Third Wave: Democratization in the Late Twentieth Century*, Norman: University of Oklahoma Press.

Hurd, E. S. (2011), *The Politics of Secularism in International Relations*, Princeton: Princeton University Press.

Ibrahim, S. E. (1995), "Liberalization and Democratization in the Arab World", in R. Brynen, B. Korany and P. Noble (eds) *Political Liberalization and Democratization in the Arab World* (Vol. 1), Boulder: Lynne Rienner, 29–57.

Ibrahim, S. E. (2004), "An Open Door. The Arab World's Liberal Tradition", *The Wilson Quarterly*, 28(2), 36–46.

Kamrava, M. (2011), *Innovation in Islam: Traditions and Contributions*, Berkeley: University of California Press.

Katouzian, H. (1999), *Musaddiq and the Struggle for Power in Iran*, London: I.B. Tauris.

Kedourie, E. (1974), *Arab Political Memoirs*, London: Frank Cass.

Kedourie, E. (1992), *Democracy and the Arab Political Culture*, Washington: Washington Institute for Near East Policy.

Kitchen, N. and Cox, M. (2011), "Just Another Liberal War? Western Interventionism and the Iraq War", in A. Acharya and H. Katsumata (eds) *Beyond Iraq. The Future of World Order*, Singapore: World Scientific Publishing, 65–84.

Lynch, M. (2005), *Voices of the New Arab Public: Iraq, al-Jazeera and Middle East Politics Today*, New York: Columbia University Press.

Maghraoui, A. (2006), *Liberalism without Democracy. Nationhood and citizenship in Egypt, 1922–1936*, Durham: Duke University Press.

Mansfield, E. and Snyder, J. (1995), "Democratization and the Danger of War", *International Security*, 20(1), 5–38.

Mirghani, O. (2012), "The Arab Spring Conspiracy", *Asharq Alawsat*, 11 October.

Monroe, E. (1963), *Britain's Moment in the Middle East, 1914–1956*, London: Chatto and Windus.

Mouffe, C. (2005), "The Limits of John Rawls's Pluralism", *Philosophy, Politics and Economics* 4(2), 221–231.

Owen, J. M. (1997), *Liberal Peace, Liberal War*, Ithaca: Cornell University Press.

Owen, R. (1995), "Socio-Economic Change and Political Mobilization. The Case of Egypt", in R. Brynen, B. Korany. and P.Noble. (eds) *Political Liberalization and Democratization in the Arab World* (Vol. 1), Boulder: Lynne Rienner

Owen, R. (2004), *State, Power and Politics in the Making of the Modern Middle East*, 3rd edition, Oxford: Oxford University Press.

Owen, R. (2012), *The Rise and Fall of Arab Presidents for Life*, Cambridge: Harvard University Press.

Peres, S. and Noar, A. (1993), *The New Middle East*, New York: Henry Holt and Co.

Ramadan, T. (2012), *The Arab Awakening. Islam and the New Middle East*, London: Allen Lane.

Rutherford, B. K. (2008), *Egypt after Mubarak*, Princeton: Princeton University Press.

Salamé, G. (1994), "Introduction: Where are the Democrats?" in G. Salamé (ed.) *Democracy without Democrats? The Renewal of Politics in the Muslim World*, London: I.B. Tauris, 1–20.

Schlumberger, O. (2007), "Arab Authoritarianism", in O. Schlumberger (ed.) *Debating Arab Authoritarianism: Dynamics and Durability in Non-Democratic Regimes*, Stanford: Stanford University Press.

Springborg, R. (2011), "Wither the Arab Spring: 1989 or 1848?" *The International Spectator* 46(3), 5–12.

UNDP. (2002), *Arab Human Development Report 2002, "Creating Opportunities for Future Generations"*, New York: UNDP.

Vatikiotis, P. J. (1991), *The History of Modern Egypt*, 4th edition, London: Weidenfeld and Nicholson.

Waterbury, J. (1994), "Democracy without Democrats? The Potential for Political Liberalization in the Middle East", in G. Salame (ed.) *Democracy without Democrats. The Renewal of Politics in the Muslim World*, London: I.B. Tauris, 23–47.

Whitehead, L. (2002), *Democratization. Theory and Experience*, Oxford: Oxford University Press.

Yapp, M. (1987), *The Making of the Modern Near East 1792–1923*, London: Longman.

Zurcher, E. Y. (1998), *Turkey: A Modern History*, London: I.B. Tauris.

Conclusion

Rebekka Friedman, Kevork Oskanian, and Ramon Pacheco Pardo

This volume examined the role of liberalism in two interrelated aspects: as an ideological source of order in global politics and as a theoretical approach within International Relations (IR) as a discipline. IR itself was born in reaction to the failure of realpolitik in the First World War, and its "first debate" centred on realists' engagement with the *empirical* failures of interwar liberal "utopianism" as a political project. At the same time, the claims of liberal theories of IR have fed back into practice through their influence on policymaking and grand strategy throughout the twentieth and twenty-first centuries, on issues as diverse as statebuilding, the treatment of authoritarian states, regional integration, and international institution building.

Liberal theorising in IR has generally focused on answering one of two types of questions. The first queries *the extent to which the liberal characteristics of a polity have an impact on its foreign policy*. This question emerged in the scholarship of liberals during the interwar period, which endorsed liberalism as a global political project and believed that states (should) make their liberal-democratic internal political philosophy the driver of their foreign policies. More recent liberal scholars seek to draw out the theoretical implications of classical liberal theory and look for empirical evidence to substantiate liberal claims. Against systemic theories of IR, liberal scholars in IR look at the impact of regime type and ideology, arguing against realist proponents of *functional identity*, that these, rather than mere capability, determine the behaviour of states. This scholarship ranges from liberal intergovernmentalists, looking at European integration (Moravcsik, 1997), to democratic peace theorists, who endorse the arguments of Immanuel Kant and liberal republicans that liberal democracies are less likely to go to war with each other (see, e.g., Doyle, 1996, Hurrell, 1990).

The second question that has occupied liberal scholarship is *the extent to which liberalism has become the defining rubric of the international system, and the implications of its ideological and institutional dominance*. Macro-level liberal IR theorists seek to provide a big picture analysis of the international system and its characteristics. John Ruggie (1983) wrote of liberalism's embeddedness as the institutional-legal expression of broadly shared legitimate goals. In this volume, building on his previous works (Ikenberry, 2002, 2006), G. John Ikenberry argued that the current American-led international liberal order was qualitatively distinct – that the United States used its unique role after its emergence as hegemon following the Second World War to restructure the international system in a way that was less threatening to other states. This liberal, American-led international society was rule based and transparent, making it more predictable. It bound the hegemon to the system and, unlike previous hegemonies, gave smaller states more reason to cooperate and bandwagon, rather than balance. In the late 1970s, when American influence had arguably waned and the international order came under threat, liberal scholars sought to explain the sustainability of this order in the face of challenges. The oil crisis, the non-aligned movement, the Vietnam War, and the economic weakening of the United States at home and abroad had expressed itself not only in a renewed isolationist sentiment domestically but also in a greater strategic reliance on alliances and international institutions. Complex interdependence and the strengthening of global institutions had seen the emergence of a resilient, self-sufficient system (Keohane and Nye, 1977). Importantly, for complex interdependence and regime theorists, liberalism had survived despite the decline of the hegemon; the liberal order had proven resilient, taking on a life of its own, bolstered by the strengthening of liberal institutions and regimes (Keohane, 1984).

Liberalism, order, and power

Insofar as the current economic crisis is a crisis of *liberalism*, these two major guiding questions of liberal scholarship, situated at the nexus between empirics and theory, become pertinent to both the future role of liberalism as an ordering ideology and its theoretical relevance in IR. G. John Ikenberry argues in his chapter that the characteristics of this US-designed, liberal international order make it more likely to survive the current dislocations of the global economy. The contemporary malaise is a crisis of American hegemony that does *not* endanger the continuity of the liberal order itself for four distinct reasons: the low likelihood of great power war, the order's integrative and expansive character, the absence of coherent alternatives, and the general alignment of major states around shared interests. In his words, the liberal world order is "easy to join and hard to overturn", and while major states like Russia and China do not necessarily define themselves as "liberal", they lack any incentive to completely replace today's fundamental institutional status quo in the face of growing security interdependence. A shift away from unipolarity will thus not result in a return to great power balancing, but it will uphold and reinforce the liberal international order.

The United States' role in the international system is intimately tied to the future of the liberal order. Charles Kupchan and Peter Trubowitz maintain that while the United States' military predominance remains strong, economic realities – deficits and the public debt burden – and political complications are weighing down on the United States' longer term ability to provide "leadership" in the contemporary world. The United States' domestic climate and politics bear significantly on American foreign policy. American society has become polarised between a revitalised conservative right and a demographically advantaged liberal left; its institutions remain in gridlock, unable to produce the compromises required for effective governance, and the liberal-internationalist foreign policies that underlay its global engagement in earlier, more prosperous decades. The legacies of military failure, perceived economic stagnation, and political polarisation in the United States now mark its internal debates, roughly splitting the erstwhile liberal-international consensus into two camps, centred on that consensus' two distinct components: the projection of American power, advocated by Republicans, and partnership with allies and international institutions, stressed by Democrats. Washington's future role in the world remains in the balance. Here, it has veered away from the costly neoconservative unilateralism of the past – which Jonathan D. Caverley describes as "*democratic neo-classical realism*" because of its combination of liberal ideology with raw hegemonic power. At the same time, the Obama administration has remained globally engaged, through its strategic presence in East Asia and the Middle East, the Global War on Terror, and its still-prominent role in the shaping of the global economy. *Economic* realities loom large in this age of crisis and stagnation, and it remains to be seen how America's reduced economic strength will, over the longer term, translate into an inability or unwillingness to uphold the post-Second World War global liberal system.

The rise of China over the past three decades forms part of these changing economic realities and directs our attention to the link between regime type and behaviour as analysts ponder the consequences of this rise for the current liberal order. Liberal orthodoxy would look sceptically upon the People's Republic's ability to adapt to the requirements of a liberally constructed world. Many consider China to be distrustful of activist liberal heresies against orthodox Westphalian sovereignty. As Margot Light argues in her chapter, the Russian Federation, in many ways, has been similarly inclined, with the perceived failure of its own liberal post-Cold War experiment reinforcing its scepticism today. However, Ren Xiao affirms Ikenberry's view that, while China remains a highly centralised bureaucratic state under one-party rule, Beijing's foreign policy continues to engage actively and constructively with the liberal institutions of global politics. Importantly, the People's Republic's reticent view of liberal international activism is not combined with an alternative ideological project; if anything, it is highly conservative, aiming to reform but not fundamentally change the institutional-legal status quo at home and abroad.

The occasional stirrings of Chinese nationalism might nevertheless indicate the dependence of such a passive outlook on China's status as an *as-yet emerging*, rather than *established* great power. Even without an explicit alternative ideological programme, China's growing economic engagement with the developing world has sometimes complicated the expansion of the liberal project. In the absence of a clear ideological vision that goes beyond the practicalities of maintaining stable single-party rule while ensuring economic growth, the future interactions between a great-power China and the foundations of the liberal world order remain an open question. For realists, power remains the crucial determining factor in any dissection of the past, present, or future shape of global politics. As Brian Schmidt and Nabarun Roy argue in their chapter, the realist emphasis on the epiphenomenal character of the liberal order augments their concern with the ability of rising powers to adapt to a liberal world. Especially for offensive realists, the prospect of Chinese regional hegemony becomes inherently threatening, regardless of the future trajectory of its domestic political system, necessitating the balancing strategies that underlie relations between the United States and other rising powers, including India. However, not unlike Ren Xiao and G. John Ikenberry, defensive and neoclassical realists, in particular, hold out the prospect of a security-seeking China working within the existing liberal system, challenging US predominance from *within* existing institutions by adopting what Randall Schweller (1999) calls a "hedging strategy". The critical question facing both realist and liberal scholars is whether China will *change* or *be changed* by this liberal world order.

Liberalism's inequalities

Importantly, *After Liberalism?* also goes beyond the great debates of liberalism and realism. The largely empirical narrative of a waning US hegemony and an emerging China cannot be divorced from the more profound contradictions inherent in liberal theory and practice. For Beate Jahn, while liberalism as a theory may be in decline in IR, liberal projects are alive and well, as expressed in current (neo-)liberal economic policies, liberal peacebuilding, and liberal organisations, law, and humanitarian intervention. However, alongside Christian Reus-Smit, Jahn notes the unequal application of liberal principles at home and abroad. Both stress the intimate link of colonialism and imperialism, and liberalism – the use of liberalism, in its classical and contemporary forms, to justify exclusionary policies and binary divisions between us versus them (liberal and non-liberal powers). For John Stuart Mill, the relationship is more complicated in his conception of self-realisation – in order for change to have meaning, it must come from societies within. Still, this does not deny Mill's support for imperialism and colonialism, and his two-tier understanding of liberal versus non-liberal powers, which is also found in the writings of John Locke.

Liberalism's unequal application in international society also links into discussions on its legitimacy. How we understand liberalism has implications for how we recognise and explain changes to the international system. For Christian Reus-Smit, Ikenberry's narrative of the liberal order is American-centric. It masks the agency of smaller states in shaping the current liberal order. In some sense, as Reus-Smit argues, Ikenberry's conception of the liberal order is closer to the conception of Hedley Bull (2002), where order is an arrangement of states. Ikenberry, Reus-Smit charges, neglects the purposive dimension of the international order. Post-colonial states take on liberal principles and demand representation. One of the major accomplishments of post-1945 anti-colonialism was to "delegitimise not only the institution of empire, but also this explicitly racist division of the world's people's into civilized and barbarian". While Reus-Smit's analysis of the newly independent states and non-hegemonic drivers is important, the empirical legacies of these normative developments are far from certain. Although empire now has stigma, hierarchy has not disappeared. Inconsistencies have always been part of the liberal order, even after moments of high energy, as in the Abyssinian crisis, when Emperor Haile Selassie's "Appeal to the League's" in June 1936, carefully crafted in the League's language, fell to the deaf ears. As Beate Jahn argues, while the successful democratisation of liberalism has been a major change, forcing governments to pursue economic growth to provide the "population with the economic benefits that maintain their stake in the system", this accountability has more often occurred on the domestic level rather than in the global sphere, where the "political fallout of these economic policies has to be borne by other states".

The binary character of liberal identities also brings its own set of risks. Liberal scholars themselves have noted inconsistencies within liberalism-as-practice, alongside its less than benign implications. For Michael Doyle, while liberal states are indeed more peaceful – at least towards each other – they have historically also found "liberal reasons for aggression" (Doyle, 1986: 1151). Indeed, for Doyle, it is important to note that it is not (political) liberalism per se, but the interaction of a liberal political system and a capitalist economy, which produces a less war-like propensity in the population. Drawing on Joseph Schumpeter's 1919 "Sociology of Imperialisms", capitalism becomes all-consuming as the population's energy is absorbed in the daily tasks of production, and capitalism, liberalism, and democracy reinforce each other in supporting a rationalised and individualised society. The scholars of this volume take Doyle's warning further, noting the implications of a norm of democracy promotion and humanitarian intervention. Liberal democracies go to war on behalf of liberal causes, most starkly expressed in humanitarian intervention.

While for Nicholas Wheeler (2002), humanitarian intervention expressed a long-standing tension between order versus justice and between solidarist and pluralist positions in international society, for others, contemporary liberal norms implicitly expand liberalism's interventionist logic. Writing within the same English School, Cornelia Navari examines the potential consequences of the intimate linking of democratisation and liberalism in practice. Navari entertains whether democratisation as a norm of international society could be used to justify intervention and non-recognition of authoritarian regimes, mostly situated in the South. While over a decade of conflict and intervention prompted by the 9–11 attacks has fused a discourse of democracy with military intervention, one could also argue that the jihadist groups around Al Qaeda have, if anything, proven more dangerous to the liberal order through the reactions they have elicited in Western societies. More than ten years since the start of the "Global War on Terror", fundamental civil liberties and due process have frayed considerably in the West as governments have become ever more intrusive of the private sphere.

Liberalism as metamorphosis

Importantly, despite these tensions within liberal theory and practice, for many of the contributors of this volume, liberalism is here to stay, albeit in a different guise. Metamorphosis is an important theme in the book – liberalism is versatile; its staying power lies in its adaptability and fungibility. For Ikenberry, if the current liberal order is experiencing a crisis, it is a crisis of liberalism's success, rather than failure. In this sense, rather than represent an E.H. Carr crisis, signifying a victory of realism over liberalism, it is a Karl Polanyi (1971) crisis, where liberal governance is troubled as a result of dilemmas and long-term shifts in the order – which can only be solved by rethinking, rebuilding, and extending that liberal order. Many of the contributors in the volume suggest that liberalism's versatility is precisely what makes it sustainable both in theory and in practice. This is a powerful argument, yet it also makes liberalism ambiguous. If liberalism consistently reinvents itself, then what does liberalism actually mean? The tendency of liberal scholars to seek to save liberalism from itself means that liberalism continues to exist despite the decline of liberal powers and uneven application of liberal principles in practice.

These questions will also determine the *future* status of liberalism as a theory and organising ideology. While Nicholas Rengger argues in favour of a dystopic liberal theory, guided by scepticism and suspicion of utopianism, he also acknowledges the tensions within dystopic liberalism between liberalism and scepticism. Dystopic liberals take a prudent approach, yet, ultimately, they also share as an end goal the protection of personal freedom. This pragmatic attitude, combining a relatively limited goal with a distrust of grand ideological programmes, makes *dystopic* liberalism adaptable to a changing world, especially in thought where the *liberal* dominates over the *dystopic*.

It is also worth stressing the increasingly globalised and pluralistic nature of international society today. As Phil Cerny points out, globalisation has both weakened and enhanced liberalism. On the one hand, the globalised world is still distinctly neoliberal, with cross-cutting institutional and market relationships that have made the state progressively powerless as liberalism's legitimate locus for decision-making. On the other hand, the neo-medieval nature of political jurisdiction in "durable disorder" does maintain some space for the liberal state as a focus for particular types of legitimacy and identification. The complex, transnational, and disorderly nature of global-isation is also reflected in the loose organisational and diverse ideological structure of the groups that have emerged in reaction to the contradictions and failings of neoliberalism. State-based alternatives to (neo-)liberalism were very much marginalised after the fall of the Soviet Union and the con-version of China. The challenge to (global) liberalism is therefore spread out globally, in what Michael Hardt and Antonio Negri (2000) have referred to as the "multitude": a collection of activist and subaltern groups adhering to alternative modes of social organisation.

The relationship of this diverse anti-globalisation movement to liberalism is complex. On the one hand, the absence of a clearly defined alternative programme makes effective change more complicated, driven as it is by radical groups that, by their very nature, reject hierarchy and centralised authority. On the other hand, these groups could function as "incubators" of left-radical alternatives to neoliberal globalisation over the long run. These left-radical alternatives could become relevant should the current economic slump worsen, leading to political instability, the discrediting of liberal insti-tutions, and an ensuing readiness to experiment with non-liberal forms of social organisation. While the chances that this change will take place seem remote, one only needs to consider the current situation in Southern Europe – especially Greece – where galvanised citizens abandon the liberal mainstream for the political "extremes" in reaction to an impotent state.

Illiberal right-wing populism, nationalism, religious conservatism, and their main non-Western counterpart – political Islam – also remain impor-tant political factors in the twenty-first century. Here, it is significant that the major wave of political change following the collapse of Communism in 1989–1991 – the Arab Spring – resulted from a combined *liberal and Islamist* challenge to the authoritarian regimes of the Middle East. As Louise Fawcett argues in her chapter, contrary to received wisdom, colonial and early post-colonial Arab (and Islamic) societies did spawn a liberal tradition, repressed during decades of authoritarian rule. With secular liberalism mostly advo-cated by the small middle classes in these societies, its initial visibility during street protests in Cairo and Tunis soon ebbed away as moderately Islamic par-ties took over the reigns of government. The main debates in these young democracies are now structured around the fault lines between secular liberals and Islamists, on the one hand, and moderate and radical Islamists, on the other. The ability of a distinctly *Arab* version of liberalism to assert itself would certainly contradict conceptions of the inevitable illiberalism of these societies, opening up the region to an internally sustained – rather than externally imposed – form of liberal politics. It would also emphasise this volume's theme of "metamorphosis", of liberalism's ability to transform and reinvent itself in response to historical, social, cultural challenges to its core assumptions.

The role of religion in IR brings us full circle in our discussion of liberalism's future as a global political project. As many have argued, the European enlightenment – central in the lineage of liberal ideology – was rooted in the secularisation of Western scientific and political thought in earlier centuries. The first liberal revolutions – in the United States and France – produced *secular* states. Significantly, however, this leading power would combine its secular system of government with a deeply – and, in the Western context, a-typically – religious society. Religious conservatism remains influential – following the revival of its right wing by the Tea Party movement. Could a change of government there result in a move away from secularism in domestic and foreign policy, with inevitable consequences for the current liberal world order? The strength of secular liberal institutions in the United States, it should be borne in mind, makes this an unlikely outcome. If anything, analysts and commentators have argued that the United States' mainstream is moving towards a more *secular* liberal future, contra the religious right's description of itself as a "Christian" nation (Campbell and Putnam, 2012). With liberal secularism still well-grounded in the last remaining superpower, and within the institutions that continue to shape order in today's world, Cox's argument about the persistence of liberalism would seem to be convincing indeed.

The present and future of liberalism remain in flux. This volume has examined challenges to liberalism in three spheres: as a theory of IR, as an American politico-economic project, and as the defining characteristic of the international system. Firstly, as a theory of IR, while the end of the Cold War reenergised liberalism, today, liberal failures abroad have bolstered its critics. Realism's many followers have adapted and reinvigorated their theory as one of the key theoretical paradigms in IR. Meanwhile, the English School, constructivism, and other approaches provide alternative explanations of the state and the evolution of the international system. Similarly, in practice, while the post-Second World War period saw the United States take the leading role in structuring the international institutional arrangement, turning the expansion and consolidation of liberal precepts into a cornerstone of American foreign policy, pro-isolationist currents within the country have increasingly questioned the benefits derived from the active spread of liberal values. At the same time, the Global Financial Crisis, the rise of non-liberal powers, and the Eurozone sovereign debt crisis have shown the limits of supra-nationalism and challenged the viability of liberalism as an ordering principle of the international system.

While these challenges to liberal theory and practice have put liberalism to test, this volume cautions against the conclusion of liberalism's demise. Present day theoretical criticisms, it is worth noting, are qualitatively distinct to earlier debates between liberals and realists in the interwar era. The continuing ability of critical views to identify inconsistencies within liberal theory is important in and of itself, expanding a literature questioning the current order's basic, political-theoretical assumptions. Within IR, critics of liberalism increasingly engage with the theory's foundational texts, going back to liberalism's roots and its own intellectual history. Two factors limit these critiques' transformational potential, however. Much of the *normative* literature itself operates within the broad confines of the liberal intellectual tradition, advocating behavioural rather than fundamental systemic change. Meanwhile, critical theorists, while united in their dismissal of (neo-)liberal ideology and practice, remain too fragmented in their post-positivism to pose a coherent, comprehensive intellectual challenge outside of specific issue areas – not unlike the groups challenging "really existing liberalism" outside of academia.

Similarly, in practice, despite internal divisions and an isolationist current within the United States, defence of free trade, the expansion of democracy, and the protection of human rights still underpin many US foreign policy actions. Neither the Bush nor the Obama administrations have refrained from seeking to advance the liberal project, whether through diplomacy or force. Reforms of global economic and financial governance are underway, and rather than create new regimes, potential challengers to the liberal economic regime have increasingly joined the liberal order, calling for more representation on more equal terms. New institutions such as the G20 have emerged, and the IMF and Bank for International Settlements are becoming more relevant and are gradually shifting power to emerging countries. North Africa and the Middle East have witnessed the greatest spread of democracy since the end of the Cold War.

Despite the many challenges and tensions facing liberalism, *After Liberalism?* suggests that both in theory and practice, liberalism is not time-bound: it has proven remarkably resilient and will, most likely, survive in the foreseeable future. Its strength lies in its own versatility and adaptability, which allows it to meet new challenges over time and remain relevant, redefining itself to meet a changing world order. The challenge facing liberalism in the future therefore may not be from outside liberalism but from within: can liberalism retain its coherence as a political project and organising principle if it continues to move away from its foundations? Can the liberal order retain the legitimacy it requires to assert itself in what is becoming an increasingly disjointed and pluralistic set of understandings, practices, and ideas? Liberalism's strength is therefore also its weakness. To the extent that the current international order is qualitatively distinct, resting on a normative institutional foundation, which has made it both more transparent and accessible, the danger of conceptual overstretch is that liberalism becomes a hollow shell, devoid the ideological purpose that has sustained it.

References

Bull, H. (2002), *The Anarchical Society: A Study of Order in World Politics,* London: Palgrave.

Campbell, D. E. and Putnam, R. D. (2012), "God and Ceasar in America: Why Mixing Religion and Politics Is Bad for Both", *Foreign Affairs*, 91(2), 34–43.

Doyle, M. W. (1986), "Liberalism and World Politics", *American Political Science Review*, 80(4), 1151–1169.

Doyle, M. W. (1996), "Kant, Liberal Legacies, and Foreign Affairs", in E. M. Brown, M. S. Lynn-Jones and E. S. Miller (eds) *Debating the Democratic Peace*, Cambridge: MIT Press, 3–57.

Hardt, M. and Negri, A. (2000), *Empire*, Harvard, MA: Harvard University Press.

Hurrell, A. (1990), "Kant and the Kantian Paradigm in International Relations Theory", *Review of International Studies*, 16(3), 183–206.

Ikenberry, G. J. (2002), *After Victory: Institutions, Strategic Restraint, and the Rebuilding of Rules after Major Wars*, Princeton: Princeton University Press.

Ikenberry, G. J. (2006), *Liberal Order and Imperial Ambition: Assays on American Power and World Politics*, Cambridge: Polity.

Keohane, R. and Joseph, S. N. (1977), *Power and Interdependence: World Politics in Transition*, Boston, MA: Little Brown.

Keohane, R. (1984), *After Hegemony: Cooperation and Discord in the World Political Economy*, Princeton, NJ: Princeton University Press.

Moravcsik, A. (1997), "Taking Preferences Seriously: A Liberal Theory of International Politics", *International Organization*, 51(4), 513–553.

Polanyi, K. (1971), *The Great Transformation: The Political and Economic Origins of Our Times*, Boston: Beacon Press.

Ruggie, J. G. (1983), "International Regimes, Transactions, and Change: Embedded Liberalism in the Postwar Economic Order", in D. S. Krasner (ed.) *International Regimes*, Ithaca, NY: Cornell University Press, 195–231.

Schweller, R. (1999), "Managing the Rise of Great Powers: History and Theory", in I. A Johnson and S. R. Ross (eds) *Engaging China*, New York, NY: Routledge, 1–32.

Wheeler, N. (2002), *Saving Strangers: Humanitarian Intervention in International Society*, Oxford: Oxford University Press.

Index

Printed and bound by CPI Group (UK) Ltd, Croydon, CR0 4YY